ECONOMIC ANALYSIS OF FARM PROGRAMS

ECONOMIC ANALYSIS OF FARM PROGRAMS

Peter G. Helmberger

University of Wisconsin

McGraw-Hill, Inc.

New York St Louis San Francisco Auckland Bogotá Caracas
Hamburg Lisbon London Madrid Mexico Milan Montreal
New Delhi Paris San Juan São Paulo Singapore Sydney Tokyo Toronto

This book was set in Times Roman by the College Composition Unit
in cooperation with General Graphic Services, Inc.
The editors were Anne Duffy, Denise T. Schanck, and Margery Luhrs;
the production supervisor was Friederich W. Schulte.
The cover was designed by Rafael Hernandez.
R. R. Donnelley & Sons Company was printer and binder.

ECONOMIC ANALYSIS OF FARM PROGRAMS

1 2 3 4 5 6 7 8 9 0 DOC DOC 9 0 9 8 7 6 5 4 3 2 1

P/N 027923-3
PART OF
ISBN 0-07-909945-9

Library of Congress Cataloging-in-Publication Data

Helmberger, Peter G.
    Economic analysis of farm programs / Peter G. Helmberger.
        p.   cm.
    Includes bibliographical references.
    Includes index.
    ISBN 0-07-909945-9 (set)
    1. Agriculture and state—United States.   2. Agricultural
subsidies—United States.   3. Agriculture—Economic aspects—United
States.   4. Agriculture—Economic aspects—United States—
Mathematical models.   I. Title.
HD1761.H475   1991
338.1'873—dc20   90-48622

ABOUT THE AUTHOR

Peter G. Helmberger received his Ph.D. in agricultural economics from the University of California at Berkeley. He has served on the faculties of Pennsylvania State University and the University of California at Berkeley and is currently professor of agricultural economics at the University of Wisconsin in Madison. He has served as the book review editor and as an associate editor of the *American Journal of Agricultural Economics* and has received several awards for scholarly work from the American Agricultural Economics Association.

To Rose M. Helmberger

CONTENTS

Appendixes

Index

IBM Software by Earl Brown and Bruce Gardner,
University of Maryland.

PREFACE

This book is intended for a semester course in farm policy for upper-division undergraduates and beginning graduate students. It is intended for students who have studied microeconomic theory at least at the intermediate level. A course in production economics beyond a principles course will likely substitute for intermediate theory. Students who have not had a course in calculus will find some of the material inaccessible, providing instructors with the opportunity to teach calculus under the guise of marginal analysis. The more mature scholars might also find the book handy to have on the shelf for quick reference to farm policy approaches and models. I should not be altogether surprised if even the sophisticates occasionally come across results that give pause for contemplation.

The book is based on lecture notes used in teaching farm policy at the undergraduate and graduate levels over the past 20 years. In the development of these notes, I have striven from the beginning to show how economic theory can be used to analyze the market and welfare effects of farm programs. Not surprisingly, this effort often gave rise to research projects and collaborative work with graduate students. The book is therefore a product of an evolutionary process, reflecting the interplay between teaching and research.

Students who master the material in the book will, I believe, have a better appreciation for the usefulness of economic theory and a good understanding of how farm programs work and with what consequences for farm output and input markets. I have tried to strike the right balance among description of program details, modeling program effects, and reviewing relevant policy researches. Whether I've succeeded others must judge. Instructors in farm policy courses will be able, of course, to tip the balance toward whatever they think is optimal through classroom discussions and supplementary readings.

Chapters 1 and 2 are introductory with the latter centering on benefit-cost concepts that are used throughout the book. The interdependence among farm output and input markets, introduced in Chapter 2, is given a more rigorous development in Chapter 3. The explicit treatment of this interdependence is one of the key features of this book.

Chapter 3 centers on the exogenous factors that have shaped U.S. agriculture in the post-World War II period, with considerable attention given to the out-migration of labor. It is relatively long and difficult for several reasons. For one thing, I've endeavored to replace the traditional bloodless entrepreneur with the notion of a family enterprise. This calls for some modifications of competitive price theory. The decision to treat explicitly the interdependency among output and input markets leads to difficult material that is nearly always treated (I can think of few exceptions) in an informal and nonrigorous manner in the textbooks on economic theory. I decided, further, to include in this chapter the theoretical underpinnings of the demand for exports because some students will likely not have studied this topic before and because others might find a review useful. Chapter 3 sets the conceptual and empirical foundation for much of the subsequent analysis in the book.

Chapters 4 and 5 both analyze in some detail the market and welfare effects of direct payments and market price supports but from quite different perspectives. Chapter 4 views these policy instruments as alternative means for elevating farm income; comparative static analysis is used to derive programs effects. International trade implications are considered in some detail. The application of market price supports to milk components used in manufacturing is explained together with some of the experience with this program since World War II.

Chapter 5 views direct payments and price supports, along with other approaches, as alternative means for stabilizing markets; the analysis is stochastic and dynamic. I expect that some instructors will find the material in Chapter 5 outside the mainstream of farm policy courses not because of the subject matter but because of the mode of analysis. Many writers discuss market stabilization in an informal way, often concluding that, yes, some form of farm market stabilization is probably a good idea. I do not believe much progress can be made in this area, however, unless the analyst uses dynamic stochastic analysis and takes advantage of recent advances in the theory of storage. Chapter 5 provides an introduction to these relatively difficult topics and supports the conclusion that if the government desires to stabilize farm markets, regardless of whether this is a sensible goal, then careful consideration should be given to the simple expedient of subsidizing private storage as the most effective way of going about it.

Federal marketing order programs for fruits and vegetables and for milk eligible for fluid use are analyzed in Chapter 6. The theory of price discrimination is called into play. The application of price discrimination (classified pricing) in the marketing of fluid-eligible milk is described in some detail, and key findings from research on U.S. dairy policy are briefly summarized.

Chapter 7 analyzes mandatory acreage and strict production control programs. The U.S. experience under acreage controls in the 1950s is briefly recounted. The programs for tobacco and peanuts are considered as examples of government-sponsored cartels. It is shown that far from generating benefits to the suppliers of farm inputs in the long run, government cartels with negotiable production rights have just the opposite effect.

Chapter 8 centers on voluntary programs in which the government uses payments and other benefits to induce farmers to idle land. The concept of the indirect profit function is developed and applied in the modeling of the farmer's decision whether to participate in voluntary programs. Present land diversion programs are explained together with their antecedents. Quantification of the effects of land diversion programs for the major crops poses difficult problems for researchers, which is, as I explain in Chapter 8, the principal reason why our knowledge in this area is in an unsatisfactory state.

Chapter 9 turns attention to farm programs for commodities that are both produced domestically and imported on a large scale. Import quotas, tariffs, and direct payments are analyzed and their welfare effects are compared. The U.S. programs for sugar and wool illustrate the use of import quotas and direct payments, respectively. The European Community's Common Agricultural Policy illustrates the use of tariffs, less now than it did in an early stage of its operation.

The external effects of agriculture on the environment are the subject of Chapter 10. Here the student learns that it makes sense from the point of view of economic efficiency to increase environmental pollution up to the point where the marginal benefit of more food consumption and production just equals the marginal cost of pollution; U.S. policies toward soil erosion and pesticide use are critically examined.

The method of analysis in the book is mainly graphic. Derivatives and partial derivatives are employed sparingly. Occasionally, economic models are expressed as systems of equations. Take-home problems given at the end of each chapter range in difficulty from simple arithmetic applications to those that may tend to be more appropriate for graduate students than for undergraduates. Some problems modify or extend in significant ways the material covered in the chapter. All require the student to use his or her knowledge of theoretical analysis to organize computations. Sections and problems marked with asterisks are intended for advanced students. Publications cited or quoted in a chapter are listed in the references at the end of the chapter together with supplementary readings.

A computer disk entitled *AGSEC: A Computer Simulation to Teach Agricultural Policy,* by Earl Brown and Bruce Gardner, is included in this book (see inside back cover). A brief description of this software, together with some discussion of its role in farm policy courses, is given in Appendix C. The software contains a user's guide and sets forth the structural model. Aside from being great fun to run, the computer program offers valuable lessons as to the political and economic consequences of farm policy choices.

Many people have helped me write this book in one way or another, and I am appreciative of their efforts. My debt to former graduate students is large as evidenced by the extent to which I have drawn upon our joint research publications. The names of John Rosine, Patricia Hutton, David Lee, Mark Lowry,

Joseph Glauber, and Mario Miranda come readily to mind. Marvin Johnson and Jung-Sup Choi, who read early drafts of several chapters, made many valuable suggestions and caught several mathematical errors. Bruce Gardner made detailed comments on Chapters 3, 4, and 6 which are gratefully acknowledged. Lydia Zepeda kindly read Chapter 10 and suggested many improvements. The following reviewers for McGraw-Hill made suggestions that caused me to change the book in significant ways, particularly in terms of topics covered: Jim Kendrick, University of Nebraska–Lincoln; Marvin L. Klein, California State Polytechnic–Pomona; Jeffrey T. LaFrance, Montana State University; Marshall Martin, Purdue University; and Haele M. G. Selassie, South Carolina State College. Kathleen Haygood and Jack Solock prepared the many diagrams and helped locate relevant data. Karen Denk typed endless revisions of the manuscript with patience and good humor. To all the people above, named and unnamed, I say thank you.

Peter G. Helmberger

ECONOMIC ANALYSIS OF FARM PROGRAMS

CHAPTER

1

Introduction

Farm programs are the product of demand and supply. Farmers, with some help from their friends in agribusiness, demand them and politicians oblige by providing a supply. The demand of farmers for farm programs that redistribute income (benefits) from consumers and taxpayers to the farm sector is inversely related to farm prosperity. The willingness of politicians to finance farm program benefits is constrained by the willingness of consumers and taxpayers to foot the bill and the demands of other interest groups for their share of government assistance.

The consorting of farmers, farm lobbyists, and politicians often leads to results that are both costly and strange. In 1986, farm programs cost the federal government about $26 billion. This amounts to $11,267 per farm. This doesn't mean that each and every farmer received a check for $11,267. As in other years farm subsidies were heavily concentrated among the largest, richest farmers, with some operators receiving subsidies in excess of $1 million. Farm program costs divided by the number of commercial farms, farms with annual sales in excess of $40,000, equaled $39,000. In addition to costing Uncle Sam an arm and a leg, farm programs have resulted in subsidized sales to the Soviet Union, destruction of commodities, and wasting land resources on a large scale. Under recent dairy programs some farmers have been paid to produce surplus milk; at the same time others have been paid to liquidate their herds. Many tobacco and peanut growers have had to pay city folk for the right to grow crops or else pay stiff government penalties. Although considerable lip service has been given to the plight of family farms, the fact remains that the number of such farms together with farm labor and the farm population have declined dramatically in the period since World War II. Farm pro-

1

grams are important, expensive, and controversial; they are a worthy subject of debate and analysis.

From another point of view, however, farm program are marvelous experiments in public policy for students who are eager to see how the tools of analysis learned in courses in economic theory can be brought to bear on real-world phenomena. Analyzing the economic effects of farm programs can be a valuable part of a student's economic education. As explained in more detail below, economic theory purports to analyze the behavior of highly idealized agents in highly idealized environments of choice. No one has ever seen a perfectly competitive market, for example, and no one ever will. The student may well ask if theory is of much value in understanding the real world. There is really only one way of answering that question and that is to have a go at it.

The objectives of this book are threefold: the first and foremost is to show how economic theory can be used to analyze farm programs or, in other words, to derive hypotheses as to their economic effects. This is accomplished through modifying competitive models to take account of government intervention and through comparing the predicted performance of markets with and without intervention. With the exception of Chapter 5, the models analyzed in this book are comparative-static models developed with the aid of graphic analysis and, occasionally, elementary mathematics. Comparative-static models compare the performance of markets in equilibrium under alternative economic circumstances such as different technologies or different farm programs. (Chapter 5 provides an introduction to dynamic stochastic modeling with an application to market stabilization policy.) Relevant dimensions of market performance include prices and quantities of farm outputs and inputs. Considerable attention is also given, however, to the benefit-cost implications of farm programs for consumers, taxpayers, farmers, and farm input suppliers.

A second major objective of this book, closely related to the first, is to acquaint the reader with a variety of farm commodity programs. The programs receiving the greatest attention are those that have been in effect in the United States off and on since World War II. Examples include marketing orders; price supports via nonrecourse loans, direct payments, or both; price supports together with production controls of various kinds; and agricultural trade policies. Many of these programs have been the object of empirical research, and some of the findings will be discussed not only because they are of intrinsic interest but also because they have implications for the empirical validity of models of farm programs. Although the focus of attention is on U.S. domestic programs, some examples from foreign countries will also be considered. The Common Agricultural Policy of the European community is a case in point.

A third objective is to apply economic theory in a study of the effects on the farm economy of changes in variables determined outside the farm sector. More particularly, the manner in which farm sector variables are affected by technological change, population growth, changes in farm input supply functions, shifts in export demand, etc., will be considered in some detail. The resulting analysis will shed considerable light on the unevenness of farm prosperity over time, the out-migration of farm labor, and the frequent pleading of farmers for government assistance.

The remainder of this chapter considers three preliminaries. The first concerns the meaning, source, and role of hypotheses in research and, more generally, in seeking to understand the blooming complexities of the real world. A second preliminary centers on the distinction between hypotheses and value judgments and the role of each in the choice of public policy. A third preliminary examines the notion of causality in economics and distinguishes between structural and reduced form behavioral relationships and between endogenous and exogenous variables.

A fourth preliminary is of sufficient importance and complexity to require a separate chapter. This preliminary is the introduction to benefit-cost analysis given in the next chapter.

1.1 ON THE IMPORTANCE OF HYPOTHESES

People use different kinds of statements in everyday communication. We make observations, issue commands, utter expletives, ask questions, and so on and so forth. One class of statements is of basic importance to science, viz., those called hypotheses. Since this book devotes considerable space to their development, some justification for doing so appears in order.

We start with a definition. A *hypothesis* is a statement (or set of statements) proposed as an explanation for the occurrence of some specified group of phenomena, either asserted merely as a tentative conjecture to guide research or accepted as highly probable in light of established facts. Basic to this definition is the word "explanation," which suggests cause-and-effect relationships. Daylight wanes and darkness descends because the planet earth is spinning on its axis away from the sun. The real price of Chicago no. 2 corn rose sharply during the summer of 1988 because a severe drought took hold in the Corn Belt. At the heart of the idea of explanation is that of causality.

Another crucial element of the above definition is the possibility, likely or remote, that a statement sets forth an explanation that is false, so that the statement itself is subject to refutation. To take a famous example, it was once proposed that night and day were the result of an earth that was both spherical and stationary, with the sun, moon, and other planets orbiting around it in a majestic sweep. When Galileo peered through his newly invented telescope, however, he discovered the moonlike phases of Venus, which could only be explained by the movement of Venus around the sun. Take an example from economics. In the early 1980s it was proposed by some supply-side economists that lowering tax rates would invigorate the American economy and cause surges in efficiency and productivity of such magnitude as to increase the tax take. Tax rates were slashed, and as government deficits soared to new heights, some economists began to question the empirical validity of the supply-side hypothesis.

Obviously, statements other than hypotheses are also subject to refutation. The claim that it is raining outside can be checked by looking out the window. The accuracy of the predicted election of a politician can be determined by counting the votes. These two examples merely help drive home the distinction between hypotheses and other statements, such as observations and predictions, that offer no element of explanation even though their truth or falsity is ascertainable.

What is the source of hypotheses? How do people arrive at these special statements? There are many sources including guesses, religion, and empirical regularities. The source of major interest here, however, is theory, more particularly, economic theory. Since the dominant theme of this book is using economic theory to develop hypotheses, there is little need to explain here how theory can be so used or to consider examples.

There is, however, one aspect of using theory in the derivation of hypotheses that merits a few comments straightway. Students often complain that the assumptions of economic theory are unrealistic and hardly worthy of consideration. However, as Ernest Nagel points out in a seminal paper on scientific methodology, the word "unrealistic" as used in this context has at least two alternative meanings that need to be recognized. First, an assumption may be said to be unrealistic because it does not provide a detailed description of all the attributes of some concrete existing object. Since the attributes of any real-world object are infinite, it would be impossible for any assumption of finite length to be other than unrealistic in this sense. It is also difficult to imagine how such statements would be of use in theory.

There is another sense, however, in which an assumption may be said to be unrealistic. According to Nagel (p. 215),

> In many sciences, relations of dependence between phenomena are often stated with reference to so-called "pure cases" or "ideal types" of the phenomena being investigated. That is, such theoretical statements (or "laws") formulate relations specified to hold under highly "purified" conditions between highly "idealized" objects or processes, none of which is actually encountered in experience.

It may be useful to elaborate a bit on Nagel's second view of unrealistic assumptions. What is meant by a highly idealized object? One frequently hears references to "smart shoppers." Some consumers seem to have a special talent for keeping tabs on prices at various retail outlets. They seem to know a lot about the attributes of competing products; they rarely make mistakes regarding products that are needed as opposed to those that are purchased and then discarded. Some shoppers are smarter than others, and the shoppers envisaged in the theory of consumer behavior are as smart as they can be. The consumer knows all the prices and which affordable commodity bundle will yield more satisfaction or utility than other affordable bundles. In this sense, the economist's consumer is highly idealized. The same can be said for other decision makers such as entrepreneurs, workers, or investors.

Modeling consists of characterizing idealized decision makers through assumption, placing these agents in environments that are also highly idealized, and then showing how choices are made. Behavioral relationships such as demand and supply functions, for example, are derived through recording how buyers' and sellers' choices vary with assumed changes in the environment. Choices lead to economic activities that determine economic performance. The question becomes whether we can learn much of interest about real economic processes through analyzing theoretical models. Here again the importance of hypotheses and the testing of hypotheses for empirical relevance take their rightful position at center stage. Happily, there are few fields as fertile for testing the empirical validity of economic theory as is U.S. farm policy.

The need for hypotheses arises out of the infinity of details that characterize the real world. Hypotheses serve as a guide to those elements of the real world that are crucial to the recurrence of whatever set of phenomena we wish to understand and to those elements that can be ignored. But how can this be done except through statements that assert causality, that assert certain events (droughts) cause other events (grain price hikes) to occur? Thus, the simple but powerful theory of demand and supply provides a reservoir of hypotheses that might explain the ups and downs of real U.S. wheat prices over time. The theory does more than just tell us that weather here and abroad, population growth, technological change, price of fertilizer, etc., are relevant variables and that we should, therefore, seek measurements of these variables (data) over time. It also provides a guide as to how the data are to be organized in providing an explanation. A severe drought at home restricts the quantity of domestic wheat production. A serious drought abroad raises the demand for U.S. wheat. Either occurrence raises the U.S. price of wheat, through curtailed domestic supply in the first instance and greater demand in the second.

Economists use economic models like an orthopedic surgeon uses x-rays. X-rays strip away skin, muscle, and veins, making it possible to see the skier's bones. Economic models strip away irrelevant detail so that one can see the variables that really matter.

In passing, we note that one frequently encounters the expression "analytical framework" in studies of agricultural economics. An analytical framework sets forth and possibly develops rigorously the hypotheses to be used in the study of some set of phenomena. In this way the writer alerts the reader to what evidence will be examined and how empirical observations will be organized.

Relying on a theory such as that of demand and supply to explain what we observe in the real world is not without risks. The theory may lead us to focus on the wrong variables, ignoring crucial elements in the process. Such risks really cannot be avoided, but they serve to remind us of the tentative nature of hypotheses and the important role of empirical tests. If it is found that on some but not all occasions, grain prices rise sharply following upon the heels of inclement weather, then the theory may need to be jettisoned or, more likely in the present example, modified to take account of possibilities that the present theory might ignore. The role of large stocks that might alleviate the effects of bad weather is a good example of phenomena often neglected in elementary expositions of the theory of demand and supply. It frequently happens that an inconsistency between theory and observation leads to the modification of the theory to take account of some new factors previously ignored.

Through using hypotheses to explain the world we observe and through testing their empirical validity, it is often found in scientific studies that some hypotheses must be rejected but that others hold up very well. In time, after considerable testing, some hypotheses may become widely accepted as true; people come to accept them as knowledge and, for all practical purposes, their tentative nature is all but forgotten.

1.2   THE ROLE OF HYPOTHESES AND VALUES IN POLICY CHOICES

In Table 1.1 let G_1 stand for a possible government program. It might involve placing a tariff on imported bicycles or supporting the price of butter. Let G_2 and G_3 stand for other possible programs, recognizing that the list of possibilities could be made as long as desired. Let C_1 be the set of economic consequences that result from putting G_1 into operation, and likewise for C_2 and G_2 and for C_3 and G_3. The consequences associated with having no program at all are denoted by C_0. Program consequences consist of all output levels and output prices, all input levels and input prices, and all taxes and income transfers. Importantly, the economic effects of government intervention on the nation's total output and its distribution among the populace can be seen through comparing C_0 with the C corresponding to whatever program is of interest. Writers sometimes refer to this procedure as the with-and-without principle for policy evaluation.

TABLE 1.1.
Three hypothetical government programs and the associated economic consequences

Program	Consequences
G_1	C_1
G_2	C_2
G_3	C_3
No program	C_0

In general, it is very unlikely that anyone would know exactly what the consequences would be for any program or for the case of no program at all. The most that can be hoped for is informed judgment, and it is here that economics has an important role to play. An important objective of economic analysis is to frame hypotheses as to the likely economic effects of various policy options, drawing upon theory and whatever evidence may be relevant. Hypotheses may be more or less detailed. The analyst might choose to ignore certain possible consequences judged to be of little importance or beyond the reach of analysis because of the weaknesses of theory, research methods, available data, or all three. Obviously, the predicted consequences would also reflect the analyst's skills and whatever research resources are available.

Hypotheses may be either qualitative or quantitative. Qualitative hypotheses identify those economic variables that will likely be affected by a program. They might also indicate whether an increase in a program variable causes an economic variable to rise or fall. Qualitative hypotheses are mainly the product of theoretical analysis, as we shall see time and time again in the remainder of this book.

Quantitative hypotheses, as one might expect, go further than qualitative hypotheses by predicting by what amounts economic variables will change (rise or fall) in response to a policy choice. Quantitative hypotheses are mainly the product of empirical research that uses economic theory and statistical techniques in the analysis of data.

An example might be instructive. Consider a program that establishes a tariff on imported bicycles. Let P equal price and T equal the level of the tariff. What is desired is some knowledge of the function $P=f(T)$, recognizing that additional economic variables will likely be of interest. On the basis of theory we might predict that an increase in T causes an increase in P. This is an example of a qualitative hypothesis. A quantitative hypothesis, on the other hand, might assert that a 10 percent increase in T causes P to rise by 8 percent. Such a conclusion might be reached by studying previous changes in tariffs and prices, recognizing that disturbing influences such as rampant domestic inflation might greatly complicate the task of separating out the "net" effects of changes in the tariff. Quantification of program effects is a major objective of empirical research.

If economists could supply quantitative or even qualitative hypotheses as to policy effects that later proved nearly always to be correct, their role in public policy formulation would be assured, though not always welcomed. Obviously, special interest groups may not want to hear what economists have to say. Lobbyists, columnists, astrologers, and others who feel that economic analysis is too important to be left to economists, are quick to press their own points of view on political leaders and the electorate and to call attention to the past failures of economists, of which there are many. The successes of economists, of which there are several, are often ignored.

Public choices reflect more, however, than beliefs or hypotheses as to the economic consequences of alternative policies. For one thing, policies have consequences that are not ordinarily thought of as economic in nature. Politicians, for example, are ever mindful of what is required to get themselves reelected. Unlovely compromises can always be struck on the argument that saving the country might require bowing occasionally to a parochial interest, be it dairy or oil. As another example, old religious fanatics welcome holy wars as a quick way to send young men to heaven, a privilege rarely extended to women and old men.

Perhaps of equal importance to noneconomic consequences in making public choices is the role played by value judgments. A *value judgment* is a statement of preference for one set of economic consequences over another set. One politician might prefer C_2 to C_1 and C_1 to C_3. Another might prefer C_3 to C_2 and C_2 to C_1. Aside from possible lies, of no interest here, statements of preference are subject to change but not refutation. Value judgments and hypotheses are quite different beasts. There is a basic and intrinsic difference between such statements as "We should help the poor" and "The diets of the poor can be improved through food stamps." The first statement is a value judgment and asserts a policy goal or objective. The second is a hypothesis and asserts causality but not advocacy.

The importance of the distinction between value judgments and hypotheses can be exaggerated. Two groups of people might both be sympathetic to the need to help the poor, but one group opposes government aid on the argument that such aid destroys individual initiative and rots moral fiber. Disagreement may arise more out of different beliefs as to program effects than different value judgments. All the more reason to study economics, striving to link accurately economic effects with alternative public policies.

There is considerable controversy among economists and others whether an economic analysis of program effects can ever be completely free of value judgments. We choose not to enter this debate. What is important to bear in mind here is that as a practical matter the extent to which value judgments pervade an economic analysis is a matter of degree. There are good reasons, however, to strive for objectivity in program analysis, eschewing value judgments according to which this or that set of effects is good or bad. Value judgments can bias efforts to assess the consequences of alternative public choices. The researcher who is against aid to the poor and who for that reason attempts to construct a theory according to which food stamps make the poor worse off and who chooses to use data selectively to support such a hypothesis runs the risk of being branded unreliable and incompetent.

To sum up, actual public choices among alternative government programs reflect beliefs as to both economic and noneconomic consequences taken together with value judgments as to which set of consequences is the most desirable. The objective of this book, as noted, is to assess the consequences of alternative farm programs. We shall strive, never with complete success, of course, to keep value judgments at bay in deriving hypotheses and in examining evidence and research studies as to program effects.

1.3 SOME NOTES ON CAUSALITY
IN ECONOMIC ANALYSIS

Consider the simple demand and supply model given in Figure 1.1. The price P_0 is said to be an equilibrium price because at this price all buyers are able to buy as much as they like and all suppliers are able to sell as much as they like. No other price will satisfy these conditions. Implicit in the theory are various arguments of a dynamic nature that explain why at any price other than P_0, activities will be undertaken by buyers, sellers, or both that impel the price to move in the direction of P_0. At a price above P_0, for example, sellers could not sell as much as they desire. Each can remedy the problem by lowering the price a bit. Buyers will discover sellers are receptive to price discounts. The result is downward pressure on price, and the pressure will continue so long as the price remains above P_0. If, on the other hand, the price is less than P_0, some buyers will be unable to buy as much as they like, a problem that can be remedied by arranging to pay sellers small price premiums. Sellers will also discover that they can raise prices and still sell as much as they like. Pressure builds to elevate prices. The theory of demand and supply consisting of Figure 1.1 together with arguments according to which price gravitates to P_0 describe a process that determines market price together with the quantities of production and consumption.

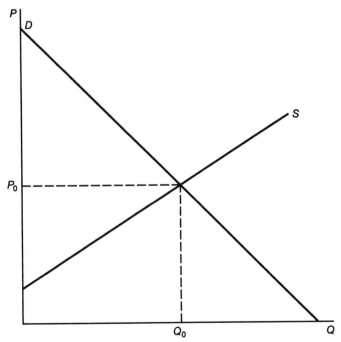

FIGURE 1.1
Demand and supply for output.

If this were all there were to the demand-supply model, it would be of limited interest. The real significance of the model resides in a set of hypotheses, not explicitly shown in the diagram, as to variables that expand or contract demand and supply and therefore cause price and quantity to change. A partial list of demand shifters includes population, per capita income, prices of related goods, and consumer preferences. Supply shifters, at least in the short run, include number of sellers, input prices, weather, and technology.

Within the context of this model, demand and supply shifters are examples of exogenous variables. Variables are said to be *exogenous* to a model or theory if their values are determined by processes not described by the model. Whereas changes in exogenous variables cause changes in endogenous variables, changes in the latter have no effect on the former. Causality flows in one direction. For example, weather can greatly influence grain prices, but the latter will have no perceptible impact on the former.

Returning to Figure 1.1, we say that price and quantity are examples of endogenous variables. Variables are said to be *endogenous* if their values are determined jointly by processes described by the theory. In the present instance price and quantity are jointly determined variables. The value of one does not determine the value of the other. It would be nonsensical in the present instance, for example, to ask whether an increase in price would cause quantity to fall. Price might rise because of an increase in demand, in which case quantity rises. On the other hand, price might rise because of a decrease in supply, in which case quantity falls. It makes perfectly good sense to inquire how a change in an exogenous variable will affect the value of an endogenous variable. To ask, however, how a change in one endogenous variable affects the value of another endogenous variable is simply an improper question.

The above discussion of demand and supply is based on graphic analysis, and we shall make great use of such analysis throughout the remainder of this book. The fact remains, however, that some models of use in the study of farm policy cannot be expressed or analyzed conveniently using graphics. For this reason it is instructive to recast much of the above discussion using elementary algebra.

The demand-supply model considered above can be expressed as follows:

$$Q_d = a - bP_d \qquad \text{demand} \qquad (1.1)$$

$$Q_s = c + dP_s \qquad \text{supply} \qquad (1.2)$$

$$Q_s = Q_d = Q \qquad \text{equilibrium condition} \qquad (1.3)$$

$$P_d = P_s = P \qquad \text{equilibrium condition} \qquad (1.4)$$

This system consists of six equations and six endogenous variables (Q_d, P_d, Q_s, P_s, Q, P). The variables Q and P are introduced to allow expressing the model in equilibrium values only, as below:

$$Q = a - bP \tag{1.5}$$

$$Q = c + dP \tag{1.6}$$

In the latter rendition of the model, four of the six equations given by (1.3) and (1.4) have been used to rid the system of four endogenous variables, namely Q_d, P_d, Q_s, and P_s. In algebra it is standard procedure to reduce the size of an equation system by eliminating variables through substitution, i.e., by getting rid of variables through giving up equations. Indeed, if the process is carried to its logical conclusion, the solution values of a consistent equation system can be found. Solving (1.5) and (1.6) for the solution values of P and Q yields:

$$P = \frac{a - c}{b + d} \tag{1.7}$$

$$Q = \frac{ad + bc}{b + d} \tag{1.8}$$

The equilibrium values for P and Q are given by (1.7) and (1.8), respectively. The value P_0 in Figure 1.1 corresponds to $(a - c)/(b + d)$ in the algebraic representation of the model, whereas Q_0 corresponds to $(ad + bc)/(b + d)$.

Now suppose we complicate the above model slightly by inserting shift variables in demand and supply. More particularly suppose Z_1 equals population such that an increase in Z_1 causes demand to expand. Let Z_2 equal technological change that expands supply. Both Z_1 and Z_2 are assumed to be exogenous. We then have:

$$Q = a - bP + eZ_1 \tag{1.9}$$

$$Q = c + dP + gZ_2 \tag{1.10}$$

Solving the system in (1.9) and (1.10) for P and Q, we have:

$$P = \frac{1}{b + d}(a - c + eZ_1 - gZ_2) \tag{1.11}$$

$$Q = \frac{1}{b + d}(bc + da + deZ_1 + bgZ_2) \tag{1.12}$$

The system given by (1.9) and (1.10) is an example of a structural model. The distinguishing feature of a *structural model* is that at least one of its equations contains two endogenous variables. In this instance both (1.9) and (1.10) contain two endogenous variables. The system given by (1.11) and (1.12), on the other hand, is an example of a reduced form model. The distinguishing feature

of a *reduced form model* is that each equation has no more than one endogenous variable. Structural models in economics provide tentative, simplified
descriptions or explanations of real-world processes. Structural models are expressions of economic theories. Reduced form models, on the other hand, are
of great use because they often allow ready derivation of the hypotheses that
are implied by the theory.

In Figure 1.2 let demand increase from D_0 to D_1 because of population
growth. As a result equilibrium price and quantity increase. The hypothesis
asserts that population growth causes P and Q to rise. It is apparent from
Equations (1.11) and (1.12) that an increase in Z_1 (population) also causes P
and Q to increase. Similarly an increase in S caused by technological change,
not shown in Figure 1.2, would cause P to fall and Q to rise, an assertion that
can be checked by examining Equations (1.11) and (1.12). The graphic and algebraic approaches lead to the same results. The advantage of the graphic approach is that it allows for the easy derivation of hypotheses when the structural model is simple, i.e., when it consists of but a few equations. The
advantage of the algebraic approach is that it allows derivation of hypotheses
in the case of structural models that are relatively complex.

In the present model it is clear that changes in P and Q are brought about
by changes in Z_1 and Z_2. What role is played by the values of the structural
parameters, i.e., by the values of a, b, e, c, d, and g in the system (1.9) and
(1.10)? An example will prove to be illuminating. Suppose that b is very close

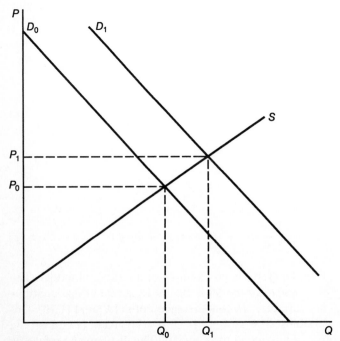

FIGURE 1.2
Supply and a shift in demand for output.

to zero, so close in fact that we can obtain good approximations by setting *b* equal to zero. This is to say, suppose that the demand for output is perfectly vertical or completely inelastic as in Figure 1.3. Now let technological change cause *S* to shift from S_0 to S_1. The effect of technological change is to decrease *P*, but *Q* doesn't change at all. The importance of the value of *b* is that it conditions the price and quantity effects of technological change. If it were true worldwide that the demand for food is highly inelastic, then technological change would not affect output very much, at least for short periods of time; it would mainly tend to lower world food prices. *Structural parameters* are important in explaining real-world events because they condition the effects of changes in exogenous variables. This explains why it is often important to have good estimates of structural parameters such as the elasticities of demand and supply.

A question raised by the above discussion is how we should consider changes in structural parameters. In many contexts it is indeed instructive to try to ascertain how the endogenous variables of a system would change in response to a change in one or more structural parameters. It should be noted that even in such cases structural parameters do not simply change of their own volition. Presumably some exogenous change or changes cause parameters to be altered, and from the point of view of the flow of causality it is still appropriate to maintain that endogenous variables change only in response to changes in exogenous variables.

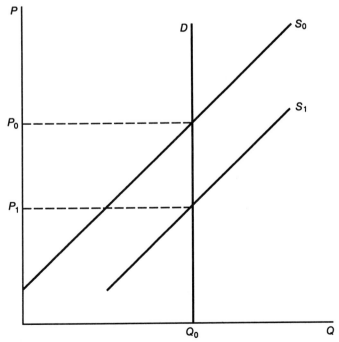

FIGURE 1.3
Demand and a shift in supply for output.

This discussion of causality in economics will be brought to a close by considering briefly the implications of a change in government policy. Since a government may be viewed as a decision maker, as are producers and consumers, one might expect economists to evolve a theory that explains government choices. Although work along this line is continuing, it is very complex. It is not always obvious, for example, just what it is that elected officials are seeking to accomplish. In what follows we shall nearly always view government choices as exogenous to the economic system. That is to say, we will inquire as to the results of this or that public choice without attempting to explain how the choices are or will be made. This does not mean, however, that we will ignore important issues that may arise when a public choice at one point in time will have effects that greatly influence public choices later on. What it does mean is that the introduction of a government program will be viewed as a shift in an exogenous variable of a given structural model or, more frequently, as a motivation for conceptualizing a new structural model.

Behavioral relationships are commonly derived for decision makers in perfectly competitive environments. The objective in much of what follows is to derive such relationships for decision makers when the environment of choice is altered by the introduction of government programs. What we shall discover is that supply and farm-level demand functions are often altered significantly by the introduction of farm programs, but they are still powerful concepts for analyzing the performance of farm products.

REFERENCES AND SUGGESTED READINGS

Hempel, Carl, *The Philosophy of Natural Science*, Prentice-Hall, Englewood Cliffs, NJ, 1966.
Nagel, Ernest, "Assumptions in Economic Theory," *American Economic Review*, 53(1963):211–219.

CHAPTER
2

Introduction to Benefit-Cost Analysis

The objectives of this chapter are to explain some of the basic concepts of benefit-cost analysis, concepts that will be used repeatedly in the remainder of this book, and to show how these concepts can be used to analyze the welfare implications of a simple farm program. The problem is this: government programs often affect the well-being or welfare of many people. Were it otherwise, it would be difficult to imagine why programs are enacted or, indeed, why people bother to form governments at all. Although it is possible to conceive of programs that are intended to make virtually everyone happier or better off, such as those intended to rid the world of smallpox and other communicable diseases, most programs will intentionally or otherwise increase the welfare of some people at the expense of others. Identifying people who will be helped and those who will be hurt and quantifying the effect in either case is what benefit-cost analysis is all about.

The previous chapter stressed the importance of economic hypotheses that link alternative programs with alternative sets of consequences. The consequences were expressed in terms of output and input quantities and prices. It is of interest to note that outputs, inputs, and prices are not only measurable but a contract involving exchange also nearly always spells them out in some detail. The same cannot be said for the increases in welfare or happiness that the parties to a transaction might enjoy. Upon leaving the supermarket, the shopper pockets a tape showing the quantities of items purchased and the prices paid. However, the tape does not show the extent of a consumer's pleasure with a special bargain on steaks or of the distress caused by the unavailability of grapes. In benefit-cost analysis, the analyst proposes to deal with the effects of programs on the well-being or happiness of the affected parties, and a very serious issue is how such effects can be measured and researched.

It is convenient to define benefit-cost concepts, explain their strengths and weaknesses, and show how they can be used in program analysis through application to one of the simplest farm programs one can imagine. The program is of interest in its own right even though we shall view it here mainly as a vehicle for an introduction to benefit-cost analysis.

2.1   MARKET PRICE SUPPORT PROGRAM

In the farm program here envisaged the government announces a support price P^+ for some farm commodity, food, say, and guarantees that through government purchases the market price will never be allowed to fall below the support level. The support level is set above the market-clearing competitive price. All food acquired by the government is promptly destroyed. Program costs are to be financed through the collection of taxes. For purposes of this chapter, we assume there is no international trade in food.

Let the private demand and supply for food be given by DD and S in Figure 2.1. The supply curve may be interpreted, for the moment, as either a short-run or long-run curve. The competitive levels of output and price equal Q_c and P_c, respectively. Now imagine the government introduces its support program, setting the support price P^+ equal to P_0^+. The government demand for food $D_g D_g$ is then perfectly flat or elastic at P_0^+. The total demand confronting the farm sector is given by the darkened, kinked curve DD_g, which is

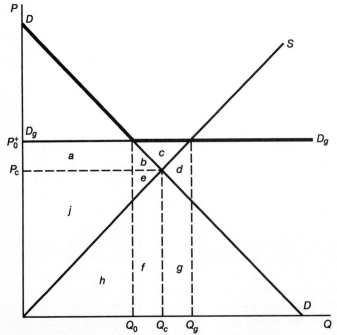

FIGURE 2.1
Supply and a change in demand due to price support.

the horizontal sum of DD and $D_g D_g$. (Here and in the remainder of this book we will often darken graphic representations of behavioral relationships that reflect farm programs.)

Equilibrium output under the program is given by the intersection of total demand and supply and equals Q_g. Some program effects are readily apparent from the diagram. Since the price is now pegged at P_0^+, consumers will only purchase output Q_0. The surplus to be destroyed is therefore $Q_g - Q_0$. Production rises from Q_c to Q_g. Consumption falls from Q_c to Q_0. Market price rises from P_c to P_0^+. The government expenditure, and therefore the total tax needed to finance the program, equals $P_0^+ (Q_g - Q_0)$.

Equilibrium in the product market translates or corresponds to equilibria in the markets for inputs used in production. In taking up the effects of the program in the input markets, we find it instructive to interpret the supply curve S as a long-run curve.

In the long run it is assumed that the free entry and exit of firms drives excess profits of all producers to zero. Firms are also able to adjust plant size to achieve the lowest possible per unit cost of production. We assume that the food industry is an increasing cost industry such that the long-run supply curve is upward sloping. The reason for increasing cost is that as the industry output expands, the price of at least one input also rises. We will often consider increasing cost industries in this book, and we will always assume that the reason for increasing costs is that at least one input price rises with industry output.

We imagine that three factors of production are required to produce food: land, labor, and producer goods. (Producer goods include machine services and the like.) Equilibrium in the product market, as depicted in Figure 2.1, requires input markets to be in equilibrium as well. Parts a, b, and c of Figure 2.2 give the supply functions for land, labor, and producer goods, respectively. We assume that the supply function for land use A is perfectly inelastic. The price support program causes land rent R to rise from its competitive value R_c to R_g. The supply function for hired labor L is upward sloping, and the program increases the wage rate W from W_c to W_g; the input of labor L rises from L_c to L_g. The supply function for producer goods K is perfectly

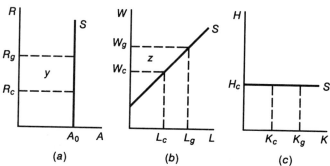

FIGURE 2.2
Supply cuves for land A, labor L, and producer goods K.

elastic. The program leaves the price of producer goods constant, but the level rises from K_c to K_g.

From the above analysis it is clear that some participants in the market for food will benefit from the price support program. Those who do will be called beneficiaries or gainers. Other people will be hurt by the program and we will call them losers. Those unaffected much one way or the other can be ignored. The question that now arises is by how much do the gainers gain and by how much do the losers lose. In what follows we will be concerned with the welfare implications of a market price support program for consumers, producers, input suppliers, and taxpayers. To figure out how much any one person would be affected would require recognizing the various hats he or she might be wearing. It might require adding up the loss incurred by a person as a consumer, say, together with the loss as a taxpayer and the gain as a supplier of labor to the food industry.

2.2   CONSUMER BENEFITS AND LOSSES

The demand of a single consumer for the product food is given by the curve d in Figure 2.3. (Frequently in this book, lowercase letters such as q will be used to indicate quantities for an individual decision maker with the corresponding capital letter Q indicating the quantity for all such decision makers taken to-

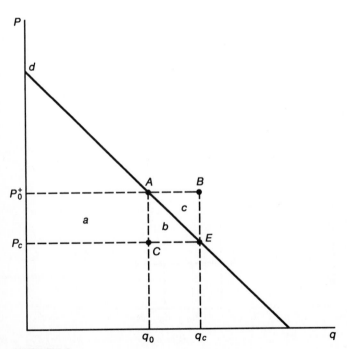

FIGURE 2.3
Measuring welfare effects of price changes.

gether.) The program under consideration would, if enacted, raise the price from P_c to P_0^+. Would the program make the consumer worse off? The answer is yes, at least according to the *principle of consumer sovereignty*. According to this principle the consumer knows best and is the best judge whether a program improves his or her welfare. Objections and exceptions come immediately to mind. Consumers are urged by the surgeon general to refrain from smoking cigarettes. The government strains to reduce the flow of hard drugs into the United States, thus restricting supply and raising prices, all for the purpose of advancing the public welfare. The principle at work in these instances seems to be that the government knows best. Commodities such as butter and red meats are in a kind of twilight zone. Decreased consumption following an increase in price might help some people avoid serious health problems due to obesity and cholesterol. At the very least, it seems, the principle of consumer sovereignty must be applied with some discretion.

There is, however, a rather more serious objection to the conclusion that a price hike caused by a government program makes the consumer worse off. This objection involves the distinction between what might be called selfish losses (or benefits) and selfless losses (or benefits). Two quite different questions might be put to our hypothetical consumer. How important is the loss due to a price hike given that no other people are affected by the program? How important is the loss given that the program generates benefits for migrant farm workers? The answers to these two questions might be quite different. A consumer loss reckoned in terms of the consumer's well-being or welfare entirely apart from the consumer's regard for the welfare losses and gains to other members of society is referred to as a *selfish loss*. A consumer loss that takes full account of the consumer's concern for the well-being of others is called a *selfless loss*. The distinction between selfish benefits or gains and selfless benefits follows accordingly. It is entirely possible that in our example the consumer is quite happy to pay a higher price if such benefits the poor. In this case the consumer enjoys a selfless gain from the program and suffers a selfish loss.

Let us suppose, however, that the consumer suffers a selfless loss as a result of an increase in price from P_c to P_0^+. The question then becomes, how much worse off is the consumer? If only we had the appropriate machine, we could strap it on the consumer's back, insert an electrode in the consumer's ear or whatever, and measure welfare directly. The machine might tell us, for example, that the consumer loses 100 utils through a price increase when full account is taken of the consumer's empathy for others. The trouble is that although individual welfare is a very important notion, like love, hate, or lust, no one has yet contrived a means for measuring it directly.

Lacking such a wondrous machine, economists have turned to monetary measures of welfare gains and losses. What is perhaps equally important, economists have largely backed away from analyzing selfless gains and losses. The reason for this is not because selfless gains and losses are unimportant. Rather, it has not been possible to devise operational measures of such changes in an individual's well-being. Indeed, measuring selfish gains and losses has proved to be quite difficult enough, and the resulting literature is rife with controversy.

This book is concerned with analyzing the benefit-cost implications of farm programs, but we will center on selfish benefits and costs. When we speak hereafter of benefits and costs (or gains and losses), it is to be understood that we speak of selfish changes in welfare.

Perhaps the most widely accepted measure of the change in a consumer's welfare due to a price increase or decrease is the change in consumer surplus *CS*. *Consumer surplus* is defined as the area under the demand curve and above the price line. The change in consumer surplus *CS* associated with a price change is given by the area under the demand curve and between the two price lines. In Figure 2.3, the area $(a + b)$ measures *CS* or the loss to the consumer because of a price hike from P_c and P_0^+. For a price decline, the area $(a + b)$ measures the consumer gain. This measure of the welfare loss for a price increase (gain for a price decrease) was originally proposed by Alfred Marshall. In time his justification for the measure came under severe criticism. Remarkably, however, after years of controversy and gallons of spilled ink, the concept of consumer surplus has recently been given a reasonably firm foundation. We will make use of recent developments in the literature on consumer surplus in a moment, but we will first try for a "low-brow" justification.

We will argue in what follows that the area $(a + b + c)$ is an upper bound of the loss to the consumer due to a price increase from P_c to P_0^+. Area (a), on the other hand, is a lower bound of the consumer's loss. One reason for taking area $(a + b)$ as the loss is that this area is roughly the simple average of the two areas $(a + b + c)$ and (a), if only demand is approximately linear. The resulting approximation may seem to be a very rough one indeed, but bear in mind that in real-world applications, there may be little difference between area $(a + b + c)$ and area (a).

Why should we view area $(a + b + c)$ as an upper bound of the consumer's loss? Suppose for the moment that the consumer is forced by the government to buy q_c at price P_0^+. The consumer would then continue to consume q_c at P_0^+ but would have $(P_0^+ - P_c)q_c$ less to spend on other goods. Clearly, $(P_0^+ - P_c)q_c$ equals area $(a + b + c)$, which would appear to be a plausible estimate of the consumer loss in dollars *if* the consumer is forced to move from point *E* to point *B*. But in actuality the consumer under the price support program is free to move from *E* to *A* and to curtail consumption after the price hike. Point *A* is definitely preferred by the consumer to point *B*. Hence, the loss associated with moving from *E* to *A* must be less than the loss associated with moving from *E* to *B*. Therefore, the consumer's loss due to the price increase is less than area $(a + b + c)$.

Why should we view area (a) as a lower bound on the consumer's loss? Suppose that prior to enactment of the program the consumer had been forced through rationing to buy only q_0 at price P_c. The consumer would voluntarily consume q_0 after the price support program is activated, but there would be $(P_0^+ - P_c)q_0$ less money to spend on other goods. Clearly $(P_0^+ - P_c)q_0$ equals area *a,* which is a plausible measure of the consumer's loss *if* the consumer moves from point *C* to point *A*. But point *E* is preferred by the consumer to point *C*. The loss associated with moving from *C* to *A* must be less than that associated with moving from *E* to *A*. Therefore, the consumer loss is greater than area (*a*).

It appears that any area less than (*a* + *b* + *c*) but greater than (*a*) might be a plausible and operational measure of the consumer's welfare loss due to a price increase. This is particularly true if area (*b* + *c*) is small. The change in consumer surplus is equal to the average of the upper and lower bounds and, as suggested above, may be used as a point estimate of the consumer loss.

A more rigorous defense for using the change in consumer surplus, area (*a* + *b*), as a measure of the welfare change associated with a price change can be launched using some applied welfare measures originally suggested by John R. Hicks. Consider the gainers and losers under some government program. According to Hicks, the maximum amount of money the gainer would be willing to pay to have the program enacted is the *compensating variation*. The minimum amount of money the gainer would be willing to accept in lieu of program enactment is the *equivalent variation*. Now consider a loser. The maximum amount of money the loser would be willing to pay in order to avoid the program is the *equivalent variation*. The minimum amount of money the loser would be willing to accept in order to make up for program costs is the *compensating variation*.

Applying these definitions to the price support program, we note that the compensating variation is the minimum amount of money the consumer would accept in order to make up for the increase in price. In other words, we could keep the consumer at the initial level of utility or welfare if we gave him or her a sum of money equal to the compensating variation and allowed the price to rise to P_0^+. This appears to many economists to be a meaningful and plausible measure of the consumer's welfare loss. In particular, it is argued that such information would be of interest to policymakers. (Were this information judged by the policymaker to be irrelevant, it could always be ignored.) The equivalent variation, on the other hand, is the maximum amount of money the consumer would be willing to pay in order to avoid the program and keep the price at P_c. In general, the compensating variation *CV* and the equivalent variation *EV* are not equal. What is wanted is a measure of the loss of welfare caused by a price hike, and we have two alternatives, plausible measures, that yield different numbers. What is more, it can be shown that the change in consumer surplus *CS* always falls somewhere between *CV* and *EV*. (See Section 2.5.)

The importance of this last result arises out of the possibility that in many real-world situations, *CV* and *EV* will be very close together. As Robert Willig has demonstrated in a seminal paper, this is very likely to be the case. Roughly speaking, if either the income elasticity for a good or the share of income normally spent on a good is small, then the compensating variation, equivalent variation, and change in consumer surplus will be very close together; each yields essentially the same estimate of either a consumer gain or loss. (Hicks was the first to show that if in fact the quantity demanded of a good is completely insensitive to a change in income, i.e., the income elasticity equals zero, then $CV = EV = CS$.) What this means is that in many applications the concept of change in consumer surplus provides a good money measure of the change in a consumer's welfare. This is important because CS is relatively easy to measure in empirical research. It is also a powerful tool in the theoretical analysis of government programs.

Thus far our attention has centered on a single consumer. Although we could not meaningfully add together the changes in utility or welfare experienced by all consumers, even if such changes could be measured, we can add together their compensating variations, equivalent variations, and changes in consumer surplus. These measures, after all, are all stated in terms of money. The welfare change for all consumers can, at least in principle, be measured by first estimating the aggregate demand and then calculating the area under the demand and between the two price lines. Returning to Figure 2.1, the aggregate loss in welfare for all consumers as a result of the price support program is given by the area $(a + b)$. In the aggregate, consumers would be willing to pay roughly area $(a + b)$ in order to avoid a program that raises price from P_c to P_0^+. Alternatively, area $(a + b)$ is roughly the amount of money that would need to be given to consumers to compensate them for having to shop at a higher price. These results are valid on the assumption that the share of income spent on food is small or, what is more likely, that the income elasticity for food is small. In the remainder of this book we will assume that one or the other (or both) of these conditions always holds.

It is illuminating to consider an example. Between 1971 and 1973, the real price of eggs at retail increased sharply from 55.1 cents per dozen to 73.9 cents. Annual per capita egg consumption fell from 25.9 dozen to 24.1 dozen. Using an arc elasticity formula yields an estimate of -0.247 as the demand elasticity, which may be a fairly good estimate. A maximum or upper-bound estimate of the annual per capita consumer loss equals ($0.739 - $0.551) multiplied by 25.9 dozen, or $4.87. A minimum or lower-bound estimate equals ($0.739 - $0.551) multiplied by 24.1 dozen, or $4.53. The difference between these two estimates amounts to 34 cents or 2 percent of the 1971 expenditure, hardly a startling sum. On the assumption of a linear demand, the annual change in consumer surplus per capita equals $4.70. If this sharp increase in the price of eggs had been brought about by a price support program, the annual welfare loss to U.S. consumers would have amounted to about $976 million, a not inconsiderable sum.

Before leaving analysis of consumer welfare, we pause to consider a serious limitation of benefit-cost analysis in general. For this purpose imagine that the government requests the economics branch of its bureaucracy to estimate Q_g and Q_0 (see Figure 2.1) prior to initiating the program. Partly on the basis of the estimates, the program is begun and it is found that the estimates of Q_g and Q_0 depart significantly from the observed values. The prediction errors could arise from two different sources. The theory could be wrong. Perhaps there exists a very large consumer cooperative that organizes a boycott of the product as a means of protesting the government's program. For this reason the observed value of Q is much less than the estimate of Q_0. Prediction errors could also arise out of faulty analysis by the economics branch. The data might have been inaccurate or the procedures used might have been inappropriate or both. Whether bad theory or bad statistical procedure is involved, the economics branch might undertake additional research in order to improve its effectiveness. Science is often served well by inconsistency between prediction and fact. If, on the other hand, the prediction errors are very small, then the evidence supports, but obviously does not prove, the empirical validity of the theory.

But now suppose that the government had also requested a measure of the loss of consumer benefits because of the program. Suppose further that an excellent estimate of DD is in hand. Measuring the area $(a + b)$ in Figure 2.1 is then a trivial matter. The economics branch might explain to government leaders that the estimate of the loss of consumer benefits is an estimate of how much money selfish consumers would be willing to pay in order to avoid the price hike. Prediction is always subject to error, however, and the question arises whether the area $(a + b)$ is a good estimate of willingness to pay. How can this question be answered? As noted in the introduction to this chapter, the ordinary market transactions of buying and selling generate data on quantities and prices that can be tabulated over time, data that can be used to check the accuracy of predicted quantities and prices. Ordinary market transactions do not involve contracts that specify consumer surpluses or amounts of money consumers would be willing to pay in order, say, to keep prices where they are. Except in the context of controlled experimental markets, quite different from markets that comprise the economy, it seems that measuring errors in the prediction of the welfare consequences of price changes is exceedingly difficult. That being the case, how can much confidence be placed in the predictions? Clearly, this is an area within economics that is much in need of further development.

2.3 BENEFITS AND COSTS TO FARM INPUT SUPPLIERS AND EFFICIENCY LOSSES

Turning to farm input suppliers we consider in turn farm labor, landowners, and suppliers of producer goods. The concepts of producer surplus and net efficiency gain (or loss) are also explained.

The analysis of program benefits to labor follows closely that for consumers. Figure 2.4 shows the labor supply function for a single worker. One measure of the worker's gain from the wage hike from the competitive level W_c to the level with the price support program in effect W_g is the Hicksian compensating variation. The compensating variation in this case is the maximum amount of money the worker would be willing to pay for the privilege of selling labor services at the higher wage rate. The equivalent variation, on the

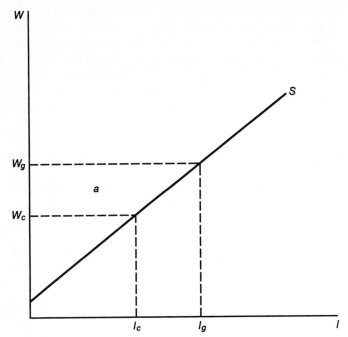

FIGURE 2.4
Measuring welfare effects of changes in the wage rate.

other hand, is the minimum amount of money needed to compensate the worker for forgoing this privilege. The change in worker surplus, given by area (*a*) in Figure 2.4, can be shown to lie always between the worker's compensating and equivalent variations. In what follows we will use the notion of the change in a worker's surplus as an approximate measure of the gain (loss) in welfare due to an increase (decrease) in the wage rate. The aggregate change in the worker's surplus can be estimated as the area between the two wage lines and above the aggregate labor supply curve.

Suppose that the aggregate farm labor supply function were flat or perfectly elastic. This might arise through the migration of workers from other geographic markets or through the transfer of workers from other jobs in response to increased demand for farm labor. In such a case a price support program would increase labor input without creating labor benefits. If all new workers are essentially indifferent toward their old jobs and their new jobs in the farm industry, then the program generates no labor benefits.

In what follows we will refer to landowners who rent their land to others (to farmers) as rentiers. From Figure 2.2 *a*, it is clear that rentiers benefit from the price support program. We take area *y* as our measure of their annual welfare gain, which equals the increase in the annual rental payments received, viz., $(R_g - R_c)A_0$.

In the study of input markets, especially the land market, it is important to distinguish between a resource and resource use. The latter is called an *in-*

put. In Figure 2.2, A_0 measures the use or input of land on, say, an annual basis. The price paid for the use of land is called *land rent,* given by R in part *a* of Figure 2.2. If all buyers and sellers of land had assumed initially, prior to the introduction of the program, that perfect competition would reign forever and that the world was stationary, with no changes in population, technology, input supply functions, etc., then the value of land V_c under competition would be given by the following simple formula:

$$V_c = \frac{R_c A_0}{i} \qquad (2.1)$$

where i equals the annual interest rate. On the assumption that all buyers and sellers assume that the price support program will last forever, once it is introduced, the value of land under government intervention is given by

$$V_g = \frac{R_g A_0}{i} \qquad (2.2)$$

With these arguments, one long-run effect of the price support program is the creation of a capital gain equal to

$$CG = \frac{(R_g - R_c) A_0}{i} \qquad (2.3)$$

Similar considerations would apply to labor, with corrections for longevity, if only markets for slaves were legal, which, fortunately, they are not.

That land can be bought and sold has very important implications for benefit-cost analysis. The price support program under consideration increases the annual flow of benefits or rental payments to rentiers by $(R_g - R_c)A_0$, as noted. At any point in time the future flow becomes capitalized in the price or value of land. Thus, with the introduction of a price support program, the rentiers find their annual payments increased; upon selling their land, they capture the present value of the future flow of benefits as well. Future rentiers receive no benefits whatever.

But now consider the man who gives up carpentry in favor of farming as a result of the price support program. The benefit is $1,000 per year. A daughter who is identical to her father except for age and sex, and who would have been a carpenter absent the program, follows in her father's footsteps and she, too, receives a benefit of $1,000 per year. Aside, perhaps, from closed-membership worker cooperatives or other special labor institutions that sell entry privileges, there is no way the initial generation of workers can usurp the benefits to subsequent generations.

In the analysis of program benefits and costs to farm producers themselves, it is necessary to distinguish between the short run and the long run. Returning to Figure 2.1, we interpret the supply curve S as a short-run supply.

It is assumed that in the short run the number of producers is fixed and that each has a fixed plant. It is also assumed that all variable input prices are held constant. On these assumptions, the supply consists of the horizontal sum of the producers' marginal cost curves. Using integral calculus it can be shown that the area under the supply curve and to the left of whatever level of output is produced equals the aggregate variable costs of all the producers. Therefore, under perfect competition the aggregate variable cost equals the area $(h + f)$ in Figure 2.1. Since total revenue is given by the product of P_c and Q_c or the area $(j + e + h + f)$, it is clear that aggregate quasi-rent to producers equals $(j + e)$. (A firm's quasi-rent is defined as total revenue minus total variable cost and is never negative. Profit, which can be either positive or negative, equals quasi-rent minus total fixed cost.) Similar reasoning indicates that under a price support program aggregate quasi-rent is given by the area $(a + b + c + j + e)$. This means that in the short run the price support program raises aggregate quasi-rent by the area $(a + b + c)$.

The *change in producer surplus due to a price change* is defined as the area above the supply curve and between the two price lines. This is equal to area $(a + b + c)$ in Figure 2.1. In the short run, the change in quasi-rent and the change in producer surplus due to the price support program amount to the same thing. The short-run case in which the prices of some variable inputs are allowed to vary jointly with product price is considered in a moment.

In the long run, assuming competitive conditions, entry is said to be free if potential entrants who elect to enter the industry experience no disadvantages in making profit not also experienced by established firms. A common proposition in the exposition of competitive theory is that entry and exit of firms force excess profits of all firms to vanish. (As we shall see in the next chapter, however, this result rests uneasily on the assumption that the supply curve for entrepreneurs is perfectly elastic.) Given this result, there is little point in wondering about the long-run effects of a farm program on the welfare of producers as such: there aren't any.

It is remarkable, however, that the concept of the change in producer surplus defined as the area above the long-run supply curve and between the two price lines can still be given an important interpretation. Returning once again to Figure 2.1, and interpreting the supply curve as long-run in nature, it can be shown that the change in producer surplus given by area $(a + b + c)$ exactly equals the sum of the rentier surplus (area y in part a of Figure 2.2) plus the worker surplus (area z in part b). In general, it can be shown in more advanced work that the change in long-run producer surplus defined as the area above the long-run supply curve and between the two price lines equals the sum of the surpluses to all inputs with upward sloping supply curves (see Just, Hueth, and Schmitz; Helmberger and Rosine.)

Even in the short run it is possible that some variable input prices are also jointly determined with product prices. All that need be assumed is that supply curves for some variable inputs are upward-sloping. In this case the change in producer surplus equals the change in quasi-rent to producers plus the surpluses accruing to the variable inputs with upward-sloping supply curves.

Thus, the change in producer surplus, whether in the short or long run, can be given a valuable interpretation. Although having a measure of the aggregate change in the surpluses to producers, inputs suppliers, or both is handy for many purposes, the necessity of examining the input markets remains if the intention is to see how program benefits are distributed among input suppliers.

The above discussion sheds light on the possible benefits or costs to suppliers of manufactured farm inputs such as fertilizers, petroleum products, tractor services, and the like. If, as in Figure 2.2c, producer goods are supplied by a constant cost industry, with a perfectly elastic supply curve, then this industry will in the long run neither share benefits nor incur costs as a result of the price support program. If, on the other hand, the producer goods industry were an increasing cost industry, then some program benefits would flow to the suppliers of inputs to that industry.

In discussions of the pros and cons of a public program it is commonplace to make reference to the program's impact on economic efficiency. The *net efficiency gain* is here defined as the sum, whether positive or negative, of all program benefits and costs. A negative sum in absolute value is called a *loss*. Returning to Figure 2.1 and assuming a long-run model, we note that the gain to input suppliers is given by area $(a + b + c)$, whereas the loss to consumers equals area $(a + b)$. The gain to producers is larger than the loss to consumers by the amount area (c). Does this mean the price support program gives rise to a net efficiency gain? Indeed not, for we have ignored taxpayers. Here and throughout this book we will simply define the *taxpayer loss (gain)* as the increase (decrease) in taxes required to pay government costs.

In Figure 2.1, the government buys $Q_g - Q_0$ at the support price P_0^+. The taxpayer loss equals $(Q_g - Q_0)P_0^+$ or the area $(b + c + d + e + f + g)$. The area c must be subtracted from this area in order to measure the net efficiency loss, which equals area $(b + d + e + f + g)$. The net efficiency loss is large relative to either the consumer loss or the producer gain, and for good reason. The purchase and destruction of a large proportion of total production is blatantly inefficient.

2.4 BENEFITS AND COSTS TO THE MARKETING SECTOR

Our analysis up to this point has assumed that producers sell their output directly to consumers. This assumption is needlessly restrictive in modeling farm programs. Farmers rarely sell their outputs directly to consumers. Farm output consists mainly of raw materials that require considerable marketing services (processing, transporting, etc.) before being placed on supermarket shelves. As a consequence, the farm gate demand is a derived demand on the part of the marketing industry.

How does this complication affect the benefit-cost analysis of our price support program? Here and throughout the remainder of this book we assume that farm output is proportional to retail output and that the marketing industry is a constant cost industry in the following sense: the marketing margin or marketing cost per unit of output does not in the long run vary with the level of output. On the assumption of proportionality, retail output may be expressed in terms of farm output equivalent. A pound of cheddar cheese, for example, can be expressed in pounds of milk required for its manufacture. The assumption of a constant marketing margin means that the retail price minus the farm-level price is constant and does not vary with the level of output. These assumptions likely approximate real-world conditions rather well and, in any event, greatly simplify analysis.

Figure 2.5 gives the competitive farm-level demand DD as before. The retail demand D_r lies above DD by a constant margin. The consumer loss as a result of the price support program was previously reported as the area under D and between the price lines P_0^+ and P_c. In the present model, output equal to Q_c is associated with a farm price P_c and a retail price P_{rc}; Q_0 is associated with a farm price P_0^+ and a retail price P_{rg}. Simple algebra will suffice to show that area $(d + e + g + h)$, the area under DD and between the two price lines associated with P_c and P_0^+, equals area $(a + b + c + d + e + f)$, the area under D_r and between the two price lines associated with P_{rc} and P_{rg}. This

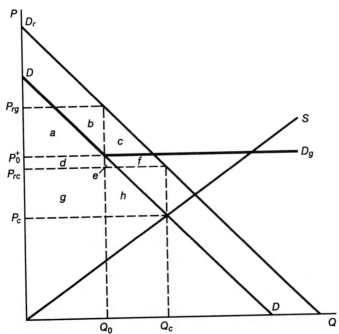

FIGURE 2.5
Measuring welfare effect of price changes in farm and retail markets.

means that the loss (change) in consumer surplus can be read as the area under either the farm-level demand or the retail demand. This is a direct consequence of the assumption of a constant marketing margin, an assumption that greatly simplifies much of the graphic analysis given in this book.

On the other hand, had we assumed that the marketing margin increases with industry output, then programs that alter prices and outputs change the marketing margin and create either benefits or costs for suppliers of inputs to the marketing industry. In this case, it can be shown that the area under the farm-level demand curve and between P_0^+ and P_c measures the consumer loss plus the loss to those suppliers of inputs to the marketing industry that have upward-sloping supply curves. (See Problem 4 at the end of the chapter.)

2.5 COMPENSATED DEMANDS AND WELFARE EFFECTS*

The conventional Marshallian demand function for a good is derived through maximizing a utility function subject to a budget constraint. A Hicksian or compensated demand function is derived through minimizing expenditure subject to the constraint of a utility function. Movement along the Marshallian curve involves holding money income constant but allowing utility to vary with price changes. Movement along the compensated curve involves holding utility constant but allowing money income to vary with price changes.

Let the Marshallian and compensated demand functions be given by (2.4) and (2.5), respectively,

$$q = D_m (P, Y) \qquad (2.4)$$

$$q = D_h (P, U) \qquad (2.5)$$

where the independent variables in (2.4) are P and money income Y and where P and utility U are viewed as given or independent in (2.5). All prices save for the good in question are held constant. According to the Slutsky equation,

$$\frac{\partial D_m}{\partial P} = \frac{\partial D_h}{\partial P} - q \frac{\partial D_m}{\partial Y} \qquad (2.6)$$

Suppose the good in question is a normal good so that $\partial D_m/\partial Y$ is positive. Then for any q, the slope of the compensated demand in absolute value is less than that for the Marshallian demand. If $\partial D_m/\partial Y$ is negative, then for any q the slope of the compensated demand in absolute value is greater than that for the Marshallian demand. These results are useful in the following graphic analysis, remembering that (2.4) and (2.5) are quantity-dependent functions but that our graphs give price-dependent demand curves. (We thus continue the long tradition in economics of trying to confuse the student as much as possible.)

In Figure 2.6, the Marshallian demand given by D_m is the same as curve d in Figure 2.3. This is the conventional demand curve encountered in elemen-

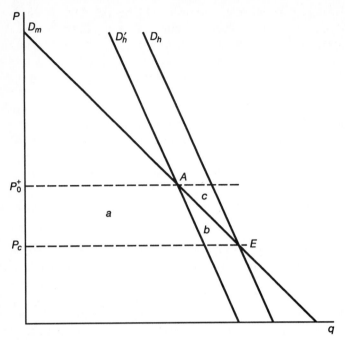

FIGURE 2.6
Measuring welfare effects of price changes using Marshallian and
Hicksian demands.

tary analysis for a consumer. For movement along a compensated demand,
utility is held constant, and, since there is an infinity of utility levels (indifference curves in two-product analysis), there is an infinity of compensated demand curves. (There is, of course, an infinity of Marshallian demand curves as
well, one for each level of money income.) The compensated demand for the
level of utility associated with point E, the initial point prior to introduction
of the price support program, is given by D_h. The compensated demand for
the utility level associated with point A, with price raised to the support level,
is given by D_h'. Notice that the compensated demands are more steeply inclined than is the Marshallian demand. The good in question must, therefore,
be normal.

It can be shown that the area under D_h and between the two price lines,
area $(a + b + c)$, is the compensating variation (see Just, Hueth, and
Schmitz). The area under D_h' and between the two price lines, area (a), is the
equivalent variation. The change in consumer surplus equals area $(a + b)$.
(Were the good an inferior good, the compensated demands would cut through
the Marshallian demand from below; they would be less steeply inclined.) As
noted earlier, if the income elasticity of the good or the share of the income
spent on the good or both are small, then area $(b + c)$ will be small as well.

Notice that if the term $\partial D_m/\partial Y$ in Equation (2.6) equals zero, then the Marshallian demand and Hicksian demands coincide. In this special case the compensating variation, equivalent variation, and change in consumer surplus are equal.

2.6 SUMMARY

This chapter provides an introduction to benefit-cost analysis. For purposes of illustration we consider a price support operation in which the government acquires and destroys whatever surplus quantity of food is necessary to raise the market price to the support level. The increased price prompts consumers to consume less and producers to produce more, hence the surplus. The production of food obviously requires inputs, and a price support operation in the product market also affects the prices and levels of farm inputs. Farmers, moreover, do not produce food for final consumption; they produce raw materials that pass from the farm gate to the retail shelf through a marketing system. Marketing firms and suppliers of marketing sector inputs will also be affected by a price support operation.

Benefit-cost analysis is applied welfare analysis; it tries to go beyond simply measuring the impacts of a program in terms of output and input quantities and prices. More specifically, benefit-cost analysis tries to measure how and to what extent the well-being, welfare, happiness—call it what you will—of the various participants in a market is affected by government intervention. A serious obstacle in such analysis is that the changes in welfare due to a change in the terms of trade are not directly measurable and are not recorded in the contracts of exchange. To finesse this problem, economists have proposed a person's willingness to pay money in order to receive the benefits of some program (or in order to avoid the costs) as a measure of the change in the person's welfare. Returning to the example of a price support program, we take as our measure of the consumers' welfare loss due to a price hike the change in consumers' surplus defined as the area beneath the market demand curve for food and between the two price lines associated with the competitive price and the price support level. This area can be shown to approximate closely, under a wide range of conditions, the total willingness of consumers to pay to avoid the onus of having to shop for food at a higher price. The short-run welfare gain to producers is measured by the aggregate increase in quasi-rent, which can conveniently be measured as the area above the short-run supply curve and between the two price lines. This area is often referred to as the *change in the producers' surplus*. Price support operations and most other farm programs entail government expenditure, and in this book we take as our measure of taxpayer loss the expenditure required to implement a program.

Increasing the demand for farm output ordinarily increases the demands for inputs. We envisage three inputs—producer goods, labor, and land—in order to emphasize the implications of the shapes of input supply curves for welfare analysis. In general we take as our measure of the welfare gain to suppliers of an input their willingness to pay for the privilege of selling inputs at a higher price as measured, approximately, by the area above the aggregate input supply curve and between the two input price lines associated with perfect competition and the price support program. In this chapter and in much of the book we assume the supply curve for producer goods is perfectly flat. Producer goods suppliers, therefore, receive no benefits from a price support program. The long-run supply curve for labor to the farm sector, on the other hand, is assumed to be upward-sloping. Increased output implies increased labor input and increased returns to labor. We take as our measure of the welfare gain to farm workers as a result of the price support program the area above the aggregate labor supply curve and between the two price lines.

In contrast to farm labor and producer goods, the supply curve for land is assumed to be perfectly inelastic. The welfare gain to initial landowners is simply the increase in the total rents they receive from farmers for the use of farmland. A very important hypothesis in farm program analysis, and one repeatedly emphasized in the chapters to follow, is that increases in rents to farmland become capitalized into the price or value of land. A price support operation, through increasing the demand for land, creates a capital gain for the benefit of initial landowners. Future landowners receive no benefit because they end up paying higher prices for the farms they buy.

The area above the output supply curve and between the two price lines measures the short-run gain to farmers, as already noted, but this area must be given an altogether different interpretation in the long run. Specifically, the area above a long-run supply curve measures the aggregate flow of long-run benefits to all farm input suppliers. This aggregate measure includes the increase in annual rents to landowners but does not include their capital gains. Notice that if all input supply functions are perfectly elastic, then the long-run output supply curve is perfectly flat and there is no long-run increase in producer surplus.

The price support operation analyzed in this chapter is blatantly inefficient, involving the production and destruction of food. Often, however, the inefficiency caused by farm programs is more subtle in nature, taking the form of a misallocation of resources as between the farm and nonfarm sectors. In all cases, however, in the chapters to follow we need a measure of the efficiency loss (or gain) caused by farm programs that are usually implemented to redistribute income. We take as our measure the sum of all benefits and costs to the various societal groups affected by the program, including consumers, producers, taxpayers, and input suppliers.

Turning to the marketing sector for farm output, we will ordinarily assume in this book that the input supply functions confronting the marketing sector, not counting the supply curve for farm output, are highly elastic. As a rough approximation the industry that produces the marketing services that get embodied in final retail consumer products is a constant cost industry in the long run. Decreases in the quantity demanded at the retail level have no long-run impact on marketing margins or on prices of marketing inputs. This has two important implications. First, the area under the farm-level demand curve and between the two price lines associated with competition and the price support program measures accurately the corresponding area under the retail demand for food. The analysis of farm-level markets can therefore tell us a lot about how consumer welfare is affected by farm programs. Second, in the analysis of the benefits and costs of farm inputs, short shrift can be given to the suppliers of inputs to the marketing sector.

PROBLEMS

1. The supply function for farm labor is given by $W = 2 + 4L$. A government program raises W from the competitive value 82 to 90. Find the increase in worker surplus.
2. Demand and short-run supply are given by

$$P = 12 - Q$$
$$P = (1/2)Q$$

(a) Find the equilibrium values for P and Q.

(b) The government adopts a price support program setting the support price equal to 6. Find the equilibrium levels of production, consumption, and the government surplus.

(c) Calculate the loss of consumer surplus, the gain in producer surplus, the increase in taxes, and the efficiency loss associated with the program described in part b.

(d) The government program will cause total variable cost to increase by how much?

3. The quantity of land equals 100. A government program raises rent from the competitive value 10 to 20. The buyers and sellers of land believed, prior to the program, that competitive equilibrium would last forever. With enactment of the program they think the program will be in effect forever.

(a) Calculate the capital gain to landowners if the interest rate is 0.05.

(b) How would the capital gain be affected if the program were enacted for a 4-year period but buyers and sellers were uncertain what would happen after the 4 years had elapsed? What is the minimum capital gain? Hint: The present value PV of \$1,000 to be received t years from today equals

$$PV = \frac{\$1,000}{(1 + 0.05)^t}$$

4. The retail demand for apples is given by $P^r = 100¢ - 1¢\,Q$ where Q is measured in pounds. Let M equal the marketing cost per pound of apples where marketing cost includes cleaning, packing, transportation, etc., but excludes the cost of the apples. In a short-run model the marketing cost per pound rises with Q as follows: $M = 0.5¢\,Q$. Graph this latter function along with retail demand and derive graphically the short-run derived demand for apples at the farm level. (Hint: Subtract vertically the marketing cost function from the retail demand function.) Give the equation for the derived farm-level demand. (Hint: Let P equal the price that handlers are willing to pay farmers. Then $P = P^r - M$.) The short-run supply curve for apples is given by $P = 2¢ + 0.5¢\,Q$.

(a) Using both an algebraic and graphical approach solve for the competitive equilibrium values for Q, P, P^r, and M.

(b) The government announces a support price for apples at the farm level with the support price set equal to 40¢ per pound. Show that the area under the farm-level demand curve and between the two price lines equals the sum of the loss in consumer surplus plus the loss of quasi-rent in the marketing industry.

5. *Consider a consumer with the utility function $u = q_1 q_2$ where u = ordinal utility and q_1 and q_2 are quantities of the first and second good, respectively. The equations for the ordinary demand curves are

$$q_1 = \frac{y_0}{2P_1} \quad \text{and} \quad q_2 = \frac{y_0}{2P_2}$$

where y_0 = initial income and P stands for price. Demonstrate that the equations for the compensated demand curves are

$$q_1 = \left(\frac{U^0 P_2}{P_1}\right)^{1/2} \quad \text{and} \quad q_2 = \left(\frac{U^0 P_1}{P_2}\right)^{1/2}$$

where U^0 = initial utility. Under competition, $P_1 = 4$, $P_2 = 9$, and $y_0 = 36$. Under a price support program for q_1, $P_1 = 9$, $P_2 = 9$, and $y_0 = 36$. Compute the compensating variation, the equivalent variation, and the change in Marshallian consumer surplus. (Hint: For computing consumer surplus, use the following results. Let $Z = a \log_e X$. Then, $dZ/dX = a (1/X)$. $\log_e 9 = 2.2$ and $\log_e 4 = 1.4$.)

6. *In a diagram draw an ordinary demand curve for good X. Assume X is inferior and that the initial price is P_1. Sketch the appropriate Hicksian compensated demand curve for measuring the compensating variation for a price decrease. Do the same for equivalent variation.

REFERENCES AND SUGGESTED READINGS

Helmberger, Peter, and John Rosine, "Measuring Producer's Surplus," *Southern Economic Journal*, 47(1980):1175–1179.

Hicks, J. R., *A Revision of Demand Theory*, Oxford University Press, London, 1956.

Just, Richard E., Darrell L. Hueth, and Andrew Schmitz, *Applied Welfare Economics and Public Policy*, Prentice-Hall, Englewood Cliffs, NJ, 1982.

Willig, Robert D., "Consumer's Surplus without Apology," *American Economic Review*, 66(1976):589–597.

CHAPTER
3

Causes of Farm Income Problems

Farm programs are not so much a product of political ideology as of circumstances that determine the level of farm prosperity. Under both democratic and republican administrations, the federal government spent billions of dollars annually on farm programs during the 5-year period 1968–1972, when annual real net farm income averaged $34.2 billion (in 1982 dollars). When real net farm income rose to $69.4 billion in 1973, major commodity programs were largely confined to mothballs, where they remained until 1977. By that year income had fallen to $29.5 billion and the 1977 Farm Bill, passed under a democratic administration, embraced many of the techniques for elevating farm income that had been tried before. Ronald Reagan entered the White House in 1980, espousing conservative causes and promising to get the federal government off the backs of American farmers. Under his administrations, real net farm income plummeted and farm program costs soared to new highs, reaching $25.8 billion in 1986. After correcting for inflation, this was more than double the highest farm program budget recorded prior to 1980.

When farm prosperity falters, farmers turn to Uncle Sam for help. To catch his attention they follow in part the advice given by Mrs. Mary Elizabeth Clyens Lease who, in 1890, suggested that farmers raise less corn and more hell. Convoys of farm tractors descend upon Washington, D.C., where they are duly tracked by TV cameras. The secretary of agriculture's limousine is pelted with eggs as it pulls away from the curb. New farm organizations spring up to carry the word to congress members. Through such means farmers put their income problems on the nation's policy agenda.

Before taking up the analysis of alternative farm policies, it is important to consider the causes of the farm income problem, to seek to understand why farm prosperity waxes and wanes. A doctor will not ordinarily treat a patient for an

35

ache without first trying to find out what is causing the pain. Prescribing a couple aspirin and a nap could be disastrous if the patient is suffering from acute appendicitis. Similarly, farm programs that fail to address the causes of farm problems might not only fail to solve them, but they might also make matters worse.

This chapter centers on the reasons for the recurrence of farm income problems. Since farm income is determined jointly by the levels of farm outputs and inputs and their respective prices, we examine first, in Section 3.1, how these variables have changed over time since World War II. We then construct an aggregative competitive model of the farm sector in Section 3.2. This model becomes the framework for a tentative explanation in Section 3.3 of the changes that have occurred in U.S. agriculture in the period since World War II. This period is divided into two subperiods, the first being 1948–1972 and the second being 1973 to the present. Because of the important role played by farm exports since 1972, the latter part of Section 3.3 includes some partial equilibrium models of international trade that extend the model of Section 3.2. A final section centers on the changing size distribution of farms.

3.1 THE CHANGING NATURE OF THE U.S. FARM SECTOR

Figure 3.1 shows the trends in the use of several farm inputs over the period 1948–1987, with 1948 serving as the base year. The downward trend in farm labor is dramatic, with the index falling from 100 in 1948 to 27 in 1987. The number of farms fell from 5 to 2.2 million. The farm population fell from 24 million to 5 million, from 16.6 percent of total population to 2.0 percent. Behind the stark numbers is a human migration that easily rivals the great migra-

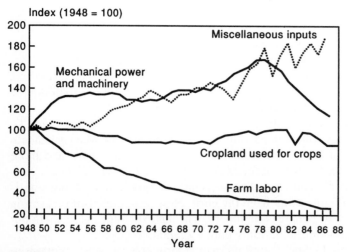

FIGURE 3.1
Trends in farm input levels, United States, 1948–1988. (From USDA, ERS, *Economic Indicators of the Farm Sector: Production and Efficiency Statistics, 1987.*)

tions of history, such as that from Ireland during the Great Potato Famine. As with other migrations, the flight from rural to urban areas was not without its toll in human anguish. It is therefore not surprising that farm families resisted the move from agriculture for an uncertain future in urban areas. And it is also not surprising that many had little understanding of the basic causes of their problems, or that they looked to the federal government for help.

Producer goods, defined as production inputs purchased from the nonfarm sector, showed marked increases in contrast to farm labor. The index of mechanical power and machinery rose from 100 in 1948 to 168 in 1979, before falling back to 116 in 1987. The index for fertilizer and other agricultural chemicals (not shown in Figure 3.1), soared to 694. The index for miscellaneous inputs such as insurance, veterinary fees, telephone, and the like, a not insignificant collection of inputs, rose to 189. The index of cropland used for crops held steady over the period 1948–1988, with the major variation caused by farm programs that offered incentives to farmers for idling land.

According to Figure 3.2, the index of all farm inputs taken together was fairly stable over the period 1948–1987, suggesting that the decline in labor was about offset by the increase in producer goods. The index of farm output, on the other hand, rose from 100 in 1948 to 175 in 1987. With inputs holding nearly constant, the index of productivity, defined as the output index divided by the input index but not shown in Figure 3.2, rose in tandem with that for output. This indicates substantial technological change about which we shall have a good deal more to say later in this chapter.

Turning to output and input pricing, we note that the index of real prices received by farmers for all farm products fell from 100 in 1948 to 42 in 1987 (Figure 3.3). The index of real prices paid for producer goods fell to 71 in 1987.

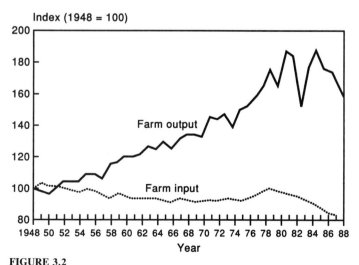

FIGURE 3.2
Trends in total farm output and input, United States, 1948–1988. (From USDA, ERS, *Economic Indicators of the Farm Sector: Production and Efficiency Statistics, 1987.*)

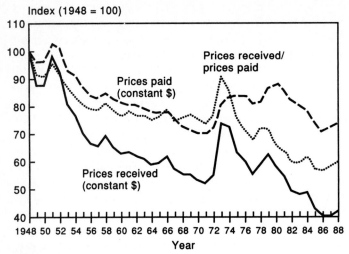

FIGURE 3.3
Trends in real prices received and paid by farmers, United States,
1948–1988. (From USDA, ERS, *Agricultural Prices,* various issues.)

The ratio of prices received to prices paid fell to 60. With technology held constant, such a decrease in the ratio of prices received to prices paid would be a fairly sure sign of depressed farm income. As we have just seen, however, technology did not hold constant.

According to Figure 3.4, the index of real farm wage rates rose from 100 in 1948 to 145 in 1988. The index of the real value of farm real estate per acre

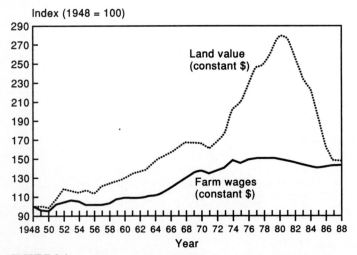

FIGURE 3.4
Trends in the real value of farm real estate per acre and real farm wages,
United States, 1948–1988. (From USDA, ERS, *Agricultural Prices,*
various issues.)

soared to 285 in 1980 and then, remarkably, fell to 147 in 1988. The fall in real land values since 1980 is unprecedented since the Great Depression. Importantly, average annual net farm income (1982 dollars) equaled $30 billion over the 5-year period 1976–1980. The corresponding figure for the 5-year period 1981–1985 was $24.3 billion. The sharp decline in real prices received by farmers along with the declines in the value of land and in farm income were merely a few indications of widespread financial distress in the farm sector in the 1980s.

What accounts for the changing pattern of resource use in the farm sector since World War II? Particularly, what have been the major factors causing farm labor to decline, even though real farm wage rates were rising? Why did land values rise so high and so steadily before taking a nose dive in 1980? What has caused the recent dramatic decline in farm prosperity? The remainder of this chapter considers these and related questions and, drawing upon agricultural economics research, tries to answer them. We begin by developing an analytical framework. In other words, we look to that part of economic theory that identifies the variables and relationships likely of importance in understanding the lurching changes that have occurred in U.S. agriculture since World War II.

3.2 MODELING THE FARM SECTOR

It is commonplace in microeconomics to model or derive behavioral relationships for an individual decision maker, whether consumer, firm, or input supplier, and then to aggregate these relationships across all like decision makers in order to obtain aggregative or marketwide behavioral relationships. Marketwide demand and supply curves are obtained, for example, through the lateral summation of the demand and supply curves of individual consumers and producers. The argument can and has been made that the aggregative relationships are of primary interest in economics, that the modeling of the individual decision maker is of interest mainly as a stepping stone. In building an aggregative model of the farm sector, we start by considering the family farm, but our major interest is in aggregative relationships.

Modeling the Family Farm

Much of the discussion of the definition of a family farm in the literature on farm policy appears to center on definitions that might be of use in taking a census. Suppose the objective is to estimate the current proportion of farms that could be classified as family farms. It seems likely that a rather elaborate set of criteria would need to be developed to cope with the rich diversity of the real world. It might also be difficult to find widespread agreement as to the criteria to be used.

Definitions play a different role, however, in the development of theory. The role of "ideal" types was discussed in Chapter 1. The firm envisaged in economic theory, for example, is governed by a highly idealized entrepreneur;

the resulting conception does not closely resemble the typical modern-day corporation.

For purposes of theoretical analysis, a *family farm* is here defined as a farm in which the major management or entrepreneurial decisions are made by the family and in which the labor input required by the farm is supplied by the family as well. It does not matter whether authority is concentrated in what might be called the head of the household or whether it is diffused among household members. Also, it will be seen presently that our model could easily be extended to allow for hired as well as family labor.

In short-run economic models of the firm, profit is defined as

$$\pi = TR - TVC - TFC \tag{3.1}$$

where π equals profits, TR equals total revenue or receipts, TVC equals total variable cost, and TFC equals total fixed cost. All quantities are flow variables, measured on a per unit of time basis, output per year, say. Total revenue equals price times output. Total variable cost is the sum of the products of variable input levels times their respective prices. It is shown in elementary analysis that total revenue and minimized total variable cost are both functions of output. Total fixed cost is cost that does not vary with output. In what follows we will break up total fixed cost into two components. One of these is the opportunity cost of the money invested in the fixed plant. We use $\overline{R}$ to denote this component. The other component, given by TE, measures the fixed cost associated with fixed labor. Some brief discussion of these components is in order.

Suppose an entrepreneur signs a contract to rent a fixed plant complete with buildings and a complement of machinery for 10 years at $10,000 per year. Subletting is disallowed. Assume the entrepreneur need devote no labor input to the enterprise so that we can forget about the fixed cost of fixed labor for the moment. Whether output is produced or not and regardless of the rate of plant utilization, at the end of each year, the $10,000 must be paid. Such would be an example of an annual fixed cost.

As an alternative, suppose the entrepreneur has the opportunity of buying the plant and that his or her retirement is planned for some future year T. The best alternative for the entrepreneur's equity capital is, say, a money market fund that pays a rate of interest equal to r. Let M_0 be the entrepreneur's initial holding of money (capital or wealth). At the end of year t, the entrepreneur's capital would equal $M_t = M_0(1 + r)^t$ if the capital were invested in the money market fund. As a special case, the entrepreneur's wealth would equal $M_T = M_0(1 + r)^T$ at the end of year T. This, of course, assumes the entrepreneur does not spend some of his or her wealth or earned interest on consumption. It also assumes a constant rate of interest.

If the entrepreneur buys the plant, we can then imagine that at the end of each year, the quasi-rent, i.e., $TR - TVC$, is deposited in the money market fund. How much must be deposited each year such that at the end of year T the sale of what remains of the plant plus the amount accumulated in the money market fund just equals M_T? To answer this question let R_t = quasi-rent deposited in the money market fund at the end of each year t, $t = 1$, $2,\ldots,T$. Further suppose that R_t equals a constant R for all t. At the end of period T the entrepreneur's wealth is given by:

$$R(1 + r)^{T-1} + R(1 + r)^{T-2} + \cdots + R(1 + r)^{T-T} + S = R\sum_{t=1}^{T}(1 + r)^{T-t} + S$$

where S equals the salvage value of the plant. Consider a particular value of R, $\overline{R}$, such that

$$M_T = \overline{R}\sum_{t=1}^{T} = 1(1 + r)^{T-t} + S$$

Therefore,

$$\overline{R} = \frac{M_T - S}{\sum\limits_{t=1}^{T}(1 + r)^{T-t}} \tag{3.2}$$

Equation (3.2) defines $\overline{R}$, the cost associated with a fixed plant. Aside from considerations of risk, an entrepreneur would (not) buy the plant if the resulting wealth at the end of year T was expected to be larger (less) than M_T. Importantly, this definition of annual fixed plant cost $\overline{R}$ is based on the notion of the opportunity cost of capital.

We now envisage a family contemplating the organization of a family farm. It is assumed that if the farm is organized, the family labor is fully committed to farm production. Off-farm employment is ignored. (Relaxing the assumption that farm family labor is fixed would complicate the analysis considerably.) The return to family labor RFL is defined as:

$$RFL = TR - TVC - \overline{R} \tag{3.3}$$

We next define the family's *transfer earnings* TE as the minimum return to family labor, the minimum RFL, that would prompt the family to organize a farm. Alternatively, TE may be defined as the minimum RFL needed to keep a family in the farming business in the long run.

Profit, or more explicitly, pure profit, may now be redefined as follows:

$$\pi = TR - TVC - \overline{R} - TE \tag{3.4}$$
$$= TR - TVC - TFC$$

where TFC is total fixed cost and equals the sum of $\overline{R}$ *and* TE. If $\pi > 0$ (or equivalently, if $RFL > TE$), then the family organizes a farm. If $\pi < 0$ (or equivalently, if $RFL < TE$), then a farm will not be organized. Notice that although $\overline{R}$ is defined on the basis of opportunity cost, the same does not apply to *TE*. There is a reason for this. Most people are quite willing to put their money in investments that yield the highest return, aside from risk considerations. Relatively few idealists would prefer to invest in "good" corporations with low returns as opposed to "bad" corporations with high returns that, for example, do business with South Africa. On the other hand, the utility or disutility of work clearly varies considerably among people according to individual preferences and the nature of the work. We might find, for example, that a family is perfectly willing to give up a job opportunity in the city that returns $30,000 to labor annually in favor of farming, which returns only $20,000 to labor. In measuring the cost of production in agriculture, the opportunity cost of labor defined as the returns to labor in the family's best nonfarm alternative is irrelevant. What matters is transfer earnings.

Corresponding to the total cost concepts are the usual average and marginal cost concepts. Average transfer earnings, *ATE* equals *TE* divided by the level of output q. Average "normal" return to investment in the fixed plant $A\overline{R}$ equals $\overline{R}$ divided by output q. Average fixed cost is the sum of *ATE* and $A\overline{R}$. Average variable cost *AVC* is *TVC* divided by q. Average total cost *ATC* equals the sum of *AFC* and *AVC*. Marginal cost *MC* is given by the first derivative of the *TVC* function.

Figure 3.5 gives a graphic representation of the average cost and marginal cost relationships. The *AFC* curve is the vertical sum of the curves for

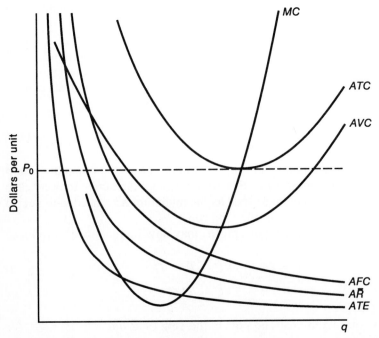

FIGURE 3.5
Short-run average and marginal cost curves for a farm.

ATE and *AR̄*. That part of the *MC* curve not below the *AVC* curve is the firm's supply curve. If we assume the plant is of optimum size, then at P_0 the farm is earning zero profit and is in both short-run and long-run equilibrium. In any event, the horizontal sum of those parts of the farms' *MC* curve not below the *AVC* curves is the industry's short-run supply curve.

It is typically assumed in long-run analysis that the number of firms is variable and that no firm is saddled with a fixed plant or with the corresponding fixed cost. We assume, however, that although the family is free to enter or exit farming in the long run, if it chooses to enter, family labor becomes fixed in agriculture. Figure 3.6 depicts the market for output in long-run equilibrium (part *b*) together with the cost curves for a farm earning no profit (part *a*). By construction, the vertical difference between *AC* and *AVC* times *q* equals the farm family's transfer earnings. At the farm's long-run equilibrium output q_c, *TE* equals $(P_c - AVC_c) q_c$. Mainly to simplify analysis, we assume that the long-run *AVC* curve, as in Figure 3.6, is the same for all families that organize family farms. (Farms that are not family farms are ignored.)

We now consider the relationship between the returns to family labor *RFL* and the number of families that would be willing to farm. As *RFL* rises, we assume that more and more families would be willing to enter farming and that the supply of family farms or farm operators is upward-sloping, as given by *S* in Figure 3.7. In other words, we assume that transfer earnings vary among households. If *RFL* is high enough, even Mick Jagger would be willing to button his shirt and start milking cows, although, presumably, the *RFL* would need be very high indeed.

It is important to realize that an implicit assumption of most economics texts is that the supply function for entrepreneurs is perfectly elastic, as given by *S'* in Figure 3.7. In this case transfer earnings do not vary among entrepreneurs or fam-

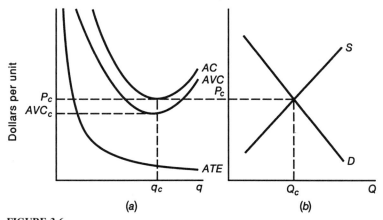

FIGURE 3.6
(*a*) Long-run average cost curves for a farm; (*b*) long-run demand and supply for the farm industry.

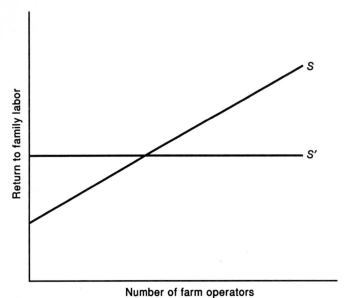

FIGURE 3.7
Supply curves for farm operators.

ilies, and in long-run equilibrium no firms enjoy excess profit. The situation is changed, however, if the supply for entrepreneurs is upward-sloping.

In Figure 3.8, we start with an initial equilibrium with demand given by D_0. The ith farm's average total cost curve is given by AC^i. The average variable cost curve is given by AVC. (No superscript is needed for AVC since all

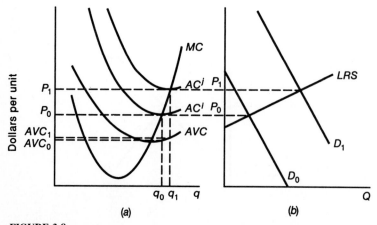

FIGURE 3.8
(a) Long-run average and marginal cost curves; (b) long-run demand and supply curves for the farm industry.

farms are assumed to have the same AVC curve.) At a price P_0, the ith farm earns no excess profit and is indifferent between a farm and a nonfarm occupation. Transfer earnings equal $(P_0 - AVC_0) q_0$. For demand D_0, the ith farm will be referred to as the marginal farm, since it earns no profit. Suppose demand increases to D_1. The higher RFL now available induces nonfarm families to enter farming. At a new equilibrium price P_1, the new marginal farm is the jth farm with transfer earnings equal to $(P_1 - AVC_1) q_1$. The ith farm now earns excess profit; the returns to its resources exceed the minimum required for entry. As demand increases, we envisage a succession of entry with old marginal farms giving way to new ones. Importantly, the usual conclusion from traditional competitive theory that no firm earns excess profit in long-run equilibrium must be discarded. Profit equals zero for the marginal farm only.

Limitations of Graphic Analysis: An Example
Involving Technological Change

Graphic analysis is both simple and illuminating for many purposes. For other purposes more powerful techniques are required. The following example, while important in its own right, illustrates the point. Demand and initial long-run supply are given by D and S_0 in Figure 3.9. A technological change shifts S from S_0 to S_1. Clearly, technological change causes price to decline and output to increase. It is also clear that consumers' welfare is increased, with the increase in consumer surplus given by the area $(a + b)$. With the initial tech-

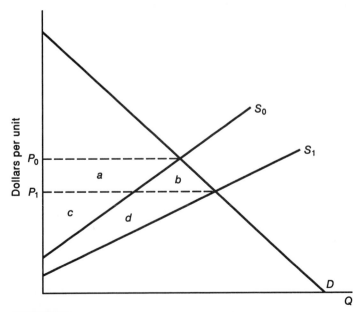

FIGURE 3.9
Demand and a shift in the supply curve due to technological change.

nology, producer surplus equaled area $(a + c)$. With the new technology, producer surplus equals area $(c + d)$. The gain in producer surplus is given by area $(d - a)$, which equals area $(c + d)$ minus area $(a + c)$. Is the gain positive or negative? It is difficult to say on the basis of graphic analysis.

Recall from Chapter 2 that the change in producer surplus equals the sum of the changes in the surpluses of all the inputs, including in the present case, the surplus accruing to family labor. The effects of technological change on agriculture have been one of the most widely discussed topics in agricultural economics. Surely we would want to know about, or at least have some idea as to, the effects of technological change on the welfare of farm families and other input suppliers; and it is sobering that elementary graphic analysis has so little to offer on these crucial issues. What is required is a model in which the interrelationships between the product market and the input markets are made explicit. Such a model provides insights as to the effects of many exogenous changes, not just technological growth. In fact, there is an entire range of important issues that cannot be analyzed without a model that integrates product and input markets in a consistent fashion. To the construction of such a model, we now turn.

An Aggregative Model of the Farm Sector

We proceed directly to long-run analysis. Let the profit function for the ith producer be given by:

$$\pi = Pq - Ra - Gk - TE \tag{3.5}$$

where π equals profit; a equals acreage farmed; k equals producer goods such as diesel fuel, fertilizer, hours of tractor use, etc., purchased from the nonfarm sector; and where P, R, and G equal, respectively, the price of output, land, and producer goods. The model could easily be expanded to include fewer aggregative input categories, as will be seen shortly. As before, TE equals transfer earnings.

The production function is assumed to have the Cobb-Douglas form:

$$q = \alpha_0 a^{\alpha_1} k^{\alpha_2} l_0^{\alpha_3} \tag{3.6}$$

where $\alpha_1 + \alpha_2 + \alpha_3 = 1$ and $0 < \alpha_i < 1$, $i = 1, 2, 3$, and where l_0 equals fixed family labor. A Cobb-Douglas (CD) production function has several interesting properties. The CD function is linearly homogeneous, meaning that a doubling of all inputs doubles output as well. The isoquant map is shown in Figure 3.10. Each isoquant is smooth and convex to the origin and does not touch either axis. Also, the expansion path, given by EPA in Figure 3.10, is linear for constant prices of a and k. The marginal cost curve on these assumptions is everywhere upward-sloping. The assumption of a CD function greatly simplifies analysis, but the simplifications come at a cost. The assumption of a CD function is restrictive, meaning that some of the conclusions reached on the basis of the resulting model might not hold for other forms of the production func-

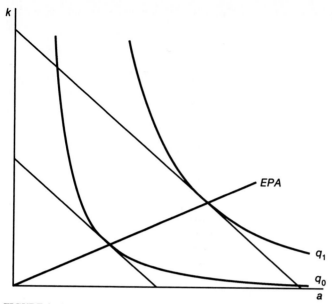

FIGURE 3.10
Isoquants and isocost lines for a farm.

tion. Fortunately, there has been some empirical research to suggest that aggregative models based on CD functions provide plausible approximations of the real world. (See, for example, Rosine and Helmberger.)

Maximizing (3.5) subject to (3.6) yields

$$R = (\alpha_1\alpha_0 a^{\alpha_1-1}k^{\alpha_2}l_0^{\alpha_3})P = P\ MPP_a$$

$$G = (\alpha_2\alpha_0 a^{\alpha_1}k^{\alpha_2-1}l_0^{\alpha_3})P = P\ MPP_k$$

(3.7)

where *MPP* equals marginal physical product. Profit maximization implies that the level of each variable input will be chosen such that its price equals its value of marginal product.

For example, let $\alpha_0=1.0$, $\alpha_1=0.5$, $\alpha_2=0.4$, and $l_0=1.0$. Then, $q=a^{0.5}k^{0.4}$. Taking the partial derivative of q with respect to a yields the marginal physical product of a: $MPP_a=0.5a^{-0.5}k^{0.4}$. Similarly, we find that $MPP_k=0.4a^{0.5}k^{-0.6}$. These expressions for MPP_a and MPP_k can be inserted in (3.7). When this is done and the two-equation system is converted to logarithms, we have

$$\log R = \log 0.5 - 0.5 \log a + 0.4 \log k + \log P$$

$$\log G = \log 0.4 + 0.5 \log a - 0.6 \log k + \log P$$

Conversion to logarithms yields a linear, two-equation system, which can be solved for log a and log k. (Recall that R, P, and G are constants from the individual farmer's point of view.) Solving for log a and log k and taking the antilogarithms yields

$$a = 0.0004R^{-6}G^{-4}P^{10}$$

$$k = 0.00032R^{-5}G^{-5}P^{10}$$

By assigning values to R, G, and P, we can quickly calculate the quantities of a and k.

As an alternative to maximizing π, recalling that TE is fixed, we could just as well have chosen to maximize the return to family labor RFL, subject to the production function:

$$RFL = Pq - Ra - Gk \tag{3.8}$$

This approach also yields the relationships given by (3.7). Since family labor is fixed, we can define its imputed wage W as follows:

$$W = \frac{RFL}{l_0} \tag{3.9}$$

We will make use of this relationship shortly.

Since all farmers are assumed to have the same production function and face the same prices, we can form the following identities:

$$Q_s = Nq, \quad A = Na, \quad K = Nk, \quad \text{and} \quad L = Nl_0 \tag{3.10}$$

where N equals the number of farm operators or families; Q_s, A, K, and L equal, respectively, the aggregate quantities of output supplied, acreage, producer goods, and family labor. In the long run, the number of farms is variable. This means that although family labor per farm is fixed, the aggregate level of family labor is variable.

We next derive aggregative relationships that are the counterparts to (3.6) and (3.7). Using (3.10), (3.6) can be rewritten as follows:

$$\frac{Q_s}{N} = \alpha_0 A^{\alpha_1} K^{\alpha_2} L^{\alpha_3} \left(\frac{1}{N}\right)^{\alpha_1 + \alpha_2 + \alpha_3} \tag{3.11}$$

But the α's sum to 1 and we can multiply both sides of (3.11) by N, yielding the aggregate production function:

$$Q_s = \alpha_0 A^{\alpha_1} K^{\alpha_2} L^{\alpha_3} \tag{3.12}$$

The aggregative relationships corresponding to (3.7) can be derived in similar fashion as the reader may verify. We postpone writing out (3.7) in aggregative form until a later point in the analysis.

It is now convenient to show that in long-run competitive equilibrium, the value of the marginal product of family labor equals its imputed wage W. According to Euler's theorem,

$$Q_s = \frac{\partial Q_s}{\partial A}A + \frac{\partial Q_s}{\partial K}K + \frac{\partial Q_s}{\partial L}L$$

$$= \frac{RA}{P} + \frac{GK}{P} + \frac{\partial Q_s}{\partial L}L \tag{3.13}$$

(The partial derivatives of Q_s with respect to the inputs are the marginal physical products.) The second expression follows because the ratio of an input's price to output price equals marginal product. Rearranging (3.13) and using (3.9) yields

$$\frac{\partial Q_s}{\partial L}PL = PQ_s - RA - GK$$
$$= N\,RFL$$
$$= Nl_0W$$
$$= LW \tag{3.14}$$

Dividing both sides of (3.14) by L we have

$$W = \alpha_3\alpha_0 A^{\alpha_1}K^{\alpha_2}L^{\alpha_3-1}P \tag{3.15}$$

What this result shows is that even though labor is fixed according to each farm, the number of farms will adjust in the long run such that the implicit wage to labor exactly equals labor's value of marginal product.

We proceed with the construction of our model by assuming that land is in perfectly inelastic supply; aggregate land input A is thus exogenous. Producer goods, on the other hand, are assumed to be in perfectly elastic supply; the price of producer goods, as opposed to their level, is exogenous. The supply function for family labor is upward-sloping. Postulating a demand function for farm output and a product market equilibrium condition together with the above assumptions allows expressing the aggregative model of the farm sector in its entirety as follows:

$Q_s = \alpha_0 A^{\alpha_1}K^{\alpha_2}L^{\alpha_3}$ Aggregate production function

$R = \alpha_1\alpha_0 A^{\alpha_1-1}K^{\alpha_2}L^{\alpha_3}P$ Rent equals land's value marginal product

$G = \alpha_2\alpha_0 A^{\alpha_1}K^{\alpha_2-1}L^{\alpha_3}P$ Price of producer goods equals its value marginal product

$$W = \alpha_3 \alpha_0 A^{\alpha_1} K^{\alpha_2} L^{\alpha_3 - 1} P \qquad \text{Wage equals labor's value marginal}$$

Wage equals labor's value marginal product   (3.16)

$$L = L(W, Z_1) \qquad \text{Family labor supply}$$

– –

$$Q_d = D(P, Z_2) \qquad \text{Demand for farm output}$$

$$Q_d = Q_s \qquad \text{Equilibrium condition}$$

The system given by (3.16) consists of seven equations and seven endogenous variables or unknowns. Recall that A (but not R) and G (but not K) are exogenous variables. In the labor supply function, Z_1 is a vector or set of exogenous (or shift) variables; Z_2 is a vector of shifters of the aggregate product demand. For example, Z_1 might contain such variables as the nonfarm wage rate, the level of unemployment, etc.; Z_2 might contain population, per capita income, etc.

The manner in which model (3.16) could be expanded to allow for hired labor can now easily be explained. Allowing for hired labor would entail adding two equations to the system, one reflecting the equating of the hired wage rate to hired labor's value of marginal product and the other postulating a hired labor supply function. Because we expect that the economic effects of changes in exogenous factors are about the same for family labor as for hired labor, we will not distinguish between the two in what follows.

As an informative exercise, consider the block of five equations above the dashed line in (3.16). This subsystem has six unknowns. Now imagine reducing the system of equations through substitution, using one equation at a time to get rid of one variable at a time but always maintaining the variables Q_s and P. If continued as far as possible, this process would eventually lead to a single equation and two unknowns, namely,

$$Q_s = S(P, A, G, Z_1) \qquad (3.17)$$

This relationship shows that the level of output depends on price and the levels of the exogenous variables A, G, and Z_1. The result is the aggregate supply, which together with the two equations below the dashed line yield a determinate system. In fact, the S and D functions together with the equilibrium condition $Q_d = Q_s$ are nothing more than the mathematical expression of the long-run demand-supply model given in Figure 3.9. If nothing else, this analysis makes clear the extent to which economic relationships are suppressed when we simply draw a long-run supply curve in a demand-supply diagram.

As another exercise consider the block of equations given by (3.16) excluding the family labor supply function. The resulting block consists of six equations and seven unknowns. Through substitution this system could be reduced to a single equation containing the two variables W and L. The resulting relationship would be a "general equilibrium" long-run demand for labor, which together with the labor supply function could be used to solve the model. A similar procedure could also be used for land and for producer goods. Importantly, the long-run product supply together with the long-run input demand functions are all implicit in (3.16).

The aggregative model given by (3.16) marshals the theory of perfect competition as a means for generating hypotheses as to the causes of changes in the U.S. farm sector. The endogenous variables are the same ones encountered earlier in our description of the trends that have occurred in agriculture since World War II. *Theory suggests three sets of exogenous factors that merit analysis and research: factors that shift product demand; factors that shift the input supply functions, including the exogenous input prices; and technological changes that alter the production function.* The assumption of a Cobb-Douglas production function, although restrictive, allows attacking a broad range of issues which would otherwise be extremely difficult to analyze.

How can the above model be used to explore the effects of changes on exogenous factors? One possibility would be to assume that the labor supply and product demand functions have a multiplicative or constant elasticity form. Then system (3.16) could be transformed into a system that is linear in logarithms. (For example, let $Q_d = a_0 P^{a_1}$.) This would facilitate finding the important reduced form relationships in which each endogenous variable is expressed as a function of all exogenous variables. The next step would involve trying to ascertain how a change in each exogenous variable affects the equilibrium values of each of the several endogenous variables. In other words, once the reduced form relationships had been derived, the next step would be to determine, if possible, the signs of the partial derivatives. This is the high road to take in the derivation of hypotheses, but it is a hard road to follow. Solving a seven-equation system simultaneously isn't easy. Fortunately, thanks to the assumption of a Cobb-Douglas production function, there is a much simpler but still powerful method of analyzing the model. The method can be easily applied, moreover, to large equation systems that simply could not be solved analytically using the high road approach as described above.

We show first that the exponents of the inputs in the aggregate production function are production elasticities. Consider, for example, α_1:

$$\frac{\partial Q_s}{\partial A} \frac{A}{Q_s} = \frac{\alpha_1 \alpha_0 A^{\alpha_1 - 1} K^{\alpha_2} L^{\alpha_3}}{\alpha_0 A^{\alpha_1} K^{\alpha_2} L^{\alpha_3}} A = \alpha_1 \qquad (3.18)$$

In words, Equation (3.18) states that the percentage change in output divided by the percentage change in land equals α_1. We also know, however, from the equality between land rent and land's value marginal product, that $(\partial Q_s / \partial A) = R/P$. Therefore,

$$\alpha_1 = \frac{RA}{PQ_s} \qquad (3.19)$$

In words, the *production elasticity* for land equals its share of total receipts. Similarly, it can be shown that

$$\alpha_2 = \frac{GK}{PQ_s} \quad \text{and} \quad \alpha_3 = \frac{WL}{PQ_s} \quad\quad (3.20)$$

The usefulness of (3.19) and (3.20) will become apparent in the discussion that follows.

For the purpose of numerical example we consider a short-run version of the model given by system (3.16). We assume that the units of measurement are such that $A = L = \alpha_0 = 1$ and that $Q_s = K^{0.5}$. On these assumptions $dQ_s/dK = 0.5K^{-0.5}$. Therefore, $G = 0.5K^{-0.5}P$. Since $K = Q_s^2$, we have $Q_s = 0.5PG^{-1}$. If $G = 10$, then $Q_s = 0.05P$, which is the aggregate short-run supply function. Let demand be given by $Q_d = P^{-0.6}$. Then, in competitive equilibrium, $P = 6.5034$, $Q = 0.3252$, and $K = 0.1058$. Notice that the product of G and K (1.058) equals 0.5 times the product of P and Q (2.1149) with allowance for rounding error. Suppose the production elasticity for land, α_1, equals 0.4 and that the production elasticity for labor, α_3, equals 0.1. Then, $R = 0.4K^{0.5}P$ and $W = 0.1K^{0.5}P$, where R is the imputed rent to fixed land and W is the imputed wage to fixed labor. Using the equilibrium values for K and P, we have $R = 0.8461$ and $W = 0.2115$. Notice that $RA = \alpha_1(PQ)$, $WL = \alpha_3(PQ)$, and $RA + GK + WL = PQ$.

3.3 EXPLAINING CHANGES IN THE U.S. FARM SECTOR

Close examination of Figures 3.1 through 3.4 appearing earlier in this chapter reveals that changes occurring in the farm sector between 1948 and 1972 differed in marked respects from those occurring since 1972. Consider, for example, the year-to-year percentage declines in farm labor. Over the 25-year period 1948–1972, these percentage declines averaged 3.8 percent. Over the 15-year period 1973–1987, the percentage declines averaged 2.3 percent. The ratio of prices received to prices paid fell rather continuously between 1948 and the early 1970s, except for the Korean war years. It then rose noticeably in 1973, fell through 1977, and then rose again in 1978. Throughout the period 1948–1972, again except for the Korean war years, farmers sought and secured government assistance year after year. This is in considerable contrast to the period since 1972.

In light of the above considerations it is convenient to explain changes in the U.S. farm sector by considering first the period 1948–1972 and then taking up the period since 1972.

The Period 1948–1972

As noted above, theory suggests that the farm sector is subject to three sets of exogenous forces. Considered in turn, these are (1) the nature of and shifts in the farm-level demand for U.S. farm output; (2) shifts in the input supply functions, including changes in the price of producer goods; and (3) technological changes that have altered the production function. Thereafter, we consider factors affecting agriculture that are rather ignored by competitive theory but which nonetheless require our serious attention.

One small matter can be dispensed with at the outset. Land available for farming was treated as exogenous in the above model. The reason for this is mainly the constancy of cropland in use over the period of interest. Changes in the level of cropland available are of little importance in explaining the transformation of U.S. agriculture since World War II. It may be noted parenthetically, however, that in an earlier epoch, particularly prior to the turn of the century, the westward movement of farmers and the wresting of land from native Americans were probably the dominant factors associated with changes in the performance of the farm sector.

MAJOR FACTORS CAUSING CHANGES IN THE FARM SECTOR: SOME THEORETICAL RESULTS. The aggregate demand for U.S. farm output at the farm level consists of three components: the demand for current domestic consumption, the demand for exports, and the demand for storage. In light of the available research we know a good deal about the first component, the domestic consumption demand. We know a good deal less about export demand, however, and still less as regards the demand for storage. One unfortunate consequence of this is that the question of the price elasticity of total farm-level demand is at present very much up in the air.

It appears that over the period 1948–1972, however, neither shifts in export demand nor private storage demand had much impact on U.S. agriculture. Farm exports as a percentage of gross U.S. farm income rose slightly over the period 1948–1956 and then leveled off at about 12 percent, where they stayed until 1973. Private storage demand, to the extent that it was allowed to flourish in the face of public stock holding, served to even out consumption, given changes in crop yields. Over a several-year period it had neither an elevating nor a depressing effect on total farm-level demand. This means that over the period 1948–1972, attention may properly be centered on domestic consumption demand.

Regarding domestic consumption demand we are mainly interested in its shape or elasticity and in its position over time. Bad world weather plus the decision of the Soviet Union to enter world commodity markets on a large scale in the early 1970s provided an excellent experiment for gauging the price elasticity of the U.S. demand for farm output. Between 1972 and 1974 the index of prices received by farmers, corrected for inflation, rose 27.8 percent. The per capita domestic consumption of farm output fell 6.4 percent. Dividing 6.4 by 27.8 yields an estimate of price elasticity of demand equal to 0.23, an estimate that is only somewhat higher than those of more sophisticated econometric studies. It will be seen presently that the inelasticity of demand for farm output played a critical role in the transformation of U.S. agriculture in the period prior to 1972.

In regard to the position of aggregate food demand there is only one important shifter of domestic consumption demand, population growth. For every 10 percent increase in population we can expect a 10 percent increase in the quantity of farm output demanded. Econometric analyses indicate that changes in per capita income, although important in the nonfarm sector, have little effect on demand for farm output. The United States is a wealthy country; most people eat to their satisfaction without regard to changes in income. Because there are no good substitutes or complements for food, we needn't be very concerned that prices of related goods might be important demand shifters.

The increase in the domestic consumption demand as a result of population growth has had a buoyant effect in U.S. agriculture. It has encouraged the greater use of all farm inputs and elevated the price of land. In the period between World War II and 1972, the year in which demand for farm exports took off, it was the dominant cause of increased farm output. Over this period, the U.S. population increased by 43.1 percent. Farm output increased by 44.4 percent.

The aggregative model of the farm sector as set forth above indicates that exogenous changes in the input markets may also affect the farm sector. These changes and their possible effects are now considered, and there is no better way to begin than by discussing a hypothesis set forth by T. W. Schultz in 1957.

According to Schultz (1957), the price of all producer goods in farming (motor vehicles, fertilizer, etc.) on the average doubled between 1940 and 1955. The price of farm labor fully tripled. He writes (p. 12), "We thus would expect widespread substitution of producer goods for human effort." Later (p. 13) he writes, "Our economic growth has been increasing the price of human effort relative to that of producer goods. In agriculture, this change in the structure of prices has made it necessary to employ a smaller labor force and a larger quantity of producer goods."

The argument can be clarified using Figure 3.11. The curve labeled Q_0 is an isoquant showing the various combinations of producer goods K and farm labor L that could be used to produce the same level of output, holding technology constant. The slope of the isocost line ISO_0 equals the price of labor divided by the price of producer goods. Cost minimization at initial input prices implies that farm labor equals L_0 and producer goods equal K_0, at the point of tangency between the isocost line and the isoquant. Suppose the ratio of the price of labor to the price of producer goods rises. Holding output constant at Q_0, labor falls from L_0 to L_1 in the new equilibrium; producer goods increase from K_0 to K_1. This is of some interest in that, as we saw earlier, labor did decline and producer goods did increase over the period in question.

A problem arises, however, if output is not held constant. Changing input prices will likely mean changes in per unit cost. Suppose, for example, that all input prices rise with the price of labor rising relative to the price of producer goods. Then the cost associated with ISO_1 exceeds that associated with ISO_0. With increased cost (or decreased cost for that matter), output would remain the same or approximately the same only if the farm-level demand for output is perfectly or nearly perfectly inelastic. As demand elasticity increases, the theoretical underpinnings of Schultz's hypothesis become weak and it is curious that he never acknowledged this to be the case in his seminal paper. Importantly, however, at the time Schultz framed his hypothesis, the farm-level demand was judged by most economists to be severely price inelastic.

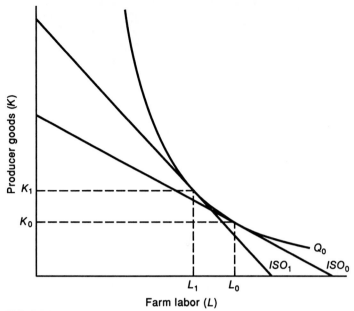

FIGURE 3.11
Isoquants and two isocost lines reflecting a change in relative input prices.

But there is another theoretical objection to Schultz's analysis. He argues that the rising price of farm labor, relative to the price of producer goods, causes a reduction in the former. The price of farm labor is almost certainly an endogenous variable, and, as we saw in Chapter 1, it is improper and basically nonsensical to argue that a change in one endogenous variable causes a change in another. In what follows we propose to clarify Schultz's analysis and to bring out more clearly the importance of the elasticity of demand.

The real price farmers paid for producer goods fell rather steadily over the period 1948–1972 (Figure 3.12). The real nonfarm wage rate, on the other hand, rose in every single year. As a consequence, the ratio of the nonfarm wage to prices paid for producer goods fell dramatically. At this juncture, the student might well ask what the nonfarm wage rate has to do with the problem. The answer is that it plays a central role in the whole analysis.

The aggregative model of the farm sector developed above allowed for exogenous shifters of the supply function for farm labor and took the price of producer goods as given, determined largely in the nonfarm sector. Intuition suggests and statistical analysis confirms that one of the most important shifters of the farm labor supply function is the nonfarm wage rate. More particularly, as the nonfarm wage rate rises, the supply function for family labor in agriculture contracts. An increase in the nonfarm wage rate, *ceteris paribus,* causes farm labor to fall and the farm wage to increase.

A decrease in the price of producer goods, *ceteris paribus,* causes both farm labor and the farm wage rate to either rise or fall depending on the elasticity of

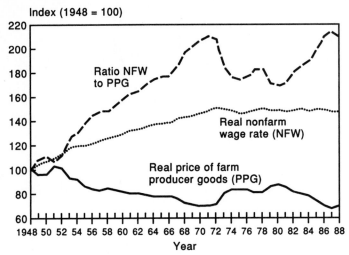

FIGURE 3.12
Trends in real nonfarm wage rate and in real price of farm producer goods,
United States, 1948–1988. (From *Economic Report of the President, 1989.*)

demand. Recall that according to (3.20), $WL = \alpha_3 (PQ)$. A decrease in the
price of producer goods lowers the cost of production, causing Q to rise and P
to fall. If demand is inelastic, PQ falls and so do W and L. In this case both the
increase in the nonfarm wage rate *and* the decrease in the price of producer
goods cause farm labor to fall. If demand is elastic, on the other hand, PQ
rises, and so do W and L. In this case the negative effect of an increase in the
nonfarm wage rate on farm labor could conceivably be offset by the positive
effect of an increase in the price of producer goods.

As it turns out, however, it seems likely that demand was highly inelastic
over the period in question, and we conclude that the increase in the nonfarm
wage rate taken together with the decline in the real price of producer goods
caused a decline in farm labor. The effect on the farm wage rate is uncertain,
but it would be entirely consistent with theory if the farm wage rate increased,
as it did in practice.

What of the level of producer goods? A decrease in the price of producer
goods, *ceteris paribus,* increases the amount of producer goods purchased.
The effect of an increase in the nonfarm wage rate by itself may be either positive or negative, however, depending on the elasticity of demand. To see this,
we note that according to (3.20), $GK = \alpha_2 (PQ)$. As the nonfarm wage rate
rises, the farm labor supply function contracts and the cost of producing farm
output rises. This causes Q to fall and P to rise. If demand is inelastic, PQ rises,
as does K. In this case, the effect of a decrease in the price of producer goods
taken together with an increase in the nonfarm wage rate must be to increase
the level of producer goods. Over the period in question the level of producer
goods did increase, just as labor fell.

If demand is elastic, then an increase in the nonfarm wage rate, *ceteris paribus,* causes PQ to fall; K falls as well. In this case the positive effect on K of a fall in its price could be offset, theoretically, by the negative effect of an increase in the nonfarm wage rate.

Was Schultz correct in arguing that an increase in the relative price of farm labor, *ceteris paribus,* causes farm labor to decline and producer goods to increase? Drawing together various strands of the above analysis, the answer is yes, if demand is perfectly inelastic and if the farm wage rate is essentially determined by the nonfarm wage rate. Absent these conditions the analysis becomes more difficult. Figure 3.12 shows that over the period 1948–1972, the real nonfarm wage rate increased and the real price of producer goods fell. These changes taken together are sufficient, *ceteris paribus,* to cause farm labor to fall and producer goods to increase if demand is merely inelastic. It needn't be perfectly inelastic. Over the period in question, as we have repeatedly stressed, demand was very likely inelastic.

How have changes in the nonfarm wage rate and in the price of producer goods affected the market for farmland? Broadly speaking the amount of land available for production given the relevant range of output and input prices is in severely inelastic supply. The question then centers on the impacts of changes in nonland input prices on land rent. Assume demand for output is inelastic. An increase in the nonfarm wage rate then causes land rent to rise. A decrease in the price of producer goods causes land rent to fall. (The logic behind these propositions is left to the student as an important exercise.) No qualitative conclusion is possible without further information. In particular, we require information as to the quantitative importance of the two countervailing effects. Quantitative analysis would also be of use in gauging the importance of the effects first cited by Schultz (1957). We will consider quantitative analysis momentarily, but we first take up the subject of technological change.

Among the various exogenous forces buffeting the farm sector, technological progress has undoubtedly received the most attention (Brandow; Cochrane; Schultz, 1945). As we saw earlier, however, not much of interest can be said in regard to the effects of technological progress on input levels and prices using graphic analysis alone.

Technological change may be defined as a change in the production function as a result of new knowledge, which lowers the per unit cost of production. Very often it consists of the availability of new or improved inputs. There are many different kinds of technological change. The two of interest here are neutral and biased change. A technological change is said to be *neutral* if, after its adoption, the ratio of any one input to any other input, labor to capital, say, remains the same as before. It is difficult to think of real-world examples of neutral technological change. One possible example of a change that comes at least close to being neutral is the introduction of hybrid seeds. The usual processes of soil preparation, fertilization, planting, and harvesting are not greatly affected. Even so, yields and production levels for given levels of inputs can rise markedly.

A technological change is said to be *biased* if the ratio of at least one input to some other input is altered. In a two-input world if the ratio of labor to capital declines, the change would be said to be biased against labor and in favor of capital. Real-world examples abound. Milking machines, tractors, corn pickers, combines, and the like come readily to mind as changes biased against labor and in favor of capital. Within the context of our aggregate model of the farm sector, an increase in α_0 is neutral, whereas a decrease in α_3 together with an equal increase in α_2 is a change biased against family labor and in favor of producer goods.

Turning to the effects of a neutral change, we take advantage of the relationship $WL = \alpha_3 (PQ)$. Because supply is increased as a result of a neutral change, Q rises and P falls. The product of W and L falls, rises, or stays the same as demand is inelastic, elastic, or has unitary elasticity. If demand is inelastic, the product WL falls, which can only happen if the position of equilibrium moves down the family labor supply function. In this case, both W and L decline and labor suffers a loss of benefits. It is true, of course, that all other inputs would fall as well.

We next consider a change biased against farm labor and in favor of producer goods. More particularly, let α_3 fall by the same amount that α_2 increases. Let $TR_0 = P_0Q_0$ and $TR_1 = P_1Q_1$ be the initial and subsequent levels of total revenue. We then have $W_1L_1 - W_0L_0 = \alpha_3(P_1Q_1 - P_0Q_0)$. If demand is elastic, the change in total revenue is positive, and since α_3 falls, it is impossible to say how labor will be affected. If demand is not elastic, however, then labor will be decreased by the technological change. As regards producer goods we note that $G_1K_1 - G_0K_0 = \alpha_2(P_1Q_1 - P_0Q_0)$. The change in question raises α_2. If demand is not inelastic, a change biased in favor of producer goods will increase K. Inelastic demand confounds the situation, however, in that α_2 rises as $(P_1Q_1 - P_0Q_0)$ falls. Even here, however, an increase in producer goods would not be inconsistent with economic theory.

These results are of considerable interest in that over much of the period since World War II, the farm gate demand was likely inelastic, and technological change was rampant. To the extent change was neutral the effect would have been to decrease all inputs. The observed decline in labor and increase in other inputs (rent in the case of land) might very plausibly have been in part the result of technological change biased against labor and in favor of other inputs.

The above discussion has largely ignored changes in the land supply, but the analytical approach can be used with advantage to show the effects of such changes as well. (See the problems given at the end of this chapter.)

Table 3.1 draws together the results of the above analysis. Upward-pointing arrows indicate positive effects; downward-pointing arrows indicate negative effects. In many cases the signs of effects cannot be derived without invoking an assumption regarding demand elasticity. Effects based on the assumption that demand is elastic are judged to be unrealistic for the period 1948–1972 and are, therefore, put in boxes to set them apart from other hypotheses. Finally, in a few cases the signs of effects cannot be determined even if a commitment is made in regard to demand elasticity. This explains the question marks.

TABLE 3.1
Qualitative effects of specified exogenous changes on endogenous farm sector variables[a]

Exogenous change	Effects on endogenous variables					
	P	Q	W	L	K	R
Demand expands	↑	↑	↑	↑	↑	↑
Nonfarm wage rate rises	↑	↓	↑	↓		
Inelastic demand					↑	↑
Elastic demand					↓	↓
Producer goods price falls	↓	↑			↑	
Inelastic demand			↓	↓		↓
Elastic demand			↑	↑		↑
Neutral technological growth[b]	↓	↑				
Inelastic demand			↓	↓	↓	↓
Elastic demand			↑	↑	↑	↑
Biased technological change[c]	↓	↑				
Inelastic demand			↓	↓	?	?
Elastic demand			?	?	↑	↑

[a]See text for the explanation of these hypothesized effects.

[b]The parameter α_0 in the production function rises.

[c]The technological change here considered is biased against labor and in favor of producer goods and land. In terms of the production function, α_3 declines and α_1 and α_2 increase.

To review the essential elements of the analysis needed to obtain the entries in Table 3.1, we note that *a useful first step in many cases is to determine how the exogenous shock affects price and output in the product market*. This is accomplished through ascertaining how exogenous change affects product demand or supply. *Second, it is useful to remember that the demand function for any input is downward-sloping*. This is particularly important for analyzing the effects of shifts in input supply functions. *Third, it is also useful to remember that the share of total receipts going to any input equals that input's production elasticity, which is constant for given technology*.

The results given in Table 3.1 are to be viewed as an internally consistent set of hypotheses drawn from economic theory. The hypotheses are internally consistent because they all spring from a single structural model. They all reflect the very same commitment as to the processes that determine performance of the farm sector.

In terms of understanding the changes that occurred in the U.S. farm sector between 1948 and 1972, the results given in Table 3.1 are subject to a serious limitation quite aside from the question of empirical validity. Although theory identifies many cause-and-effect relationships, it tells us little in regard to the question whether an effect is important or not or whether one effect is offset by another. In every column of Table 3.1 one can find arrows that point up and others that point down. What is required is quantitative analysis designed to measure the magnitudes of the various effects so that we can ascertain how the positive effects on a variable such as labor are or are not offset by negative effects.

MAJOR FACTORS CAUSING CHANGES IN THE FARM SECTOR: SOME QUANTI-TATIVE RESULTS. Quantification of the cause-and-effect relationships suggested by theory is a major objective of empirical research, and attention now centers on research findings that may be useful in gauging the importance of some of the effects considered above. These findings are summarized in Table 3.2. The model employed in this research was essentially the same as that developed earlier [see Equation system (3.16)]. U.S. farm exports were assumed to be exogenous. The farm-level demand was estimated to be severely inelastic.

The results given in Table 3.2 confirm that technological growth together with exogenous input price changes (increases in nonfarm wage rates and decreases in real producer goods prices) exerted strong downward pressure on farm labor over the period 1948–1972, easily offsetting the buoyant effect of population growth. Technological change by itself tended to decrease the use of producer goods. This suggests that the negative effect of neutral change outweighed the positive effect of change biased in favor of producer goods. Population growth together with input price changes caused an expansion in the use of producer goods in spite of the negative effect of technological progress. Farm input price changes along with population growth caused rent to farmland to more than double. (Later, we will see that farm programs were also important in explaining the increase in rent to farmland.)

According to Table 3.2, farm input price changes essentially determined the returns to farm labor. More particularly, farm and nonfarm wage rates were

TABLE 3.2
Factors causing changes in the U.S. Farm Sector: 1948–1972[a]

	Effect on farm sector variables				
Exogenous factors	Labor, billion hours	Producer goods, billion real $	Rent, $/acre	Wages, $/hour	Farm output, billion real $
Technological growth	−9.1	−3.6	−1.02	−0.22	1.5
Farm input prices[b]	−6.5	2.5	9.56	1.10	2.2
U.S. population	3.4	7.1	5.83	0.13	10.3
Miscellaneous[c]	0.2	1.7	4.57	0.03	1.7
Estimation errors	1.2	0.9	0.01	0.02	1.0
Observed changes, 1948–1972	−10.7	8.6	18.95	1.02	11.8
1948 value	16.8	13.7	7.47	0.58	25.6

[a]Producer goods and farm output are in 1957 dollars.

[b]Includes changes in the nonfarm wage rates together with changes in prices of producer goods such as fertilizer, petroleum, chemicals, and the like, along with use of items such as tractors and combines.

[c]Includes the consumer price index, farm exports, changes in farm commodity stocks, changes in land supply, and farm programs. Because these five additional variables often tended to cancel each other out and were not individually important in explaining farm sector changes, they were grouped together in a miscellaneous category.

Source: Adapted from Rosine and Helmberger.

not equal, but changes in the latter were the dominant cause of changes in the former. This is an important result for it indicates that, given the preferences of people for farm versus nonfarm work, the returns to nonfarm labor largely determine the returns to farm labor in the long run. The incomes of farm families come from returns to their labor and equity capital. If returns to these resources are determined largely in the nonfarm sector, how then can farm programs elevate farm income in the long run? We will return to this question time and time again in the chapters that follow.

As indicated earlier the dominant cause of the growth in farm output over the period 1948–1972 was the increase in the U.S. population, a finding consistent with Table 3.2. Because of the inelasticity of demand, the effect of technological change was mainly to lower prices, not increase output.

A FARM PROBLEM: EXCESS CAPACITY OR OBSOLETE CAPACITY? It is not uncommon for agricultural economists to argue that the farm sector was characterized by excess capacity over much of the period 1948–1972. The term "excess capacity" is not always carefully defined, but is sometimes used to mean the "excess production" resulting from government programs, programs that set prices above market-clearing levels. A different interpretation will be adopted here.

By *excess capacity* we mean the existence of production assets (buildings, machines, and land) in such quantity that their optimum short-run use does not yield a normal return on the investment in those assets. Consider an industry in which specialized plants and equipment are purchased in anticipation of demand growth. Suppose that after the investments have been made, demand does not grow or that the growth is less than expected. It is in such circumstances that excess capacity could be expected to develop. Entrepreneurs will not earn a normal return on their investments; assets will be allowed to depreciate without replacements. Over time the level of plant capacity and equipment is adjusted downward to fit the new demand situation.

It does not appear that U.S. agriculture was characterized by excess capacity, as here defined, over the period 1948–1972. Producer goods flowed into the farm sector in large quantities. Farmland was both highly specialized according to agriculture and constant (Figure 3.1), but the price of land rose steadily. The influx of producer goods along with the dramatic increase in land rent are hardly the telltale signs of excess capacity. It is more precise to say that U.S. agriculture was characterized not so much by excess capacity as by the wrong kind of capacity. There were too many farmers and too much labor. The plants and equipment were appropriate for more labor than efficient production required. In industry the ratio of labor to capital is adjusted through layoffs, new investments in plant and equipment, or both. In agriculture the substitution occurs when one farm operator leaves for an urban occupation and a remaining operator takes over an additional farm, expanding acreage, buying bigger tractors and combines, and often abandoning unwanted farm buildings. Used, out-of-date farm machinery often sells at a fraction of its original price because of both depreciation and obsolescence.

The Period Since 1972

The U.S. farm sector appears to have been affected in the years since 1972 by some exogenous forces that were like and some that were unlike those experienced in the earlier years. Technological progress occurred as before, continuing to exert pressure on labor to exit farming. Interestingly, *since about 1972, the real nonfarm wage rate ceased its upward trend* (see Figure 3.12), a development that bodes ill for the U.S. labor force. Likewise, the upward trend in the ratio of the nonfarm wage rate to the price of producer goods stalled in the early 1970s and actually fell for several years before seemingly resuming its upward movement again in 1980. The Schultz hypothesis appears to have been inapplicable over much of the period since 1972, a factor that likely accounts in part for the lessened pace of the out-migration of labor from agriculture.

Easily the most important new factor affecting farm prosperity since 1972, however, was the large but unsteady growth in the demand for farm exports. Prior to 1972 farm exports accounted for approximately 13 percent of gross farm income (cash marketing receipts plus value of inventory changes). By 1980, this percentage had more than doubled, reaching 27.6. The decline in exports since 1980 has been associated with the largest decline in farm prosperity since the Great Depression of the 1930s. Because the objective here is to explain the changes that have occurred in agriculture since 1972, it is essential that export demand and export supply be moved to center stage. We begin by examining their theoretical underpinnings.

THEORY OF EXPORT DEMAND AND EXPORT SUPPLY. In the graphic analysis that follows, we ignore transportation costs and the use of different currencies by different countries. The demand and supply for food for the rest of the world (ROW) are given by D_r and S_r in part *a* of Figure 3.13. For each price, subtract the quantity supplied from the quantity demanded and plot the absolute difference in part *b* using the following rule: quantities that are algebraically negative are plotted in the second quadrant; quantities that are algebra-

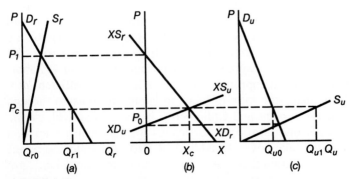

FIGURE 3.13
Derivation of the demand and supply for U.S. farm exports.

ically positive are plotted in the first quadrant. This gives the offer curve labeled $XS_r XD_r$. For prices below P_1, the quantity demanded in the ROW exceeds the quantity supplied and that part of the offer curve in the first quadrant, labeled XD_r, is the ROW's demand for exports from the United States. For prices above P_1, quantity demanded in the ROW is less than quantity supplied, and that part of the offer curve in the second quadrant, labeled XS_r, is the ROW's supply for exports to the United States. (It will soon be evident that it is the export demand that is most relevant in our analysis.)

The demand and supply for food in the United States are given by D_u and S_u in part c of Figure 3.13. Subtracting laterally the demand from the supply, but otherwise following the procedure described above for the ROW, and plotting the result in part b yields the offer curve labeled $XS_u XD_u$. For prices below P_0, the quantity demanded in the United States exceeds the quantity supplied, and the part of the offer curve in the second quadrant is the U.S. demand for exports from the ROW. For prices above P_0, the quantity demanded in the United States is less than the quantity supplied, and that part of the offer curve in the first quadrant is called the U.S. supply for exports.

Equilibrium in the world market is given by the intersection of XD_r and XS_u in part b of Figure 3.13. Competitive price equals P_c. Only at this price will world consumers be able to buy as much as they desire at the same time that world producers are able to sell as much as they desire. The United States exports $(Q_{u1} - Q_{u0})$ to the ROW. The ROW imports $(Q_{r1} - Q_{r0})$ from the United States. By construction, $X_c = (Q_{u1} - Q_{u0}) = (Q_{r1} - Q_{r0})$.

This simple model of pricing is useful in understanding the factors affecting the demand for U.S. farm exports. Economic theory identifies many factors that shift demand and supply in foreign countries. Any of these factors has the potential, at least, of shifting the demand for U.S. exports. Suppose increased income abroad raises the demand for food. This exogenous shock would expand D_r and XD_r, causing world food prices to rise and increasing U.S. exports.

The graphic analysis given above ignores transportation cost and multiple currencies. We now take up an analysis that allows for these complicating factors. To simplify exposition, we will model the market for the commodity wheat instead of that for food.

The demand and supply for wheat for the ROW are given by

$$Q_{rd} = a - bP_r$$
$$Q_{rs} = c + dP_r$$

(3.21)

where Q_{rd} equals quantity demanded, Q_{rs} equals quantity supplied, and P_r equals the price of wheat in, say, German marks. Wheat is chosen as a proxy for farm output. German marks are chosen for illustration. On the assumption of a perfect market for foreign currencies any foreign currency would do as well. Without trade, $P_{r0} = (a - c)/(b + d)$. The export demand for the United States is the excess demand for the ROW. Assuming $P_r \leq P_{r0}$, $(Q_{rd} - Q_{rs})$ yields the ROW's excess demand for wheat:

$$Q_e = (a - c) - (b + d)P_r$$
$$= i - jP_r \qquad (3.22)$$

where parameters i and j equal $(a - c)$ and $(b + d)$, respectively. This equation is the algebraic counterpart of XD_r in part b of Figure 3.13.

In order to obtain the export demand for the United States, we use (3.22) along with an arbitrage condition given by

$$P_r = \alpha \, (P_u + T) \qquad (3.23)$$

where α equals the number of marks that can be purchased with 1 dollar; P_u equals the U.S. price of wheat in dollars; and T equals the per unit cost of transportation in dollars, assumed constant. We call α the foreign exchange parameter. The easiest way to understand the logic behind (3.23) is to consider an example. Suppose the price of wheat in the United States is \$4.00, letting T equal \$2.00. Assume further that 1 mark buys 2 dollars so that 1 dollar buys ½ mark. Then $\alpha = $ ½ and the price of wheat in the ROW equals 3 marks. If the ROW price were more than 3 marks, profit could easily be gained by using marks to buy dollars and using dollars to import U.S. wheat. This would have the effect of increasing the U.S. price and decreasing the ROW price. If the price in the ROW were less than 3 marks, then too much wheat would have been imported; losses to importers could be reduced by buying less U.S. wheat, causing the U.S. price to fall and the ROW price to rise. This explains why under competitive conditions and free trade, the arbitrage condition given by (3.23) must hold.

The demand for exports in the United States can now be derived. We substitute the right-hand side of (3.23) into (3.22) in place of P_r, giving

$$Q_e = i - j\alpha \, (P_u + T) \qquad (3.24)$$

which is the demand for U.S. farm exports.

The model of the U.S. wheat market can now be set forth as follows:

$$
\begin{array}{lll}
Q_d = m - nP_u & \text{U.S. domestic demand} & \\
Q_e = i - j\alpha \, (P_u + T) & \text{U.S. export demand} & \\
Q_s = w + vP_u & \text{U.S. supply} & (3.25) \\
Q_s = Q_d + Q_e & \text{Market-clearing condition} &
\end{array}
$$

The system given by (3.25) has four equations and four unknowns. Solving for P_u, we have

$$P_u = \frac{1}{j\alpha + v + n}(m + i - w - j\alpha T) \qquad (3.26)$$

In order for this model to make sense, $m + i - w - j\alpha T > 0$. Equation (3.26) is a reduced form relationship, and we can use it to derive hypotheses in regard to how changes in T and α affect P_u, and, for that matter, the performance of the entire international wheat market. It is clear by inspection that a 1 dollar increase (decrease) in T causes P_u to decline (rise), but by less than 1 dollar. By inspection an increase (decrease) in α also causes P_u to decline (rise). A fall in P_u *is associated with* an increase in Q_d and with decreases in Q_e and Q_s. Note that it would be improper to say Q_s and Q_e fall *because P_u declines*. They fall because either T, α, or both increase. (Solving for the reduced forms for Q_d, Q_e, and Q_s is left to the student.)

What does it mean to say α increases? We had previously considered an example in which 1 mark buys 2 dollars so that 1 dollar buys half of 1 mark. Now imagine that the exchange rate changes such that 1 mark buys \$1.75 and 1 dollar buys 0.57 of 1 mark. Then the exchange rate parameter increases from 0.5 to approximately 0.57. When the dollar strengthens in exchange markets, when a dollar buys more foreign currency than previously, α rises and P_u falls. Contrariwise, when the dollar weakens, α falls and P_u rises.

Of interest, too, are the effects of changes in T and α on the ROW wheat market. The reduced form relationship for P_r can be derived by substituting the right-hand side of (3.26) for P_u in (3.23), which leads to:

$$P_r = \frac{\alpha[m + i - w + (v + n)T]}{j\alpha + v + n} \tag{3.27}$$

To find the effects of changes in T and in α we form the partial derivatives of P_r with respect to T and α as follows:

$$\frac{\partial P_r}{\partial T} = \frac{\alpha(v + n)}{(j\alpha + v + n)}$$
$$\frac{\partial P_r}{\partial \alpha} = \frac{(v + n)[m + i - w + (v + n)T]}{(j\alpha + v + n)^2} \tag{3.28}$$

Recall that structural parameters are such that $(m + i - w - j\alpha T) > 0$. It follows that $(m + i - w) > 0$. Although increases in T and α cause the U.S. price of wheat P_u to decline, these exogenous changes cause the ROW price of wheat P_r to rise. The associated changes in the ROW wheat market include a rise in production and a decline in consumption.

APPLYING THE THEORY OF EXPORT DEMAND. We now consider changes in the demand for U.S. farm exports since 1972. We start by examining the effects of changes in the exchange rates between dollars and foreign currencies. Then we return to the shifters of foreign demand and supply functions.

An index of the multilateral trade-weighted value of the U.S. dollar is plotted on the left-hand vertical axis of Figure 3.14 for the period 1967–1988. The value of U.S. farm exports is plotted on the right-hand vertical axis. The the-

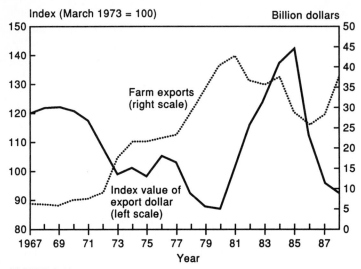

FIGURE 3.14
Trends in farm exports and in value of export dollar, Unied States,
1967–1988. (From *Economic Report of the President, 1989.*)

ory set forth above predicts that as the dollar weakens against other currencies, U.S. farm exports will rise. This is exactly what happened in the period
1971–1973 and again, though to a lesser extent, in 1977–1980. On the other
hand, as the dollars strengthens, U.S. farm exports can be expected to fall.
This is what happened in the period 1981–1985. Notice, too, the rise in farm
exports since 1986 and the continuing decline of the dollar.

One might well ask why exchange rates change the way they do, but answering this question would take us too far afield. Suffice to say that prior to
1971, the United States relied on a fixed-exchange-rate system, with the U.S.
dollar pegged at $35.00 per ounce of gold. In 1971 and again in 1973, the dollar
was devalued (the price of gold was dropped) and finally allowed to float. At
the present time the exchange rate must be viewed as an endogenous variable
in the context of economywide models, a variable that is greatly affected by
monetary and fiscal policy.

The above analysis ignores several important factors affecting U.S. exports,
factors that will receive attention at various points in what follows. *It is clearly
the case, however, that exports are sensitive to changes in the value of the
dollar.* Now that export demand has become important to U.S. farm prosperity, changes in the exchange rate are, or at least ought to be, of major concern
to farm families. It is possible that in the years ahead monetary and fiscal policies may exert a greater impact on farm income than do farm programs. Finally, the value of the dollar had begun a downward swing against other major
currencies in 1986. This will surely serve to expand export demand once again
(Figure 3.14).

Although changes in the exchange rate between dollars and foreign currencies have played an important role in shifting the U.S. demand for farm exports since 1972, there is more to the story than that. First, the Soviet Union has historically had grave problems with its highly centralized agricultural system and with what appears to be a weather pattern characterized by severe instability. Historically, stocks were drawn down and its citizens were expected to tighten their belts in periods of short supply. In 1972, however, after a particularly poor harvest, the Soviet Union entered world grain markets on a large scale. Though its purchases have varied a lot from year to year, on average it has become a major food-importing nation (see Table 3.3).

Second, China's trade policies have also played a role in the determination of U.S. farm exports. A highly irrational agricultural policy in the 1970s, intended in part to make the various provinces self-sufficient, caused massive food shortages, which necessitated substantial food imports in the late 1970s and early 1980s. Liberalization of the Chinese economy, beginning in 1979, has apparently had a handsome payoff in terms of increased agricultural productivity. Recently, China has exported significant amounts of both corn and soybeans.

TABLE 3.3
U.S. farm exports to the rest of the world and to selected regions, 1971–1986 (billion 1977 dollars)[a]

Year	World	Europe excluding USSR	USSR	Asia excluding Japan and China	Japan	China	South America	Africa
1971	13.738	5.638	.055	2.748	1.941	.000	.684	.525
1972	15.673	6.108	.723	2.908	2.393	.097	.700	.495
1973	19.429	6.838	1.012	3.170	3.295	.632	1.027	.641
1974	18.803	6.544	.256	3.611	2.974	.558	.951	.973
1975	20.842	7.404	1.079	4.248	2.935	.076	1.068	1.102
1976	22.546	8.636	1.458	3.940	3.493	.000	.968	1.156
1977	23.636	8.962	1.037	4.121	3.857	.064	.901	1.362
1978	27.985	9.710	1.607	5.034	4.224	.546	1.465	1.522
1979	29.953	10.176	2.461	5.054	4.530	.853	1.547	1.397
1980	32.986	11.005	.838	5.252	4.889	1.768	2.030	1.790
1981	32.343	10.119	1.243	5.417	4.897	1.460	2.063	2.064
1982	30.267	10.174	1.546	5.467	4.591	1.244	1.801	1.850
1983	28.202	8.466	1.151	5.674	4.884	.425	1.659	1.920
1984	27.197	6.903	2.071	5.404	4.879	.441	1.484	2.138
1985	24.201	6.180	1.603	4.688	4.508	.131	1.383	2.073
1986	24.589	7.038	.621	5.065	4.817	.058	1.373	1.881
1987	27.084	7.306	.885	6.084	5.399	.342	1.204	1.666
1988	29.439	6.661	1.783	6.710	6.064	.602	1.082	1.897

[a]Nominal values deflated by the index of prices received for crops, U.S., 1977 = 100.

Source: U.S. Department of Agriculture, *Foreign Agricultural Trade of the United States, Calendar Year 1988*, Economic Research Service, Internatonal Economics Division; and the earlier reports in this series.

Third, although per capita food consumption in the United States is quite insensitive to changes in income, the same cannot be said for the less developed nations. Many of these nations have large populations with not much to eat. With rising incomes many of them are becoming important food importers. This is particularly true of the so-called newly industrialized countries such as Taiwan and South Korea. The slow growth rates and staggering debts in much of the less developed world during the 1980s have been important causes of the decline in the demand for U.S. farm exports.

A fourth factor worth mention is the Common Agricultural Policy (CAP) of the European community (EC). This policy has been in effect since the late 1960s. We will have more to say about the CAP in Chapter 9. Suffice to say here that the CAP has been the dominant factor in converting the EC from a food deficit to a food surplus region. Exclusive of the Soviet Union, Europe accounted for about 23 percent of real U.S. farm exports in 1988, down from 41 percent in 1971 (see Table 3.3). Between 1980 and 1986, U.S. farm exports fell by $8.4 billion (1977 dollars), and Europe, again exclusive of the Soviet Union, accounted for 47 percent of this decline. China accounted for an additional 20 percent of the decline.

A final factor that may have contributed to the recent decline in U.S. exports is U.S. farm programs that set minimum prices for several farm commodities and idled millions of acres, possibly making the United States a residual world supplier. (See Chapter 8.)

EXPORTS AND ELASTICITY OF DEMAND*. The growth in the demand for U.S. farm exports, particularly since 1972, is important not only because of its implications for the position of aggregate farm-level demand but also for its shape or curvature. Shape is important because, as we have seen, demand elasticity conditions in a crucial manner the effects of changes in exogenous factors. Although the U.S. domestic demand for food is highly inelastic, the elasticity of export demand, particularly in the long run, is another matter. The elasticity of the export demand reflects the elasticity of both the ROW demand and supply. To see this more explicitly, let the ROW demand and supply be given by

$$Q_{rd} = D_r(P_r)$$

$$Q_{rs} = S_r(P_r)$$

(3.29)

The special assumption of linearity considered earlier is dropped. The demand for U.S. exports may then be written as follows:

$$Q_e = D_r(\alpha P_u + \alpha T) - S_r(\alpha P_u + \alpha T)$$

(3.30)

using (3.23).

Differentiating Q_e with respect to P_u and then converting the expression into one involving elasticities, we have

$$\frac{\partial Q_e P_u}{\partial P_u Q_e} = \left(\frac{\partial D_r}{\partial P_r} \frac{P_r - \alpha T}{Q_{rd}}\right)\frac{Q_{rd}}{Q_e} - \left(\frac{\partial S_r}{\partial P_r} \frac{P_r - \alpha T}{Q_{rs}}\right)\frac{Q_{rs}}{Q_e} \qquad (3.31)$$

The expression to the left of the equality sign is the elasticity of the demand for U.S. farm exports. As T approaches zero, the first parenthesized term on the right-hand side approaches the elasticity of ROW demand; the second parenthesized term approaches elasticity of ROW supply. Even though ROW domestic demand is inelastic, the export demand might be elastic because of the elasticity of ROW supply. The evidence indicates that although the supply for total farm output is inelastic in the short run both here and abroad, it likely exhibits a good deal more elasticity in the long run. There have been several sharp price declines both here and abroad followed by slight declines in output. Yet when one studies the remarkable differences in the amount of inputs per acre of land across countries, as between the United States and Japan, for example, the conclusion that emerges is that farm output may be quite sensitive to price in the long run.

On the basis of cross-country comparisons, Willis Peterson estimates that the elasticity of long-run supply is in the range 1.25 to 1.66. What this means is that under competitive conditions worldwide, the demand for U.S. farm exports would be quite elastic in the long run. The importance of this conclusion is diminished by the many imperfections arising out of (1) the centralized buying decisions of the Soviet Union, China, and other countries; (2) the existence of farm programs both here and abroad; and (3) other impediments to free trade.

The relevance of the above discussion to total U.S. demand for farm output can be clarified by expressing total demand as the sum of domestic and export demand as follows:

$$Q_u = Q_d + Q_e$$
$$= D_d(P_u) + D_e(P_u) \qquad (3.32)$$

Differentiating Q_u with respect to P_u and converting this into an expression involving elasticities, we have

$$\frac{\partial Q_u}{\partial P_u} \frac{P_u}{Q_u} = \left(\frac{\partial D_d}{\partial P_u} \frac{P_u}{Q_d}\right)\frac{Q_d}{Q_u} + \left(\frac{\partial D_e}{\partial P_u} \frac{P_u}{Q_e}\right)\frac{Q_e}{Q_u} \qquad (3.33)$$

The elasticity of total demand is equal to the weighted sum of the domestic and export demand elasticities. (Domestic and export elasticities are given in parentheses to the right of the equality sign.) The weights are given by the ratios of domestic consumption and exports to total quantity demanded. Statistical analyses of expressions like (3.33) have led some researchers to believe that in the long run, the aggregate demand for farm output has become elastic in recent years as the proportion of total output accounted for by exports has reached record levels. The issues involved are complex, however, and much remains to be learned. At present there is considerable uncertainty as to the elasticity of total demand confronting U.S. agriculture.

Uncertainty as to long-run demand elasticity complicates predictions as to how the farm sector will be affected by exogenous shocks in the future, including, importantly, the effects of continued technological change. Suppose, for example, that long-run demand has become elastic in the period since 1972. Does this mean that technological change will create more, not less, room for labor in agriculture? That it will be more output-expanding and less price-contracting than in the period prior to 1972? These questions are of fundamental importance and as yet unanswered.

Another factor that complicates analysis of the effects of future technological change is the mobility of knowledge. Some technological changes that originate in the United States likely will be adopted quickly by other developed and developing nations. Likewise, changes pioneered abroad may be quickly adopted here. Technological change affects the rest of the world supply and, therefore, the U.S. aggregate demand. Consequently, U.S. demand and supply have become interdependent. Even if aggregate demand is elastic because of exports, technological change may both expand supply and contract demand; its effect may be mainly to lower prices without expanding U.S. output, just as in the period 1948–1972. This is good news for society but not for farmers.

Miscellaneous Exogenous Factors Affecting the Farm Sector

The competitive model is useful in identifying the exogenous forces that have shaped the U.S. farm sector since World War II. One should always be mindful, however, of factors that may have a bearing on the issues at hand, even if these factors cannot be conveniently integrated into the competitive model. In the remainder of this chapter we consider two such factors. These are labor immobility and monopoly elements in the markets for farm products and inputs.

LABOR IMMOBILITY. Suppose the demand and supply curves for farm labor are given by D and S_0 in Figure 3.15. The supply curve S_0 is drawn on the assumption that farm workers (both hired and family) have definite but misguided perceptions as to the advantages and disadvantages of city life. With better information on available jobs, returns to labor, cultural opportunities, and other amenities of urban centers, the labor supply curve would, we assume, be given by S_1. The inaccurate assessment of urban life depresses the earnings of farm workers and increases farm labor input. This is one possible interpretation to be given to the term "labor immobility." With this interpretation, farm labor would find the move to urban centers a happy surprise, and there is some anecdotal evidence that such experiences are not uncommon.

An important study by Hathaway and Perkins suggests, however, that farm labor, particularly hired labor, is generally quite mobile, with considerable

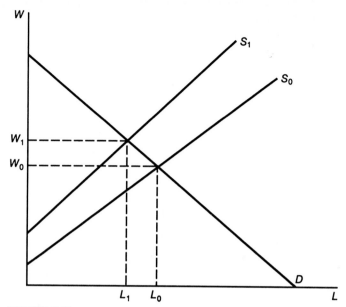

FIGURE 3.15
Demand and a shift in the supply for farm labor due to perceived
change in nonfarm alternatives.

movement to and from the farm sector as workers seek the optimum place of
employment. They found that for every 10 workers leaving agriculture during
the mid-1950s, 9 returned. Whether the movement of labor to and from agriculture is as fluid today as it was during the time of their study is an important
question.

In addition to calling attention to the fluidity of movement of labor between
the farm and nonfarm sectors, Hathaway and Perkins also noted the likelihood
of inadequate investment in the education of rural people, particularly rural
youth. Because education has historically been supported by state and local
taxes, poor states and localities, which are often of a predominantly rural char-
acter, have had inadequate educational systems relative to the more prosper-
ous urban areas. The spatial dimension of the farm sector and the high birth-
rates in rural areas, high relative to urban areas, have doubtless exacerbated
the problem. Low levels of educational achievement cloud urban opportunities
and promote inefficiency in agricultural production as well.

MONOPOLY ELEMENTS IN FARM PRODUCT AND INPUT MARKETS. In the
aggregative model considered above it was assumed that farmers were confronted with a derived demand for their output. Strictly speaking, such a curve
may be drawn only on the assumption of perfect competition in the marketing
of farm products. But competition in the marketing sector is not perfect, and
the consequences for the farm sector can be seen by considering Figure 3.16.

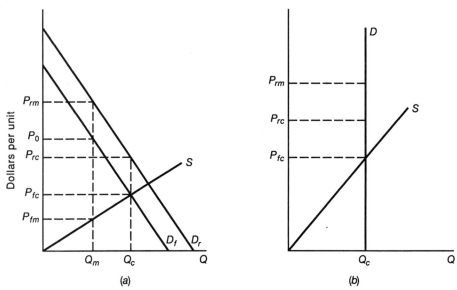

FIGURE 3.16
Effects of monopoly power on the marketing channel for farm output.

The long-run demand curve given by D_f in part a shows, as the competitive demand for any input shows, the highest price that can be paid for alternative levels of input (output from the farmers' point of view) subject to the constraint that all necessary marketing costs are covered by total receipts from consumers. The curve labeled D_r is the retail demand. When perfect competition output equals Q_c, farm price equals P_{fc}, and the retail price equals P_{rc}. The marketing bill equals $(P_{rc} - P_{fc})$ times Q_c. If competition is not perfect, if monopoly elements exist among marketing firms and labor unions, then marketing costs will be excessive. This lowers farm output to Q_m. Farm price falls to P_{fm} and the retail price rises to P_{rm}. The excessive marketing costs given the quantity Q_m equals $(P_0 - P_{fm})Q_m$.

Assessing the importance of the effects of monopoly elements on farm income requires distinguishing between the market for farm outputs and that for farm inputs. The former involves firms that market farm outputs for domestic consumption and those that export outputs for foreign consumption. Two quite different marketing channels are involved.

The competitiveness of the industries that comprise the marketing channel for farm output consumed domestically is the subject of a literature that is both vast and replete with controversy. Fortunately, it is not necessary to review this literature, for whatever conclusions can be supported, it is reasonably clear that any monopoly elements in this marketing channel for farm output have little long-run impact on the farm sector. The main reason for this is that the demand for domestic consumption is highly inelastic. To make the point through exaggeration of an essential truth, suppose that the demand is perfectly inelastic as in part *b* of Figure 3.16. Here we let $(P_{rm} - P_{rc})Q_c$ equal the excessive marketing costs due to monopoly. The farm price is given by P_{fc}. Quashing market power through vigorous antitrust regulation would increase consumer welfare, but farm price and output would not be affected. The point is this: if consumers insist on consuming a given amount of food Q_c, with little regard for price, then that amount of food will only be forthcoming if the competitive price P_{fc} is paid to farmers. The market will not be in equilibrium unless output equals Q_c. The dissolution of monopoly elements, if possible, would serve to increase benefits to consumers, but farm producers would not share significantly in the spoils.

As regards the marketing channel for the export of farm outputs, particularly of grain, not much can be said because little is known. U.S. grain exports are dominated by five large, diversified, multinational companies that maintain worldwide market information systems. All five are closely held private corporations. They compete in world markets with a limited number of private exporters from other nations and state trading nations such as Canada and Australia. Nearly all the actors in this arena are very secretive about their transactions. As a consequence little is known at present about the consequences of monopoly elements for the performance of major export markets. The available data do not allow the relevant research to go forward. It seems quite possible that the multinational companies enjoy excess profit, decreasing U.S. farm output and prices and generating benefits for domestic consumers.

On the farm input side the only input market of interest in connection with monopoly is that for producer goods. The markets for hired labor and land are characterized by selling (or renting) industries with extremely low levels of concentration. An increase in the price of producer goods, as engineered by monopolistic or oligopolistic farm input supply industries, might but need not harm farm families. An increase in the price of producer goods causes the farm output supply function to contract; output falls and price rises. With inelastic demand and a Cobb-Douglas production function, farm labor and farm labor returns both increase. (See Problem 3 at the end of this chapter.) Farmland rent also increases. With elastic total demand, the elasticity being the result of exports, increasing the price of producer goods can hurt the interests of both farmers and landowners. If exogenous input prices rise in the United States relative to prices paid by farmers in foreign nations, then clearly U.S. farmers will be disadvantaged in world markets.

It is fortunate that farmer-owned cooperatives play an important role in the marketing of farm inputs. Because cooperatives are nonprofit institutions, they can and likely do interject vigorous competition in markets that might otherwise be oligopolistic.

3.4 SOME NOTES ON THE SIZE DISTRIBUTION OF FARMS

The analysis of the U.S. farm sector up to this point has been aggregative in nature. As such it has ignored the considerable heterogeneity that characterizes agriculture. Farmers produce a vast array of commodities, not just a single product called food. They farm land of uneven quality under widely varying climatic conditions. Some farm in heavily populated areas, such as Illinois, where off-farm employment opportunities are relatively plentiful. Others, as in the Dakotas, farm land located many miles from the nearest town.

To be sure, competitive models can be constructed that encompass much more of agriculture's diversity than has the model considered above. Modeling choices become increasingly difficult, however, and the resulting equations become increasingly numerous as one seeks to model multiple products, farm versus off-farm employment decisions, alternative land tenure arrangements, and the like. The resulting models are the appropriate material for textbooks more advanced than this. Instead of pursuing this line of inquiry we turn our attention to farm programs and program analysis. There is, however, one assumption of our aggregative approach that merits further discussion in light of agriculture's diversity. This is the assumption of identically sized farms. In fact, size varies considerably among farms (Table 3.4), with the largest farms accounting for ever larger shares of total sales with the passage of time (Table 3.5). It is important to realize that with inflation, growth in farm size according to annual sales or some other measure of size might not accurately reflect growth in the real size of operations. The information given in Tables 3.4 and 3.5 is based on procedures that separate out the effects of inflation. Size is measured in 1982 dollars.

In 1982, farms with annual sales less than $40,000 accounted for 71.7 percent of all farms and only 10.9 percent of total sales. Those with sales in excess of $500,000 accounted for a scant 1.2 percent of all farms but 32.5 percent of total sales. Farms with sales in excess of $250,000 increased their percentage of total sales from 36.6 percent in 1974 to 47.6 percent in 1982. The average assets of farms with sales in excess of $100,000 in 1985 were well over 1 million in nominal dollars. Commercial farming has become the province of the well-to-do, not the simple yeoman tilling the soil with a few rudimentary tools.

The data given in Tables 3.4 and 3.5 indicate that the notion of an optimum-sized firm, a notion often encountered in the theory of perfect com-

TABLE 3.4
Percentage of total farms accounted for by constant dollar farm size groups (1982 dollars) for 1974, 1978, and 1982

	Percentage of farms with sales of				
Year	$500,000 and over	$250,000 to $499,999	$40,000 to $249,999	Less than $40,000	All farms
1974	0.7	1.5	22.8	75.0	100.0
1978	1.0	2.1	25.4	71.5	100.0
1982	1.2	2.6	24.5	71.7	100.0

Source: Reimund, Donn A., Nora L. Brooks, and Paul D. Velde, *The U.S. Farm Sector in the Mid-1980's*, U.S. Department of Agriculture, Economic Research Service, Agricultural Economic Report No. 548, May 1986.

TABLE 3.5
Percentage of farm sales accounted for by constant dollar farm size groups (1982 dollars) for 1974, 1978, and 1982

Year	Percentage of farms with sales of				
	$500,000 and over	$250,000 to $499,999	$40,000 to $249,999	Less than $40,000	All farms
1974	25.2	11.4	46.0	17.4	100.0
1978	29.7	13.2	43.6	13.5	100.0
1982	32.5	15.1	41.5	10.9	100.0

Source: Reimund, Donn A., Nora L. Brooks, and Paul D. Velde, *The U.S. Farm Sector in the Mid-1980's*, U.S. Department of Agriculture, Economic Research Service, Agricultural Economic Report No. 548, May 1986.

petition, is rather restrictive. For some purposes it is better to think in terms of an optimum size distribution of firms. The heterogeneous conditions in agriculture together with the notion of an optimum size distribution negates neither the usefulness of aggregative analysis nor the hypotheses derived therefrom. Indeed, this chapter has dealt at some length with the substitution of purchased inputs, to a large extent composed of capital plant and equipment, for labor. The technological changes that have occurred in agriculture together with the declining price of capital goods relative to wage rates have doubtless increased the advantages large farms have over small farms and has shifted the optimum size distribution of farms toward larger operations. In 1985, the ratio of sales to total assets equaled 0.381 for farms with sales in excess of $500,000 and 0.086 for those with sales less than $40,000. Small farms tend to be labor-intensive, and it has been these farms that have been hurt the most by the exogenous factors that continue to reshape U.S. agriculture.

The increasing dominance of large farms has important implications for the analysis of farm programs. The concentration of farm program benefits among the largest and most well-to-do farmers has caused a storm of controversy and, as we shall see in the following chapters, has precipitated a number of interesting policy proposals.

3.5 SUMMARY

The U.S. farm sector has undergone important changes in the period since World War II. Farm labor declined dramatically, whereas inputs purchased from the nonfarm sector—equipment, pesticides, commercial fertilizers—increased steadily. Although the index of total farm inputs has declined slightly, that for output has trended upward, indicating significant technological change. As further evidence of technological change, the ratio of the index of prices received by farmers to the index of prices paid decreased by more than 50 percent since World War II. The real returns to farm labor trended upward before stagnating in the 1970s. The real returns to farmland rose steadily until 1980 and then plummeted. The rapid rise of land values in the decade of the 1970s was approximately offset by the decline in the 1980s.

An explanation of these changes requires an analytical framework, a set of hypotheses that tentatively assert causal relationships between the endogenous variables that describe the farm sector, on the one hand, and exogenous (or shift) variables determined outside the farm sector, on the other. The hypotheses developed in this chapter are based on the seven-equation aggregate model in (3.16) of the farm sector consisting of an aggregate Cobb-Douglas production function; three conditions, each equating the value of the marginal product of an input to its price (for land, producer goods, and farm labor); an upward-sloping supply function for farm labor; an aggregate farm-level demand for output; and, finally, an equilibrium condition asserting that output supply equals output demand. The supply curve for land is assumed to be perfectly inelastic, and that for producer goods is assumed to be perfectly elastic. Exogenous variables include factors that shift product demand, factors that shift input supply functions, and both neutral and biased technological change.

With few exceptions it is possible to predict on the basis of the aggregate model how a change in any one of several exogenous variables affects the equilibrium values of all the endogenous variables of the system, depending in many instances on whether aggregate demand is elastic or inelastic (see Table 3.1). For example, it is shown that if the farm labor supply curve contracts to the left as a result, say, of an increase in the nonfarm wage rate, then the prices of farm output and farm labor increase; farm output and farm labor decrease. The input of producer goods and the rent to farmland increase if demand is inelastic and decrease if demand is elastic. A useful theorem in the derivation of the hypotheses reported in Table 3.1 asserts that an input's factor share of total farm receipts equals that input's production elasticity, which remains constant in the absence of biased technological change.

Quantitative analysis indicates that over the period 1948–1972, technological change and the increased price of labor relative to the price of producer goods were the dominant factors explaining the massive out-migration of labor from the farm sector. The growth in farm output and the expanded use of producer goods were attributable mainly to population growth. Price changes in the nonfarm sector, particularly the increase in the nonfarm wage rate, largely explained the increases in land values and in the returns to farm labor prior to 1972.

Many of the factors that buffeted the farm sector in the period 1948–1972, such as technological change, continued to be important factors in the period since 1972. An important exception was the upward trend in the ratio of nonfarm wages to the price of producer goods, which came to an abrupt end in 1973. In addition, a set of new and destabilizing factors emerged in the wake of a remarkable increase in U.S. farm exports beginning in 1973. The factors in question are the exogenous shifters of farm export demand including foreign exchange rates together with all of the demand and supply shifters in the other countries.

We have much to learn in regard to the shape (short- and long-run elasticity) of the export demand for U.S. farm output and the importance of the various demand shifters suggested by economic theory. Still, it appears likely that the weakening of the dollar in the 1970s together with the decisions of the Soviet Union and China to import large quantities of grain and the inclement weather in many parts of the world were important reasons for export demand growth in the 1970s. During the 1980s, on the other hand, the dollar strengthened in currency markets, which had the effect of decreasing export demand. Other factors contributing to the decline in export demand included (1) expanded farm output in the European community due to high price supports and rapid gains in productivity; (2) the debt crisis confronting several of the developing nations such as Brazil and Mexico; and (3) the recovery of China's agriculture following on the heels of farm policy reforms.

PROBLEMS

1. The price of a farm complete with a set of machines is $100,000. A potential buyer has the necessary cash but plans to retire in 5 years. If the buyer does not become a farmer, her money will be invested in a money market fund where it will earn an annual interest of 10 percent. The buyer's transfer earnings equal $30,000 per year. At the end of 5 years, the buyer estimates the farm will be worth $90,000. Calculate the annual total fixed cost if she decides to organize a farm.

2. The production function for a farmer is given by $q = a^{1/2} l_0^{1/2}$ where l_0 is fixed family labor. Land rent equals 2 per acre. Let $l_0 = 16$. Transfer earnings equal 10 per year. Derive the equations for the average variable cost, marginal cost, and average total cost functions and sketch their graphs.

3. Let $q = \alpha_0 a^{\alpha_1} l_0^{\alpha_2}$ be the production function for a representative farm. Fixed family labor is given by l_0 and a is a purchased input. The number of farms in the industry is held constant. Show that with an inelastic demand an increase in the price of a causes aggregate quasi-rents to increase.

4. Demand and supply for the rest of the world (ROW) are given by

$$Q_{rd} = 20 - 0.5P_r$$

$$Q_{rs} = 2 + P_r$$

Domestic demand and supply for the United States are given by

$$Q_d = 16 - 0.5P_u$$

$$Q_s = 3.5P_u$$

Price P_r is measured in British pounds and P_u is measured in dollars. One pound buys $1.60 in the foreign exchange market. It costs 80 cents per unit to transfer output from the United States to the ROW.

(a) Derive the export demand for the United States.

(b) Find the equilibrium levels for P_r, P_u, Q_d, Q_s, Q_{rd}, Q_{rs}, and the level of U.S. exports Q_e.

(c) The exchange rate changes such that 1 pound buys $1.50. Find the new export demand and compare it with the initial export demand.

(d) As an alternative to (c), suppose the transfer cost per unit rises to 90 cents. Find the new export demand and compare it with the initial export demand.

5. The model given by the system of Equations (3.16) was based on the assumption that land was in perfectly inelastic supply. Suppose we relax that assumption such

that land made available for farming increases as land rent rises. In this case, A becomes an endogenous variable.

(a) Add the appropriate column to Table 3.1 and, where possible, find the signs for the effects of the specified exogenous changes on A.

(b) Also, suppose the supply of land shifts to the right. How will this exogenous change affect the endogenous variables of the system?

6. *The aggregate production function is given by $Q = \alpha_0 A^{\alpha_1} L^{\alpha_2}$. The supply function for L is given by $L = bW^d$. A and P are assumed to be exogenous. Derive the reduced form relationships for the endogenous variables.

7. *The aggregate production function is given by $Q = \alpha_0 A^{\alpha_1} L^{\alpha_2}$. The demand for output is $P = \beta Q^\gamma$. Both A and L are exogenous. Let L increase and A decrease at the same time. What restrictions must be placed on the system such that the combined effect of the two changes will be to increase land rent?

8. *The production for livestock is given by $H = H(F_n, A_p, L_h, K_h)$ where H = output of livestock, F = crop output, A_p = acres of pasture, L = labor, and K = purchased inputs. The production function for crops is $F = F(A_c, L_f, K_f)$ where A_c = acres of cropland. Subscripts denote use of input, with h denoting livestock and f denoting food for human consumption. Construct a long-run comparative static model of the farm sector. Briefly explain each structural equation.

REFERENCES AND SUGGESTED READINGS

Brandow, G. E., "Policy for Commercial Agriculture, 1945–71," *A Survey of Agricultural Economics Literature*, Vol. 1, ed. Lee R. Martin, University of Minnesota Press, Minneapolis, 1977.

Cochrane, W. W., *Farm Prices, Myth and Reality*, University of Minnesota Press, Minneapolis, 1958.

Gardner, Bruce L., ed., *U.S. Agricultural Policy: The 1985 Farm Legislation*, American Enterprise Institute, Washington, DC, 1985.

Hathaway, Dale E., and Brian B. Perkins, "Farm Labor Mobility, Migration, and Income Distribution," *American Journal of Agricultural Economics* 50(1969):343–353.

Peterson, Willis L., "International Farm Prices and the Social Cost of Cheap Food Policies," *American Journal of Agricultural Economics*, 61(1979):12–21.

Rosine, John, and Peter Helmberger, *An Aggregative Analysis of the U.S. Farm Sector: Past Trends and Future Prospects*, Wis. Agr. Exp. Sta. Res. Bul. No. R2733, University of Wisconsin, Madison, June 1975.

Schultz, T. W., *Agriculture in an Unstable Economy*, McGraw-Hill, New York, 1945.

Schultz, T. W. "The United States Farm Problem in Relation to the Growth and Development of the United States Economy," *Policy for Commercial Agriculture*, Joint Economic Committee, 85th Congress, 1st Session, 1957.

Spitze, R. G. F., and Marshall A. Martin, eds., *Analysis of Food and Agricultural Policies for the Eighties*, North Central Regional Research Publication No. 271, Illinois Bulletin 764, University of Illinois at Urbana-Champaign, November 1980.

Tweeten, Luther, *Foundations of Farm Policy*, University of Nebraska Press, Lincoln, 1970.

U.S. Department of Agriculture, *Agricultural-Food Policy Review: Commodity Program Perspectives*, Economic Research Service, Agricultural Economic Report No. 530, July 1985.

CHAPTER
4

Direct Payment and Price Support Programs without Production Controls

In this chapter we analyze and compare two alternative programs that can be used to elevate farm prices and incomes through setting a floor or lower bound on prices received by farmers. The first to be modeled is a *direct payment scheme* in which the government establishes a target price and pays, when necessary, a direct payment per unit of output equaling the target price minus the market price. This assures an effective farm price no less than the target. (A direct payment is made only if the market price is less than the target.) The second scheme to be modeled, a variant of that considered in Chapter 2, is called a *market price support program*. Under this program the government keeps the market price from falling below a support level through government purchases and disposal of the resulting surplus in foreign or secondary markets. Throughout this chapter we will either assume no international trade or that some of the farm commodity is or can be exported.

The latter part of this chapter considers the current U.S. program for milk used in manufacturing, which illustrates price support operations. In Chapter 9, which centers on commodities that are imported, we will consider the U.S. program for wool. This program illustrates the use of direct payments.

In the case of direct payments, price supports, and other kinds of subsidy programs, it often becomes necessary to invoke trade restrictions to keep foreign producers from receiving program benefits. Section 22 of the Agricultural Adjustment Act of 1933 gives the president broad authority to do just that. The instruments at his disposal include import quotas, tariffs, or both. In this chapter we assume that adequate safeguards are in effect to keep foreign producers

79

from taking advantage of domestic direct payment and price support operations.

4.1   DIRECT PAYMENTS

In a direct payment program, the government makes payments to farmers
based on output, target price P^*, and market price P. More specifically, the
farmers' output is sold at the market price P. If the market price equals or
exceeds the target price P^*, the government does nothing. If the market price
is less than P^*, then the government sends the farmer a check equal to
$(P^* - P)q$ where q equals the farmer's output. The direct payment per unit
equals $(P^* - P)$. In real-world applications, it is important that the direct payment per unit be set equal to the target price minus a market price as opposed
to the price actually received by the farmer. This encourages farmers to get the
best prices possible for their outputs.

Direct Payments with No International Trade

The U.S. domestic demand curve DD and supply curve SS are given in Figure
4.1. The intersection of these curves gives the competitive price P_c and the
competitive output Q_c, assuming international trade does not exist. Demand
shows how much buyers would purchase at alternative market prices with or
without a direct payment program.

In order to find the market equilibrium under the direct payment program, we need a relationship that shows how much farmers would be willing to
supply at alternative market prices. For any market price less than the particular target price P_0^* in Figure 4.1, the farmer receives a per unit direct payment
that brings the real price up to P_0^*. Therefore, for any market price less than
P_0^*, the effective farm price equals P_0^* and, in the aggregate, farmers produce
Q_g. For any market price in excess of P_0^*, the farm price equals the market
price. On these arguments, the supply curve showing how much farmers
would be willing to produce at alternative market prices is given by the darkened, kinked curve SS_g in Figure 4.1. The intersection of DD and SS_g gives the
market equilibrium under the program. Equilibrium market price and output
equal P_g and Q_g, respectively. Notice that in equilibrium all farmers are able to
sell as much as they want at the effective farm price P_0^*. Buyers are able to buy
as much as they want at the market price P_g. All market participants are therefore in equilibrium.

The farmer producing output q receives a check from the government
equal to $(P_0^* - P_g)q$. The equilibrium direct payment per unit equals
$(P_0^* - P_g)$. Total government expenditure is given by $(P_0^* - P_g)Q_g$ where Q_g
equals total farm output (Figure 4.1).

The benefits and costs to various economic groups are readily apparent.
Because production is subsidized, the price to consumers falls. Consumer benefits are given by the area $(c + d + e)$. The area $(a + b)$ may be interpreted as

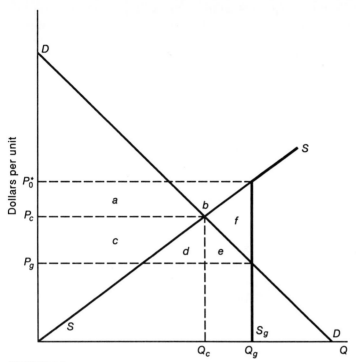

FIGURE 4.1
Effects of direct payments.

the increase in quasi-rents to initial farmers if the supply curve is assumed to be a short-run curve. Otherwise, in the long run, the area $(a + b)$ must be interpreted as the benefits to farm input suppliers such as farm workers, landowners, etc. The taxpayer loss is given by the area $(a + b + c + d + e + f)$. Subtracting the benefits to consumers and producers from the taxpayer loss leaves the area f as the efficiency or "deadweight" loss. Area f may be interpreted as the net cost to society of effecting a redistribution of income from taxpayers to consumers and farm producers (or farm input suppliers).

Quasi-rents to farmers increase by the amount area $(a + b)$ in the short run, but these short-run benefits need not be spread evenly across farmers like butter on a slice of bread. As we saw in Chapter 3, the largest farms account for a much larger share of farm output than other farms; farm sizes are extremely uneven. Roughly speaking, the benefits of a direct payment program vary among farmers in direct proportion to the size of operation. The concentration of the short-run benefits of farm programs among the largest farmers has provoked considerable controversy. Several programs that involve direct payments, more often than not involving production controls as well, place an upper limit on the size of the direct payment farmers may receive. The Food Security Act of 1985, for example, places a $50,000 limit on the total payment a farmer may receive through participation in major crop programs. Several loopholes exist, however, that allow many big farms to skirt the legislation's intent.

An alternative to a $50,000 or other limit on payments is to scale payments according to income, level of output, or some other measure of size. One possibility is to set the direct payment received by the farmer equal to the product of three terms: the farmer's output; the target price minus the market price; and a factor, call it the E-factor, that varies inversely with farm income or total income from all sources as reported on federal income tax forms. The E-factor might be set equal to 1 for low incomes, for example, and be allowed to decline to 0 at some sufficiently high level of income, say $20,000. (Perhaps the E-factor could be based on a 3- or 4-year moving average of total incomes.) In this way the concentration of farm program benefits among farmers with high incomes might be avoided. Another effect, unfortunately, would be the subsidization of inefficient operations due to wrong farm size, poor management, submarginal land, and the like.

The aggregative model of the previous chapter can be used to make some rough approximations of the long-run welfare effects of a direct payment scheme for the whole of U.S. agriculture. Suppose the supply function for farm labor is given by

$$L = b_0 W^{b_1} \tag{4.1}$$

where, as before, L equals labor and W equals the return to farm labor. The elasticity of the labor supply function is given by the parameter b_1; b_0 is simply a multiplicative constant. A graph of such a supply curve is given by S in Figure 4.2 with L plotted on the vertical axis. If we assume that a direct payment program causes W to increase from the competitive value W_c to the new level W_g, then the benefit to farm labor is given by the area under the S curve and between W_g and W_c. Using integral calculus it can be shown that this area equals

$$LB = \frac{1}{b_1 + 1}(W_g L_g - W_c L_c) \tag{4.2}$$

where LB equals farm labor benefits. Recall that if the production function is Cobb-Douglas, then $WL = \alpha_3 (PQ)$, where α_3 is labor's production elasticity. Making the appropriate substitutions we have

$$LB = \frac{\alpha_3}{b_1 + 1}(P_0^* Q_g - P_c Q_c) \tag{4.3}$$

Rosine and Helmberger have estimated that for the U.S. farm sector b_1 equals 1.9. To estimate α_3, we divide returns to all farm labor in 1984 by total farm

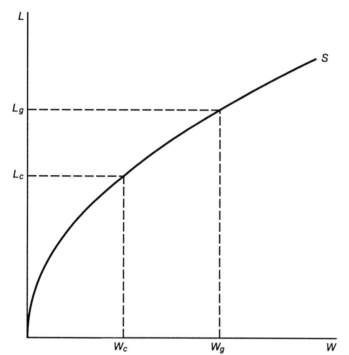

FIGURE 4.2
Welfare effects of direct payments on farm labor.

receipts, which yields the number 0.124. (Recall that an input's production elasticity equals its share of total receipts.) Using these estimates and (4.3), we find that long-run farm labor benefits equal about 4.3 percent of the increase in total receipts to the farm sector (including direct payments) caused by a direct payments program. *It does not seem likely that increasing the total receipts to the farm sector is an effective means for elevating significantly the long-run returns to farm labor.*

Landowners would likely fare much better. We take Albert Yeboah's estimate of 0.2 as the total returns to land divided by total receipts. Since the land supply function is highly inelastic, land's long-run annual benefit from a direct payments program about equals its share, 20 percent, of the increase in total receipts (including direct payments) to farmers. In addition, as we saw in Chapter 2, when a landowner sells his (her) farm, the future stream of benefits becomes capitalized into the value of that farm. Therefore, a direct payment program creates a capital gain for initial landowners.

Some rough approximations may be illuminating. We take as our estimate of the competitive total receipts to U.S. farmers the actual receipts in 1984, which equal $174.4 billion. Suppose that a direct payment program causes the effective farm price to increase by 10 percent and that the long-run elasticity of farm supply equals 0.7. Such a direct payment program for all of agriculture would cause receipts (including direct payments) to rise to $205.3 billion. The increase in annual benefits to labor equals 4.3 percent of the increase in total receipts, or $1.33 billion. The annual benefits to landowners equal 20 percent of the increase in total receipts, or $6.18 billion. The remainder of the increase in total receipts, $23.4 billion, is spent on operating inputs such as gas and oil and on the use of plant and equipment. The estimate of supply elasticity used in making these calculations is probably too low. (See the reference to Willis Peterson in Chapter 3). A higher estimate of supply elasticity would lead to still lower estimates of benefits to labor and land.

If the stream of benefits to land is assumed to continue in perpetuity and if we take 0.08 as our estimate of the interest rate, then the capital gain to initial landowners—those who owned the land at the time of the program's enactment—equals $77.2 billion. Many farmers own land, of course, and would benefit from increased returns to labor as well as through capital gains to landowners. *There is little reason to expect, however, that future generations of farmers would be helped very much by the program.*

Even so, it would be a grave mistake to suppose that future farmers would not support continuation of a program once begun. On the contrary, having purchased land at a price that reflects increased returns due to the program, future farmers could be expected to resist vigorously its termination for fear of suffering capital losses. The government would likely find termination of a well-established program very difficult.

The above analysis requires modification if the program is assumed applicable to only one of several farm industries that make up the farm sector. For one thing, the elasticity of the supply of labor to one among several farm industries, to dairy, say, likely exceeds that for the farm sector as a whole by severalfold. We can simply forget about long-run benefits to farm labor in this case. Assessing the returns to landowners is made difficult by the unevenness of land quality. Some land has a comparative advantage in dairying. Other land has a comparative advantage in wheat. A direct payment program for dairying would be most beneficial to owners of land with the greatest comparative advantage in dairying. Land that was barely bid away from wheat as a result of the program would generate scanty benefits to its owners. Little more can be said regarding benefits to landowners on theoretical grounds. Research would be needed for each farm industry, and even then it is not altogether clear that current research methods and available data could be relied upon to yield solid estimates.

Direct Payments with International Trade

The foreign trade implications of a direct payment program have been largely ignored up to this point, and we now propose to correct for this omission. The objective in what follows is to analyze the effects of a direct payment program in the context of international trade. Analysis may proceed on the assumption that U.S. sales in the world market are small relative to total trade and have no effect on the world price. This is often referred to as the small country assumption. The large country assumption means that the international transactions of a country are large relative to total world trade and do affect significantly the world price. Four cases may be analyzed according to whether the United States is assumed to be (1) a small food exporter, (2) a large food exporter, (3) a small food importer, or (4) a large food importer. The first two cases are now considered with the emphasis given to the large country assumption. Analysis of cases 3 and 4 is postponed to Chapter 9 where a direct payment program is compared with import quotas and tariffs.

Certain graphic relationships given in Figure 4.3 are the same as those appearing in Figure 3.13 in the previous chapter, with slightly different notation. Thus, D_r and S_r in part a are demand and supply for the rest of the world (ROW); D_u and SS_u in part c are domestic demand and supply for the United States; and XD_r and XS_u in the first quadrant of part b are the ROW demand and the U.S. supply for exports. Recall that XD_r is derived by subtracting laterally S_r from D_r; XS_u is derived by subtracting laterally D_u from SS_u.

Now consider a U.S. direct payment program, with the target price set at P_0^* in part c and with direct payments made to domestic producers only. The program changes the domestic U.S. supply curve from SS_u to the kinked, darkened curve SS_g. This alters the U.S. supply for exports. In order to find the new supply for exports we subtract laterally D_u from SS_g. That is to say, for each possible market price, subtract the quantity demanded in the United States from the quantity supplied. This yields the new supply for exports given by the kinked, darkened curve XS_uG^* in part b of Figure 4.3. The intersection of XD_r and XS_uG^* gives the new world equilibrium price P_g^*, which is less than P_c. U.S. exports increase from X_c to X_g^*. Centering on part c, we see that U.S. producer benefits equal area $(a + b)$; consumer benefits equal area c. U.S. taxpayers pay area $(a + b + c + d + e)$ in increased taxes. Therefore, the efficiency loss to the United States, abstracting from foreign benefits and costs,

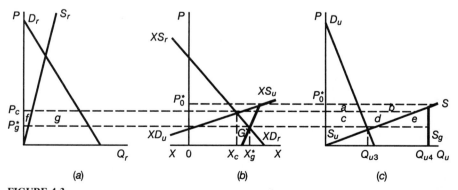

FIGURE 4.3
Effects of direct payments on the domestic and world markets.

equals area $(d + e)$. Consumer benefits in the ROW equal area $(f + g)$ in part a, whereas the producer loss in the ROW equals area f.

Two conclusions from the above analysis merit emphasis. First, because the United States is an exporter of the good in question, a direct payment program generates net benefits to the ROW, given by area (g). Second, the efficiency of a direct payment program as a means for generating benefits to U.S. farmers decreases with increases in the importance of farm exports. The second conclusion follows directly from the first. In the absence of trade, a lower price generates benefits to domestic consumers but not to foreign consumers. With trade the U.S. taxpayer picks up the tab for the benefits accruing to foreign and domestic consumers alike.

Although the above analysis is based on the large country assumption, it is easy to see what modifications would be required by the small country assumption. Specifically, on the latter assumption the ROW demand for U.S. exports is perfectly flat. Direct payments leave the market price and U.S. consumption unaffected even though U.S. exports to the ROW go up. In this situation, a direct payment program transfers benefits from U.S. taxpayers to U.S. producers; consumers are not affected.

4.2   MARKET PRICE SUPPORTS COMPARED WITH DIRECT PAYMENTS

The market price support program analyzed in Chapter 2 assumed that surplus production acquired by the government was destroyed. This is not a very interesting farm program. The destruction of crops and animal products as a means for elevating farmers' incomes has been adopted by governments both here and abroad but on a limited basis and mainly as a short-run emergency measure. The physical destruction of food on a large and continuous scale would be difficult for politicians and farm leaders to justify, particularly when there are alternatives that may be more cost effective. One of these alternatives involves government sales of the surplus in a foreign or secondary market.

Domestic demand DD for a primary market and competitive supply SS are given in Figure 4.4. The price the product would fetch in a secondary market, such as the price of corn used in making ethanol, is given by P_w. Equilibrium price is given by the intersection of DD and SS. A market price support program alters the demand confronting farmers as we saw in Chapter 2. If the support price equals P_0^+ in Figure 4.4, then the government's demand is given by $D_g D_g$. Total demand is given by the darkened, kinked curve DD_g. Market equilibrium with a price support program is given by the intersection of SS and DD_g. Equilibrium price equals P_0^+; equilibrium output equals Q_g. At price P_0^+ the primary buyers buy Q_0. Assume the government acquires the surplus $Q_g - Q_0$ and sells it in the secondary market at price P_w. Benefits to producers equal area $(a + b + c)$; losses to consumers equal $(a + b)$. The loss to taxpay-

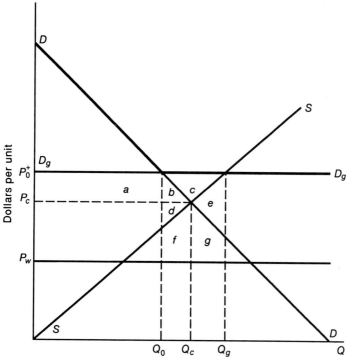

FIGURE 4.4
Effects of market price support.

ers is given by area ($b + c + d + e + f + g$). The efficiency loss equals the loss to taxpayers minus area c, viz., area ($b + d + e + f + g$). (The area c is the excess of the producer gain over the consumer loss.)

The model given in Figure 4.5 is based on the assumption that the United States is a large food exporter under perfect competition worldwide. (The demand and supply curves in the absence of government intervention are the same as those given in Figure 4.3.) Under a price support program, the government sets the domestic market support price at P_0^+ in part c of Figure 4.5. Imports are not allowed, and whatever surplus is acquired by the U.S. government in the domestic market is dumped in the world market. Because the United States is a large exporter, its farm program affects the world price.

The domestic market price support program changes the U.S. domestic demand from DD_u to DD_g. In order to derive the U.S. supply for exports, we ask, how much the United States would export at alternative world prices? At any world price less than P_0^+, the United States would export X_g^+ because this equals the U.S. quantity produced Q_{u4} minus the U.S. quantity consumed Q_{u2} at the support price P_0^+. For any world price in excess of P_0^+, the United States would export as much as under competition. The U.S. price support

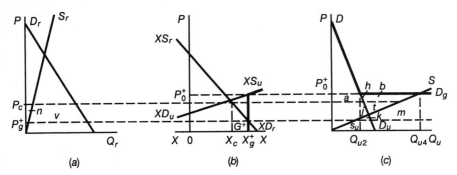

FIGURE 4.5
Effects of market price support on the domestic and world markets.

program, therefore, shifts the export supply from XS_u to the darkened, kinked curve $XS_u G^+$ in part b. The world price is now given by the intersection of XD_r and $XS_u G^+$. The U.S. price support program lowers the world price from P_c to P_g^+ and raises the domestic price from P_c to P_0^+. U.S. exports rise from X_c to X_g^+.

The support price P_0^+ in Figure 4.5 was set equal to the target price P_0^* in Figure 4.3 in order to facilitate comparative analysis. *Relative to direct payments, a price support program increases U.S. exports and lowers the world price.* The basic reason for this is that under direct payments the price to U.S. consumers is lowered, which encourages domestic consumption. Price support raises the U.S. price, which discourages domestic consumption, but the quantity of output produced domestically is the same in both cases.

Turning to benefit-cost implications, we note that the price support program generates a gain to U.S. producers equal to area $(a + h + b)$ in part c, Figure 4.5. [This area equals area $(a + b)$ in part c, Figure 4.3, in the case of direct payments.] Consumers lose area $(a + h)$, due to the higher price. U.S. taxpayer cost is given by area $(b + h + j + k + m + t)$. The efficiency loss equals area $(h + j + k + m + t)$. ROW consumers gain area $(n + v)$, which exceeds area $(f + g)$ in part a of Figure 4.3. ROW producers lose area n, which exceeds the loss given by area f in Figure 4.3.

Regarding the comparative analysis of direct payments and price supports, we note that the efficiency loss, from the point of view of the United States, is larger for the price support program than for direct payments as can readily be seen by comparing Figures 4.3 and 4.5. The reason for this is not difficult to see. As noted, U.S. production is the same in both cases, but with direct payments domestic consumers pay the same low price as foreign consumers. Price support involves dumping in the foreign market. It might also be noted that if the U.S. domestic demand curve were perfectly inelastic, then the effects of the two programs in the world market would be the same. This is of some importance in light of the severe inelasticity of U.S. domestic demand.

Is a market price support program better than a direct payment program? The welfare implications considered above, including the efficiency loss, are certainly relevant considerations in trying to answer this normative question. Three other considerations are worth mentioning, however. First, the concentration of benefits among the largest, wealthiest farmers might be more easily avoided under direct payments than under price supports. In fact, avoiding the concentration of benefits under a market price support program appears to be nearly impossible.

A second consideration concerns a value judgment often invoked in discussions of income redistribution, viz., that benefits should not be distributed in a manner demeaning to recipients. It has been argued, for example, that farmers would prefer to receive their subsidies disguised in the form of above-market-clearing prices, with the government engaged in product dumping, than in the form of checks from the U.S. treasury. The latter smacks of welfare. The former can be seen, with eyes slightly veiled, as the result of hard work and "fair" prices.

A third consideration can be explained with the aid of Figure 4.6. Here it is assumed that the target price or the support price equals P_0^* and that government surpluses in the case of price supports are destroyed. The tax re-

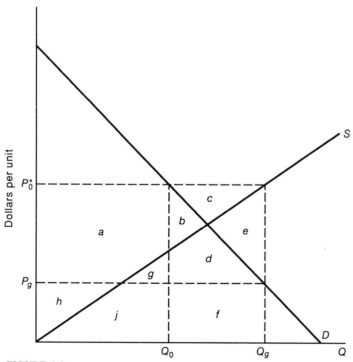

FIGURE 4.6
Tax bills and food bills under direct payments and market price support.

quired to finance a direct payment program equals area $(a + b + c + d + e + g)$; that for a price support program equals area $(b + c + d + e + f)$. Both programs yield the same benefits to farmers, aside from the cost of "demeaning" benefits, but the tax bills differ. Which program places the greater drain on the U.S. treasury? Notice that the area $(b + c + d + e)$ is common to both tax bills. Hence, whether the direct payment tax exceeds, equals, or is less than the price support tax turns on whether area $(a + g)$ exceeds, equals, or is less than area f. If demand is elastic, area f exceeds area $(a + g)$; direct payments cost the government less than do price support operations. Contrariwise, if demand is inelastic, area $(a + g)$ exceeds area f, and the direct payment tax exceeds the price support tax. This is one reason why farm lobbyists sometimes argue for price supports as opposed to direct payments. *If demand is inelastic, farmers get more bang for the buck if the buck is spent removing the commodity from the market than if it is spent on direct payments. The bang is even bigger if the surplus can be sold in a secondary market.*

Returning to Figure 4.6, we note that food expenditures equal area $(a + g + h + j)$ under price supports and area $(f + h + j)$ under direct payments. Area $(h + j)$ is common to both. With elastic demand, area $(a + g)$ is smaller than area f; the food bill is less under price supports than under direct payments. With inelastic demand, area $(a + g)$ exceeds area f; the food bill is greater under price supports than under direct payments. Food bills and tax bills are important to bear in mind for it is through such expenditures that farm benefits are financed.

4.3   THE MARKET PRICE SUPPORT PROGRAM FOR MILK USED IN MANUFACTURING

The federal government indirectly supports the market price for milk and milk components (fat and nonfat solids) used in manufacturing an array of dairy products. The support system is indirect in that the government offers to buy butter, cheese, and nonfat dry milk in bulk containers at announced prices. The objective is to put a floor on the price received by farmers through putting floors on prices of manufactured products and counting on keen competition to do the rest. The distinction between milk and milk components is important because much of the raw milk produced in the U.S. is separated into its component parts, with some sold in fluid form (skim milk) and some sold for manufacturing (milk fat used in butter). A separate program exists for raw milk and milk components going into fluid milk consumption, a program that will be analyzed in a subsequent chapter on marketing orders. Hereafter, when we refer to milk used in manufacturing, we mean all components used in manufacturing. The same applies to milk used in fluid consumption.

We assume for simplicity that the supply function for milk used in manufacturing is independent of the supply for milk for fluid consumption. Figure

4.7 gives the free market wholesale demand $D_w D_w$ for manufactured dairy products (cheese, say) in terms of the raw milk equivalent, the free market derived demand for milk at the farm level $D_f D_f$, and the milk supply curve S. The vertical distance between $D_w D_w$ and $D_f D_f$ is the marketing margin required to convert a hundredweight of milk into a given amount of manufactured product, with the margin assumed constant for all levels of output. In the absence of government intervention the equilibrium wholesale price, farm-level price, and output equal, respectively, P_{wc}, P_{fc}, and Q_c.

It would be awkward for the government to buy raw milk directly from farmers because of milk's perishability. To assure that farmers receive a minimum milk price P_f^+, the government offers to buy an unlimited quantity of manufactured product at the so-called announced price, at P_w^+ in Figure 4.7. With the program in effect, total wholesale demand $D_w D_w'$ becomes perfectly elastic at price P_w^+ and total farm-level demand $D_f D_f'$ becomes perfectly elastic at P_f^+, at P_w^+ minus the marketing margin. Supply intersects the new demand (perfectly elastic in the relevant range) at output equal to Q_g. The program elevates the farm price from P_{fc} to P_f^+ and expands output from Q_c to Q_g. One trick the government must perform is to set P_w^+ at such a level as to assure that farmers receive no less than P_f^+ for their milk, a trick that is not always

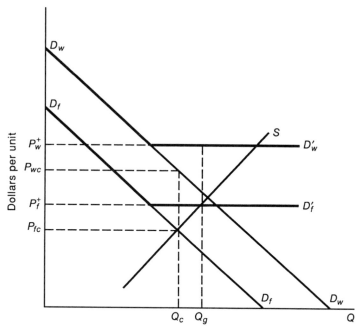

FIGURE 4.7
Supporting the price of milk through supporting the prices of manufactured dairy products.

carried off with aplomb. Another much more difficult trick is getting rid of the surplus.

The history of the milk price support program over much of the period since World War II has been uneventful, at least when viewed from the perspective of recent years. Support levels were kept rather close to market-clearing prices; surplus accumulation and disposal did not pose insurmountable problems. Before recounting a bit of this history in more detail, however, we pause briefly to consider the notion of parity price, a notion that has receded in importance as politicians have come to understand the law of supply and demand.

The current price of a commodity is said to be at *full parity* if a unit of it has the same purchasing power today as it did in some base period. The strategy has been to choose some time period in which farmers were doing very well relative to other periods. If a bushel of wheat today buys as much gingham and calico as it did back in the good old days of 1910–1914, then the present price of wheat is said to be at 100 percent of parity. (As a kindness to the reader, the details of parity price calculations are left to other publications.) As another example, in 1980–1981, the support level for milk used in manufacturing equaled $12.80 per hundredweight (3.5 percent butterfat). This was 80 percent of parity. At 100 percent of parity, the support price would have equaled $16.00. In much of the period since World War II, price support levels were specified in terms of percentages of parity, with many farmers and farm leaders pushing for price supports equal to, or at least near, 100 percent of parity.

In their quest for government assistance many farmers have viewed parity prices as a policy objective, the idea being that if they received prices equal to 100 percent of parity, they would then be about as well off as they would have been in the base period. The logic does not wash. Technological change lowers production costs even if all input prices remain the same. Maintaining parity prices through farm programs then elevates returns to family labor above that received in the base period. To cite another problem, if product demand declines, the market-clearing price declines as well. Although farmers might like prices maintained at full parity, a price support program could lead to expensive surplus disposal. Transfers of benefits from consumers and taxpayers to producers would rise. Over much of the period since World War II, price support levels as percentages of parity generally drifted downward, in recognition of changes in many factors including the effect of technological progress. As noted, the role of parity prices in U.S. farm programs is of much less significance today than it once was.

The Agricultural Act of 1949 required that the price of milk be supported between 75 and 90 percent of parity, a provision that was continued until October 21, 1981. Since that time the support price has been established by the government at specific levels. In the interval between World War II and the early 1980s, the support price as a percentage of parity varied between 75 and 90 percent with no apparent trend. On the two occasions when the government surplus became a serious problem, in 1953–1954 and again in 1961–1962, when the surplus exceeded 8 percent of industry production, the government lowered the support prices and the problem went away. The main outlets for surplus butter and cheese have been donations to the school lunch program and domestic programs for the needy, with occasional subsidized sales abroad. Surplus nonfat dry milk has been more of a problem. Here the government has resorted to a wide range of disposal activities on a more-or-less continuing basis including school lunches, programs for the needy, foreign donations, and subsidized sales abroad.

The price support program for milk has been seriously constrained by the lack of secondary markets that could easily absorb government surpluses. It is obviously in the best of interests of U.S. farmers in general to move toward free trade since the U.S. is a large net exporter of food. It is difficult for Uncle Sam to stoutly defend free trade in international trade negotiations and at the same time systematically dump on a large scale surplus production of major farm products in world markets. But clearly, if support prices for milk are held high enough for long enough, then the governmϵnt will have no alternative but to dump in world markets or limit production. In the 1980s, the government resorted to both of these devices as the surpluses of dairy products rose to unprecedented levels.

Table 4.1 provides data on the more recent history of the milk price support program. After many years of modest milk surpluses, the surplus rose to 8.2 billion pounds, 6.4 percent of total milk production, in 1979–1980. Government expenditures exceeded $1 billion. Although support prices rose in the following 2 years, support levels as a percentage of parity fell to 72.9 percent in 1981–1982. Thereafter, the support price was lowered substantially both absolutely and as a percentage of parity, reaching 49.6 percent of parity in the latter part of 1987–1988. Still, the milk surplus remained at high levels. Government expenditure soared to over $2 billion. One important reason for the growth in production was the collapse of feed prices, which allowed profitable milk production at the announced support prices. Reduced farming opportunities outside dairying and continuing gains in productivity were contributing factors.

New program devices were soon brought up to do battle with surplus production. Although the support price remained at $13.10 per hundredweight (cwt) in 1983, the same as in 1982, the government collected deductions from farmers' milk checks in order to defray part of the treasury outlays. A 50 cent per cwt deduction effective April 16, 1983, was raised to $1.00 per cwt, effective September 1, 1983. In addition to lowered support levels and deductions after 1983, the government opted for a 15-month voluntary milk diversion program beginning January 1, 1984. Under the diversion program, milk producers were paid $10 per cwt for reductions in milk production, where the reductions had to equal between 5 and 30 percent of milk marketings in a base period. Approximately one-fifth of the commercial milk producers participated in the diversion program. Finally, under an 18-month milk production termination program beginning April 1, 1986, milk producers were given the chance of en-

TABLE 4.1
Milk used in manufacturing: farm-level price, support price, support price as a percentage of parity, total milk production, USDA net market removals, and net government expenditure, United States, 1976–1977 through 1987–1988.

Year	Farm price, $/cwt	Support price, $/cwt	Support price percentage of parity, %	Milk production, billion lb	USDA net market removals, billion lb	Removals as percentage of production, %	Net government expenditure, million $
1976–1977[a]	8.65			122.2	6.9	5.6	714.3
Oct. 1–Mar. 31		8.26	81				
Apr. 1–Sept. 30		9.00	82				
1977–1978	9.30			121.7	3.2	2.6	451.4
Oct. 1–Mar. 31		9.00	82				
Apr. 1–Sept. 30		9.43	86				
1978–1979	10.86			122.5	1.1	0.9	250.6
Oct. 1–Mar. 31		9.87	80				
Apr. 1–Sept. 30		10.76	87				
1979–1980	11.75			127.3	8.2	6.4	1,279.8
Oct. 1–Mar. 31		11.49	80				
Apr. 1–Sept. 30		12.36	86				
1980–1981	12.71			131.7	12.7	9.6	1,974.8
Oct. 1–Mar. 31		12.80	80				
Apr. 1–Sept. 30		12.80	80				
1981–1982	12.66			134.7	13.8	10.2	2,239.2
Oct. 1–Oct. 20		13.49	75				
Oct. 21–Sept. 30		13.10	72.9				

Period							
1982–1983	12.66			138.8	16.6	12.0	2,600.4
Oct. 1–Mar. 31		13.10	69.1				
Apr. 1–Sept. 30		13.10	69.1				
1983–1984	12.47			136.7	10.4	7.6	1,594.6
Oct. 1–Nov. 30		13.10	64.9				
Dec. 1–Sept. 30		12.60	62.4				
1984–1985	12.08			140.2	11.5	8.2	2,185.0
Oct. 1–Mar. 30		12.60	59.1				
Apr. 1–June 30		12.10	56.8				
July 1–Sept. 30		11.60	54.4				
1985–1986	11.31	11.60	54.6	145.1	12.3	8.5	2,416.5
1986–1987	11.42			141.5	5.4	3.8	1,237.5
Oct. 1–Dec. 31		11.60	54.1				
Jan. 1–Sept. 30		11.35	52.9				
1987–1988	10.97			144.9	9.7	6.7	1,039.9
Oct. 1–Dec. 31		11.10	51.9				
Jan. 1–Sept. 30		10.60	49.6				

[a]Support prices are announced for periods less than a year, following passage of the Food and Agricultural Act of 1977.

Source: Adapted from Agricultural Stabilization and Conservation Service, *ASCS Commodity Fact Sheet: 1988–89 Dairy Price Support Program*, U.S. Department of Agriculture, April 1989.

tering contracts with the Commodity Credit Corporation (CCC) through submitting bids to dispose of their entire dairy herds and to terminate production for a minimum of 5 years. Thus, it came to pass in the mid-1980s that the government had evolved a manufacturing milk program that relied on price supports to encourage milk production and a payment program to do just the opposite. The whys and wherefores of milk check deductions as opposed to a decrease in the support level are analyzed in the next section.

Dairy price supports transfer benefits from domestic consumers and taxpayers to dairy producers in the short run and to the suppliers of dairy farm inputs in the long run, particularly to the owners of land with a comparative advantage in milk production. Discussion of these issues and related research findings is postponed until after a discussion of milk marketing orders, when a more comprehensive appraisal of national dairy policy will be given.

4.4 MARKET PRICE SUPPORTS AND DEDUCTIONS*

Confronted with troublesome surpluses of manufactured dairy products, the government in 1983 introduced producer assessments instead of simply lowering the support price. The question is, why producer assessments? We explore this question here not only because of its relevance to dairy policy but also because of its potential relevance to other commodities as well. What we find is that a hundredweight assessment, in comparison to an equivalent drop in the support price, increases the extent to which the remaining producer benefits are financed through higher food prices as opposed to higher taxes. This is of some importance in that the tax system, with its heavy emphasis on the income tax, is roughly proportional; a food tax is highly regressive.

To see the likely economic effects of the producer assessment program, let P_1 be the support price in Figure 4.8. At this price, farmers produce Q_4, but buyers will only purchase Q_1 for distribution in commercial channels. Therefore, the government surplus equals $(Q_4 - Q_1)$. Letting a, b, c, d, and e equal the areas of rectangles formed by the dashed lines (ignoring the solid lines), the cost to taxpayers of government purchases equals area $(b + c + d + e)$. Now consider a 50 cent per cwt deduction or assessment. Letting the deduction equal the distance $(P_1 - P_2)$, the effective support price to producers is P_2. At this latter price producers are only willing to produce Q_3; the cost of buying the surplus equals area $(b + d + e)$. The total deductions from milk producers, on the other hand, amount to area $(a + b)$. Hence, the government (i.e., taxpayers) saves area $(a + b + c)$ in comparison with the original program.

The major effects of the new program are as follows. (1) Benefits to milk producers fall by the area given between the two price lines P_1 and P_2 and above the supply curve. (2) As noted, the new net cost to taxpayers (total cost of purchases minus total deductions) falls by the area $(a + b + c)$. (3) Consumers of dairy products are unaffected since the support level remains at P_1. (4) Benefits to recipients of free or low-priced manufactured dairy products

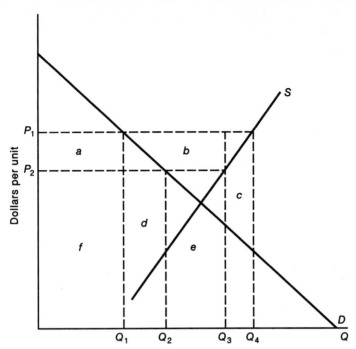

FIGURE 4.8
Effects of deductions compared with cuts in the level of price support.

(the cheese give-away program, for example) decline because surplus production falls by $(Q_4 - Q_3)$.

Why the deduction? Why not simply lower the support price to P_2? In this latter case production falls to Q_3 and the amount flowing into commercial trade channels increases to Q_2. Surplus production therefore falls to $(Q_3 - Q_2)$, which of course is less than under the 50 cent deduction. The new cost to taxpayers amounts to area e. Is area e, the cost to taxpayers with the lower support price, less than area $(e + d - a)$, the net cost to taxpayers with the 50 cent deduction? All hinges on the elasticity of the demand for milk. Total revenue equals area $(a + f)$ for Q_1 and area $(d + f)$ for Q_2. Area f is common to both. If demand is inelastic, area $(a + f)$ exceeds area $(d + f)$ and area a exceeds area d. The tax bill is lower with the assessment than with the comparable drop in the support level. The opposite obtains if demand is elastic. On the basis of available econometric analysis (Hutton and Helmberger, for example) it appears that the U.S. demand for milk is highly inelastic, particularly in the short run. Consequently one would expect the cost to taxpayers to decline more with the 50 cent deduction than with a 50 cent decrease in the support price. Note that the loss of benefits to producers is the same in either case. *An important point not to miss is that the deduction, in comparison with a cut in the support price, tends to shift the financing of a given level of pro-*

ducer benefits away from the income tax in favor of higher dairy product prices to the consumer (i.e., a higher food "tax").

4.5   SUMMARY

Direct payments and price supports are two alternative ways of putting a floor on the effective prices received by farmers. In the case of direct payments, the farmer sells all output at the market price and then receives a direct payment per unit of production equaling the difference between a target price and the market price. As a consequence, the supply for farm output becomes perfectly inelastic for market prices less than the target level. In the case of price supports, the government stands willing to acquire a sufficient amount of farm output to drive the market price up to the support level. The domestic demand for farm output becomes perfectly elastic at the support level. The surplus commodity may be destroyed or, what is more likely, sold abroad or in a secondary market.

Turning to program effects, we note that neither direct payments nor price supports are very effective in generating benefits to farm labor. The reason for this is that returns to farm labor now account for less than 15 percent of total farm receipts. In this sense, farm labor is no longer as important an input as it once was. Farming has become a very capital-intensive business. Also, the farm labor supply function appears to be quite elastic, and input suppliers tend not to receive benefits if their response to input price change is elastic. The major beneficiaries of programs that put a floor on farm prices are the initial landowners who receive capital gains. Although consumers are hurt by a price support operation, a direct payment program is as much a consumer subsidy program as it is a farmer subsidy program. Also, because the United States is a large world food exporter, price supports and direct payments generate benefits to foreign consumers; foreign producers are hurt. The trade effects of both approaches are likely to be very similar, however, because the domestic demand for food, particularly at the farm gate level, is highly inelastic.

The program for milk components (fat and nonfat solids) used in manufacturing dairy products illustrates price support operations. The federal government acquires butter, cheddar cheese, and dried skim milk in order to elevate prices of these products in wholesale markets. This in turn allows dairy manufacturing plants to pay higher prices to their milk suppliers. Over much of the period since World War II, the milk price support level was closely aligned with the market-clearing price; surplus dairy products ordinarily did not give rise to serious disposal problems. The school lunch program together with food programs for the needy were able to absorb most of the surpluses of butter and cheese. The situation changed drastically in the 1980s, however. As a percentage of total milk production, surplus output rose to a high of 12 percent in 1982–1983 and remained high over much of the decade. The government lowered the price support level sharply, and various new devices, including the dairy herd buyout program, were introduced in order to bring surplus production under control. Substantial quantities of surplus products were dumped in foreign markets. Largely because of the impact of drought on feed supplies in 1988, surplus production was no longer a major problem in 1989.

PROBLEMS

1. Under competitive conditions, food demand and supply are given by $P = 10 - Q$ and $P = (1.0)Q$, respectively. Calculate equilibrium market price, production, and consumption for each of the following regimes. Calculate change in consumer surplus, change in producer surplus, government expenditure, and the efficiency loss for the three farm programs given by parts b, c, and d.
   (a) Perfect competition.
   (b) A direct payment program with the target price equal to 7.
   (c) A price support program with the support price equal to 7. (Assume the government surplus can be sold for bird seed at a price equal to 2.)
   (d) The farm program includes *both* the programs described under parts b and c above except that the support price is set at 4 instead of 7.

2. The U.S. demand and supply for food are given by $D_u = 10 - P_u$ and $S_u = 4P_u$. The rest of the world (ROW) demand and supply for food are given by $D_r = 10 - P_r$ and $S_r = (1.0)P_r$. Calculate market prices and the levels of production, consumption, and exports (imports) for both regions for the following U.S. regimes.
   (a) Perfect competition.
   (b) The United States adopts a direct payment program with the target price equal to 3.
   (c) The United States adopts a price support program with the support level equal to 3.

3. *The aggregate production for food is given by $Q = L^{0.5} A^{0.5}$, but the supply of land A is fixed at $A = 16$. The supply function for labor is given by $L = W^2$. Food demand is given by $Q = P^{-0.5}$. Under a direct payment program, the target price is set equal to 0.2. Calculate program benefits to labor and the increase in land rent per unit of land.

REFERENCES AND SUGGESTED READINGS

Houck, James P., *Elements of Agricultural Trade Policies*, Macmillan, New York, 1986.

Hutton, Patricia, and Peter Helmberger, *Aggregative Analysis of U.S. Dairy Policy*, Wisconsin Agricultural Experiment Station Bulletin No. R3191, College of Agricultural and Life Sciences, University of Wisconsin, Madison, 1982.

Knutson, Ronald D., J. B. Penn, and William T. Beohm, *Agriculture and Food Policy*, Prentice-Hall, Englewood Cliffs, NJ, 1983.

Rosine, John, and Peter Helmberger, *An Aggregative Analysis of the U.S. Farm Sector: Past Trends and Future Prospects*, Wisconsin Agricultural Experimental Station Research Bulletin No. R2733, University of Wisconsin, Madison, June 1975.

U.S. Department of Agriculture, *Dairy: Background for 1985 Farm Legislation*, Economic Research Service, Agricultural Information Bulletin No. 474, September 1984.

U.S. Department of Agriculture, *Farm Commodity and Related Programs*, Agricultural Stabilization and Conservation Service, Agricultural Handbook No. 345, March 1976.

U.S. Department of Agriculture, *Review of Existing and Alternative Federal Dairy Programs,* Economic Research Service, Staff Report No. AGES 840121, January 1984.

Yeboah, Albert O., *An Aggregative Analysis of U.S. Agriculture: Impact of Farm Programs and Exogenous Changes,* unpublished Ph.D. dissertation, University of Wisconsin, Madison, 1980.

CHAPTER

5

Market Stabilization Programs*

In the previous chapter, price support and direct payment programs were considered as alternative means for elevating farm prices and incomes. This chapter continues the analysis of these programs but from a rather different perspective. More particularly, we seek in this chapter to analyze price supports and direct payments together with other programs as alternative means for stabilizing farm markets, where stabilization might or might not be linked to the elevation of farm income as a twin objective.

Writers often cite the extreme volatility of farm prices as evidence that farm markets tend to be unstable. The argument is frequently made that price variation is excessive and that government intervention is required to bring more stability to the market. Presumably, price stabilization is not an end in itself, however, and it is natural to inquire first, why price volatility, even extreme volatility, is inimical to the public interest and second, what steps the government might take to reduce volatility to an acceptable or optimum level.

Although not always convincing, many reasons have been given in support of the view that farm price stabilization programs can be used to serve the public interest. First, although farm production may be inherently unstable, subject to the vagaries of weather, locusts, and God knows what, the needs of people for food are remarkably stable. Food production is often discontinuous over time, as in the case of major field crops with harvests occurring once a year. Desired food consumption, on the other hand, is continuous and stable, with three square meals being the order of the day. It is thus perfectly clear that food storage is an economic activity of vital importance. Storing food in periods of plenty for consumption in periods of scarcity stabilizes both consumption and price.

---

* This specialized chapter may be more appropriate for the advanced student.

A second reason why price stabilization programs are often supported is the belief that wide swings in prices are often associated with wide swings in farm income. The idea here is that, other things being equal, such as average income, farmers would prefer stable as opposed to unstable incomes. Capital markets could, of course, allow farmers to enjoy a stable flow of consumption over time even though incomes bounce about, but capital markets are often poorly developed and imperfect.

One must be careful, however, in supposing that programs which stabilize price also stabilize farm income. Much depends on the source of instability. Farm prices and incomes might move together in lock-step fashion because of cyclic changes in exchange rates or in national income. In such cases it may be true that price stabilization programs stabilize farm income. If, on the other hand, price instability is caused mainly by sharp changes in crop yields, then it is possible, and indeed likely, as we shall soon see, that programs which stabilize prices destabilize farm income.

Consider the following hypothetical example. The harvest of an exotic wild mushroom is unstable because of variability in rainfall. Price rises during years of low yields and falls during periods of high yields. The government proposes to stabilize price through storage operations that are very expensive, much more expensive than private storers could afford. If the demand for mushrooms has unitary elasticity, then the incomes of gatherers will be perfectly stable with unstable production. Changes in prices are negatively correlated with changes in output such that the product of price and output always remains exactly the same. Price stability achieved through government storage in this situation destabilizes income.

A third reason why price stabilization might be a sensible government objective pertains to marketing costs. Marketing margins for farm output might be a good deal lower if the flow of farm output from production and storage through the marketing channel is regular and stable so that processing and distributing plants operate at full capacity day in and day out. Periods of idle capacity and worker layoffs alternating with periods of overtime and multiple shifts are not conducive to low marketing costs. It might also be inefficient and risky for processing firms to undertake the storage necessary to assure the continuity of their operations. Storage might more efficiently be carried out by specialized firms.

As a final reason why governments might seek to stabilize farm prices, consider the effects of risk on farm production. Often farmers commit inputs to crop production uncertain as to the weather and uncertain as to the price at harvest time. Risk may be costly in that farmers would be willing to pay to avoid it if given the opportunity to do so. A stabilization program that decreases the riskiness of production in effect decreases the cost of production, encouraging farmers to expand output. The question remains, however, whether a program that stabilizes price stabilizes farm income as well, thus making farm production less risky.

As noted above, we are mainly concerned in this chapter with the analysis of farm programs intended to stabilize markets. This is in contrast to most of the material covered in this book, centering as it does on programs intended to elevate farm prices and incomes. Another contrast arises out of the different mode of analysis used in this chapter. Other chapters rely, one hopes with some success, on comparative static analysis, analysis that examines and compares markets in alternative positions of equilibrium. Such analysis is subject to several limitations, limitations that become very serious in studies of price stabilization issues. What is required is analysis that allows for random or stochastic elements and deals more explicitly with market dynamics. The nature of such analysis will become clear as we progress. As a primer, however, it is necessary to introduce some tools of analysis common to the field of statistical inference. This we do in the next section. Attention is thereafter centered on models of pricing and storage under uncertainty with and without government intervention.

5.1 RANDOM VARIABLES AND PROBABILITY DISTRIBUTIONS

A random variable is a variable that takes on different numerical values with relative frequencies or probabilities that we assume are known. Such a variable may be continuous or discrete. The annual amount of rainfall or the average annual temperature are examples of continuous variables that an economist might treat as random. A random variable that assumes distinct values only is called *discrete*. It will be convenient to develop the material in this chapter assuming that all random variables are discrete. Examples are developed below.

Consider tossing a fair coin on the convention that a random variable is assigned the value 1 when the coin turns up "heads" and 0 when it turns up "tails". Lex X represent the random variable with $X_1 = 1$ and $X_2 = 0$. Subscripts are used to indicate specific values. If the coin is tossed a large number of times, we would expect that $X = 1$ one-half the time and $X = 0$ one-half the time. We say the probability of getting heads, that $X = X_1$, is one-half; similarly for tails. The probabilities sum to 1 if we assume away the possibility that a coin upon landing balances on its edge. Worse assumptions are made in this book.

As another example, consider the amount of rainfall that occurs at a specific geographic location where the U.S. Weather Bureau just happens to keep a close record of annual rainfall. Since water is for all practical purposes perfectly divisible, annual rainfall may be thought of as a continuous variable. To avoid the difficulty of working with continuous variables, we may think of a discrete variable that measures with acceptable accuracy a continuous phenomenon. The following convention might be adopted as an example: if less than one-tenth of an inch of rain falls, we say no rain fell. If the rainfall is between 40.1 and 40.2 inches, we say that we had 40.1 inches. Thus we measure rainfall in terms of small intervals of a tenth of an inch of rain, starting from zero rainfall and ranging upward to whatever. In any one year t we may not be able to predict very well how much rain will fall in the subsequent year, year $t + 1$, but, on the basis of a long historic record, we might still be able to make such statements as: the probability of getting 10.9 inches of rain next year is one-sixteenth. That is to say, we may think of the amount of rain that falls each year as a discrete random variable and from historical records calculate the probability that the amount of rain will equal, roughly, this or that value.

More generally, let X be a random variable that takes on n distinct values. We say that $X = X_i$ where i ranges over the values $1, 2, 3, \ldots, n$. Let the probability that $X = X_i$ be given by p_i for all i. The expected value or mean of the random variable EX is defined thus:

$$EX = p_1 X_1 + p_2 X_2 + \cdots + p_n X_n \tag{5.1}$$

The variance of X is defined thus:

$$VX = p_1(X_1 - EX)^2 + p_2(X_2 - EX)^2 + \cdots + p_n(X_n - EX)^2 \tag{5.2}$$

These two concepts, expected value and variance, are of basic importance in the analysis that follows. We pause again, however, to consider an example.

A gambling house offers the following game: a coin is tossed once. If a head appears, the customer wins $200. If a tail appears, the customer pays $100. The customer may play the game only once. The expected value or mean of X in this case equals $50, given by $(½)\$200 - (½)\$100$. The variance, it may be noted, equals $22,500. (Customers who are said to be averse to risk would be willing to pay less than $50 to play the game; those who enjoy risk would be willing to pay more than that.) In light of the participation in state lotteries and the success of gambling houses, it appears that many people would be delighted to play this game if there were no charge at all. Of course, the house would in the long run take a terrible beating unless it sold drinks at high prices and hired Wayne Newton to sing.

Suppose a second game is offered, however, such that if a head appears, the customer gets $50,000, but that if a tail appears, the customer pays the house $49,900. The expected value of X in this game is the same as before, $50, but presumably few people would be willing to play the game. Many people can afford to drop $100 but a $49,900 loss would be out of the question. The trouble with this latter game in comparison with the first is that the variance of the payoff X is very large, equaling almost $2.5 billion. This example ought certainly to suggest that in the study of random processes, it may be very useful to know more about the probability distribution of a random variable than simply its mean or expected value. The variance has been shown to be of great importance in many applications.

We next consider linear functions of random variables. Suppose that $Y = f(X)$ where X is random. Then Y is random as well, and it is extremely useful for analytical purposes to know how the mean and variance of Y can be found given the mean and variance of X. At this juncture we simply state a number of results together with a few examples, leaving proofs to the references given at the end of the chapter. If $Y = a + bX$, then

$$EY = a + bEX \tag{5.3}$$

where a and b are constants. It may be noted that the expected value of a constant is the constant itself. Also, we have

$$VY = b^2 V(X) \tag{5.4}$$

It is often useful to compare the variability of one variable with that of another. For this purpose a useful measure of variability, expressed in percentage terms, is the coefficient of variation CX defined as

$$CX = \frac{(VX)^{1/2}}{EX} \, 100 \tag{5.5}$$

The expected values and variances of different variables may be expressed in different units such as bushels of corn and hundredweights of milk. The coefficient of variation would allow comparing the variability of corn production with that of milk production.

We now consider an example that illustrates the application of the above concepts in an economic model. Let the demand for the wild mushrooms mentioned earlier be given by $P = 10 - Q$. The harvest H of mushrooms is a random variable such that $H = 8$ with $p = 0.5$ and $H = 6$ with $p = 0.5$, where p equals probability. We assume that $Q = H$, which makes price a random variable. The value of EP may be estimated in two ways, through using the definition of expected value given by Equation (5.1) or through applying the formula given by Equation (5.3). Using the former we have $P = 4$ with $p = 0.5$ and $P = 2$ with $p = 0.5$ so that $EP = 3$. Using the latter approach, we note first that $EQ = 7$. It follows that $EP = 3$. The value for VP may also be estimated in two ways, through applying the definition given by Equation (5.2) or through applying the formula given by Equation (5.4). Using the former, we have $VP = (\frac{1}{2})(1^2 + 1^2)$, so that $V(P) = 1$. Using the latter approach, we note first that $VQ = 1$. Therefore, $VP = 1$ as well. The total revenue TR received by the gatherers of mushrooms equals price times harvest: $TR = 10H - H^2$. We cannot calculate $E(TR)$ and $V(TR)$ using Equations (5.3) and (5.4) because total revenue is not a linear function of H. Because the probability distribution for H is simple, however, we can easily estimate $E(TR)$ and $V(TR)$ using the definitions. When this is done, we find that $E(TR) = 20$ and $V(TR) = 16$. Turning to mushroom consumers we see that consumer surplus TCS equals 18 when $H = 6$ and 32 when $H = 8$. Therefore, $E(TCS) = 25$ and $V(TCS) = 49$.

Which is more variable, price or consumption? To answer this question we use the coefficient of variation. Applying Equation (5.5) we have $CP = 33.3$ percent and $CQ = 14.3$ percent. Price is relatively more unstable than consumption. Perhaps this is what we should expect when demand is inelastic in the relevant price (or quantity) range. Exogenous changes in supply cause large relative price changes and small relative quantity changes.

Now that the nature of performance under competition has been specified in some detail, we introduce a government price stabilization program. In order to keep life simple we make some assumptions that are whimsical and strange. We assume the government, through a secret process, is able to store mushrooms without cost and that it has a very large stock of mushrooms on hand. The government launches a price stabilization program in which it sells one unit of its stock when the harvest H equals 6 and buys one unit when the harvest equals 8. The government's initial stock is so large that, as a practical matter, it need never worry about a string of bad harvests that would deplete its stock. As a result of this program, price is completely stabilized at its expected value under competitive conditions. We have $P_g = 3$, $EP_g = 3$, and $VP_g = 0$, where the subscript g indicates the presence of the government program. The following results can also be calculated: $E(TR_g) = 21$, $V(TR_g) = 9$, $E(TCS_g) = 24.5$, and $V(TCS_g) = 0$.

We may now compare market performance with and without the price stabilization program. What we find is this: the government program does not affect the expected price, raises the expected returns to the gatherers of mushrooms, and lowers the expected consumer surplus. The variance of both price and consumer surplus is reduced to zero, and the variance of total revenue falls from its competitive value, 16, to the program level, 9. It appears that the gatherers of mushrooms would be made better off by this program. Expected revenue rises and the variance falls. Consumers might or might not be made worse off because both the expectation and the variance of consumer surplus fall. The fundamental problem, which will not be explored in this chapter, is that we have not specified a utility function for the consumer that describes the consumer's preference for stability.

The above analysis of a price stabilization program illustrates analysis of stochastic models, models that contain random variables. The analysis must not be taken seriously, however, because the assumptions are too restrictive. Assuming that $Q = H$ under competition does not allow for the possibility of private storage. If storage is feasible, it is improper to compare the performance of a market with and without a government storage program on the assumption that private storage never occurs. This is particularly true if the carrying cost per unit is small relative to differences in prices over time. Assuming the government need never be concerned about running out of stocks is also restrictive, particularly in the early years of program operation, before the government has had any chance to accumulate stocks. The gathering of food growing in the wild is largely for the birds; except for a few primitive tribes, humankind long ago developed technologies that have rendered food gathering obsolete. What is required is analysis that allows for planting, harvesting, and storing in a world of uncertainty.

As an aside it may be noted that in the typical articulation of supply-and-demand analysis, demand is assumed to be that for consumption only. The current demand for stocks for future consumption is nearly always ignored. A possible reason for this is that the theoretical underpinnings of the demand for consumption are well developed and can be found in any basic textbook in economics; the underpinnings of the demand for stocks, on the other hand, have only recently been developed. The demand for stocks is of considerable importance for an applied discipline such as agricultural economics that must come to grips with markets in which storage is prevalent. Explanations of monthly and quarterly prices must, for many crops, recognize that in the period immediately following harvests, the demand for stocks greatly exceeds the demand for consumption. The development of the theory of demand for stocks in the following sections is of value in its own right, quite without regard to its role in the analysis of government programs.

5.2 A MODEL OF INTRAYEAR PRICING AND STORAGE

Consider a farm product that is produced annually. The harvest is completed at some point in time, and the product can be and is stored for two periods, 2 months, say. After that the product turns into garbage. Although intrayear storage is possible, interyear storage is not. In this respect our hypothetical product is not unlike late summer potatoes or onions.

Let demand in the first, postharvest month or period be given by

$$Q_1 = a - bP_1 + u_1 \tag{5.6}$$

where u_1 is a random or stochastic term and the subscript 1 indicates period 1. Although known in period 1, the value of u_1 is not known beforehand. This means that the position of demand cannot be known in advance. The initial expectation of u_1 formed prior to period 1, $E_0 u_1$, equals zero.

A market-clearing condition states that

$$Q_1 + I_1 = H_0 \tag{5.7}$$

where I_1 equals the quantity of output committed to storage for consumption in the second period and H_0 equals total harvest, which is known. If I_1 were treated as an exogenous variable, we could solve for Q_1 and P_1 since we have two equations. Such an assumption would be wholly inappropriate, however, in light of our objective, which is to develop a theory of pricing and storage.

In order to get on with our task, we begin by modeling the decisions of arbitrageurs, entrepreneurs who organize storage operations. Arbitrage involves purchasing a product in a low-price market and selling it in a high-price market. The two markets might be linked in space by a transportation system or in time by commodity storage. If carried out on a sufficient scale, arbitrage tends to equate market prices subject to differentials that arise because of the per unit cost of transfer or storage.

The profit function for an arbitrageur who buys the product at the beginning of period 1 and sells it at the beginning of period 2 may be expressed as follows:

$$\pi_2 = P_2 q - P_1 q - Kq - iP_1 q \qquad (5.8)$$

where π_2 equals profit earned in the second period; q is the amount purchased in period 1 for resale in period 2; K equals the per unit cost of storage, possibly paid to a grain elevator; and i is the monthly rate of interest. Total revenue is given by $(P_2 q)$. By definition, the total carrying cost equals the sum of three components: $(P_1 q)$ is the cost of acquiring the commodity in period 1; (Kq) is the total storage cost; and $(iP_1 q)$ is the opportunity cost of committing money to holding stocks as opposed to earning interest in a bank. We assume the cost Kq is not actually paid until the sale of q occurs.

It is assumed that in period 1, the second-period price is unknown but that all arbitrageurs have the same subjective expectation as to what that price will be. We let $e_1 P_2$ be the subjectively expected price. The price expectation is said to be subjective because for the moment we make no commitment as to how it is formed. Perhaps all arbitrageurs contract with the same consulting firm or view last year's second-period price as the best predictor of this year's second-period price.

The expected profit function may be written

$$e_1 \pi_2 = q[e_1 P_2 - P_1 (1 + i) - K] \qquad (5.9)$$

where $e_1 \pi_2$ equals expected profit. We assume that competition in the storage industry is keen and that many firms with storage facilities could easily enter the market if excess profits were expected. On these arguments, aggregate storage operations will be of such magnitude that all expected excess profits are destroyed. If $e_1 \pi_2 = 0$, then Equation (5.9) can be written with $e_1 P_2$ as a function of P_1 thus:

$$e_1 P_2 = P_1 (1 + i) + K \qquad (5.10)$$

Equation (5.10) is typical of an arbitrage condition that equates price in one market with either price or expected price in another.

At this point in the argument we set aside the model of pricing and storage for the first period in order to focus on the second. For the second period we have

$$Q_2 = c - dP_2 + u_2 \qquad (5.11)$$

$$Q_2 = I_1$$

where the expectation of u_2 formed in period 1, E_1u_2, equals zero. Solving for P_2 we have

$$P_2 = \left(\frac{1}{d}\right)(c - I_1 + u_2) \tag{5.12}$$

The mathematical expectation of P_2 as formed in the first period is given by

$$E_1P_2 = \left(\frac{1}{d}\right)(c - I_1) \tag{5.13}$$

Equation (5.13) is called the *expected price function*. It relates the expected second period price to the carryout I_1. In light of (5.13) how should we suppose arbitrageurs form their expectations? At this juncture we adopt Muth's famous hypothesis of rational expectations, which in the present context asserts that

$$e_1P_2 = E_1P_2 \tag{5.14}$$

According to this hypothesis, arbitrageurs understand the pricing system. Although they cannot predict what u_2 will be, they do know what the parameters of system (5.11) are. (They also know the probability distribution for u_2, which will be seen to be an important point later on.) Muth's suggestion is that arbitrageurs not only understand how the market system works, but that they also are able to take advantage of all relevant information available at the time price expectations are formed. In this sense then, Muth assumes that price expectations are rational.

The structural model for period 1 may now be specified, using (5.14) to rid the system of the subjective price expectation e_1P_2. We have

$$Q_1 = a - bP_1 + u_1$$

$$Q_1 + I_1 = H_0$$

$$E_1P_2 = P_1(1 + i) + K \tag{5.15}$$

$$E_1P_2 = \left(\frac{1}{d}\right)(c - I_1)$$

Our four-equation system has four unknowns or endogenous variables, namely, Q_1, P_1, I_1, and E_1P_2. (It is assumed that $I_1 > 0$.) This system can be reduced to a three-equation system by equating the right-hand sides of the last two equations, thus eliminating E_1P_2. We are then left with the first-period demand, the market-clearing condition, and a function that is called the demand for storage, which is given by

$$I_1 = c - dK - d(1 + i)P_1 \qquad (5.16)$$

This function shows how much arbitrageurs will commit to storage in the first period depending on the first-period price. The demand for stocks is downward-sloping. Increases in K lower the demand; increases in i cause its slope to increase in absolute value, with stocks taken as the dependent variable. The reduced form equations (solution) for the three-equation system described immediately above are given by

$$P_1 = \frac{a + c - dK - H_0 + u_1}{b + d(1 + i)}$$

$$I_1 = \frac{bc - ad(1 + i) - bdK + d(1 + i)H_0 - d(1 + i)u_1}{b + d(1 + i)} \qquad (5.17)$$

$$Q_1 = \frac{ad(1 + i) - bc + bdK + bH_0 + d(1 + i)u_1}{b + d(1 + i)}$$

It becomes quickly apparent that raising K causes P_1 and I_1 to fall; Q_1 rises. Raising H_0 causes P_1 to fall, but I_1 and Q_1 increase. The effects of changes in i are somewhat less apparent. Raising i causes P_1 to fall, but since P_1 and Q_1 are negatively related, it must be true that Q_1 rises. Since harvested supply is fixed at H_0, an increase in Q_1 means that I_1 falls. This can be checked directly by differentiating the reduced form for I_1 with respect to i and showing that the first derivative is negative. (To get the correct result, one must recognize that the numerator of the reduced form expression for a positive P_1 must itself be positive.)

The reduced form for E_1P_2 is given by

$$E_1P_2 = \frac{(1 + i)(a + c - H_0 + u_1) + bK}{b + d(1 + i)} \qquad (5.18)$$

The manner in which E_1P_2 is affected by changes in H_0, K, and i is left to the student. The variance of P_2 may also be derived. Going back to Equation (5.12), we see that I_1 may be replaced by its solution value. Taking the variance of P_2, we have

$$V_1P_2 = \left(\frac{1}{d}\right)^2 V_1u_2 \qquad (5.19)$$

Although we do not know in the first period what P_2 will be, we do know or can calculate its expected value and variance.

A graphic analysis is given in Figure 5.1 where DD_c and D_s are the demands for consumption and storage and DD is aggregate demand. (For the moment ignore DD_g.) If the harvested supply is given by Q_{14}, then Q_{12} will be consumed in the first period and Q_{13} will be purchased by arbitrageurs for consumption in the second period. Equilibrium first-period price is given by P_{10}. We know further that $Q_2 = Q_{13}$ and that $E_1 P_2 = P_{10}(1 + i) + K$. What P_2 will equal cannot be known until u_2 is known. Only time will tell. As to the effects of changes in exogenous variables, we note that the effects of an increase in H_0 are obvious and require no discussion. An increase in the storage cost K lowers the demand for stocks D_s. An increase in the interest rate i lowers the demand for stocks, decreasing its slope in absolute value. (To see this, rewrite 5.16 with P_1 dependent.) Once we know how changes in K and i affect D_s, graphic analysis can be employed to show the resulting consequences for P_1, I_1, and Q_1.

We now take up a numerical example that is crucial to the remainder of this chapter. It frequently happens in economics, and in other sciences for that matter, that structural models are developed that are of sufficient complexity as to defy obtaining analytical solutions. Nonlinear systems come quickly to mind. Such models may nonetheless be of great value because their structural parameters may be estimable. In that case, computers may be used to obtain

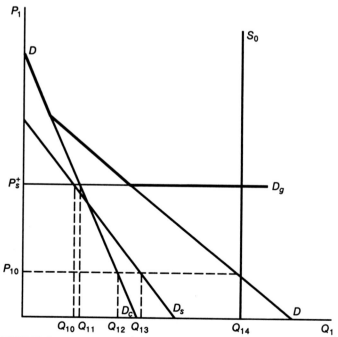

FIGURE 5.1
Effects of market price support on intrayear pricing and storage.

solutions to quantified systems that are very large or complex or both. We touch on this matter because the structural models of relevance to the phenomena of pricing and storage under uncertainty can rarely be solved analytically as in the above linear model. Computational methods must be employed. In the numerical example that follows, we use a computational method to derive the expected price function, a method that can be used in complex, nonlinear systems.

For the first period we have $Q_1 = 10 - P_1$; $H_0 = 8$; $K = 1$; and $i = 0$. From the above analysis we then have $E_1P_2 = P_1 + 1$. For the second period, we have $Q_2 = 12 - 2P_2 + u_2$. Also, $u_2 = +2$ with probability ½ and $u_2 = -2$ with probability ½. Notice that $E_1u_2 = 0$. We now estimate the expected price function using a method that differs significantly from the method described above.

First, we do not know in advance what I_1 will equal, but just suppose that it equals 2. Then, using the information given above, we see that when $u_2 = +2$, P_2 equals 6; when $u_2 = -2$, P_2 equals 4. Hence, the expected second-period price conditional on $I_1 = 2$, which we write $E_1(P_2|I_1 = 2)$, equals 5. Similarly, it can be shown that $E_1(P_2|I_1 = 6)$ equals 3. In fact we can assign many different values to I_1, computing the expected price in the second period for each value. Suppose we record this information in Figure 5.2 for $I_1 = 2$ and

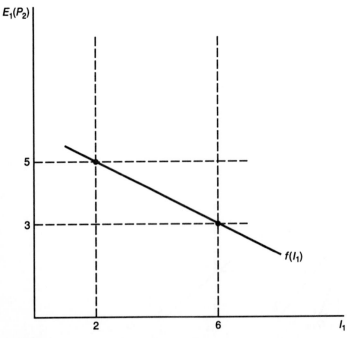

FIGURE 5.2
Deriving intrayear expected price function using computational methods.

$I_1 = 6$. By fitting a linear line through the two points we have a graphic representation of the expected price function. Of course, we could derive many such points, connecting all neighboring points with a straight line and using the resulting spline function as an approximation for the expected price function. The approximation can be made as close as we desire through taking a sufficiently large number of values for I_1. In the present case, however, two points will do very well because the expected price function is linear as shown below. Using the point-slope formula for deriving the equation for a linear line, we have the following: $E_1P_2 = 6 - 0.5I_1$. The demand for storage in the first period is $I_1 = 10 - 2P_1$. We have as the solution: $P_1 = 4$; $Q_1 = 6$; $I_1 = 2$; and $E_1P_2 = 5$.

It will be convenient in what follows to have a name for this roundabout procedure for deriving the expected price function. We will refer to this procedure as *computational rational expectations modeling,* or CREM for short. CREM is computational because it is applicable to models in which all structural parameters except those of the expected price function are known or have been estimated. Numerical as opposed to analytical methods are employed. CREM also relies on the rational expectations hypothesis of Muth.

The student might well ask at this point, however, why we should bother to use CREM when a direct procedure is available. After all, $P_2 = 6 - 0.5I_1 + u_2$ and taking the expectation of P_2 yields the expected price function directly. Madness sometimes has a method, however. As it turns out CREM can be used to generate excellent approximations of the expected price function in cases where the direct method fails completely. A case in point is the model analyzed in Section 5.3 below.

We now briefly consider a three-period model in which the initial supply H_0 may be stored and consumed over three periods instead of only two. The objective is to further clarify the derivation of expected price functions. The structural model for the third period is given by

$$Q_3 = g - hP_3 + u_3$$

$$Q_3 = I_2$$

(5.20)

Absent an expected price function, the structural model for the second period is

$$Q_2 = c - dP_2 + u_2$$

$$Q_2 + I_2 = I_1$$

(5.21)

$$E_2P_3 = P_2(1 + i) + K$$

That for the first period is given by (5.22):

$$Q_1 = a - bP_1 + u_1$$

$$Q_1 + I_1 = H_0 \tag{5.22}$$

$$E_1 P_2 = P_1(1 + i) + K$$

System (5.21) consists of three equations and the four unknowns P_2, Q_2, I_2, and $E_2 P_3$. System (5.22) is similarly incomplete. In order to complete models (5.21) and (5.22), we examine the last period first. We notice that

$$P_3 = \frac{1}{h}(g - I_2 + u_3)$$

$$\tag{5.23}$$

$$E_2 P_3 = \frac{1}{h}(g - I_2)$$

assuming that $E_2 u_3 = 0$.

If we add the second equation from (5.23), the expected price function, to system (5.21), then the unknowns for the second period may be found. When this is done, we have for P_2

$$P_2 = \frac{c + g - hK - I_1 + u_2}{d + h(1 + i)}$$

$$\tag{5.24}$$

$$E_1 P_2 = \frac{c + g - hK - I_1}{d + h(1 + i)}$$

The latter of these two equations can be added to system (5.22), thus completing that system and allowing solutions to be found for the first period. CREM could also be used to complete the systems, if only all the structural parameters given in systems (5.20), (5.21), and (5.22) were known. There would be little incentive to use this procedure for the simple linear model at hand. In any event, the crucial idea in the derivation of the expected price function for the current period is to solve for price in the last period first, finding the expected price function for the second-to-last period, and working backward to the present.

We now return to the two-period case in order to consider the following question: How might a price support operation as analyzed in the previous chapter affect the performance of the two markets separated by time but linked through storage? We will not dwell on the question at any length here, but some conclusions can be quickly reached by going back to Figure 5.1. We must first note, however, that in practice price support programs for U.S. farm commodities involve not only support levels but release levels as well. In addition to assuming that the government stands willing to buy as much of the product as necessary in order to keep price from falling below the support level P_s^+, we assume that it stands willing to sell everything it owns if price rises above the release level P_r^+. Often, release levels have been only slightly above support levels.

In the present instance, if the support price is less than P_{10}, nothing happens. The government program is inoperative. Suppose, however, that P_s^+ exceeds P_{10} as in Figure 5.1. Then the government's demand becomes perfectly elastic at P_s^+. Total demand is given by DD_g. Two cases are of interest depending on the release level P_r^+. If $P_r^+ > P_s^+(1 + i) + K$, then arbitrageurs may still expect to earn normal profits by buying in the first period at P_s^+ and selling in the second period at P_2. With P_r^+ set above P_s^+ by more than the carrying charge, consumers buy Q_{11} for first-period consumption (Figure 5.1). Arbitrageurs buy Q_{10} for second-period consumption. The government acquires $Q_{14} - (Q_{10} + Q_{11})$, which must be gotten rid of one way or another in the second period. (Late summer potatoes might be fed to cows, for example).

A second case of interest occurs if $P_r^+ < P_s^+(1 + i) + K$. Under this condition, private storage disappears. The government purchases what it must in the first period to elevate price to P_s^+. It disposes of as much as it can for consumption in the second period at P_r^+ or, possibly, at a price in excess of P_r^+ determined by equating government stocks to Q_2. If P_s^+ exceeds P_{10}, the government stock will always exceed what the private stock would have been in the absence of the program but with the first-period price equal to P_s^+. Private storage will never occur if P_s^+ exceeds P_{10} and $(P_r^+ - P_s^+)$ is less than the carrying cost per unit. Under these circumstances, the government need not necessarily become saddled with a surplus to be disposed of in a secondary market. Or, perhaps to think of it in a different way, the second-period market becomes a secondary market, no pun intended.

Something like this has occurred from time to time in the U.S. dairy price support program. During the spring, flush months, when market prices would have fallen to low levels in the absence of a government program, the government acquired butter, cheese, and nonfat dried milk, commodities that were subsequently returned to the market in months of tight supply. Marketing firms relied on the government to carry part of the inventory.

5.3 INTERYEAR STORAGE OF FIELD CROPS WITH AND WITHOUT GOVERNMENT INTERVENTION

In this section we first consider a model of competitive pricing and interyear storage of field crops in which the source of market instability is the variation in random yields. We then analyze the effects of alternative government programs aimed at market stabilization.

Competitive Pricing and Storage

Consider the market for a field crop. Quantity demanded for consumption Q_t is a downward-sloping function of price P_t:

$$Q_t = D(P_t) \tag{5.25}$$

where the subscript t indicates the crop year or period. Acreage planted in period t is an upward-sloping function of the expected price at harvest time, in period $t + 1$:

$$A_t = S(E_tP_{t+1}) \tag{5.26}$$

This function assumes that farmers make their acreage planting decisions on the basis of the price they expect will prevail when they harvest their crops in period $t + 1$. The price expectations are rational in that growers understand the economic system and take full advantage of all the relevant information available to them when the expectations are formed. The crop is planted in period t, but the yield depends on subsequent weather. Therefore, production equals acreage planted the previous year A_{t-1} times current random yield per acre Y_t. That is,

$$H_t = A_{t-1}Y_t \tag{5.27}$$

By definition,

$$H_t + I_{t-1} = Q_t + I_t \tag{5.28}$$

where, as before, I_t is the carryout from one crop period to the next.

Storage is carried out by arbitrageurs. As in the previous section, we assume that keen competition does not allow expected profits from arbitrage to be positive. Unlike the previous section, however, we do allow for zero storage. In broad terms, we might expect that in periods of bountiful harvests the carryouts would be positive. In periods of small harvests due to drought or whatever, nothing would be stored for future consumption. The arbitrage condition is given by

$$E_tP_{t+1} \le P_t(1 + i) + K \tag{5.29}$$

where K equals annual storage cost paid at the end of period t and i equals the annual rate of interest. If $E_tP_{t+1} < P_t(1 + i) + K$, as might happen in periods of small harvests, nothing is committed to storage by arbitrageurs and $I_t = 0$. If expected returns from arbitrage are normal, then $I_t > 0$ and $E_tP_{t+1} = P_t(1 + i) + K$. (This equality might also hold as a special case with $I_t = 0$.)

We now take stock of our modeling effort thus far. Either the inequality or the equality of condition (5.29) must hold. If the former holds, we have but four equations, (5.25) through (5.28), with which to solve for the five unknowns Q_t, P_t, A_t, H_t, and E_tP_{t+1}. In this case $I_t = 0$. (Notice that H_t is an endogenous random variable since it depends on random current yield Y_t and lagged acreage planted.) If, on the other hand, the equality of (5.29) holds, then I_t need not and likely will not equal zero, and we have five equations with which to solve for six unknowns. Clearly, our model is incomplete as it stands.

To close the model we assert that

$$E_t P_{t+1} = f_t(I_t, A_t) \tag{5.30}$$

A full and rigorous justification of (5.30) will not be given here; the reader is referred to the references at the end of the chapter for that. It is plausible to suppose, however, that the price arbitrageurs and farmers expect will prevail in the next period is sensitive to the acreage planted in the current period together with the amount of the carryout. Increases in planted acreage lower expected future prices. Increases in the carryout have a similar effect. It is also difficult to imagine other variables that would affect expected prices, unless we allow for exogenous variables that shift, for example, the demand for consumption. In what follows, all such shift variables are held constant.

In order to provide further justification for including (5.30) in our model, we now suggest how this equation could be estimated in the context of empirical research. This is where computational rational expectations modeling (CREM), as introduced in the previous section, comes into play.

We envisage a horizon, a distant period T. Arbitrageurs and farmers pay no attention to what might happen in periods beyond period T as they form, in period t, their expectations in regard to period $t + 1$. It may be useful to adopt the whimsical idea that all market participants expect the world to come to an end at the close of period T. That being the case, we may safely equate A_T and I_T to zero; we need not bother with $E_T P_{T+1}$. We cannot predict what P_T will equal, but we do know that

$$A_{T-1} Y_T + I_{T-1} = D(P_T) \tag{5.31}$$

Solving for P_T, we have

$$P_T = g_T(A_{T-1} Y_T + I_{T-1}) \tag{5.32}$$

In words, P_T is a function of the total available supply. We assume Y_T takes on any one of several specified values with known or estimated probabilities. If, in addition, we have estimates of the structural parameters for equations (5.25) and (5.26) and we know the values for i and K, we can then estimate $E_{T-1} P_T$ for alternative sets of values for A_{T-1} and I_{T-1}. Here's how. Choose specific values for A_{T-1} and for I_{T-1}. Then, for each value of Y_T, calculate P_T. Since the probabilities associated with the various values for Y_T are known, we also know the probabilities for the associated values for P_T, which allows calculating the expected price in period T conditional on the specified values for A_{T-1} and I_{T-1}. For the values $A_{T-1} = A_0$ and $I_{T-1} = I_0$ in Figure 5.3, for example, the vertical distance to point B measures the associated value for $E_{T-1}P_T$. Other sets of values for A_{T-1} and I_{T-1}, as shown in Figure 5.3, include (A_0, I_1), (A_1, I_0), and (A_1, I_1). In each case the vertical distance above the point measures $E_{T-1}P_T$. The surface $BCKL$ is like a tabletop resting on uneven legs. Once the lengths of the table legs are estimated, one can use interpolation to estimate the height of the table, the value of $E_{T-1}P_T$, for any point in the rectangular area directly beneath the tabletop. One may then imagine a surface above the $A_{T-1}I_{T-1}$ plane consisting of a great many small tabletops. This surface is our estimate of Equation (5.30) for $t = T-1$. Given this estimate, we then have a determinate system for $T-1$, which allows estimating $E_{T-2}P_{T-1}$ for many sets of values for A_{T-2} and I_{T-2}. This, in turn, allows estimating the expected price function for period $T-2$, which completes the model for $T-2$. In this manner we can work our way back from the horizon, period T, to the current period t. On the basis of experience with computational models it appears that a horizon of 5 years will often provide excellent approximations for the expected price function for period t.

With an estimate of Equation (5.30) for period t, the current demand for storage can be estimated. The right-hand side of (5.30) is substituted for the left-hand side of Equation (5.29). The resulting equation may then be rewritten with P_t expressed as the dependent variable as follows:

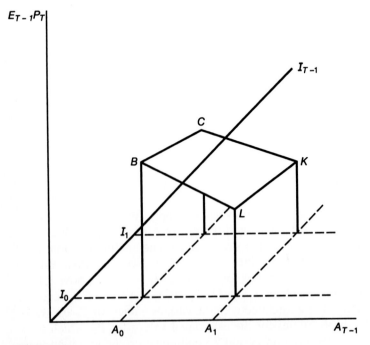

FIGURE 5.3
Deriving interyear expected price function using computational methods.

$$P_t \geq \frac{f_t(I_t, A_t) - K}{1 + i} \tag{5.33}$$

The demand for storage is defined for all prices such that condition (5.33) holds as an equality.

The resulting model of pricing and storage is given a graphic representation in Figure 5.4. We make the simplifying assumption that acreage is fixed by either nature or, perhaps, a government program. [Alternatively, we could interpret the demand for storage as a general equilibrium function that takes into account the relationship between A_t and I_t obtained by substituting the function f_t from (5.30) for $E_t P_{t+1}$ in (5.26).] The demands for consumption and storage in the current period t are given by DD_c and D_s, respectively. Total demand is given by DD. Available supply S equals the sum of the carryout from the previous period I_{t-1}, which might equal zero, plus the current harvest $H_t = A_{t-1}Y_t$. If, because of a drought, say, S is very small, equaling S_0, then price equals P_0 and the entire supply is consumed. With a bountiful crop, the supply is given by S_1. Price then equals P_1, Q_1 is consumed, and I_1 is stored for future consumption.

The above model of pricing and storage is an example of a model that is both stochastic and dynamic. It is stochastic because it contains random vari-

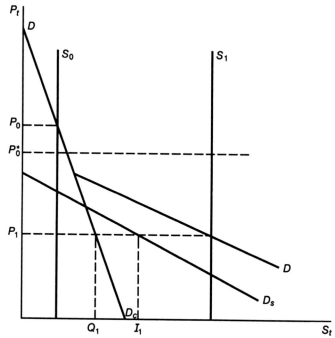

FIGURE 5.4
Competitive pricing and interyear storage of output.

ables. It is dynamic because the equilibrium values of the endogenous variables in period t affect those for period $t + 1$.

It is no longer proper to speak of short-run and long-run effects of changes in exogenous variables, as in the case of comparative static analysis. To see the significance of this, suppose that in period t the value of K drops. How will this affect the values of the endogenous variables in period t, $t + 1$, and in all other future periods?

Suppose that all structural parameters have been estimated, including the probability distribution for yield Y_t and that the initial values for acreage planted and the carryin are known. Using simulation analysis, it is then possible to mimic how the market might perform in all future periods. Time is plotted on the horizontal axis in Figure 5.5 with P_t plotted on the vertical axis and letting 1, 2, 3, etc., stand for future periods. A computer is programmed to generate a future time path of random values for Y_t according to its probability distribution. Given a value for Y_1, the equation system is solved for period 1. The solution values for A_1 and I_1 allow finding the solution for period 2 given the value for Y_2 picked by the computer. Continuing in this vein, we can trace out what might happen in all future periods. Price might follow the pattern given by the dashed line L_1 in Figure 5.5. Suppose that many thousands of such time paths for P_t are simulated in this manner, each displaying its own unique pattern reflecting the random values for Y_t picked by a computer. It would then be possible to estimate for P_t its expected value and its variance for

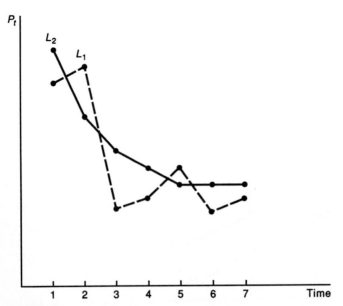

FIGURE 5.5
Simulated expected prices through time due to exogenous shock.

$t = 1, 2, 3, \ldots, n$ since for each t we would have a large random sample of values for P_t and, it might be added, for all other endogenous variables as well.

Suppose that the curve L_2 in Figure 5.5 shows the expected values for P_t estimated in this way and that eventually, in year 5, the expected value becomes stable. It becomes stable in that it does not vary from one year to the next after year 4. We would then say the system has reached its steady-state equilibrium in year 5. It is important to recognize that the expected values for all future years are formed in the initial period. We could not possibly predict in the current period the expected price in period 10 conditional on what actually happens in period 9 because we have no way of knowing what will, in fact, happen in period 9. The notion of a steady-state expected value for an endogenous variable set into motion by a change in an exogenous variable within a dynamic stochastic model is the counterpart to the notion of a new long-run equilibrium value in comparative static analysis resulting from an exogenous shock. The concept of steady-state values will be used repeatedly in what follows.

The only exogenous variables to appear in the above model are K and i. The reason for this is that our interest is centered mainly on storage and its implications for pricing. An important question that arises, therefore, concerns how changes in K and i affect the expected values and the variances of the endogenous variables. We will explore this question in some detail in a moment.

Here we compare briefly the performance of the U.S. soybean market with and without a storage industry, relying on a study by Helmberger and Akinyosoye. Although perhaps interesting, the results have limited policy implications in that governments are not in the habit of dissolving private storage without at the same time instituting public storage. Helmberger and Akinyosoye found that the steady-state expected values for soybean production, consumption, and price were essentially the same in a no-storage regime as in a perfectly competitive storage regime. In comparison with a no-storage regime, however, competitive storage lowered the steady-state variance of price and the variance of consumption by 66 percent and 57 percent, respectively. The variance of production rose somewhat. These findings indicate that in the theoretical analysis of price stabilization programs, the assumption that private storage does not exist may be highly restrictive, depending on the commodity.

Another interesting finding of the Helmberger-Akinyosoye study is that although competitive storage is effective in avoiding precipitous drops in price, it is not effective in avoiding occasional price hikes that are substantial. The reason for this is that storage can be relied upon to keep prices from sagging to very low levels. With no stocks on hand, nothing can be done to forestall a sharp price rise due to crop failure. What this means is that society cannot count on private storage to avoid sharp price hikes and, particularly in the context of a developing nation, famine.

Price Stabilization Programs

We now consider four forms of government intervention as alternative means for increasing market stability under otherwise competitive conditions. The first is a price support program involving both a support price and a release level. Various levels of support are considered with the release level P_r^+ set equal to 120 percent of the support level P_s^+. As will be seen shortly, one effect of a price support program, if only the support level is set high enough, is to wipe out the private storage industry. This is the assumption made for simplicity in Figure 5.6, where no demand for private stocks appears. As in the previous chapter a support program gives rise to a government demand for stocks D_g that is perfectly elastic at P_s^+. Consumption demand is given by DD_c. Total demand is given by DD_g.

Price support operations may also alter postharvest supply as in Figure 5.6. The current harvest is given by Q_0. The government-held stock equals $(Q_2 - Q_0)$ and the release level equals P_r^+. For any price less than P_r^+, the government stock is held back. (It is possible, of course, that depending on economic conditions, the government might add still more to its stock in order to keep price from falling below the support level.) The government stands

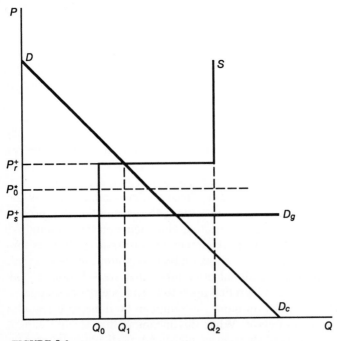

FIGURE 5.6
Effects of buffer-stock and direct price support programs.

willing to throw its entire stock on the market if price reaches or rises above P_r^+. Importantly, the manner in which the step-supply function S is changed as a result of the program depends on the level of government stocks. Without stocks, as might readily occur in long periods of drought, the supply curve might not be affected at all, being perfectly inelastic and consisting solely of current harvest. In Figure 5.6, the government is able to prevent price from rising above P_r^+ through diminishing its stock from $(Q_2 - Q_0)$ to $(Q_2 - Q_1)$. Market price equals P_r^+ and consumption equals Q_1.

The competitive market model given above must be modified in order to allow for a price support program. Importantly, the expectation of P_{t+1} as formed in period t becomes a function of A_t, I_t, and G_t where the latter equals government stocks. Both private and government stocks must be included as independent variables because private and government behavior differ in significant respects.

A second form of government intervention is a direct payment program. Suppose the target price is given by in Figure 5.4. If supply is given by S_0, market price exceeds the target and no payments are made. If supply is given by S_1, the direct payment per unit equals $P_0^* - P_1$. A direct payment program in this case drives a wedge between the market price and the effective price received by farmers. Within a dynamic stochastic model it is necessary to estimate two expected price functions, one for the market price and another for the effective price received by farmers. In what follows we will let W_t equal the market price and P_t equal the farm price. When direct payments do not apply, $P_t = W_t$.

A third form of government intervention involves both direct payments and price support operations. Let the target price be given by P_0^* in Figure 5.6. Because the market price equals P_r^+, no direct payment is made. If the step-supply function were shifted to the right by a sufficient amount, however, a low market price would entail direct payments. Notice, however, that if $P_0^* < P_s^+$, then the direct payment program becomes ineffective.

A fourth form of government intervention involves subsidies to the private storage industry, subsidies that lower the effective carrying cost for commodity stored from one year to the next. In what follows we will be concerned with a subsidy program that lowers both the cost of storage K and the rate of interest i paid for loans for holding stocks. It may be supposed that arbitrageurs are made eligible for receiving low-interest loans from the government.

To summarize, we postulate a competitive market for a field crop. In any year t, harvest reflects current yield together with the planted acreage decisions of the previous year. At harvest time, the output must be allocated between current consumption and storage for future consumption. Decisions regarding planted acreage and stocks are based on the price that is expected to prevail in the future. We then imagine that a government program is begun after harvest is completed and that the program is continued for all future periods. We expect the system to achieve a steady-state solution, eventually, in which the expected values and the variances of all the endogenous variables, formed when the government intervention is begun, remain constant from one year to the next. The question becomes how do price stabilization programs, as identified above, affect the steady-state performance of commodity markets? To answer this question we rely on a quantitative study by Glauber, Helmberger, and Miranda (GHM). We first present their quantitative model and then summarize their main results.

The GHM model is given by

$$Q_t = 5.18P_t^{-0.61}$$

$$Q_t + G_t + I_t = H_t + I_{t-1} + G_{t-1}$$

$$A_t = 13.0(E_t P_{t+1})^{0.89} \tag{5.34}$$

$$H_t = A_{t-1} Y_t$$

$$E_t P_{t+1} \le 1.09P_t + \$0.36$$

where Q_t equals the quantity of U.S. soybeans demanded for domestic consumption and export, measured in billions of bushels; P_t equals dollars per bushel; I_t and G_t are private and government stocks, respectively; A_t equals acreage planted, in millions of acres; and Y_t equals yield per acre. Yield is assumed to be a random variable with mean equal to 29.84 bushels per acre. (The probability distribution for yield was assumed to be log-normal with a coefficient of variation equal to 17.43 percent.) Computational rational expectations modeling was used to estimate the expected price functions for the competitive case as well as for cases involving government programs. Simulation analysis was used to generate large random samples of all endogenous variables for each year after a program was begun.

Tables 5.1, 5.2, and 5.3 and much of the discussion that follows are taken from the GHM study. Table 5.1 gives for various combinations of support prices and price targets the steady-state mean farm price $\overline{P}$, including direct payments, if any; mean market price $\overline{W}$; and the steady-state coefficients of variation of farm price CVP, of market price CVW, and of producer quasi-rent CVQ. Quasi-rent equals producer revenue minus the compounded cost of production. (The latter is measured by the area under the expected acreage supply curve and to the left of acreage planted, all times expected yield.) The estimates given for zero support and target prices are for the purely competitive regime, which allows for competitive storage. The remaining estimates in the first row are for a pure direct payment program. Those given along the diagonal are for a simple price support program with the release price equaling 120 percent of the support price. Without direct payments, market and farm prices are the same, as already noted. Other estimates are for the buffer-payment

TABLE 5.1
Estimates of steady-state values for mean farm price $\bar{P}$, mean market price $\bar{W}$, and for coefficients of variation of farm price CVP, of market price CVW, and of producer quasi-rent CVQ[a]

Support price	Variable	Target price							
		0.00	$4.50	$4.75	$5.00	$5.25	$5.50	$5.75	$6.00
0.00	$\bar{P}$	5.71	5.72	5.73	5.77	5.84	5.92	6.04	6.18
	$\bar{W}$	5.71	5.71	5.70	5.65	5.55	5.44	5.30	5.13
	CVP	19.4	19.4	18.8	17.4	15.0	12.5	9.90	7.2
	CVW	19.5	19.5	19.6	19.7	19.9	20.2	20.5	20.8
	CVQ	12.7	12.8	14.0	15.5	17.0	19.5	22.3	25.0
4.50	$\bar{P}$		5.71	5.72	5.75	5.80	5.87	5.95	6.07
	$\bar{W}$		5.71	5.69	5.65	5.57	5.48	5.34	5.15
	CVP		19.1	18.4	16.8	14.6	12.0	8.6	4.8
	CVW		19.1	18.9	18.8	18.5	17.7	16.2	13.2
	CVQ		12.7	13.7	15.6	17.9	21.2	24.8	28.3
4.75	$\bar{P}$			5.70	5.72	5.76	5.81	5.87	6.00*
	$\bar{W}$			5.70	5.66	5.59	5.52	5.41	5.24
	CVP			16.8	15.2	12.8	10.0	6.7	0.0
	CVW			16.8	16.4	15.6	14.4	12.4	8.2
	CVQ			13.8	15.8	18.6	22.6	27.2	30.5
5.00	$\bar{P}$				5.67	5.71	5.74*	5.87*	6.00*
	$\bar{W}$				5.67	5.62	5.54	5.50	5.44
	CVP				12.0	9.1	4.9	2.1	0.0
	CVW				12.0	10.7	8.6	8.3	8.3
	CVQ				15.9	19.3	23.7	27.4	30.5
5.25	$\bar{P}$					5.74*	5.82*	5.93*	6.08*
	$\bar{W}$					5.74	5.70	5.66	5.62
	CVP					8.3	6.3	4.1	2.2
	CVW					8.3	8.3	8.2	8.1
	CVQ					17.6	21.2	24.6	27.7

[a]Cells marked with asterisks indicate policies that give rise to explosive mean government stocks. Price is in dollars per bushel. Coefficients of variation are in percentages.

program that involves both direct payments and price supports. A support price above the target price renders the latter irrelevant, which accounts for the triangular array of estimates. The cells marked with asterisks identify policies that lead to explosive government stocks such that the expected value of government stocks tends to infinity.

Table 5.1 contains several interesting results. First, a $5.25 price support level, which is well below the mean competitive price of $5.71, causes mean government stocks to explode. With price support operations in place, increases in deficiency payments can also give rise to explosive stocks through encouraging production. In what follows we will be concerned with non-explosive policies unless otherwise noted.

TABLE 5.2
Average consumer gain CS, average producer gain PS, average government expenditure GE, and deadweight loss DL[a]

Support price	Variable	Target price							
		0.00	4.50	4.75	5.00	5.25	5.50	5.75	6.00
				Millions of dollars					
0.00	CS	0	3	30	122	279	475	719	1,012
	PS	0	7	48	148	307	506	750	1,038
	GE	0	10	80	279	608	1,024	1,547	2,180
	DL	0	0	2	9	22	43	78	130
4.50	CS		−6	23	98	221	368	573	814
	PS		7	43	136	275	444	665	947
	GE		4	70	245	521	859	1,335	1,974
	DL		2	4	11	24	47	98	212
4.75	CS			−24	40	134	249	396	599*
	PS			41	119	246	396	593	901
	GE			44	195	436	734	1,146	1,865
	DL			26	37	56	88	157	365
5.00	CS				−73	0	91*	195*	313*
	PS				111	235	393	600	869
	GE				177	420	748	1,199	1,810
	DL				139	185	264	403	628
5.25	CS					−216*	−143*	−64*	26*
	PS					265	434	659	941
	GE					524	901	1,395	2,053
	DL					474	610	801	1,086

[a]Cells marked with asterisks indicate policies that give rise to explosive government stocks. Welfare measures are calculated as the amortized average over the first 50 years of program operation.

Second, for any support price, the higher the target price is, the higher the mean farm price and the lower the mean market price. This is what we would expect from our study of direct payments in the previous chapter. In the present model, price support operations lower the mean farm price in the steady state, but the important point is that the effect is not large. Mean price is not affected very much because whatever is withheld from consumption in one period is returned to the market later on. The "surplus" is not dumped in secondary markets or destroyed as assumed in the previous chapter.

Third, price support and direct payment programs both stabilize the effective farm price, but for a given price floor, the former is more effective than the latter. For a $5.00 price target, for example, direct payments lower CVP from the competitive value 19.4 percent to 17.4 percent; a $5.00 price support lowers CVP to 12.0 percent. The combination of price supports and direct payments can be quite effective in lowering price variability without at the same time causing government stocks to explode.

TABLE 5.3
Estimates of steady-state values for mean farm price $\bar{P}$; coefficients of variation of farm price *CVP* and of quasi-rent *CVQ*; average annual consumer benefits *CS*, producer benefits *PS*, government outlays *GE*, and deadweight losses *DL* for various storage subsidy programs[a]

	Storage subsidy (cents per bushel)				
	0.04	0.12	0.20	0.28	0.36
	Interest subsidy[b]				
Variable	0.01	0.02	0.04	0.06	0.07
$\bar{P}$	5.71	5.70	5.69	5.67	5.66
CVP	19.0	17.7	15.4	11.8	7.2
CVQ	12.8	13.0	14.5	18.5	24.5
CS	−5.7	−16.2	−37.1	−75.1	−147.5
PS	13.2	36.7	81.8	156.2	272.2
GE	8.1	25.2	64.8	150.4	337.8
DL	0.6	4.6	20.1	69.3	213.1

[a]Price is dollars per bushel. Coefficients of variations are in percentages. Average annual gains (losses) are amortized over the first 50 years of program operation. Welfare measures are in millions of dollars.
[b]If the interest subsidy equals 0.01, for example, the real rate of interest paid on a storage loan is 1 percent less than the commercial rate.

Fourth, a pure direct payment program destabilizes market price slightly. This is important in that it is often argued that market stability is conducive to the efficiency of processing and marketing operations. More efficient marketing becomes a possible justification for market stabilization programs. The need for stabilizing the human consumption of food should also be kept in mind. Because direct payment programs stabilize effective farm prices without stabilizing other dimensions of market performance, they should probably not be viewed as market stabilization programs.

Fifth, Table 5.1 shows that, although the programs under consideration stabilize farm price, they destabilize quasi-rent. For any price support, raising the target price causes the coefficient of variation of quasi-rent (*CVQ*) to rise. For relatively low targets, $4.75 or less, raising the price support has little effect on *CVQ*. For higher targets, however, raising the support level causes *CVQ* to rise, the more so the higher the target. Thus, of those programs considered, the one involving a price support of $4.50 and a target of $6.00 stabilizes price the most; it also destabilizes quasi-rent the most. The reader is referred to the references at the end of the chapter for an explanation of these results. We merely note here that under competitive conditions the relationship between yield and price is negative. To some extent, a decrease in yields under competitive conditions is offset, in terms of stabilizing total revenue, by higher prices. The farm programs of interest here tend to undermine this negative correlation.

Finally, several results from the GHM study, not apparent from Table 5.1, are briefly summarized. Price supports destabilized production slightly, but the variability of consumption was lowered considerably. In fact, the percentage reductions in the variability of consumption were roughly the same as for price. Direct payments, on the other hand, stabilized production and destabilized consumption, although in both instances the effects were small. Although direct payments lowered slightly steady-state mean private storage, the effect of price supports was both negative and substantial. A pure price support program with the support level $4.75, well below the mean competitive price, decreased mean private storage by 77 percent. Price variation creates the potential for making profit through storage. Limiting price variation through price support operations destroys that potential.

How do price support and direct payment programs affect consumers, producers, and taxpayers? Again drawing upon the GHM study, we note that Table 5.2 gives their estimates of average annual consumer and producer gains (losses), average annual governmental expenditures, and average annual deadweight losses. The measure of consumer gain (loss) is the expected change in Marshallian consumer surplus caused by the introduction of a farm program into a competitive market. The measure of producer gain (loss) is the expected change in quasi-rent. The efficiency loss equals the sum of producer and consumer gains (losses) minus government expenditures.

In order to understand further the estimates given in Table 5.2, it is important to consider the dynamics of government programs. In the early periods of program operation a price support program tends to remove output from the market. Mean annual prices rise above competitive levels, benefiting producers and hurting consumers and taxpayers. In order to capture these dynamic effects the discounted sum of mean annual gains (losses) over the first 50 years of program operation were estimated and the amortized average gains (losses) per year were then calculated. (The amortized average equals the constant amount of money that would need to be invested in a savings account each year such that the present value of this flow of investments would exactly equal the discounted flow of program benefits over 50 years of program operation.) The same procedure was used for programs involving direct payments, although in this case the system was found to move quickly, in a few years, to the steady-state solution.

Again focusing on nonexplosive policies, for any price support, the average annual consumer gain, producer gain, government expenditure, and efficiency loss rise with increases in the target price (see Table 5.2). On the other hand, holding the target price constant and allowing the support price to increase causes both the average consumer and producer gains to diminish. Although average government expenditures also decline, the efficiency loss rises. The consumer losses and producer gains associated with a pure price support program are caused to a large extent by the high prices in the early years of program operation, when mean government stocks are on the rise. The gains to producers are relatively small, however. Consider a pure price support program with the support level set equal to $5.00. The producer gain equals a mere 2.3 percent of the competitive mean quasi-rent.

With few exceptions, the effects of programs that subsidize private storage operations are qualitatively similar to those of a nonexplosive price support program (see Table 5.3). Lowering the private carrying charge through subsidized credit and storage payments causes both mean farm price and price variation to fall. Quasi-rent is destabilized. Producers gain at the expense of consumers and taxpayers. In contrast to price supports, however, mean private stocks rise. A storage subsidy program that reduces the private rate of interest to 2.2 percent, for example, eliminating entirely other carrying charges, causes mean private stocks to rise by 717 percent, from 65 million to 466 million bushels.

The estimated program effects given above raise the issue of the cost effectiveness of various programs in achieving government objectives. Figure 5.7, taken from the GHM study, provides graphic relationships between the coefficient of variation of price (*CVP*) and annual government expenditure (*GE*) for four stabilization programs. The graphs for storage subsidies, pure price supports, pure direct payments, and the program that involves both price supports and direct payments are labeled *SS, LP, DP,* and *DPL,* respectively. The storage subsidy program involves subsidized storage as well as subsidized interest rates. The graph for the storage subsidy program is truncated at $338 million because this level of expenditure is associated with the near-zero carrying charge given in Table 5.3. Similarly, the graph for a pure price support program is truncated at $524 million, the highest expenditure for this program given in Table 5.2. The buffer-payment program of interest here involves a $4.75 price support. The graphs for a pure direct payment program and a buffer-payment program are truncated at $608 million in order to facilitate comparison with the other programs.

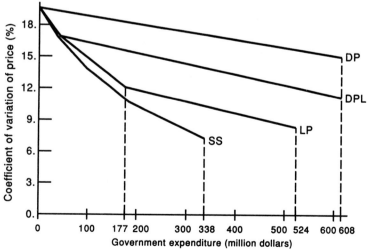

FIGURE 5.7
Effects of alternative market stabilization programs on price variability.

A storage subsidy program is the cheapest way of buying price stability. For an expenditure of $338 million, for example, *CVP* can be decreased from 19.5 percent, the competitive level, to 7.2 percent, yielding a reduction of 12.3 percentage points. The corresponding reductions for the price support, buffer-payment, and direct payment programs are, respectively, 9.2 percent, 5.7 percent, and 2.5 percent. Of the nonexplosive programs considered, however, the one involving a support price and target of $4.50 and $6.00, respectively, yields the lowest *CVP*, 4.8 percent (Tables 5.1 and 5.2). It also costs nearly $2 billion annually.

According to the GHM study, whether government expenditure or efficiency loss is taken as the measure of program cost, storage subsidies are more efficient than price supports in stabilizing market price. The likely reason for this result is the flexibility of a subsidized market mechanism in comparison with the price support mechanism analyzed here. Consider, for example, a period of bountiful years and growing stocks. Given storage subsidies, the minimum price that will induce still further growth in stocks declines, whereas the support price remains constant. Stocks may be drawn down with storage subsidies in operation even though price is less than the fixed release price. For given levels of either government expenditure or efficiency loss, steady-state mean stocks are much greater with price supports than under storage subsidies. Consider annual government expenditures equal to $177 million, for example. Mean steady-state stocks equal 546 million bushels under price supports and 261 million bushels under storage subsidies.

The above discussion calls attention to several suggestions for increasing the efficiency of government buffer-stock schemes. Reflecting a multitude of earlier suggestions, Rausser and Foster have recently argued for the following (p. 20): "On the basis of a specified price level, the Commodity Credit Corporation (CCC) would buy or sell a certain amount of commodity for every one percent decrease or increase in the market price around this specified level. The specified price would be linked to the level of stocks—the larger the supplies, the lower the targeted price." It remains to be seen, however, whether the Rausser-Foster scheme or other government-operated buffer-stock schemes would be as efficient as a simple program of private storage subsidies. Importantly, in a world of structural change, storage subsidies obviate the need for the government to change from time to time the "specified price level" and its relationship with the level of stocks.

5.4   SOME NOTES ON CHOICE OF MODEL

This chapter and the previous chapter examined the effects of price supports and direct payments on the basis of quite different models. As a consequence, the hypotheses as to program effects differ in some important respects, particularly as regards price supports. On the basis of comparative static models, a price support program has no effect on market performance unless the support level is above the competitive price. And if the support level is above the competitive price, then governments stocks will become infinite unless surpluses are destroyed or dumped in secondary markets. In this chapter we have seen, however, that a price support program can have substantial impacts on market performance without leading to infinite government stocks; neither physical destruction of output nor dumping need be involved. A support program can, moreover, lead to exploding government stocks even if the support level is below the mean competitive price.

There are important lessons to be learned here. Economic models are intended to draw attention to the causal relationships that are of major importance in understanding real-world phenomena. The student must always be aware of the possibility that a model overlooks completely variables and relationships that are vital to understanding the effects of whatever program may be of interest. In addition, where alternative models are available for predicting economic effects, choice of model is tantamount to choice of predictions. Great controversies in economics can often be traced to the choice of different models by different analysts. The way to resolve controversies in such situations is through testing the various economic models for their ability to explain and predict economic phenomena. It may not always be easy, however, to ascertain whether this or that model is the more accurate representation of the real world. Testing for the empirical validity of alternative models itself becomes a source of controversy.

In a somewhat different vein, the above analysis centered on stabilization programs where market instability was attributable to variation in crop yield. Stabilization through commodity storage appeared to be feasible and perhaps even appropriate. Stabilization via commodity storage may be quite inappropriate, however, if the source of instability is not yield variation.

History teaches that farm prosperity may rise or fall over long periods of time because of changes in technology or demand. Take the latter case, where the demand for farm commodities has fallen to a low level and where it will remain for several years. Suppose further that the government attempts initially to shore up farm prosperity through the acquisition of stocks. After 2 or 3 years, stocks might reach high levels with substantial government expenditures required to pay for costs of storage. The downward pressure on farm prices and incomes will not have disappeared, however, and the further accumulation of stocks may become untenable. Dumping stocks, on the other hand, would simply exacerbate an already bad situation. Stock accumulation under these circumstances invites production controls, controls that soon create problems of their own, as will be seen in Chapters 7 and 8. We may conclude that manipulation of commodity storage through price support operations or subsidized private storage might be an appropriate policy instrument where market instability is due to the year-to-year fluctuations in yield, but that other approaches might be needed for dealing with instability caused by changes in farm-level demand or technological growth that are substantial and that may persist over an unknown but possibly large number of years.

5.5 SUMMARY

The view that government intervention is needed to stabilize farm commodity prices and markets is widely held. Many arguments have been advanced in favor of this view. Food production, for example, is very uneven, particularly in the case of annually produced field crops, whereas the food requirements of people and animals are stable from day to day. As another example, it has been found that stabilizing the flow of a farm commodity through the marketing channel lowers per unit marketing costs.

Unfortunately, comparative-static analysis is of limited usefulness in the study of market instability and of measures the government might adopt in order to alleviate excessive price variation. New tools of analysis are required. More particularly, we require models that are both stochastic and dynamic, models that contain random variables that cannot be predicted with complete accuracy, such as annual rainfall, and in which optimal decisions at one point in time cannot be made without paying attention to what might happen in future periods. When such models are developed for farm commodity markets, storage and price expectations become crucial elements. Except for simple cases, the analyst must not count on being able to find analytical solutions for the resulting models of pricing and storage. Computational rational expectations modeling (CREM) is introduced in this chapter as one means for dealing with such models.

In this chapter we consider a competitive model of pricing and storage for an annually produced field crop. Consumption demand for the commodity in period t is downward-sloping. Acreage planted in period t depends on the price farmers expect to prevail in period $t + 1$. Total supply available for consumption and storage in period t equals the harvest (acreage planted in year $t - 1$ times random yield in period t) plus the carryin (if any) from period $t - 1$. Arbitrage conditions prevent the price expected in period $t + 1$ plus storage cost, all discounted to present value, from exceeding the present price in period t. Price expected in period $t + 1$ is a function of acreage planted and the ending inventory in period t.

Four approaches to price and market stabilization are considered within this otherwise competitive setting. Two of these are a direct payment program and a price support operation that involves both a support price and a release level. (The latter approach is often caller a buffer-stock program.) Thus, the present chapter continues the analysis of the two methods of putting a floor on prices received by farmers that was begun in the previous chapter. The perspective here is quite different, however. Whereas Chapter 4 considered these programs as a means for raising farm prices, this chapter centers on stabilizing farm prices. One of the remaining two programs combines both price supports and direct payments. The other simply subsidizes the carrying of stocks by private agents with no further interference on the part of the government.

The effects of these four stabilization programs are considered within the context of a quantified model for soybeans using CREM and stochastic simulation. Some of the major findings are as follows. First, a price support or buffer-stock program can be used to stabilize market price without giving rise to infinite government stocks. It is necessary, however, to keep the support level well below the mean competitive price. Second, direct payments can be used to stabilize the effective price received by farmers, but neither market price nor consumption is stabilized. A direct payment program, although perhaps well suited for elevating farm income, should probably not be viewed as an appropriate way to stabilize commodity markets. Third, programs that tend to stabilize prices received by farmers also tend to destabilize quasi-rents. The basic reason for this, broadly speaking, is that price stabilization tends to destroy the negative correlation between yield and price that is characteristic of competitive conditions. When yields fall, prices rise. This negative correlation is conducive to stabilization of total revenue. Fourth, of the price stabilization programs considered, that involving subsidies to private holders of stocks is the most cost-effective. This is the case whether government outlay or efficiency loss is taken as the measure of cost. A substantial advantage of a simple storage subsidy program is that it gets the government out of the guessing game whether the present price is too high or too low relative to prices that will likely prevail in future periods.

PROBLEMS

1. Let X be a random variable that takes on the value of the number of dots appearing on the upper face of a tossed die. Calculate the mean, variance, and coefficient of variation of X. How would your answers change if X equaled the number of dots plus 2? Alternatively, how would your answers change if X equaled the number of dots times 2?
2. Let X be a random variable with mean $\overline{X}$ and variance σ^2. Define a new random Y such that $Y = 10 - 2X$. Find the expressions for the mean and variance of Y.
3. On the last day of August, an exotic wild berry matures and is harvested. The berries can be consumed in September or stored and consumed in October. Storage beyond October is impossible. Demand in September is given by $Q_1 = 36 - P_1^2$. Storage cost equals 2 and the interest rate is 0. The quantity harvested in the season of interest equals 20. Demand in October is given by $Q_2 = 39 - P_2^2 + \mu_2$ where $\mu_2 = +3$ with probability 0.5 and $\mu_2 = -3$ with probability 0.5. Calculate the equilibrium values for P_1, Q_1, I_1, and $E_1 P_2$ using computational rational expectations modeling. The approximation of the expected price function is to be based on only two points, those associated with $I_1 = 0$ and $I_1 = 42$.

REFERENCES AND SUGGESTED READINGS

Cochrane, Willard W., and Yigal Danin, *Reserve Stock Grain Models, the World and the United States, 1975–85*, Minn. Agr. Exp. Sta. Tech. Bul. 305, University of Minnesota, 1976.

Gardner, Bruce L., *Optimal Stockpiling of Grain*, Lexington Books, Lexington, MA, 1979.

Glauber, Joseph, Peter Helmberger, and Mario Miranda, "Four Approaches to Commodity Market Stabilization: A Comparative Analysis," *American Journal of Agricultural Economics* 71(1989):326–337.

Glauber, Joseph, Mark Lowry, Mario Miranda, and Peter Helmberger, *Theory of Pricing and Storage of Field Crops with an Application to Soybeans,* Wis. Agr. Exp. Sta. Bul. R3421, University of Wisconsin, Madison, January 1988.

Gustafson, R. L., *Carryover Levels for Grain: A Method for Determining Amounts That Are Optimal under Specified Conditions,* U.S.D.A., Tech. Bul. 1178, 1958.

Helmberger, Peter, and Vincent Akinyosoye, "Competitive Pricing and Storage under Uncertainty with an Application to the U.S. Soybean Market," *American Journal of Agricultural Economics* 66(1984):119–130.

Johnson, Jr., Aaron C., Marvin B. Johnson, and Rueben C. Buse, *Econometrics: Basic and Applied,* Macmillan, New York, 1987.

Lowry, Mark, Joseph Glauber, Mario Miranda, and Peter Helmberger, "Pricing and Storage of Field Crops: A Quarterly Model Applied to Soybeans," *American Journal of Agricultural Economics* 69(1987):740–749.

Massell, Benton F., "Some Welfare Implications of International Price Stabilization," *Journal of Political Economy* 78(1970):404–417.

Miranda, Mario, "Analysis of Rational Expectation Models for Storable Commodities under Government Regulations," Ph.D. dissertation, University of Wisconsin, Madison, 1985.

Miranda, Mario, and Peter G. Helmberger, "The Effects of Price Band Buffer Stock Programs," *American Economic Review* 78(1988):46–58.

Muth, J. F., "Rational Expectations and the Theory of Price Movements," *Econometrica* 29(1961):58–62.

Newbery, David M. G., and Joseph E. Stiglitz, *The Theory of Commodity Price Stabilization,* Oxford University Press, New York, 1981.

Peck, Anne E., "Implications of Private Storage of Grains for Buffer Stock Schemes to Stabilize Prices," *Food Research Institute Studies* 16(1977–78):125–140.

Plato, Gerald, and Douglas Gordon, "Dynamic Programming and the Economics of Optimal Grain Storage," *Agricultural Economics Research* 35(1983):10–22.

Rausser, Gordon C., and William E. Foster, "Managing Farm Supply," *Choices,* Third Quarter, 1987:18–21.

Salant, Stephen W., "The Vulnerability of Price Stabilization Schemes to Speculative Attack," *Journal of Political Economy* 91(1983):1–38.

Samuelson, Paul A., "Intertemporal Price Equilibrium: A Prologue to the Theory of Speculation," *The Collected Papers of Paul A. Samuelson.* ed. J. E. Stiglitz, pp. 946–984, MIT Press, Cambridge, 1966.

Smith, Adam, *The Wealth of Nations,* University of Chicago Press, Chicago, 1976. (Originally published in 1776.)

Waugh, Frederick V., "Does the Consumer Gain from Price Instability?" *Quarterly Journal of Economics* 58(1944):602–614.

Working, Holbrook, "The Theory of the Price of Storage," *American Economic Review* 39(1949):1254–1262.

Wright, Brian D., and Jeffrey C. Williams, "The Economic Role of Commodity Storage," *Economic Journal* 92(1982):596–616.

CHAPTER

6

Marketing Order Programs

Federal marketing orders are programs that regulate specified marketing activities of commodity handlers (first buyers). Orders are issued and supervised by the U.S. secretary of agriculture. The legislative authority for these programs is the Agricultural Marketing Agreement Act of 1937 as amended by several subsequent farm bills. As will become clearer in a moment, this legislation is merely enabling legislation; it does not mandate the organization of programs. Rather, the programs must have widespread producer support, be judged by the secretary to be effective in achieving legislative objectives, and be limited to specified regulatory activities. Since these programs do not entail treasury outlays, they are often referred to as "self-help" programs.

The regulatory provisions of marketing orders vary as between fruits, vegetables, and other specialty crops, on the one hand, and milk used in fluid consumption, on the other. For convenience we will refer to the crops for which orders may be issued as FVS (fruits, vegetables, and specialties) crops. Most fruits and vegetables used for canning and freezing are excluded. Specialty crops include, for example, nuts, dates, cranberries, and spearmint. In 1981, there were 47 federal marketing orders for FVS crops. According to a U.S. Department of Agriculture (USDA) study more than 50 percent of the fruit and tree nuts produced in the United States and 15 percent of the vegetables produced, measured on value basis, were marketed under federal orders. Although the legislation allows for programs that control the level of crop production through producer allotments, such control has been of very limited importance. Of much greater importance are programs that seek to control the disposition of whatever farmers elect to produce. For this reason the allocation of output among alternative markets will be of major interest in this chapter. Some attention will also be given to advertising and product promotion. (A

1981 study by the USDA discusses still other permissive regulatory activities such as quality control, data collection, and research.)

Under federal milk marketing orders, the minimum price paid for grade A milk (milk eligible for fluid use) is set by the government, the price depending on how the milk is used. Many states have similar milk pricing programs. Under milk orders, milk is often allocated to two classes, to Class I for fluid use and Class II for manufactured products such as butter, cheese, and nonfat dried milk. (Many orders have a relatively unimportant separate class for milk and milk components used in "soft" manufactured dairy products such as cottage cheese and ice cream. For simplicity we will ignore this class use.) The resulting system of pricing is often referred to as *classified pricing,* and virtually all fluid milk is so priced, if not under a federal program, then under a state program. Whereas orders for FVS crops affect price indirectly through market allocation provisions, milk orders affect prices directly.

As to program objectives, the enabling legislation makes reference to the need for establishing "orderly" marketing conditions and assuring that returns to producers are equitable and at such levels as to assure adequate supplies at more stable prices to consumers. The legislative objectives sound innocent enough, but key terms such as "orderly marketing" are not given operational definitions. There are good reasons for believing, however, that the intention here as for other farm programs has been to find ways to enhance producer prices and incomes at, implicitly, someone else's expense. The legislation explicitly prohibits using marketing orders to maintain prices above parity levels.

The organization of marketing order programs usually involves the following steps: A proposed order program is formulated by either an industry group or the secretary of agriculture. A public hearing is held to allow all interested parties to enter evidence and express their views. On the basis of evidence presented both at and after the hearing, the secretary, at his or her discretion, may organize a referendum in which producers have the right to vote against or in favor of a program with specified regulatory provisions. Producer acceptance of a program requires approval on the part of two-thirds of those producers voting in the referendum or on the part of those producers producing two-thirds of the commodity. Programs may be terminated by the secretary or by producers who both produce more than half the output and request termination. Administration of programs for FVS crops is generally by a committee of producers, or of producers and handlers. Committee actions are subject to approval by the U.S. secretary of agriculture. Milk orders are administered by market administrators appointed by the secretary of agriculture.

In this chapter we first consider models of marketing order programs for FVS crops. An illustrative example of such a program, that for California-Arizona navel oranges, is then discussed. Attention is then centered on federal milk orders and on an analysis of national dairy policy, taking into account price supports, milk orders, and dairy import quotas. A final section considers the question whether milk orders are needed to achieve efficient market performance.

6.1 MODELING MARKETING ORDER PROGRAMS FOR FRUITS, VEGETABLES, AND SPECIALTY CROPS

Four alternative programs are considered. The first involves product destruction only. The second involves price discrimination. The third treats product destruction and price discrimination taken together. A fourth program involves the collection of funds from producers for product advertising. All assume the emergence of a control authority upon the initiation of a marketing order program. The control authority may be viewed either as the secretary of agriculture or a committee of producers and handlers who submit recommendations to the secretary, recommendations that may be accepted with perhaps only a perfunctory appraisal of their merits.

Product Destruction

We begin as usual on the assumption of a perfectly competitive market; equilibrium price and output are given by P_c and Q_c in part *a* of Figure 6.1. A marketing order program is introduced in which a control authority has no say as to the level of production but can decide how much output is to be sold and how much, if any, is to be destroyed. For the moment, and strictly for convenience, we assume the control authority takes physical possession of the crop, sells all or some part of it to private buyers (handlers), and distributes the proceeds to farmers. It is assumed that the collection, sales, and possible destruction of some of the commodity are costless activities. On these assumptions, the price or average return per unit of output received by each producer is determined by

$$AR = \frac{PQ}{Q_s} \tag{6.1}$$

where AR equals the average return to the farmer, P equals the price paid by buyers, Q equals the quantity sold to buyers, and Q_s is the total output of farmers. If $Q_s > Q$, then $(Q_s - Q)$ is destroyed.

We assume the objective of the control authority is to maximize AR for whatever level of Q_s is produced. This can be done by choosing a value of Q such that the numerator of the right-hand side of (6.1) is as large as possible for all possible values for Q_s. In part *b* of Figure 6.1, the level of sales Q_0 yields the largest total receipts from buyers. At this point marginal revenue equals zero. To the left of Q_0, marginal revenue is positive; to the right it is negative. The demand over the range of sales less than Q_0 is elastic. Over the range of sales larger than Q_0, demand is inelastic. Demand is said to have unitary elasticity at Q_0. Consider any level of output less than Q_0—Q_1, say. From part *b* of Figure 6.1, if Q_1 is produced and the control authority were to sell less than Q_1, total revenue would be less than TR_1. Clearly, total revenue can be maximized by selling all that is produced. We have

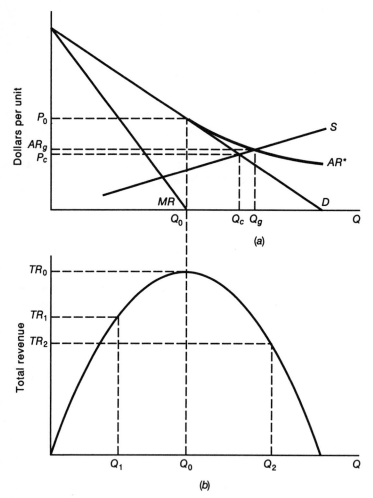

FIGURE 6.1
Effects of product destruction under a marketing order.

$$AR^* = \frac{PQ_s}{Q_s} \qquad Q_s \leq Q_0 \qquad\qquad (6.2)$$

where AR^* is the maximized value of AR given Q_s and where P is the price associated with the sale of all that is produced. The case where Q_s is less than or equal to Q_0 is trivial because all output is sold, just as under perfect competition and without government intervention. The average revenue to the farmer equals the price paid by the buyer. This is what happens if demand is elastic in the relevant range.

Next, consider any output Q_s larger than Q_0. Take Q_2, for example. From part b of Figure 6.1, the control authority could increase receipts above TR_2 by not selling all that is produced. In fact if Q_2 is produced, total receipts and therefore AR can be maximized if and only if Q_0 is sold and $(Q_2 - Q_0)$ is destroyed. In fact for any $Q_s > Q_0$, receipts can be maximized by selling Q_0 and getting rid of $Q_s - Q_0$. Therefore, we have the function

$$AR^* = \frac{P_0 Q_0}{Q_s} \qquad Q_s > Q_0 \qquad (6.3)$$

where AR^* again equals maximized average receipts. Notice that the numerator of the right-hand side of (6.3) equals the constant TR_0. Over the relevant range of Q_s, (6.3) is a rectangular hyperbola, a graph of which, labeled AR^*, is given in part a of Figure 6.1. Given the supply curve S, equilibrium output and average receipts to producers are given by Q_g and AR_g, respectively, where supply and the AR^* curve intersect. If farmers produced less than Q_g, the control authority could return to them a price larger than AR_g, which would induce them to increase production. If output were larger than Q_g, the control authority could only return a price less than AR_g, which would serve to lower production. With the program in effect, $Q_g - Q_0$ is destroyed and the price to handlers rises from P_c to P_0.

   A numerical example might be instructive. Let demand be given by $Q_d = 10 - P_d$ and supply by $Q_s = 4P_s$. Under competition $Q_d = Q_s$ and $P_s = P_d$. Solving this simple system yields the competitive solution $P_c = 2$ and $Q_c = 8$. The total revenue function is given by

$$TR = P_d Q_d = 10 Q_d - Q_d^2 \qquad (6.4)$$

(This expression for TR is obtained by first writing P_d as a function of Q_d and then forming the appropriate product.) Maximizing TR with respect to Q_d we have

$$\frac{dTR}{dQ_d} = 10 - 2Q_d = 0 \qquad (6.5)$$

The Q_d that maximizes TR equals 5; the corresponding price is also 5, and maximized total revenue equals 25. Since the competitive price is less than 5, we can be sure a marketing order program will entail product destruction. The equilibrium can be found by solving the following equation system:

$$AR^* = \frac{25}{Q_s}$$

$$Q_s = 4P_s \qquad (6.6)$$

$$AR^* = P_s$$

The third equation of this system simply states that in equilibrium the supply price equals the maximized average returns from the control authority. From the viewpoint of the producer, average receipts returned by the control authority displaces the role of price paid by buyers under competition. Solving we find that $Q_g = 10$ and $AR_g^* = 2.5$. Surplus production equals 5. Price to buyers is increased from 2 to 5.

It can be shown that the loss of benefits to consumers equals 19.5. If S is interpreted as a short-run supply, the gain in quasi-rent to producers equals 4.5. If S is a long-run curve, then the gain of 4.5 accrues to input suppliers. In either case, the efficiency loss equals 15.5. The details of the calculations are left to the student. (The student should bear in mind that a short-run supply is likely to be steeper or less elastic than a long-run supply.) Importantly, the efficiency loss involved in the transfer of benefits from consumers to producers is relatively large. This is what one should expect from a program that is as blatantly wasteful as this one.

A particularly interesting case is given in Figure 6.2. Here it is assumed that in the long run the farm industry is a constant cost industry with a perfectly flat or elastic supply curve. In the short run, supply is quite inelastic. This case may be realistic for tree crop industries, which require small propor-

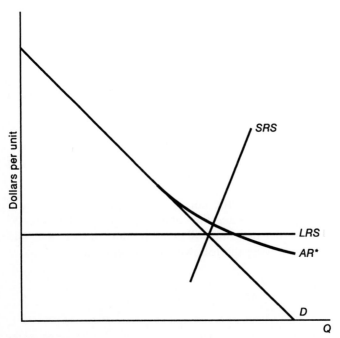

FIGURE 6.2
Effects of product destruction given a constant cost farm industry.

tions of the nation's available farm input supplies and, for this reason, have highly elastic long-run supply curves. In the short run, because of the lag between the planting of trees and tree maturity, production may respond very little to price changes. In this setting, producers might reap substantial gains from a product destruction program in the short run, with no lasting gains to themselves or to anyone else in the long run.

In the above analysis, the control authority was assumed to take possession of the crop. This assumption is unnecessary. Program results can be secured much more conveniently by the control authority through simply issuing correctly specified orders to first handlers. Consider, therefore, an order that allows the control authority to dictate to all handlers the proportion β of the crop that can be marketed for consumption and the proportion $(1 - \beta)$ that must be destroyed. We consider the case where demand is inelastic, such that product destruction takes place. Then $0 < \beta < 1$. Also, we proceed directly to long-run analysis. A behavioral relationship for the ith handler, bound by the order, is given by

$$q_i = \beta q_{di} \tag{6.7}$$

where q_i equals the output the handler is allowed to market, q_{di} equals the amount purchased from producers, and β is the factor of proportionality announced by the control authority. How can the optimal value for β be chosen? If demand is inelastic, the control authority knows that no more than Q_0 should be allowed to go to the market. It need merely set β equal to the ratio of Q_0 to Q_s. Then, aggregating across all N handlers we have

$$\sum_{i=1}^{N} q_i = \frac{Q_0}{Q_s} \sum_{i=1}^{N} q_{di}$$

$$= \frac{Q_0}{Q_s} Q_d \tag{6.8}$$

where Q_d is the aggregate amount purchased from all farmers. Since total purchases Q_d must equal total sales Q_s in equilibrium, we have

$$\sum_{i=1}^{N} q_i = Q_0 \tag{6.9}$$

How can we be sure that under an order program with this regulatory provision producers will receive a price equal to AR_g in part a of Figure 6.1? If only Q_0 is allowed to go to market, then P_0 times Q_0, or TR_0, is the maximum amount of money handlers can pay producers and still break even, covering all marketing costs. (We retain the assumption that product destruction is costless merely to simplify analysis.) If handlers paid less than TR_0 to farmers, then marketing margins would be inflated by excess profit. This would attract the entry of new handlers who would bid up the price. If, on the other hand, handlers paid more than TR_0, then the marketing margin would be less than that required to cover all marketing costs. Losses would be incurred and some handlers would exit the market. This would allow the price paid to farmers to fall. Perfect competition among handlers therefore assures that for whatever quantity Q_s is supplied, $Q_s > Q_0$, the total receipts to farmers will equal TR_0 if only Q_0 is allowed to go to market. Therefore, we have

$$AR^* = \frac{P_0 Q_0}{Q_s} \qquad Q_s > Q_0 \qquad (6.10)$$

With this relationship the model of price determination becomes the same as for the case where the control authority takes possession of the crop. The control authority need merely find the value for Q_0, announce that β equals the ratio of Q_0 to Q_s, and let the market mechanism do the rest.

Crucial to the above analysis is the assumption of keen competition among handlers. If competition is not keen, if the buying industry were characterized by monopsony or high-order oligopsony, with substantial barriers to entry, then it would be very unlikely that total receipts to farmers could be increased through product destruction. In this structural setting direct price setting by the government might be more appropriate than output allocation devices. Concern with monopsony elements has historically been of greater concern in markets for fluid milk than for FVS crops. This might explain why milk orders set minimum prices rather than trying to affect prices indirectly.

Price Discrimination

Consider a perfectly competitive market in which buyers can be broken up into two groups, groups h and k. (The following analysis can be easily generalized to handle three or more groups). The demand for group h is given by D_h in part a Figure 6.3, together with the corresponding marginal revenue curve MR_h. Demand and marginal revenue curves for group k are given in part b. Aggregate demand, given by the lateral summation of D_h and D_k, is given by D in part c. Under competition, the law of one price to all buyers would prevail such that if Q_1 is produced, then all buyers would pay price P_1. Equilibrium price and output would be determined by the intersection of total demand and supply, the latter not shown in Figure 6.3.

Now assume a marketing order program is begun. The control authority takes possession of the crop and is permitted to allocate the crop between the two groups of buyers in any way it pleases (again, assuming the control authority takes possession of the crop is strictly for convenience). Product destruction and output control are not permissible regulatory activities. We also

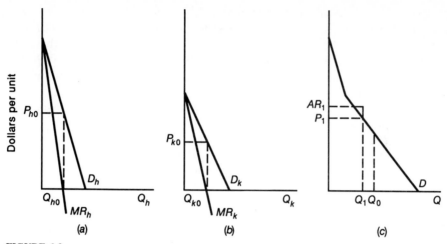

FIGURE 6.3
Price discrimination under a marketing order increases the farm price.

assume the control authority can forestall arbitrage between the *h*-buyers and the *k*-buyers. That is to say, the authority can prevent the buyers in one group from selling to the buyers in the other group. For example, the *h*-buyers might buy the product for canning, say, and the *k*-buyers buy for distribution for fresh consumption. As another example, suppose the *h*-buyers are exporters and the *k*-buyers buy for the domestic market. Government control over exports and imports may be used to forestall arbitrage.

The average return to farmers is calculated using

$$AR = \frac{P_h Q_h + P_k Q_k}{Q_s} \qquad (6.11)$$

where P_h equals the price paid by the *h*-buyers and Q_h equals the quantity they buy. Similarly for P_k and Q_k. Other terms are as defined previously. Assume the objective of the control authority is to maximize *AR* for whatever level of Q_s is produced. This can be accomplished either by selling everything in one market or the other or by allocating supplies to the two markets in such manner as to equate the marginal revenues. Consider the first option first. Suppose everything is sold to the *h*-buyers and that the resulting marginal revenue MR_h is higher than the maximum marginal revenue for the *k*-buyers MR_k. In that case *AR* is maximized. Otherwise, if $MR_h < MR_k$, the allocation scheme is not optimal. A similar argument applies to selling all the output to the *k*-buyers with nothing sold to the *h*-buyers.

Perhaps a more interesting case, however, is where optimization requires selling at least some output to each group of buyers. As noted above, maximization of *AR* in this case requires that the marginal revenues for the two groups of buyers be equated, viz., that $MR_h = MR_k$. The easiest way to see that this is true is to suppose that the marginal revenues are not equated. Suppose, for example, that $MR_h = 10$ and $MR_k = 5$. If one unit of the commodity is shifted from the k-buyers to the h-buyers, then the total receipts from the k-buyers fall by 5, but the total receipts from the h-buyers rise by 10, yielding a net increase of 5.

More rigorously, we can proceed to maximize AR for $Q_s = Q_1$ (see Figure 6.3) using the expression

$$AR = \frac{D_h(Q_h)Q_h + D_k(Q_k)Q_k}{Q_h + Q_k} \tag{6.12}$$

where the demands are given by $P_h = D_h(Q_h)$ and $P_k = D_k(Q_k)$. Notice that $Q_1 = Q_h + Q_k$. Taking the partial derivatives of AR with respect to Q_h and Q_k and setting those derivatives equal to zero yields $MR_h = MR_k$. (Second-order conditions will be satisfied if the demands are downward-sloping.)

At this juncture we can make use of the following relationship between price and marginal revenue for the h-buyers:

$$MR_h = P_h\left(1 + \frac{1}{E_h}\right) \tag{6.13}$$

where E_h equals the elasticity of demand for the h-buyers. The derivation of this result is left to the student. (Hint: Express demand as a price-dependent function, form the expression for total revenue as a function of Q_h, and then differentiate total revenue with respect to Q_h. Similarly for MR_k.) Equating marginal revenues yields

$$P_h\left(1 + \frac{1}{E_h}\right) = P_k\left(1 + \frac{1}{E_k}\right) \tag{6.14}$$

If $E_h = E_k$, then $P_h = P_k$.

We hasten to add, however, that it is extremely unlikely that demand elasticities will be equal, and we assume in what follows that such a condition does not obtain and that $E_h \neq E_k$. In this case, prices will differ as between the two groups of buyers and price discrimination can be used to raise AR above the competitive price for any given level of output. We have plotted the maximized value of AR, AR_1, against Q_1 in part c of Figure 6.3. Of course, $AR_1 > P_1$. Having performed this operation for Q_1, it is clear that we can repeat the operation for many values of Q_s. Connecting these points together yields an important curve given by AR^* in Figure 6.4. This curve is a geometric representation of

$$AR^* = f(Q_s) \tag{6.15}$$

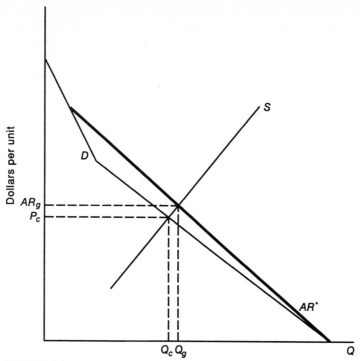

FIGURE 6.4
Effects of price discrimination under a marketing order.

This function shows the maximized values of AR for all levels of Q_s. The AR^* curve in Figure 6.4 is merely a linear approximation of a true nonlinear curve. Also, the AR^* and D curves coincide for small levels of output. Over this range of output all output is sold to the h-buyers and price discrimination does not occur. In what follows we will ignore these small, troublesome levels of output.

Equilibrium with the order program in effect is given by the intersection of the supply curve and the AR^* curve in Figure 6.4. The program increases the price to producers from the competitive price P_c to AR_g; output increases from the competitive output Q_c to Q_g. Producers receive a gain in the short run, but in the long run the gain accrues to farm labor and landowners. In either case the gain can be measured as the increase in producer surplus.

We next take up the effects of price discrimination on consumers, considering first the case where the elasticities of demand E_h and E_k are larger than 1 in absolute value. In other words, the demands are elastic in the relevant range. Taking an example, let $E_h = -3$ and $E_k = -2$. Using (6.14) we can readily determine that $P_k = \frac{4}{3}P_h$. Price discrimination raises the price to the k-buyers relative to the price paid by the h-buyers. As a general rule, with elastic demands, price discrimination raises the price to buyers with the less elastic demand relative to the price paid by the buyers with the more elastic demand. Using advanced analysis it can be shown further that with elastic demands, a marketing control program raises absolutely the price to those buyers with the least elastic demand and lowers the price to buyers with the more elastic demand. Thus, the buyers with the more elastic demand are program beneficiaries. It's the consumers with the less elastic demand who pick up the tab and who may be forgiven for objecting to calling the program a self-help program.

Now suppose that over the relevant range of output the demands are inelastic, that maximizing AR without product destruction means equating negative marginal revenues. Again taking an example, let $E_h = -\frac{1}{2}$ and $E_k = -\frac{1}{3}$. Using (6.14) we can readily determine that $P_h = 2P_k$. Clearly $P_h > P_k$. Here price is higher in the more elastic (least inelastic) market relative to price in the less elastic market. In fact, simple algebra can be used to show that, in general, when the two demands are inelastic, price discrimination raises price in the more elastic market and lowers price in the less elastic market, which is just the opposite of what occurs when demands are elastic. The claim often encountered in textbooks that price discrimination tends to raise prices in the least elastic market relative to those in more elastic markets usually reflects analysis of a price-discriminating pure monopolist who would not in any event produce to the point where demands are inelastic.

Price Discrimination Coupled with Product Destruction

The above analysis of a marketing order program that allows for price discrimination can be easily generalized to allow for product destruction as well. Since the control authority takes output produced as exogenous, we can consider how the authority's decisions change as output changes. Start with a level of output such that marginal revenues in both markets are positive, i.e., consider $Q_s < (Q_{h0} + Q_{k0})$ in Figure 6.3. For any such level of output the authority can maximize AR to producers through practicing price discrimination. Since marginal revenues in both markets are positive, product destruction would lower grower returns. Suppose output increases to the point where $Q_s = Q_0 = Q_{h0} + Q_{k0}$. Now marginal revenues are both equated to zero. No matter how much is produced, it would be impossible for the control authority ever to return more than $TR_0 = P_{h0}Q_{h0} + P_{k0}Q_{k0}$ to producers. With product destruction the control authority would never increase its sales to the point where marginal revenues would become negative. Hence,

$$AR^+ = \frac{TR_0}{Q_s} \qquad Q_s > Q_0 \qquad (6.16)$$

where AR^+ equals the maximized average return to growers allowing for both price discrimination and product destruction.

The aggregate demand and the AR^* curve from Figure 6.4 are repeated in Figure 6.5. For all Q_s less than Q_0, the AR^* and AR^+ curves coincide, and it does not matter that the control authority could destroy output if it chose to do so. If the supply curve intersects the AR^+ (or AR^*) curve to the left of Q_0, no product destruction will occur in equilibrium. To the right of Q_0, however, the AR^+ curve becomes a mathematical hyperbola and lies above the AR^* curve. Over this range of output the curve AR^+ depicts the function given by (6.16). If the supply curve intersects the AR^+ curve to the right of Q_0, then product destruction will occur. Total production will be increased relative to the competitive output Q_c and relative to the output Q_g under a simple price discrimination program. The same applies to the average returns to growers. The level of product destruction in equilibrium is given by $(Q_g^+ - Q_0)$.

The above analysis is based on the assumption that the control authority takes possession of the crop. As shown below, this assumption can be relaxed in favor of simply allowing the control authority to issue certain regulatory orders.

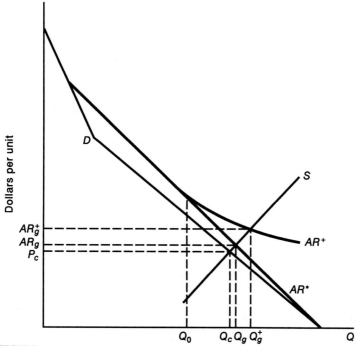

FIGURE 6.5
Effects of price discrimination and product destruction under a marketing order.

Price Discrimination with or without Product Destruction: An Algebraic Treatment*

A long-run competitive model of commodity pricing is given by

$$P_h = a - bQ_h$$

$$P_k = c - dQ_k$$

$$P_s = S(Q_s) \qquad (6.17)$$

$$P_s = P_h = P_k$$

$$Q_s = Q_h + Q_k$$

where the first and second equations are long-run derived demands for the h-buyers and the k-buyers, respectively. The third equation is long-run supply. The remaining equations state market equilibrium conditions. Linear demands are chosen to simplify the mathematics.

Let q_h and q_k equal, respectively, the quantities which a representative handler sells to the h-buyers and the k-buyers. Under a marketing order,

$$q_h = B_h q_d$$

$$q_k = B_k q_d \qquad (6.18)$$

$$B_h + B_k = 1$$

where q_d is the quantity purchased from farmers, B_h is the proportion of purchases that must be sold to the h-buyers, and B_k is the proportion that must be sold to the k-buyers. Because product destruction is for the moment not allowed, B_h and B_k sum to 1.

The aggregate quantity demanded Q_d equals the aggregate quantity supplied Q_s. Through announcing a value for B_h (or B_k), the control authority determines how total supply is allocated between the two product markets. (We assume arbitrage between the two groups of buyers is prohibited.) Under our assumptions,

$$AR = \frac{P_h Q_h + P_k Q_k}{Q_s} \qquad (6.19)$$

where Q_h and Q_k are the aggregate quantities marketed in the two markets. For any Q_s, the numerator of the right-hand side of (6.19) is the maximum amount of money handlers could pay farmers and still cover all marketing costs. Under competition, with no barriers to entry, the maximum that could be paid will be paid. Otherwise, marketing margins would contain excess profit, profit that would attract new handlers. Entry would, in turn, cause the price paid to farmers to rise.

This being the case, the problem confronting the control authority is to figure out a rule that specifies the value of B_h (or B_k) for all possible values of Q_s such that AR is maximized. Once such a rule is derived a clerk can carry out the necessary computations, announcing the value of B_h for whatever Q_s is observed.

Since the total amount demanded by handlers Q_d equals the amount supplied by growers Q_s in equilibrium, we have

$$AR = \frac{P_h B_h Q_s + P_k B_k Q_s}{Q_s}$$

$$= \frac{Q_h}{Q_s}(a - bQ_h) + \frac{Q_k}{Q_s}(c - dQ_k) \qquad (6.20)$$

In order to maximize AR subject to the restriction that the entire crop is sold, we form the Lagrangian expression L:

$$L = \frac{Q_h}{Q_s}(a - bQ_h) + \frac{Q_k}{Q_s}(c - dQ_k) + \lambda(Q_s - Q_h - Q_k) \qquad (6.21)$$

Setting the partial derivatives of L with respect to Q_h and Q_k equal to zero, we have

$$\frac{\partial L}{\partial Q_h} = \frac{a - 2bQ_h}{Q_s} - \lambda = 0$$

$$\frac{\partial L}{\partial Q_k} = \frac{c - 2dQ_k}{Q_s} - \lambda = 0 \qquad (6.22)$$

Therefore, $a - 2bQ_h = c - 2dQ_k$, which is to say that the marginal revenues in the two markets are equated. Also, $Q_h + Q_k = Q_s$. Solving for Q_h and Q_k, we have

$$Q_h = \frac{a - c + 2dQ_s}{2(b + d)}$$

$$Q_k = \frac{c - a + 2bQ_s}{2(b + d)} \qquad (6.23)$$

and,

$$B_h = \frac{a - c + 2dQ_s}{2(b + d)Q_s}$$

$$B_k = \frac{c - a + 2bQ_s}{2(b + d)Q_s}$$

(6.24)

The optimal rule, the rule that specifies the values for B_h and B_k that maximize AR for all Q_s, is given by (6.24). Since B_h and B_k together with P_h, Q_h, P_k, and Q_k are all functions of Q_s, we have

$$AR^* = f(Q_s)$$

(6.25)

A geometric representation of this function is given by AR^* in Figure 6.4. It shows the maximized values of AR for all values of Q_s.

If product destruction is a permissive regulatory activity, then

$$AR^+ = AR^* = f(Q_s) \qquad Q_s \leq Q_0$$

$$AR^+ = \frac{P_{h0} Q_{h0} + P_{k0} Q_{k0}}{Q_s} \qquad Q_s > Q_0$$

(6.26)

where Q_{h0} and Q_{k0} are the quantities in the two markets associated with zero marginal revenues. Notice that for $Q_s \leq Q_0$, the AR^+ function and the AR^* function are the same.

The conclusion to be drawn from this analysis is that it is unnecessary for the control authority to actually take possession of the crop. Formulating and implementing the optimal regulatory order is all that is required.

Product Advertising and Promotion

Several marketing order programs provide the vehicle for producers to join together in advertising their output. With a homogeneous product, there is little chance for a successful advertising program on the part of a single producer. The chances for success are not all that promising even in the case of marketing cooperatives. The problem is a classic example of free-riding. A producer or group of producers pays the advertising cost, but all producers receive the ensuing benefits.

We assume a marketing order program in which handlers are directed to deduct z per unit of output for all output purchased. The proceeds are passed along to the control authority, who then hires advertisers to throw up billboards, buy television time, and all the rest. The individual farmer receives $P' = (P - z)$ per unit of output where P equals market price and z is the deduction.

Competitive supply and demand absent the marketing order are given by S and D in Figure 6.6. The curve labeled S' lies above S by the amount z. Since

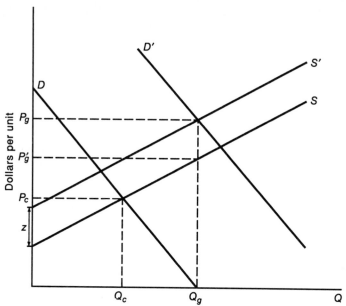

FIGURE 6.6
Effects of product promotion.

farmers will make their production plans according to P' instead of P, the curve S' is the supply curve with the marketing order in place. If the advertising campaign has no impact on demand, then the order lowers both farm price and output and raises the price to consumers, not a pretty picture. On the other hand, suppose the advertising campaign lifts demand from D to D' in Figure 6.6. This is, of course, the way the program is supposed to work. The price received by farmers rises from P_c to P_g' where $P_g' = P_g - z$. By moving S' and D' around in various ways, the student can explore many alternative sets of economic effects that might result from the program.

How might the control authority set z? A plausible objective is the maximization of P'. A calculating control authority could presumably do a good job of maximizing P' if controlled market experiments were used to gauge advertising's effectiveness. There is always the possibility, of course, that farmers could be tricked by advertisers into believing that advertising is effective when it is not.

Product advertising and promotion will not receive much attention in the remainder of the book. Consequently, this is about as good a place as any to point out an inherent danger in trying to solve farm income problems through advertising. If advertising can be used to elevate returns to producers of citrus, why not apply the same solution to lamb, jam, and cabbage? There is always the possibility of an advertising war in which only the advertisers do well. Neither farmers nor consumers need benefit. On the other hand, U.S. consumers are already well fed and fatted. Advertising food consumption in general hardly seems an idea whose time has come.

Some Notes on the Marketing Order Program for Navel Oranges

Marketing order programs exist for a wide range of fruits, vegetables, and specialty crops, and many of these programs have been the object of empirical research. A study by the USDA (1981) provides a useful survey. It concludes (p. i):

> In recent years, the orders for hops and spearmint oil, California-Arizona navel oranges, valencia oranges, and lemons, and perhaps the walnut and filbert orders, seem to have been used in ways that result in significant resource misallocations. Losses from resource misallocation for the remaining orders appear relatively small.

In what follows we will consider briefly the marketing order for California-Arizona navel oranges as an illustrative example. The production of navel oranges is concentrated in California and Arizona. As compared to oranges produced elsewhere, Florida and Texas, particularly, navel oranges have distinct advantages for out-of-hand eating. Advantages include sweetness, easy peeling, and absence of seeds. (Florida oranges are relatively better suited for juice production.) Navel oranges tend to mature in November and store remarkably well on the tree for 2 to 5 months. Once picked, oranges are moved into consumption within weeks because refrigerated storage is expensive and has adverse effects on fruit quality. Navel oranges can be and are used in the manufacture of orange juice, but the potential for processing is limited by the competition from Florida and elsewhere.

A federal marketing order has been in effect for California-Arizona navel oranges since 1933. The present order, dating back to 1953, authorizes a handler prorate, size standards, and marketing research. Size standards used to place restrictions on the sizes of oranges that may be marketed fresh are rarely used. Under the prorate, the maximum quantity each handler may ship to the domestic fresh market (the continental United States and Canada) is set weekly. In this way the order regulates the flow of navel oranges from the tree to the table over the several months of the marketing year. Harvested oranges not sold in the domestic market are sold abroad or to the domestic processing industry.

As is typical of the administration of orders for fruits, vegetables, and specialty crops, a local committee representing the interests of the industry plays a central role in operating the program. The Navel Orange Administrative Committee consists of five growers, five handlers, and a nonindustry member. (Most handlers are members of farmer marketing cooperatives such as Sunkist and Pure Gold.) This committee determines the weekly prorate levels, levels that are subject to review and approval by the U.S. secretary of agriculture.

Although oranges from Florida and Texas are sold in the domestic fresh market, navel oranges from California-Arizona (C/A) are of dominant importance, accounting for nearly 70 percent of U.S. fresh marketings. The shares of the world fresh market and the domestic juice market accounted for by C/A navel oranges are very small. This suggests the likelihood that the demand for navel oranges for domestic fresh consumption is a good deal more inelastic than are the demands for export or for processing. The latter demands are likely to be elastic. This raises the possibility of elevating average returns to C/A navel orange producers through practicing price discrimination, through restricting shipments to the domestic fresh market, and, in effect, allocating the remaining output to the export and processing markets.

Research tends to confirm what critics of the order for navel oranges often allege, namely, that it leads to price discrimination. Powers, Zepp, and Hoff estimate that the elasticity of demand in the fresh market is about -0.5. Variation in the quantity of navel oranges allocated to processing appears to have no effect whatever on the grower price. In other words, the demand for oranges for processing appears to be perfectly elastic. Powers et al. estimate that in the short run, suspension of the prorate in a normal season would result in a 16 percent increase in shipments to the domestic fresh market with an associated decline in the use of oranges in processing. Total revenue to growers would fall by 10 percent. These findings tend to support the earlier conclusions of Thor and Jesse. Powers et al. also estimate that with suspension of the order in a normal-supply season, economic rents to growers would fall by $12.7 million. Consumer surplus would rise by $30.2 million. The estimated gain in economic efficiency through abolishing the deadweight loss was $17.6 million.

6.2 MILK MARKETING ORDERS

Consider a local fluid milk market in isolation from the rest of the dairy industry except that limited production of manufactured products is sold in a national market. The market might consist of a large city and a surrounding milkshed, an area producing the city's fluid milk needs. The demand for Class I milk, milk used in fluid consumption, is given by D_I in Figure 6.7; that for Class II milk, milk used in manufacturing, is given by D_{II}. Statistical analysis has shown that in the relevant range the demand for milk for fluid use D_I is highly inelastic. There are good reasons for believing that D_{II}, on the other hand, is highly elastic. For one thing, the market for manufactured dairy products, such as butter and cheese, is national in scope. Milk production in a local milkshed is likely to be very small relative to the nation's supply, so that variations in local production would have little impact on national price. The support program for manufacturing milk also means that the Class II demand becomes perfectly elastic at the support price. For present purposes we will take D_{II} as being perfectly elastic. The vast difference between the elasticities of D_I and D_{II} cre-

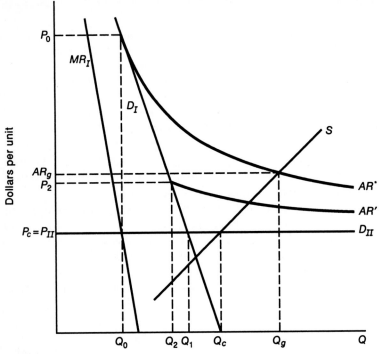

FIGURE 6.7
Effects of a milk marketing order.

ates a grand opportunity for using price discrimination to raise returns to dairy producers, an opportunity recognized by producers for well over half a century.

Equilibrium under competitive conditions is given by the intersection of supply and aggregate demand. Equilibrium price and output are given by P_c and Q_c in Figure 6.7, with Q_1 going to fluid consumption and $(Q_c - Q_1)$ going to manufacturing.

Again, for simplicity, we assume that upon the organization of a milk order, the control authority takes possession of all milk and sells some of it to Class I handlers and the rest to Class II handlers. Receipts are pooled and producers are paid an average price:

$$AR = \frac{P_I Q_I + P_{II} Q_{II}}{Q_s} \qquad (6.27)$$

where the subscript I identifies Class I price (quantity) and subscript II identifies Class II price (quantity). Maximizing AR requires equating marginal revenues from sales in the two classes such that $MR_I = MR_{II} = P_{II}$. (Class II price equals Class II marginal revenue because D_{II} is perfectly elastic.) Linear demand D_I means that marginal revenue MR_I falls twice as rapidly as does price with increases in Q_1. Therefore, $MR_1 = P_{II}$ at Q_0, where $Q_0 = \frac{1}{2}Q_1$ (see Figure 6.7). Hence, for all $Q_s > Q_0$,

$$AR^* = \frac{P_0Q_0 + P_{II}(Q_s - Q_0)}{Q_s} \tag{6.28}$$

where AR^* is the maximized value of AR for all relevant values of Q_s and where $Q_{II} = Q_s - Q_0$. A graph of (6.28) is given by AR^* in Figure 6.7. In the milk marketing literature AR^* is often referred to as the blend price and (6.28) is called the *blend price function*.

The intersection of S and AR^* gives the market equilibrium under the milk marketing order. Equilibrium output and average revenue are given by Q_g and AR_g, respectively. Classified pricing (price discrimination) raises the price of milk sold in the bottle from P_c to P_0. The quantity of milk sold in the box is increased from the competitive level $(Q_c - Q_1)$ to $(Q_g - Q_0)$.

The objectives of milk orders are achieved in practice without the government taking possession of milk. As in the case of FVS crop orders, the desired results can be achieved through issuing the correct regulatory orders. Each month the office of the milk market administrator calculates the quantities of milk going to Class I and Class II on the basis of records obtained from handlers. Knowing Class I and Class II prices and quantities and the quantity of milk supplied allows calculating the blend price to producers using (6.28). Each handler must pay a price no less than the announced blend price to producers for milk delivered the previous month regardless of the handler's use of the milk and regardless of how any individual producer's milk was used. The result is called *marketwide pooling*.

Crucial to marketwide pooling is the operation of the producer settlement fund. Notice that the blend price AR_g in Figure 6.7 exceeds the maximum price handlers could pay for milk used in manufacturing and still break even. (The maximum price is given by D_{II} or P_{II}.) Clearly Class II handlers would not be able to pay the minimum blend price without financial assistance. Here's where the producer settlement fund comes into play. Each Class II handler receives a payment from the fund equal to $(AR_g - P_{II})$ times the quantity of milk used in manufacturing. In total, Class II handlers receive $(AR_g - P_{II})$ $(Q_g - Q_0)$ from the fund. Where does this money come from? Notice that in Figure 6.7, the Class I price P_0 is a good deal higher than the blend price AR_g. Each Class I handler must pay into the fund an amount equal to $(P_0 - AR_g)Q_0$. It is left to the student to demonstrate, as an algebraic exercise, that

$$(P_0 - AR_g)Q_0 = (AR_g - P_{II})(Q_g - Q_0) \tag{6.29}$$

The producer settlement fund is self-financing and allows all handlers to pay no less than the calculated blend price AR_g.

The pricing of milk in milk order programs is a good deal more complicated than the above analysis suggests, however. This is true for two major reasons. The first pertains to the manner in which Class I prices are set in the real world as opposed to the simple model developed above. The second has to do with the role of large milk marketing cooperatives who need not and do not accept minimum prices as the optimal prices for their member-producers.

The enabling legislation for milk orders does not specify that milk market administrators should seek to maximize the blend price. In fact, the maximizing assumption is very unrealistic. It is unrealistic because it would lead to a fluid milk price that is too high to be accepted politically. Consumer groups would likely bring the whole apparatus crashing to the ground. An alternative to the maximizing assumption is to view the Class I price as an exogenous variable, chosen by the market administrator in a rather arbitrary manner. Returning to Figure 6.7, let P_2 be the Class I price where, clearly, P_2 is less than P_0. In this case the blend price function becomes

$$AR' = \frac{P_2 Q_2 + P_{II}(Q_s - Q_2)}{Q_s} \tag{6.30}$$

The graph of this function is given by AR' in Figure 6.7. The new market equilibrium is given by the intersection of S and AR'. The important point is that the analysis developed above can be applied for any Class I price the milk market administrator might care to choose. One can imagine a whole family of AR curves, each associated with a different Class I price.

The above discussion is deficient in that it leaves open the question of how Class I prices are set in practice. To address this question it is necessary to back away from the analysis of a single milk marketing order operating in isolation from all others and to recognize that the United States, at least east of the Rocky Mountains, is blanketed by many milk orders. In 1982, for example, there were 49 federal milk orders that regulated the marketing of 81 percent of all fluid grade milk produced in the United States. In addition 13 state orders, whose operations often resemble those of federal orders, regulated the marketing of an additional 17 percent of the fluid grade milk produced. U.S. fluid milk markets are regulated markets.

In the years following World War II, Class I prices were based on evidence presented at local hearings and were set more-or-less independently among orders. During this period, however, isolated local fluid milk markets were giving way to highly interrelated local and regional markets because of improvements in milk quality, refrigeration, transportation equipment, and road networks. If prices are set independently among interrelated markets, then the resulting spatial pattern of prices might prove difficult to rationalize on the basis of demand and cost factors.

In view of these developments and the need for price alignment among interrelated markets, the USDA in the early 1960s turned toward using the manufacturing milk price, more particularly, the Minnesota-Wisconsin (M-W) price series, as a mover of Class I prices in all federal milk orders. The Class

I price is set equal to the M-W price plus a Class I price differential. Class I price differentials vary among orders but are directly related to the cost of transporting milk from Eau Claire, Wisconsin, to the respective order markets. Differentials tend to be the highest in those markets farthest from Eau Claire (southern Florida) and the lowest for markets nearby (Minneapolis–St. Paul). The M-W series was chosen as a Class I mover because it is the best available indicator of changes in the nationwide supply-and-demand situation; when adjusted by an appropriate differential, it measures the cost of supplies from the midwest; and it provides for a means of coordinating changes among milk markets. In summary, Class I prices form a very definite spatial pattern rising to ever higher levels with the distance from Eau Claire and with the entire spatial pattern shifting up and down with the increases and decreases in the M-W price series. (Complex pricing devices are used to discourage shipments of milk into order markets where milk production is sufficient to serve Class I needs.)

As indicated above, milk marketing cooperatives also play a significant role in fluid milk pricing. In fact classified pricing was pioneered by local marketing cooperatives prior to passage of the enabling legislation for milk orders. According to a study by the USDA, the major cooperative association represented at least 80 percent of the producers in a third of the milk orders in December 1980. These tended to be orders in small markets, however, that accounted for only 17 percent of the milk marketed in all order markets. On the other hand, 13 percent of the orders in which the major cooperative represented less than 30 percent of the producers were in large markets, markets accounting for 41 percent of the total milk marketed under orders.

In many fluid milk markets, marketing cooperatives have negotiated so-called over-order premiums for their producers. These premiums are payments over and above Class I prices. For example, in April of 1986, the simple average premium over 35 cities equaled 83 cents per hundredweight; this amounted to 6 percent of the simple average of prices paid by handlers. The premiums ranged as high as $2.24 per hundredweight in Carbondale, Illinois, and in St. Louis, Missouri. Some writers argue that over-order premiums are evidence of monopolization by dairy cooperatives and call for prosecution of cooperatives under antitrust laws. Others have argued that the payments reflect local demand-supply conditions and are functional in that premiums are payments for services which cooperatives provide for handlers.

A study by the USDA (1984, p. 53) concludes as follows:

> Over-order payments generally do not appear to reflect abuse of market power by cooperatives. In fact, some apparently do not cover the cost of services that cooperatives provide to fluid processors. But it is unlikely that all over-order charges can be justified on the basis of costs of providing services. Averages hide substantial variability among markets: some over-order payments seem clearly out of line with adjacent markets and some reflect price discrimination beyond that associated with order Class I differentials. Wherever the level of over-order payments has exacerbated surplus Grade A milk production or where effective

Class I prices are maintained above costs of alternative supplies, inefficiencies are engendered.

Table 6.1 provides some relevant information for appraising the economic effects of federal milk orders. Average regional Class I differentials tend to increase with the distance of the region from Eau Claire, Wisconsin, the highest differential being in the south Atlantic region. With few exceptions the price for milk allocated to manufacturing was $11.03, the Minnesota-Wisconsin price for 1988. Except for Minnesota and Wisconsin, nearly all the milk produced in the United States is now eligible for fluid consumption. Because of this and because grade A and grade B milk have become virtually perfect substitutes in production, the distinction between manufacturing milk and milk eligible for fluid consumption is no longer of much importance. What this means is that for the most part handlers for milk used in fluid consumption now compete with milk manufacturers in essentially the same markets. The product under consideration, milk, is one of the most homogeneous products one is ever likely to encounter in the real world. Thus, the Class I price differentials shown in Table 6.1 suggest widespread discrimination in the pricing of the nation's milk output.

It is sometimes argued that Class I price differentials are required to assure availability of milk for fluid consumption at all times. The arguments are not cogent for various reasons to be noted shortly. Here we simply point out that in both the north Atlantic and east north central regions less than half the fluid-eligible milk delivered to handlers is allocated to fluid use (see Table 6.1). The claim that Class I price differentials are needed in these areas to assure an adequate supply of milk for fluid use is amusingly absurd.

TABLE 6.1
Class I prices, Class I differentials, blend prices, Class I sales, and Class I utilization rates, by region, 1988

Region	Average Class I price,[a] $/cwt	Average Class I differential,[a] $/cwt	Average blend price,[a] $/cwt	Total Class I sales, million lb	Average Class I utilization,[b] percent
North Atlantic	13.99	2.93	12.61	10,504	46.6
South Atlantic	14.44	3.30	13.94	4,720	83.7
East north central	12.67	1.56	11.97	11,957	37.7
West north central	12.47	1.35	11.59	3,487	21.1
East south central	13.52	2.40	13.00	1,596	75.8
West south central	13.85	2.73	13.14	6,093	57.6
Mountain	13.06	1.94	12.13	2,842	48.2
Pacific	12.76	1.64	11.68	1,943	37.9
All markets	13.33	2.11	12.55	43,144	43.1

[a]Simple averages of market order statistics by region.

[b]Weighted average of market order utilization rates.

Source: U.S. Department of Agriculture, *Federal Milk Order Market Statistics 1988 Annual Summary*, Agricultural Marketing Service, Stat. Bul. 783, July 1989.

The data given in Table 6.1 are useful in explaining why some economists argue that federal milk orders tend to undermine the competitive position of dairy farmers who rely mainly on markets for manufacturing milk, namely those located in Minnesota and Wisconsin. The effect of price discrimination to increase both milk production and the share of output going into manufacturing would, if restricted to one small market, have little impact on areas that rely mainly on the manufacturing milk market. But when this effect is ubiquitous, then the result might well be to lower national prices for milk used in manufacturing. The effect of orders to depress the manufacturing milk price is particularly large in areas that have (1) a large population, (2) a comparative advantage in milk production, and (3) high Class I price differentials. In 1988, federal milk orders transferred through price discrimination about $308 million (11 percent of total receipts) from north Atlantic fluid milk consumers to milk producers as an implicit inducement to increase milk production. Given the reluctance of the federal government to dump large quantities of surplus dairy products on the international market year after year and given the extremely limited domestic outlets for surplus milk (how much butter can schoolchildren eat during the noon hour?), the manufacturing milk price support program may not be able to offset the depressing effect that milk orders have on manufacturing milk prices.

6.3 BENEFITS AND COSTS OF U.S. DAIRY POLICY

U.S. dairy policy is a three-legged stool. One leg is the price support program for milk used in manufacturing. This program has been used, particularly in recent years, to elevate prices received by farmers above market-clearing levels. A second leg consists of strict import quotas, under Section 22, that keep imports of butter, cheese, and other manufactured dairy products from undermining the domestic support program. U.S. dairy product prices are two to three times higher than prices in the small international market. The third leg is classified pricing under milk orders, which is used to raise the blend price to producers in areas close to large metropolitan areas.

The following discussion of dairy policy benefits and costs is based on a study by Hutton and Helmberger, who considered four dairy policy options as alternatives to the continuation of the present program. Their benefit-cost estimates are based on economic conditions prevailing in 1977, which, though dated, may be more representative of dairy policy in the period since World War II than are the more recent years of unprecedented government surpluses.

Dairy import quotas are maintained under all policy options considered. Under option I, classified pricing through federal and state programs is discontinued and competitive pricing is assured through strict enforcement of antitrust laws. The Class I price is determined by equating the values of fat and nonfat solids in fluid milk with the corresponding manufacturing values. The performance of the dairy industry is modeled by aggregate supply and demand, recognizing the impact of net government acquisitions on farm gate demand. Under option II, classified pricing is maintained in that a Class I price differential is assumed, but price support operations are discontinued. Government net acquisitions of fat and nonfat solids are set equal to zero. The Class I price differential is set at $1.66 per hundredweight. Under option III classified pricing and price supports were maintained, but dairy import quotas were increased to their 1973 values. Imports of fat and nonfat solids were increased by 75 million and 254 million pounds, respectively. These increases represent roughly a doubling of 1977 fat imports and a quadrupling of 1977 nonfat imports. Under option IV, both classified pricing and price supports are dropped, but imports are maintained at their 1977 values.

As is our custom in this book, consumer benefits (losses) are measured by the area under long-run demand and between the appropriate two price lines. Benefits accrue to the consumer if dairy prices drop under the policy option considered; the opposite is true if dairy prices increase. Benefits (losses) to dairy input suppliers are measured as the area above the long-run supply curve and between the two price lines. Exogenous exports, stock changes, and farm use take on different values depending on changes in policy. Tax savings (or increases) occur because government expenditures for fluid milk distribution (school lunch, etc.) and fat and nonfat acquisitions depend on price levels. Consumer benefits that occur because of a fall, say, in fat and nonfat prices for imports also entail equal losses to foreign countries. The net efficiency benefits equal the sum of benefits and costs but are only approximations in that some costs (administrative costs, for example) are excluded. The changes in the value of stocks are ignored because these are one-time changes as opposed to benefit and cost flows.

The results of cost-benefit analysis are given in Table 6.2. All four policy options result in net gains to consumers, net losses to farmers, and tax savings. The last column is perhaps the most interesting in that it gives the benefits and costs associated with eliminating dairy programs except for import quotas. In the long run, eliminating dairy programs under 1977 conditions would have caused a transfer of benefits amounting to a little more than $1 billion from dairy producers (dairy input suppliers) to fluid milk consumers; efficiency benefits would have equaled $492.8 million. Consumers of fat and nonfat solids in the form of manufactured dairy products would have been affected very little. The gains accruing to these consumers through dropping price supports about equaled the losses incurred through dropping classified pricing. Increasing fat and nonfat imports to 1973 levels, by 75 million and 254 million pounds, respectively, would have caused a decline of nearly $400 million in producer benefits.

Because dairy programs raise farm-level milk prices, benefits are concentrated among the largest milk producers. As capital requirements continue to increase in the dairy industry, as in other farm industries, the benefits from programs that elevate farm prices above competitive prices will increasingly flow to the relatively well-to-do.

TABLE 6.2
Long-run annual costs and benefits from changes in national dairy policy relative to the actual 1977 policy[a]

	I Drop classified pricing	II Drop price supports	III Increase imports to 1973 level	IV No program except import controls
	Millions of Dollars			
Fluid milk consumers	748.0	397.1	198.4	1,123.9
Fat solids consumers[b]	−131.6	204.4	15.2	64.4
Nonfat solids consumers[b]	−281.7	222.8	178.5	−70.5
Milk producers	−336.0	−813.7	−397.8	−1,152.4
Tax savings[c]	3.6	−485.6	−29.3	−527.1
Total receipts to foreign countries[d]	9.7	−9.7	−13.0	−0.7
Net efficiency benefits[e]	12.0	486.5	10.6	492.8

[a]See text for details as to the various policy options.

[b]Fat and nonfat solids in manufactured dairy products.

[c]Tax savings accrue because either the prices of fluid milk, fat solids, and nonfat solids decrease or because government net acquisitions of fat and nonfat solids fall to zero. It should be born in mind that the government distributes some fluid milk.

[d]Changes in total receipts to foreign countries arise out of exogenous imports of fat and nonfat solids valued at various prices.

[e]Net efficiency benefits equal the sum of annual costs and benefits. Administrative costs of the programs are not considered in this calculation.

Source: Hutton, Patricia, and Peter Helmberger, *Aggregative Analysis of U.S. Dairy Policy*, Research Bulletin R3191, College of Agricultural and Life Sciences, University of Wisconsin, Madison, January 1982.

The above results with regard to classified pricing may be supplemented by findings from other researchers. Several writers have examined the effects of various institutional factors, including classified pricing, on the extent to which the spatial patterns of milk prices and outputs conform to those patterns that would be expected under conditions of competitive equilibrium. One of the earliest studies was by West and Brandow; they found that in 1960 there were large discrepancies between observed and estimated competitive spatial patterns. They wrote that under competitive conditions (p. 727), "Class I prices dropped sharply in the Northeast and less markedly in the Lake States. Prices of manufacturing milk rose in all areas, especially in the Northeast." This general conclusion was supported by the more recent work of Ruane and Hallberg for 1967 and Hallberg, Hahn, Stammer, Elterich, and Fife for 1975. For example, Ruane and Hallberg (p. 34) conclude that under an economically efficient (competitive) milk marketing system, "Production and blend prices would be lower in all regions except the North Central Region and the exporting regions of the West. Producer receipts would have been substantially lower in the Northeast and the South, but considerably higher in the Lake States and the Corn Belt."

The results of these spatial studies of milk marketing add credence to a conclusion reached above: classified pricing tends to lower both the market and the support price for milk used in manufacturing, which is counter to the interests of midwestern producers who rely heavily on the manufacturing outlet.

6.4   ARE FEDERAL MILK ORDERS HARMFUL TO CHILDREN?*

That federal milk orders and their counterpart state programs can be and are used to elevate blend prices and incomes for milk producers located close to large metropolitan areas is beyond serious doubt. What appears to be more in doubt is whether federal milk orders are needed to improve the performance of milk markets, whether the performance of fluid milk markets would be unsatisfactory without government intervention. Regarding this issue there is need for elucidation.

It may be useful to begin assessing the likelihood of market failure in the absence of government-sponsored classified pricing through analyzing fluid milk pricing in the preregulation years and then suggesting how economic changes that have occurred since then necessitate changing the analysis. The share of the fluid milk business accounted for by milk producer-distributors declined in the years following the turn of the century in favor of specialized distributors with heavy investments in fluid milk plants. One effect was increased levels of concentration, and there is evidence of collusive behavior among handlers. The demand for milk for fluid use was nearly perfectly inelastic then much as it is today. The extent to which handlers could secure excess profits depended on how well they could play the oligopoly game and how high they could raise marketing margins without prompting the entry of new firms. In this situation handlers had every incentive to maintain reserves of milk for the fall and winter months of short supply and to pay prices to producers that were adequate to elicit adequate supplies. There is no evidence of shortages of milk for fluid consumption, not that it would have been the end of the world if such shortages caused sharp price hikes to occur from time to time. Each handler was mindful, of course, of the need to pay no more for milk than did competitors.

The market failure receiving the most attention in these early years after the turn of the century was the extreme price rigidity in retail markets and the likelihood that marketing margins were larger than necessary to provide the required marketing services (see Gaumnitz and Reed). Under these circumstances consumers may have been and probably were exploited to some degree, but there is little reason to suppose that milk producers were exploited. With a nearly perfectly inelastic demand for their output and an upward-sloping farm-level supply function for milk, fluid milk handlers had to pay a competitive price, else they would not have received adequate supplies. Analysis of farm milk prices in the 1920s tends to confirm the hypothesis. In both

New York and Wisconsin the mean monthly prices for fluid use milk exceeded the corresponding mean for all milk, with the two series moving together in close harmony as economic conditions changed. The fluid-manufacturing price differentials reflected many factors including site values and production cost differentials. The evidence also shows that variation in milk prices over time was relatively low in comparison with that for other farm products.

Vexed as always with their role as price takers and recognizing the gains made possible by inelastic demand and the knowledge that higher farm prices could easily be passed along to consumers, farmers formed bargaining cooperatives. Flat pricing did not work well in this situation, however, because fluid handlers had different fluid utilization rates. Early research shows that classified pricing was invented by farmer cooperatives as a means for increasing prices received (Gaumnitz and Reed, p. 105). Price stability and the need for fluid milk reserves were matters of secondary importance.

Why should milk market performance in the dimensions of time, space, and form not be workable in today's economy without the intervening hand of government? The usual instances of market failure arise out of public goods, externalities, and imperfect competition. Milk is not a public good and externalities are not at issue. This leaves imperfections caused by market structure, lack of information, and risk.

The market power of milk handlers, at one time a force to be reckoned with, has since been dissipated by structural change. Chains have integrated backward into fluid milk processing, accounting for nearly 20 percent of the business (Manchester). Farmer cooperatives account for another 15 percent. Large bargaining associations have taken over many of the collection and balancing activities previously performed by handlers, negotiating terms of sale for member-producers. Some writers worry about the excessive clout of bargaining cooperatives. The evidence seems to indicate that cooperatives have a statistically significant but economically modest positive effect on returns to milk producers through negotiation of over-order premiums. There are good reasons to believe that the power of cooperatives would be even less in the absence of orders.

A number of objections can be raised against the argument that orders should be maintained because they increase price stability. Price instability and uncertainty are not the same thing. With stable fluid milk demand and a seasonal pattern of production costs, for example, the price of milk might follow a seasonal pattern that is not only predictable but is efficient as well. Moreover, it is by no means clear that optimal price variability in Tallahassee, say, should coincide with the variability of the M-W price series. The question is all the more pertinent when the M-W price is stuck fast at the support level. The decision to let the Class I price structure move with the M-W series was one of administrative convenience.

There are several good reasons why the U.S. dairy sector would perform well in the absence of federal and state milk orders. Instability together with uncertainty are caused by inelastic supply-and-demand functions containing stochastic terms with large variances. The farm-level demand for milk does not contain the destabilizing element of exports to foreign nations that afflicts the stability of markets for many farm commodities today. The supply function for milk is much less affected by the weather than are supply functions for crops.

Several other factors are relevant. First, technological developments in milk production, refrigeration, and transportation have destroyed the isolation of milk markets characteristic of the preregulation era. The possibility of interregional trade increases the elasticity of supply for deficit fluid milk markets and increases the elasticity of demand in surplus areas. Second, milk has become a more homogeneous commodity as grade B milk production has fallen drastically and as the grade A/B cost differential has all but disappeared. What we have then is a homogeneous product with several outlets. In this situation the storage of manufactured products makes up for the difficulty of storing fluid milk as such in that stored products can be disgorged during periods of peak demand for milk for fluid use. (As developed in the previous chapter, the theory of storage indicates that storage demands tend to be much more elastic than consumption demands.) Third, reconstituted and blended milk offers exciting new possibilities for the better coordination of production and consumption of all dairy products. Fourth, the decline in the seasonality of production coupled with changes in feeding practices indicate a marked decline in the seasonality of production costs. This means that the seasonal pattern of milk production can be tailored to fit the seasonal pattern of consumption through modest price differentials. Finally, the forward integration of cooperatives into collection, balancing, and manufacturing combines the opportunity of achieving economies of size and the assurance that concentration in procurement will not be inimical to the interests of farmers. This increases still further the likelihood of better coordination of supplies and demands.

Federal milk orders must be viewed mainly as income redistribution schemes that generate benefits for milk producers located close to large metropolitan areas. The benefits come at the expense of fluid milk consumers and milk producers who rely very heavily on manufacturing as the outlet for their milk. The case for government intervention as a means of increasing milk marketing efficiency was never very strong, not even in the preregulation years. At present there is no case at all. Federal milk orders are not good for children.

6.5 SUMMARY

Federal order programs impose regulations on firms that market farm output as a means for increasing returns to farmers. Orders for certain fruits, vegetables, and specialty (FVS) crops might specify, for example, how a harvested crop is to be allocated among alternative outlets, as between the fresh and processed market, say. Product destruction might also be a permissible regulatory activity. Federal milk orders specify minimum prices handlers may pay for milk according to whether the milk is allocated to fluid consumption or to manufacturing. In practice, order programs do not control directly the amount farmers produce. Obviously, however, farmers' output decisions will depend upon the prices they receive. Whereas milk orders affect prices directly, orders for FVS crops affect prices indirectly through controlling quantities allocated to alternative markets. The economic effects are much the same in either case.

Order programs may be used to elevate returns to farmers through taking advantage of price discrimination and, possibly, product destruction. Under perfect competition the law of one price prevails. If a product is homogeneous, then all buyers pay the very same price. Theoretical analysis shows, however, that the total receipts from the allocation and sale of a given level of output, such as between two groups of buyers, say, or between two markets, will only be maximized if the marginal revenues between the two markets are equated. Equating marginal revenues implies charging different prices to the two groups of buyers. (It is necessary in practice to prevent price arbitrage.) If product destruction is also allowed, then product sales might be limited in order to keep marginal revenues from becoming negative.

Marketing orders can thus be used to elevate returns to farmers for whatever level of output they decide to produce, increasing quasi-rents in the short run and generating benefits to suppliers of inputs with upward-sloping supply functions in the long run. In the absence of product destruction, some consumers will also be made better off, relative to the competitive outcome, because the price they pay falls. If marginal revenues are positive, the consumers with the more inelastic demand (or the consumers with the more elastic demand if marginal revenues are negative) pay a higher price as a result of the marketing order; these consumers finance the benefits to both the farm sector and to other consumers. Product destruction tends to hurt all consumers regardless of relative demand elasticities. Marketing order programs are often called self-help programs because they do not involve significant government outlays.

The most important application of the marketing order approach to farm policy involves the marketing of grade A milk. Federal milk orders together with state milk control programs that often mimic federal orders essentially blanket the nation and account for nearly all grade A milk marketed. Under milk orders, milk used for fluid consumption is called Class I milk. Milk allocated to manufacturing is called Class II or Class III milk. Orders specify the minimum prices fluid milk handlers may pay for milk depending on how the milk is classified. The demand for milk for fluid use is highly inelastic, and minimum Class I prices exceed by a substantial margin the prices paid for milk allocated to manufacturing uses in all federal orders. The widespread price discrimination in the marketing of grade A milk as a result of federal orders hurts consumers of fluid milk. It seems likely that milk orders also undermine the competitive position of midwestern milk producers who must rely heavily on the market for manufactured dairy products. The reason for this is that the production of milk in geographic areas with large population centers is encouraged by federal milk orders. This effect is particularly important in the northeastern part of the country, an area that appears to have a comparative advantage in milk production and which also receives big subsidies through the milk order system.

PROBLEMS

1. Demand is given by $P_d = 40 - 2Q_d$. Short-run supply is given by $P_s = 0.5Q_s$. A marketing order is initiated that allows for product destruction. The objective of the order is to maximize average revenue per unit received by farmers, i.e., the farm price.
   (a) Calculate competitive output and price.
   (b) Calculate the equilibrium levels of production, consumption, surplus to be destroyed, and the farm price under the marketing order.
   (c) Calculate the gain in producer benefits, the loss of consumer benefits, and the efficiency loss.
2. The buyers of a product are grouped into two groups, the h-buyers and the k-buyers. The demands of the h-buyers and the k-buyers are, respectively, $P_h = 20 - 2Q_h$ and $P_k = 10 - 0.5Q_k$. Short-run supply is perfectly inelastic with output equaling 10. A marketing order is initiated that allows for price discrimination but not product destruction.
   (a) Calculate competitive equilibrium output and price. How much is purchased by the h-buyers? By the k-buyers?
   (b) Calculate the average returns to farmers under the order together with the prices and consumption levels for both the h-buyers and the k-buyers. Calculate the elasticities of demand for the equilibrium levels of consumption. Are both groups of buyers hurt by the program? Explain, relating welfare implications to demand elasticities.
   (c) Answer part b on the assumption the supply equals 20 instead of 10.
   (d) Answer part b on the assumption the supply equals 20 *and* assuming product destruction is a permissible regulatory activity. How much output is destroyed?
3. The demand for milk for fluid consumption is given by $P_1 = 10 - \frac{1}{2}Q_1$. The price for milk used in manufacturing is fixed at 3. A milk order is in effect.
   (a) Let output equal 16. Find the Class I price that maximizes total revenue for this level of output. Explain why any increase in milk output would be allocated to the manufacturing use.
   (b) Suppose the supply for milk is given by $P_s = \frac{1}{5}Q_s$. Find the equilibrium level of output on the assumption the market control authority wishes to maximize the average revenue (or blend price) to farmers. Compute payments to and from the producer settlement fund.
4. *The demands for the h-buyers and the k-buyers are, respectively, $P_h = 10 - 2Q_h$ and $P_k = 8 - Q_k$. A marketing order is in effect that allows for price discrimination but no product destruction. Derive the equation for the AR^* curve.

REFERENCES AND SUGGESTED READINGS

Gardner, Bruce L., "Price Discrimination or Price Stabilization: Debating with Models of U.S. Dairy Policy," *American Journal of Agricultural Economics*, 66(December 1984):761–775.

Gaumnitz, E. W., and O. M. Reed, *Some Problems Involved in Establishing Milk Prices,* Agricultural Adjustment Administration, U.S. Department of Agriculture, Marketing Information Series DM-2, September 1937.

Hallberg, M. C., D. E. Hahn, R. W. Stammer, G. J. Elterich, and C. L. Fife, *Impact of Alternative Federal Milk Marketing Order Pricing Policies on the United States Diary Industry,* Pennsylvania Agricultural Experiment Station Bul. No. 818, Pennsylvania State University, May 1978.

Hutton, Patricia, and Peter Helmberger, *Aggregative Analysis of U.S. Dairy Policy,* Research Bul. No. R3191, College of Agricultural and Life Sciences, University of Wisconsin, Madison, January 1982.

Jesse, Edward V., and Aaron C. Johnson, Jr., *Effectiveness of Federal Marketing Orders for Fruits and Vegetables,* Economics and Statistics Service, U.S. Department of Agriculture, Agricultural Economic Report No. 471, June, 1986.

La France, Jeffrey T., and Harry de Gorter, "Regulation in a Dynamic Market: The U.S. Dairy Industry," *American Journal of Agricultural Economics,* 67(1985):821–832.

Long, D. H., and M. C. Hallberg, "Measuring Producers' Advantage from Classified Pricing," *American Journal of Agricultural Economics,* 64(1982):1–7.

Manchester, A. C., *Dairy Price Policy: Setting, Problems, Alternatives,* ECSC, U.S. Department of Agriculture, Agricultural Report No. 402, April 1978.

Powers, Nicholas J., Glenn A. Zepp, and Frederic L. Hoff, *Assessment of A Marketing Order Prorate Suspension: A Study of California-Arizona Navel Oranges,* Economic Research Service, U.S. Department of Agriculture, Agricultural Economic Report No. 557, June 1986.

Ruane, J. J., and M. C. Hallberg, "Spatial Equilibrium Analysis for Fluid and Manufacturing Milk in the United States," Pennsylvania Agricultural Experiment Station Bul. No. 783, Pennsylvania State University, August 1972.

Thor, Peter K., and Edward V. Jesse, *Economic Effects of Terminating Federal Marketing Orders for California/Arizona Oranges,* Economic Research Service, U.S. Department of Agriculture, Technical Bul. No. 1664, November 1981.

U.S. Department of Agriculture, *A Review of Federal Marketing Orders for Fruits, Vegetables, and Specialty Crops: Economic Efficiency and Welfare Implications,* Agricultural Marketing Service, Agricultural Economic Report No. 477, November 1981.

U.S. Department of Agriculture, *Farm Commodity and Related Programs,* Agricultural Stabilization and Conservation Service, Agricultural Handbook No. 345, March 1976.

U.S. Department of Agriculture, *Review of Existing and Alternative Federal Dairy Programs,* Economic Research Service, Staff Report No. AGES 840121, January 1984.

West, D. A., and G. E. Brandow, "Space-Product Equilibrium in the Dairy Industry of the Northeastern and North Central Regions," *Journal of Farm Economics,* 46(1964):719–736.

CHAPTER
7

Price Supports and Production Controls

The idea that governments can elevate farm income through market price support programs is widely held both here and abroad. Often the debate centers not on whether price support is an appropriate means but rather on how high the support level should be. As we saw in Chapter 4, however, price supports can give rise to a whole set of nasty problems associated with commodity surpluses. Storage can become very expensive. Dumping surpluses in world markets causes competing exporters to complain of unfair competition. Lower prices in the developing nations cause their farmers to cut back production. Not surprisingly, it seems that once price supports have become firmly entrenched among farmers and farm leaders as the appropriate means for elevating farm income, the search for a way to avoid surplus production leads inexorably to production controls.

Production controls take many forms, and understanding how they work and with what economic effects requires a variety of models. This chapter centers first on voluntary and mandatory acreage controls. We then examine some historical experience with these policy instruments in the case of corn, wheat, and cotton. A model of a government-sponsored cartel is then developed, and we examine the applicability of this model to tobacco and peanuts. Attention is finally centered on Class I base quota programs for milk.

7.1 PRICE SUPPORTS AND ACREAGE ALLOTMENTS

Figure 7.1 gives the competitive demand DD_c and supply SS_c for one among several farm commodities. The supply curve SS_c shows how much farmers would be willing to produce at alternative prices allowing for changes in acre-

169

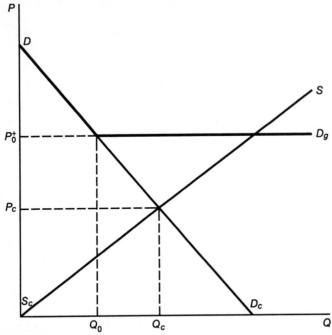

FIGURE 7.1
Desired production under market price support program.

age planted. Presumably acreage increases with increases in price. As we saw in Chapter 4, a price support program puts a kink in the demand at the support level, at P_0^+ in Figure 7.1. With the introduction of a price support program, the demand confronting farmers changes from DD_c to DD_g.

We now assume that the government links its price support operation with an acreage allotment program. A national acreage allotment A^+ is defined as an acreage adequate to produce a crop that together with the current inventory is sufficient for estimated domestic and export needs including normal ending carryover. The national acreage allotment is distributed among farms on a proportionate basis, taking the competitive acreage as the base acreage. If it is estimated that the national allotment equals 90 percent of the aggregate competitive acreage A_c, then each farm's allotment would equal 90 percent of the farm's acreage under competition.

Suppose farmers would produce Q_0 at price P_0^+ if the acreage they were allowed to plant to the program crops were equal to A_0. If the support price is set at P_0^+, then the national acreage allotment A^+ would equal A_0. If all farmers abided by the acreage allotments attached to their farms and if farmers without allotments kindly refrained from entering production, then a price support program would not give rise to surplus production. The "if" is a big one, however. The question becomes, what inducements can the government offer to assure compliance with acreage allotments?

At this juncture it is important to understand some of the details of actual price support operations. The Commodity Credit Corporation (CCC) is an agency of the federal government authorized to enter into market transactions in order to achieve farm program objectives. If a price support program is in effect for a field crop such as wheat, then after harvest the farmer may obtain a loan from the CCC equal to the farmer's output times the support price. The loan, plus interest, may be repaid within 9 to 12 months when the farmer sells the commodity for cash. The farmer need not pay back the loan, however, if he or she decides to turn over possession of the commodity to the CCC at the expiration of the loan. The farmer must hold the commodity in safe storage until either it is sold for cash and the loan is repaid or the commodity is turned over to the government. Obviously, if the price of the commodity during the period of the loan does not rise above the price support level (to be more precise, above the support level plus the accumulated interest per unit of output), then the farmer maximizes profit by turning over the stored commodity to the CCC.

Under voluntary acreage allotments, only those farmers who plant acreage less than or equal to their allotments are eligible for price support loans from the CCC. Farmers who plant more than their allotments receive the market price for their outputs. A voluntary program involving price supports, allotments, and nothing more is of minor historical significance, however, and our analysis of it will be very brief.

Consider the farmer trying to decide whether to participate in a voluntary acreage allotment program. If the market price equals (or exceeds) the support price, complying with an acreage allotment would lower the farmer's profit. At a price equal to P_0^+, profit maximization would entail planting more than the competitive acreage and a good deal more than the acreage allotment. It is possible, of course, that the price support level is so low in relation to an arbitrarily determined acreage allotment that no farmers would participate. In this case the program would be of little interest.

Let us suppose, however, that some participation occurs in a position of market equilibrium. It follows that the market price must be less than the support level, else no farmer would join the program. Therefore, the entire output of farmers participating in the program will be turned over to the government through the nonrecourse loan system. Private demand will be met entirely by farmers who do not participate in the program. Linking price supports with acreage allotments in the manner suggested above, with the national allotment equaling A_0, greatly reduces the benefits to the farm sector in comparison with a price support program free of allotments. Although the introduction of acreage allotments does not eliminate the problem of surplus production, the magnitude of the problem is certainly reduced.

The obvious alternative to voluntary allotments is mandatory allotments. We assume that under a mandatory program, all farmers who abide by their acreage allotments have access to the nonrecourse loan system as a means of price support just as in the case of the voluntary program. Those who exceed their acreage allotments, however, are not only ineligible for nonrecourse loans but are subject to large fines, incarceration, or both. We assume the penalties are sufficiently onerous as to command 100 percent participation.

Figure 7.2 is the same as Figure 7.1 except that we have added two new supply curves, one each for two alternative national acreage allotments. (Forget about price supports for the moment.) Suppose the government sets the national acreage allotment A^+ at the competitive acreage A_c. The resulting supply curve is given by SS_g', coinciding with SS_c for prices equal to or less than P_c but rising more steeply than does SS_c as price rises above P_c. The shape of SS_g' can be justified as follows: For any price received equal to P_c or less, the allotment would not be binding; farmers would not desire to plant acreage in excess of their allotments. For changes in price in this price range, farmers would vary acreage planted exactly as they would under perfect competition. If price rises above P_c, however, farmers would want to plant more than their allotted acreages. In contrast to supply response under competition, output can be expanded only through intensification on fixed acreage. The resulting supply response is less elastic than under competition. Indeed, with constant yields, the upper part of SS_g' would be perfectly inelastic.

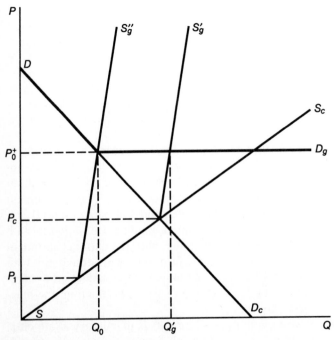

FIGURE 7.2
Effects of mandatory acreage allotments.

Let A_1 be the competitive acreage that would be planted if price equaled P_1. In this case the supply curve with a mandatory allotment set equal to A_1 is given by SS_g''. This curve coincides with SS_c for prices equal to or less than P_1 and rises more sharply with price increases in the range of prices above P_1 than under competition. The reasoning is the same as in the case where the allotment was set at A_c. Obviously, one can imagine a family of kinked supply curves, one each for every possible level of national acreage allotment.

We can now take up the question of market equilibrium under a mandatory acreage allotment program with price supports, allowing for the possibility, important in practice, that the allotment is set in a more-or-less arbitrary manner. Perhaps the simplest case is where the allotment is set equal to A_1. Equilibrium is given by the intersection of DD_g and SS_g''. Market price exactly equals the support price. Production equals consumption, and the surplus ordinarily associated with price support operations vanishes. If the allotment is set at less than A_1, the market price rises above the support level. If the allotment is set larger than A_1, market price will fall to the support level and stay there. Surplus production will again appear. Take, for example, the case where the allotment is set equal to A_c, the equilibrium acreage under perfect competition. Equilibrium is then given by the intersection of SS_g'. and DD_g. Output equals Q_g' and, since private buyers will only buy Q_0 at the equilibrium price P_0^+, the difference $(Q_g' - Q_0)$ is the surplus. Clearly, if the acreage allotment is large enough, it will have no effect at all and the resulting program is identical to a simple price support program.

Mandatory acreage allotments together with price supports can be used to generate benefits to the farm industry. For any given support level, the larger the allotment, the greater the benefits up to the point where the allotment is no longer binding. Short-run benefits tend in the long run to become capitalized into the values of farms to which allotments have been attached. Consumers, and taxpayers, too, if a surplus develops, are made worse off, as are producers of related farm commodities. Acreage allotments chase acres from the program crop to nonprogram crops, reducing the latter's prices. If the allotments may not be bought or sold independently of the farm to which they were originally attached, then another program effect is the freezing of the spatial pattern of production. This could cause inefficient production in light of technological change, better roads, and other factors that might shift the comparative advantage in the production of the program crop from one region of the country to another.

7.2 APPLICATION OF ACREAGE ALLOTMENTS IN THE 1950s

A voluntary acreage allotment program was in effect in the United States for wheat, corn, and rice in 1950 and for corn in 1954 through 1958. During 1956–1958, the program for corn was also linked with a soil bank program to be discussed in the next chapter.

The experience with voluntary acreage allotments under the corn program shows some of the limitations of this approach. Over time, the price support level was lowered from $1.62 per bushel in 1954 to $1.36 in 1958. As a percentage of the support level, the market price of corn ranged from 72 to 85 percent over the same period. The support price exceeded the market price by a significant margin in every year; government stocks increased in every year as well, rising from 25 percent of corn production in 1954 to 34 percent in 1958. (This was in spite of the diversion of land from corn production under the soil bank program.)

Mandatory acreage allotments were in effect for both wheat and upland cotton for the years 1954–1963 and for rice during 1955–1973. In practice the programs were referred to as acreage allotment and marketing quota programs, with the marketing quota referring not to a specific quantity of output but to whatever output was produced on the farm's allotment. When marketing quotas were in effect, excess production, defined as production on acreage in excess of the allotment, was subject to steep penalties. Mandatory allotments were not imposed on farmers without their widespread support. More particularly, allotments were not imposed on all farmers unless at least two-thirds of those voting in a referendum approved their use. In the various referenda organized by the secretary of agriculture, farmers either approved marketing quotas (mandatory acreage controls) or price support levels were slashed.

The legislation governing mandatory acreage allotments for wheat and cotton specified minimum national acreage allotments. Through much of the 1950s, the minimum national acreage allotment for wheat was 55 million acres. Given the levels of price support together with other economic circumstances, this minimum allotment was too large to avoid surplus production. Referring back to Figure 7.2, we note that the supply curve for wheat was well to the right of SS_g'' for most years.

The support price for wheat was lowered from $2.24 per bushel in 1954 to $1.78 in 1960. Over this same period, end-of-year stocks owned by the government rose from 976 million bushels to 1,243 million bushels (92 percent of the 1960 production). The period 1961–1963 was one of transition from a rigid program to programs that better reflected market circumstances. Even so, government stocks remained high and large quantities were dumped in foreign markets.

Wheat exported under a variety of government programs that subsidized exports exceeded commercial (free market) exports in every year; substantial quantities were practically given away. The main vehicles for moving surpluses into the international market had their origins in the Agricultural Development and Trade Assistance Act of 1954, commonly referred to as Public Law 480. Under Public Law 480, substantial quantities of wheat, dried skim milk, soybean oil, and other surplus commodities were sold to foreign governments either for foreign currencies or under generous long-term loans. Lesser amounts were donated to foreign governments and various relief organizations for distribution among the needy.

In the case of cotton, the national acreage allotment was lowered from 21 million acres in 1954 to 16 million in 1963. The price support level ranged from 32.31 cents per pound to 35.08 cents over this same period, with no upward or downward trend. As in the case of wheat, the program was plagued by large government stocks and the need to subsidize exports. Many writers objected strenuously to the cotton acreage control program in the face of increased competition from artificial fibers and foreign producers. It is uncertain, however, by how much production, acreage, and exports actually fell as a result of the program. Prior to 1956, when subsidization of cotton exports was begun, the United States was surely a residual supplier of cotton. U.S. cotton production equaled about 73 percent of foreign production over the 3-year period 1951–1953 when mandatory acreage controls were not in effect. With controls in effect, the corresponding percentages for 1954 and 1955 were 55 percent and 52 percent, respectively.

7.3 STRICT PRODUCTION CONTROLS

Returning to Figure 7.1, we have seen that the quantity demanded at the support price P_0^+ equals Q_0. Rather than trying to control production indirectly through acreage controls, the government might instead attempt to set production at Q_0 through production quotas. Several mechanisms can be used to control production, with virtually the same economic consequences. We will choose a method that lends itself to analysis.

Consider a farm industry in short-run competitive equilibrium. Prior to planting time the government announces a program involving the support price P_0^+. Production rights are issued in the form of certificates. A farmer receives a certificate for every unit of production, a bushel, say, that he or she is entitled to market. (Certificates could, of course, be issued in various denominations as in the case of money.) A farmer with 10,000 certificates may, for example, market no more than 10,000 bushels. Certificates are to be surrendered to the buyer (marketing firm) at the time the output is sold. Stiff penalties are assessed on farmers who market or attempt to market output in excess of their holdings of certificates.

How are certificates distributed among farmers? Each farmer is assigned or given a production base measured in bushels and equal to the output produced in short-run competitive equilibrium. Notice that the production base is assigned to the farm operator, not the farm owner. The base is an asset in that it entitles the farmer to receive his or her share of the total certificates issued each year for all years to come. In total, base production equals competitive production, and certificates are issued in an amount that equals some percentage of base production. A farmer with a base of 15,000 bushels, for example, might receive only 10,000 certificates. The percentages might vary from year to year depending on the level of demand. In this manner the bases and certificates are distributed over time in what might be called an equitable manner.

Short-run models ordinarily assume a fixed number of firms, each with a fixed plant. For purposes of short-run analysis we will also assume that the distribution of certificates is also fixed. This is important to bear in mind because in long-run analysis we will assume that both the bases and the certificates may be bought and sold.

A program of price support and strict production control can be used to elevate quasi-rent in the short run. This can most easily be seen if demand is inelastic in the relevant range. In this case total revenue increases and the aggregate variable production cost declines as production is lowered.

The quasi-rent to farmers may be maximized by setting output equal to that associated with the profit-maximizing solution for a perfect cartel. The demand DD_c and supply SS_c from Figure 7.1 are duplicated in Figure 7.3. The SS_c curve is the horizontal summation of the farmers' marginal cost curves. Associated with the demand curve is a marginal revenue curve MR. Under competition, price is equated to the marginal cost of production. Maximizing quasi-rent, on the other hand, involves equating marginal revenue and marginal cost. The intersection of MR and SS_c gives Q_g as the output that maximizes quasi-rent. We assume the support price P^+ is set equal to the demand price P_0^+ for output Q_g. In this scheme, the price support system is not of much importance. It is the setting of the aggregate level of certificates that determines market performance.

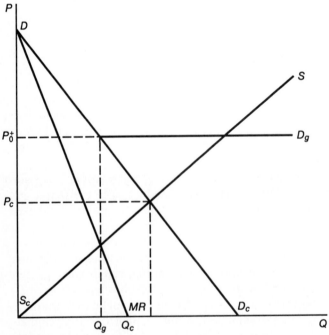

FIGURE 7.3
Short-run effects of a production control program.

Quasi-rent is elevated with no cost to the taxpayers. Outpus falls from Q_c to Q_g. Price rises from P_c to P_0^+. Consumers will not be pleased.

Turning to long-run analysis, we assume that certificates and bases may be bought and sold. Purchase of one year's certificates is equivalent to renting the base for that year. Purchasing the base is equivalent to purchasing an asset that entitles the buyer to a future stream of certificates. We assume the government allows markets to develop for the production rights it has created.

The question we now address is how prices of certificates and bases are determined. Figure 7.4 gives the demand curve DD_c and the long-run competitive supply curve SS_c. The marginal revenue curve is again given by the curve labeled MR. A long-run supply curve shows the minimum average cost of producing various levels of aggregate output allowing for changes in jointly dependent input prices such as land rent. Multiplying output times minimum average cost yields minimum total cost. In this manner minimum total cost can be linked functionally to industry output. The first derivative of this function with respect to output yields the marginal cost curve MC in Figure 7.4. The intersection of MC and MR gives the output Q_g that maximizes the difference between total revenue $P_g^+ Q_g$ and total cost of production $(ATC_g Q_g)$. We will refer to this difference as the *cartel residual*.

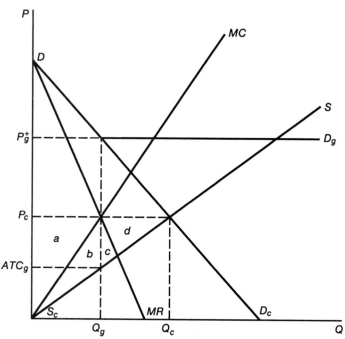

FIGURE 7.4
Long-run effects of a production control program.

If the market for certificates is characterized by perfect competition, then the price of certificates equals $(P_g^+ - ATC_g)$. A fundamental theorem of economics is that with many relatively small firms and no barriers to entry, the price of output and the prices of inputs will adjust such that the marginal firm earns zero profit. (Recall from Chapter 3 that for the marginal farmer the implicit return to family labor exactly equals the family's transfer earnings. Here as there we assume an upward-sloping supply function for family labor.) In the long run, with the exit of the initial recipients of certificates from the industry, entry requires the purchase of certificates, bases, or both. To simplify analysis, with no loss in generality, we assume that all farmers gain the right to produce through the annual purchase of certificates. Assume that bases are owned by retired farmers, country lawyers, school teachers, and such. The new generation of farmers would have no profit advantages over potential entrants. Production and sales require certificates. Certificates therefore become an essential marketing or sales input and as such the price of certificates must be consistent with zero profit for the marginal firm.

In long-run equilibrium the average cost of production equals the minimum cost of production ATC_g, with all farms achieving optimum size. Were this not true, a potential entrant could enter with an optimum-sized operation, pay a higher price for certificates than established farmers are paying, and still enjoy a profit. With production cost minimized, the maximum price of certificates equals $(P_g^+ - ATC_g)$. Were this not true, the potential entrant would be willing and able to pay more for certificates than the going price and still enjoy a profit. It is essentially a bidding process that assures that the cost of production will be minimized and that the price of certificates will be maximized, subject to the constraint that the marginal farm earns zero profit.

The above arguments can be recast in the following manner. The long-run profit function for the farmer under the production control program is given by

$$\pi = P^+ q - C(q) - TE - Uz \tag{7.1}$$

where $C(q)$ is the production cost function, U equals the price of certificates, and z equals the level of certificates purchased. As before (Chapter 3), TE equals the farmer's transfer earnings. Since $q = z$ under the program, (7.1) can be rewritten as follows:

$$\pi = (P^+ - U)q - C(q) - TE \tag{7.2}$$

where $(P^+ - U)$ may quite properly be viewed as the real or net price received by the farmer. Profit maximization requires that the cost of production be minimized and that the real price be equated to the marginal cost of production. Free entry, on the other hand, requires that for the marginal firm $\pi = 0$. (Note that free entry simply means that established farms have no advantages over potential entrants.) Setting $\pi = 0$ and dividing both sides of (7.2) by q yields:

$$(P^+ - U) = ATC_g \qquad (7.3)$$

where ATC_g is average total cost of production including transfer earnings. Condition (7.3) will only be satisfied for the marginal farm in Figure 7.4 if $U_g = P_g^+ - ATC_g$. With the support price set at P_g^+ in Figure 7.4 and output set at Q_g, there will be neither a surplus nor a shortage. As in the short-run case the price support system is largely redundant. Also, strict production control need not necessarily involve maximizing the cartel residual. A lower support price together with a higher quota simply lessens the difference between total revenue and total production cost.

Raising the support price above the competitive level, adjusting production accordingly, generates benefits to the initial generation of farmers at the expense of consumers. The benefits to initial farmers consist of increased quasi-rent in the short run plus the capital gains they receive when they retire and sell their production bases. Returning to Figure 7.4, the cartel residual equals $(P_g^+ - ATC_g)Q_g$ every year. On the assumption that the program is continued in perpetuity, the program generates a capital gain to initial farmers equal to

$$CG = \frac{(P_g^+ - ATC_g)Q_g}{i} \qquad (7.4)$$

where CG equals the capital gain and i equals the interest rate. The interest rate is assumed constant.

Although the government-sponsored cartel can be used to generate increases in quasi-rents in the short run, the program generates losses to the farm sector in the long run. Referring to Figure 7.4, we note that output falls from Q_c to Q_g. The demands for inputs required for production also decline. This means that the prices of all inputs with upward-sloping supply curves decline as well. The aggregate loss of benefits to input suppliers is given by area $(a + b + c + d)$.

The loss of benefits to farm input suppliers, particularly to landowners and suppliers of labor, could be quite significant if the price is raised to the level associated with the solution for a perfect cartel and if the program is applied to the whole of agriculture. If, on the other hand, the program is applied to only one among several farm commodities, then it is likely that all input supply functions would be highly elastic. The loss of benefits in this case might be of negligible importance.

Three miscellaneous comments are in order. First, once a long-run equilibrium is reached, one must expect that the new generation of base holders will resist vigorously any attempt to terminate the program. The holders of the production rights would in that event suffer capital losses just as the initial farmers who received the production rights gratis from the government enjoyed capital gains. The political resistance to change might be quite powerful if the new generation of farmers generally purchase bases rather than certificates upon entry into agriculture.

Second, if the production rights are assigned to the owners of farmland, as opposed to farm operators, then the initial capital gains would accrue to landowners, not farm operators. As in the case of mandatory acreage allotments, this approach would tend to freeze the spatial pattern of production unless the production rights were made negotiable.

Third, making the certificates and bases negotiable facilitates efficiency in production as well as the transferring of production rights from one generation of farmers to another. There are alternative means, however, for facilitating the transfer of production rights. The government might insist that all such rights must be returned to the secretary of agriculture upon retirement of farmers. This would surely encourage the expansion and longevity of father-offspring operations, with dubious consequences for efficiency. If the secretary sells the bases to the highest bidders, then the government itself becomes the long-run recipient of the program's benefits, but this would seem to be a bizarre way for the government to raise revenue. A national lottery also comes to mind. If properly organized such a lottery would create winners and losers in much the same way that state-operated lotteries do. Tickets could be sold with the prize being the opportunity to establish an optimum-sized farm, say, and to sell output at a price above the cost of production.

7.4   PROGRAMS FOR TOBACCO AND PEANUTS

The previous section centered on the theory of strict production control. In this section we consider the farm programs for tobacco and peanuts not only to illustrate the theory of production control but also because these programs are of intrinsic importance.

There are many kinds of tobacco and, with one or two exceptions, production control programs are in effect for all of them. Mandatory acreage allotments were in effect for flue-cured tobacco from 1948 through 1964, for burley tobacco from 1948 through 1970, and for several minor types for 1948 to the present time. (Flue-cured and burley tobacco are easily the most important types of tobacco grown in the United States.) Both flue-cured and burley tobacco have a great many different grades; price support operations involve establishing a wide array of support prices, one for each grade. An effort has been made, with considerable success, to restrict production to the point such that the U.S. average price to farmers across grades is less than the average support level. Commodity surpluses have occurred mainly when the relative support prices for the various grades were inconsistent with private demand and supply.

In 1965, poundage quotas were instituted as the effective method of supply control for flue-cured tobacco. The grower was not only governed by the acreage allotment system but also could produce no more than his or her share of the national poundage quota. The poundage quotas have tended to be the binding constraint. Poundage quotas were instituted for burley tobacco in 1971 and acreage allotments were simply abolished. Thus, what started out as a mandatory acreage control program as analyzed in Section 7.1 above evolved into a strict production control program as analyzed in Section 7.2.

One way of assessing the economic effects of the tobacco production control program is to ask what would happen if the program were abruptly terminated. Sumner and Alston researched this question at some length in a 1984 study. Major findings include the following: (1) the farm price of tobacco would fall by 20 to 30 percent; (2) U.S. tobacco production would increase by between 50 and 100 percent with a consequent increase in the farm inputs required for production; (3) exports of U.S. tobacco would increase by about 100 percent; (4) tobacco production would move to, and become more heavily concentrated in, counties that have a greater comparative advantage in tobacco than they did when acreage allotments were first established.

One of the most fascinating economic hypotheses as to the effects of government cartelization of an industry has to do with the capitalization of program benefits into the value of the production rights. Initially, the right to produce flue-cured or burley tobacco could only be obtained through buying or renting a farm to which the acreage allotment had been attached. The early research on tobacco programs showed quite convincingly that farms to which allotments had been attached were of substantially greater value than were comparable farms without allotments.

Intracounty lease and transfer of flue-cured tobacco allotments were authorized in 1961. What this means is that a grower could lease an allotment from anyone who owned a farm to which the allotment had been attached and grow a crop on another farm located in the same county. The buying and selling of allotments, however, was not authorized. The lease and transfer of burley tobacco allotments within counties was not authorized until 1971.

The leasing of allotments and poundage quotas gave rise to countywide markets, with several interesting consequences. One of these was that city folk became the owners of production rights, leasing allotments and poundage quotas to growers. An article in the *Wall Street Journal* (June 15, 1982) reported the following:

> Thanks to a government price-support program, Carolina Power & Light Co., which grows no tobacco, will earn $92,813 this year from tobacco farming. Duke University, in nearby Durham, N.C., doesn't grow tobacco either, but it will get $7,960. And like other nonfarmers—including the wife of a U.S. senator, a Catholic church, and an airport—Lloyd Massey, who no longer grows tobacco, will get thousands of dollars too.
>
> Mr. Massey and the others get the money by leasing out to farmers the rights to grow and market tobacco. The federal government gave the rights nearly

50 years ago to then-active tobacco farmers. By now, says a recent General Accounting Office report, only about 26% of the individuals and institutions who own such rights, called allotments and quotas, actually grow tobacco themselves.

Forcing farmers to pay city dwellers and corporations for the right to grow a crop of tobacco is perhaps the ultimate obscenity of farm programs. In the case of the tobacco program, the congressmembers from the tobacco states eventually came to see they had a problem on their hands; they were soon designing new legislation not so much to solve the problem as to cover it up.

A law passed in 1982 together with more recent legislation required corporations, utilities, and other nonfarm entities to sell their production rights to tobacco growers by December 1, 1984. Forfeiture was the price of noncompliance. Lease and transfer of flue-cured tobacco quotas were abolished completely in 1987. At present, owners of a flue-cured quota may grow the quota on land to which the quota is assigned or rent to a grower who will do the same. The quota may also be sold but only to an active grower in the county. The lease and transfer of burley tobacco quotas are still allowed, but quotas attached to land no longer in agricultural production must be sold to growers.

The upshot of the legislation passed since 1982 has been to link more closely the ownership of tobacco production rights to growers or to individuals who share with growers the risks involved in tobacco production. The real problems associated with government cartelization of a farm industry are not addressed. First, the problem of appearances remains in that the legislation does not restrict ownership of production rights to growers who continue to make payments for the right to produce. According to an article by Grise (p. 27), much of the tobacco quota is still "owned by nongrowers, with the result that growers must pay one-fourth to one-third of the selling price of tobacco for the right to produce the crop." But this problem of appearances merely calls attention to a more basic issue.

The economic theory of rent and a great body of evidence on the pricing and rental of assets indicate that the present tobacco program does not generate benefits to present growers. Tobacco growers must pay for the right to produce and sell tobacco at a price in excess of the cost of production, whether they rent a tobacco farm from a country doctor or buy the farm outright. In the latter case the annual payments go to a finance institution in the form of annual mortgage payments as opposed to annual rental payments to the doctor. As noted above, the program restricts production and the demands for farm inputs used in production. Since the supply functions for nonland inputs, particularly for labor, are probably very elastic, the present program neither hurts nor benefits the suppliers of farm inputs actually used in tobacco production.

This does not mean, however, that no one would be hurt by ending the program. In the study referred to above, Sumner and Alston estimate that program termination would eliminate $800 million in annual income to quota owners, many of whom are farmers who have paid for the discounted flow of future benefits. The political support for continuation of the program is strong.

The above discussion of the theory of governmental cartelization and its application to the tobacco industry raises one last important question. How should a program that has plainly outlived its usefulness, if, indeed, it ever had any in the first place, be discontinued? If the tobacco program is discontinued, should the owners of tobacco quotas be compensated for their losses? Compensation might take the form of the purchase by the government of all production quotas at some percentage of their market value. Compensation linked with program termination might be a package that would sell politically. Without compensation many tobacco farmers would suffer substantial decreases in incomes; many would doubtless go bankrupt. Still some people might argue that owners knew when they purchased the production rights there was a chance such rights might be made worthless by program termination. They were speculating the program would be continued, so goes the argument, and should be made to face whatever outcomes materialize.

Turning to the program for peanuts, we find that, as in the case of tobacco, the present program started out as a mandatory acreage allotment program. Such allotments were in effect from 1949 through 1977. Over most of this period the national acreage allotment was set equal to the legally specified minimum of 1.61 million acres. This level of acreage together with the levels of price supports, which were substantially above world prices, often gave rise to large surpluses of peanuts. In 1971 more than a third of the crop was acquired by the government. Stocks were kept in check through the diversion of peanuts from food use to crushing and exports. (Crushing yields peanut oil used in cooking and peanut meal used in feeding animals.)

The 1977 Farm Bill changed the peanut program in significant ways and set its evolution off in a new direction. The peanut grower was still subject to a mandatory acreage allotment, but the grower was assigned a poundage quota as well. Peanuts produced on alloted acres but beyond the quota were called additional peanuts and the support price for "additionals," being based on the world market conditions for peanuts and the expected price of peanuts for crushing, was much less than for quota peanuts. Quota peanuts were mainly grown for domestic edible use; additional peanuts were grown mainly for export and crushing. In 1978, the national average support prices for quota and additional peanuts were 21 cents per pound and 12.5 cents, respectively.

The Agricultural Act of 1981 further modified the peanut program, and few program changes have been made since then. Because of the Food Security Act of 1985, the mandatory acreage allotment is no longer in force. Poundage quotas are still in effect, limiting the amount of peanuts allocated to domestic edible use. Any farmer is free to produce the so-called additional peanuts, including farmers subject to quotas who wish to produce more than their quotas. Additional peanuts are subject to marketing controls, however, that prevent them from competing freely in the domestic food market. Moreover, the support price for quota peanuts remains much higher than for additionals, equaling 30.37 cents per pound for quota peanuts in 1988, and 7.49 cents for additionals. Under the 1985 bill, the penalty for marketing peanuts for domestic edible use in excess of the farm poundage quota is 140 percent of the loan level for quota peanuts. As under the 1981 act, additional peanuts may be purchased from growers solely for the purpose of crushing and export. Owners may sell or lease farm poundage quotas within a county.

In effect the federal government has cartelized the production of peanuts for domestic edible use. The production of peanuts for crushing or export has been largely set free of governmental control. Because of this segregation of the peanut production industry into two separate and unequal parts, the cartel model analyzed in the previous section requires modification if it is to be of use in analyzing economic effects.

The long-run economic effects of the current peanut program can be analyzed with the aid of Figure 7.5. The demand for domestic food consumption is given by DD. We assume that the demand in the world market or in the processing market is perfectly elastic at price P_w. (This assumption may be justified because U.S. peanut oil and peanut meal constitute a small component of the total world oilseed complex.) Total farm-level demand in the United States is given by the kinked curve DD_t in Figure 7.5. The intersection of the supply curve S and DD_t gives the competitive equilibrium price P_w and output Q_c, with Q_1 consumed domestically and $(Q_c - Q_1)$ exported or crushed.

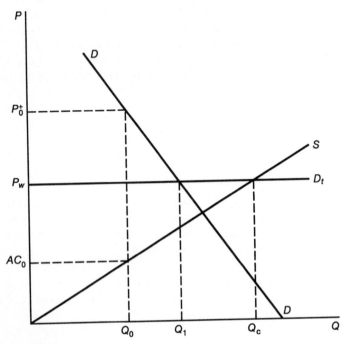

FIGURE 7.5
Effects of controls on production for the domestic market.

With the support price for quota peanuts (those going into domestic edible use) set at P_0^+, the national poundage quota must be set at Q_0 if the quota is to equal exactly the quantity demanded. We next ask how much will be produced for the world market at alternative prices. We know that the farmers will produce Q_0 for domestic food consumption. At this level of production, the long-run average cost of production equals AC_0. If the world price were below AC_0, nothing would be produced for the world market. If price rises above AC_0, however, then farmers will expand production beyond Q_0 and the excess will be made available in the world market. Equilibrium is again given by the intersection of DD_t and S. The equilibrium price for additional peanuts and total output under the peanut program are given by P_w and Q_c. Because of the program, the output of peanuts for the world market increases from $(Q_c - Q_1)$ to $(Q_c - Q_0)$. The cost of production equals P_w in the long run. This means that the per unit cost of the right to sell quota peanuts at the high price P_0^+ equals $(P_0^+ - P_w)$.

The major benefits of the peanut program have probably accrued to the initial recipients of peanut acreage allotments, the original form of the production rights. (Poundage quotas were distributed free of charge to the holders of allotments.) According to the U.S. Department of Agriculture, about half of the national poundage quota is owned by peanut growers, with the remainder owned by nongrowers. As in the case of tobacco, some peanut growers who lease a quota pay city dwellers handsomely for the privilege of growing quota peanuts. Quota rents or lease rates, which vary widely, may be approximated as follows. The average contract price for additional peanuts for export for the 1981–1983 crops is estimated to be about $380 per ton, $140 per ton lower than the average support price for quota peanuts. If we take $380 per ton as roughly equaling P_w in Figure 7.5 and $520 as equaling P_0^+, then the lease rate $(P_0^+ - P_w)$ equaled $140 per ton, or 27 percent of the sales price for quota peanuts.

The cartelization of the production of peanuts for domestic edible use has, of course, raised consumer prices of such products as peanut butter, salted peanuts, peanut candy, and the like. Peanut butter accounts for about half of the domestic edible use. The U.S. Department of Agriculture estimates that the peanut program has elevated the price consumers pay for peanut butter by about 13.5 percent.

Taxpayers are no longer greatly affected by the peanut program as they once were when substantial surpluses were being generated. At present, the production of quota peanuts about equals the domestic edible use, and the loan rate for additional peanuts is well below both the export market price and the current crush value.

7.5 THE CLASS I BASE QUOTA PLAN FOR MILK*

Consider a market for milk both for manufacturing and fluid use subject to a price support program for Class II milk with the support level equaling P_{II}.

The demand for fluid or Class I use is given by D_I in Figure 7.6; that for milk used in manufacturing, Class II milk, is given by D_{II}. The supply curve is given by S. Equilibrium price equals P_{II} with the quantity Q_0 going to fluid consumption and the quantity $(Q_c - Q_0)$ going to manufactured use.

If the desired Class I price P_I under a milk order is given by P_I' in Figure 7.6, then output Q_I' would be required for fluid needs. Under the Class I base quota plan analyzed here, the aggregate market quota is set equal to Q_I'. It is distributed among milk producers on a proportionate basis according to their shares of total milk production under a price support program. Each farmer receives P_I' for quota milk only but is free to market as much milk as desired for manufacturing purposes. (Notice the similarity of this program to the current peanut program as described in Section 7.4.) Equilibrium milk production remains at Q_c with $(Q_c - Q_I')$ going into manufacturing. Relative to a typical milk order, total milk production does not increase.

There is no doubt that such a program can be used to increase quasi-rents to milk producers in the short run. There is a difficulty in the long run, however, that is typical of government-sponsored cartels. Suppose the quotas are assigned to farmers, rather than to farms, and that owners are free to sell or lease them to milk producers. Then the benefits of the program become capitalized into the value of production rights.

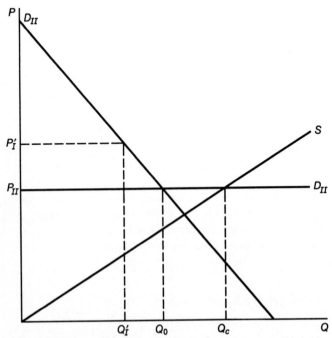

FIGURE 7.6
Effects of Class I base quota plan.

Returning to Figure 7.6, the average cost of actually producing milk is equal to P_{II}, regardless whether the milk goes to fluid or manufacturing use. Therefore, the quota use value or lease rate equals $P_I' - P_{II}$. The aggregate capital gain CG to farmers who receive the Class I base quotas free of charge equals:

$$CG = \frac{(P_I' - P_{II})Q_I'}{i} \tag{7.5}$$

where i equals the interest rate. (We assume that market participants believe the program will go on forever.) Since total output is the same under a simple price support program with or without a base quota plan, there will be neither benefits nor costs to milk producers in the long run. Present and future consumers of fluid milk will, through paying higher prices, finance the gain to the first generation of milk producers. The program obviously increases the capital required to enter the dairy business.

Equilibrium under the conditions set forth in Figure 7.6 implies that the quota use value U exactly equals $(P_I' - P_{II})$. If $(P_I' - U) < P_{II}$, the milk producer would make more money producing for the manufacturing market than for fluid use; through the bidding process, the lease rate would fall. If $(P_I' - U) > P_{II}$, producers could make more money producing Class I base quota milk than milk for manufacturing. The lease rate would be bid up. Would it be possible in long-run equilibrium for $(P_I - U) > P_{II}$? Yes, but only if the market in question, unlike that depicted in Figure 7.6, had no comparative advantage whatsoever in producing milk for manufacturing. The market would have to be a high-cost market. Southern Florida might be an example.

For a limited time, from 1965 through 1976, legislation allowed for the use of the Class I base quota plan as an alternative to marketwide pooling in federal milk orders. The actual experience with the plan was quite limited. Although widely used in Canada and western Europe, the only present application in the United States is in California under that state's milk control program.

The California milk pricing program is a good deal more complicated than the Class I base quota plan analyzed above, but it does entail negotiable quotas that give producers who own them marketing rights to the higher-priced, fluid milk market. So-called overbase milk is priced according to its estimated market value in the production of butter and nonfat dry milk. Farmers are perfectly free to produce as much overbase milk as they choose. Quota milk, used in fluid milk and yogurt, receives a higher price that changes according to changes in milk production costs, the overbase milk price, and average weekly earnings of California manufacturing employees. The amount of milk a farmer may sell for fluid use is strictly limited by the amount of quota the farmer owns.

According to a study by Jesse and Cropp, the average monthly price difference between quota milk and overbase milk in 1981 was $1.36 per hundredweight. Converting from a hundredweight of overbase milk to quota milk, produced on a daily basis, would provide $496.40 in extra revenue to the milk producer for an entire year ($1.36 times 365). How much would it have cost the farmer to buy the extra quota needed to obtain $496.40 in additional revenue? The answer for 1981 was $2,871.00. This represents a 17.3 percent annual return on investment assuming no appreciation or depreciation in quota value. For comparison, the prime interest rate in 1981 averaged 18.9 percent.

7.6 SUMMARY

If price support operations are used to elevate the market price above the market-clearing level, then the government gets stuck with surplus production. To avoid surpluses, governments often turn to production controls. Programs that involve both price supports and mandatory acreage allotments (limitations) were the dominant approach to farm price and income problems in the United States in the 1950s.

Applied to wheat and cotton, mandatory acreage allotments were excessive in light of price support levels. The result was surplus stocks and subsidized exports. A serious problem with mandatory acreage allotments is that they tend to switch acreage from program crops to nonprogram crops. Acres taken out of wheat were largely used to produce feedgrains. The program for corn, which involved price supports and voluntary acreage allotments, generated massive surpluses in the late 1950s.

Mandatory acreage control programs for tobacco and peanuts gave way to strict production control programs in the 1960s and 1970s. Production control programs are essentially government-sponsored cartels, and cartel theory is useful in understanding their likely economic effects. Under competitive conditions, production is pushed to the point where price equals marginal cost. In the case of a government cartel, however, and assuming the objective is the maximization of the difference between total industry receipts and total cost of production, the level of output is chosen so as to equate marginal revenue and marginal production cost. (Production cost is defined to exclude the cost of production rights.) Cartelization tends to raise price and restrict output relative to competitive levels. With atomistic structure—i.e., many relatively small established and potential farm producers—the smaller level of output will be produced in a least-cost manner, and this means that cartelization restricts the demands for farm inputs. Far from generating long-run benefits to farm input suppliers, farm labor, and landowners, cartelization has just the opposite effect. It imposes costs on all farm input suppliers with upward-sloping supply functions.

Who benefits from government cartelization? The answer is those parties who receive the production rights from the government free of charge. The value of the capital gain to the initial recipients of the production rights, on the assumption of a perpetual cartel, equals the discounted future stream of the annual differences between industry receipts and industry production costs.

The empirical research on the government tobacco and peanut cartels strongly supports the validity of cartel theory. It has been estimated in the case of tobacco, for example, that an abrupt termination of the program would cause the prices received by farmers to fall drastically. Output, on the other hand, would increase by between 50 and 100 percent. Annual income in the form of rents to the owners of the production rights, totaling about $800 million, would simply disappear.

PROBLEMS

1. Demand is given by $Q_d = 100 - P_d$. Under competitive conditions, yield Y rises with price received P_s according to the following relationship: $Y = 2 + 0.01P_s$. In addition, acreage planted A rises with P_s according to the following relationship: $A = 4P_s$. Quantity supplied equals yield times acreage. Find the equilibrium values for price, yield, acreage, production, and consumption under the following regimes. Also, where appropriate, calculate the government surplus.
   (a) Perfect competition.
   (b) A market price support program is in effect with physical destruction of any surplus that develops. The support price P^+ equals 15.
   (c) A mandatory acreage allotment program is in effect along with a market price support program. The support price again equals 15. The acreage allotment equals 42.
   (d) Find the acreage allotment that would avoid the surplus and peg the market price at the support level under part c.
2. Demand is given by $P_d = 22 - Q_d$. All producers are identical, and the aggregate short-run supply is given by $P_s = 2 + \frac{1}{2}Q_s$. The government announces a strict production control program, imposing production quotas on producers.
   (a) Find the level of output that maximizes industry quasi-rent and calculate the increase in quasi-rent under the program in comparison with competitive equilibrium.
   (b) Suppose the long-run supply is given by $P_s = \frac{1}{10}Q_s$. Find the level of output that maximizes the difference between industry total revenue TR and industry total cost TC. Let the interest rate equal 10 percent. All market participants believe the production control program will last forever. Calculate the total capital gain to producers who receive the production rights free from the government.
3. The domestic "food" demand and long-run supply for peanuts are given by $P_d = 30 - Q_d$ and $P_s = \frac{1}{2}Q_s$. The demand for peanuts for export and crushing is perfectly elastic at a price equal to 12. Under the peanut program the government sets the quota for peanuts for domestic edible use at 15. The price support is set at 18.
   (a) Calculate the surplus and the cost to the government assuming that surplus quota peanuts are sold in the world market.
   (b) Find the production quota for food-use peanuts that would maximize the difference between industry total revenue and industry total cost.

REFERENCES AND SUGGESTED READINGS

Bimbaum, Jeffrey, and Janet Guyon, "Changes Loom in Programs for Tobacco," *Wall Street Journal*, June 15, 1982, p. 29.

Cochrane, Willard W., *Farm Prices: Myth and Reality*, Minneapolis, University of Minnesota Press, 1958.

Cochrane, Willard W., and Mary E. Ryan, *American Farm Policy, 1948–1973,* Minneapolis, University of Minnesota Press, 1976.

Grise, Verner N., "The Tobacco Program: Recent Changes and Issues in the Eighties," *Tobacco: Outlook and Situation Report,* U.S. Department of Agriculture, Economic Research Service, TS-187, March 1984.

Halcrow, Harold G., *Food Policy for America,* McGraw-Hill, New York, 1977.

Jesse, Edward V., and Robert A. Cropp, *Milk Pricing and Pooling in California,* University of Wisconsin Extension, Madison, A3318, January 1985.

Paarlberg, Don, *American Farm Policy: A Case Study of Centralized Decision-Making,* Wiley, New York, 1964.

Sumner, Daniel A., and Julian M. Alston, *Consequences of Elimination of the Tobacco Program,* North Carolina Agricultural Research Service, North Carolina State University, Bul. 469, March 1984.

U.S. Department of Agriculture, *Peanuts: Background for 1985 Farm Legislation,* Economic Research Service, Agr. Info. Bul. No. 469, September 1984.

U.S. Department of Agriculture, *Tobacco; Background for 1985 Farm Legislation,* Economic Research Service, Agr. Info. Bul. No. 468, September 1984.

CHAPTER
8

Farm Programs That Idle Land

As explained in the previous chapter, mandatory acreage control programs were the dominant approach to farm price and income problems in the United States in the 1950s. As applied to tobacco and peanuts, this approach gave way to government-sponsored cartels. In the case of major crops, acreage controls gave way to programs that involved government payments designed to induce farmers to idle land on a voluntary basis. This is the dominant approach to farm price and income problems today.

This chapter centers on the analysis of voluntary land diversion programs. A concept that is extremely useful in the study of such programs, and, indeed, of voluntary programs in general, is that of an indirect profit function. This concept is defined and developed in the next section. Sections 8.2, 8.3, and 8.4 then set forth three alternative land diversion programs and analyze their economic effects using the concept of an indirect profit function. Section 8.2 considers a program in which the government makes payments per acre diverted. Section 8.3 analyzes a program that combines voluntary land diversion and price support protection for participating farmers. Land diversion payments are based on acres planted. Section 8.4 analyzes a program that combines voluntary land diversion coupled with direct payments. The remainder of the chapter then takes up farm programs for feedgrains, wheat, cotton, and rice, all of which rely heavily on land diversion.

8.1 THE INDIRECT PROFIT FUNCTION

Consider the firm's ordinary or direct profit function as often encountered in economic analysis:

$$\pi = Pq - C(q) \tag{8.1}$$

where $C(q)$ is the total cost function and other variables are as defined earlier. (Transfer earnings can be safely ignored for present purposes.) Assuming perfect competition, Equation (8.1) has two unknowns, q and π. Another equation is required in order to obtain a solution. A second equation can be obtained by assuming profit maximization, which implies equating price to marginal cost. (This is true only if marginal cost is not less than minimum average cost.) With this assumption, profit maximization implies

$$P = \frac{dC}{dq} \qquad \frac{dC}{dq} > 0 \tag{8.2}$$

Importantly, marginal cost is given by dC/dq, which, in general, is a function of output q. Rewriting (8.2) with q dependent yields

$$q = S(P) \qquad \frac{dS}{dP} > 0 \tag{8.3}$$

where $S(P)$ is the supply function for q. Equations (8.1) and (8.2) constitute a structural model. Equation (8.3) is the reduced form or solution for q. We can now substitute $S(P)$ for q in (8.1), yielding the reduced form or solution for π:

$$\pi = P(S(P)) - C(S(P))$$
$$= \pi^*(P) \tag{8.4}$$

This reduced form is called the *indirect profit function*. The function π^* shows the maximum profit that can be obtained for various levels of price. It is instructive to take the first derivative of (8.4) with respect to price:

$$\frac{d\pi^*}{dP} = S(P) + \frac{dS}{dP}P - \frac{dC}{dq}\frac{dS}{dP}$$
$$= S(P) + \frac{dS}{dP}\left(P - \frac{dC}{dq}\right) \tag{8.5}$$

But, since $P = dC/dq$, we have

$$\frac{d\pi^*}{dP} = S(P) \tag{8.6}$$

Thus, the first derivative of π^* with respect to price yields the optimum level of output as a function of price. This is, or course, the firm's supply function. Moreover, the second derivative of π^* with respect to price is larger than zero because the firm's supply curve is upward-sloping. This tells us what we need to know in order to give a graphic representation of the indirect profit function.

The curve labeled π^* in Figure 8.1 is such a representation. Figure 8.1 is drawn on the assumption that price P_0 equals minimum average cost of production. For prices less than P_0, the firm produces nothing. As price rises above P_0, production occurs and profit rises at an increasing rate with increases in price. There is an intuitive explanation for this result. At price P_1, let $q = q_1$. Profit equals π_1. If price increased but the firm held output constant, profit would rise linearly because $\pi = Pq_1 - C(q_1)$ and $d\pi/dP = q_1$. Through altering its output in response to a price increase, however, and through making sure that price always equals marginal cost, profit can be made to increase by more than q_1. If P moves from P_1 to P_2, profit rises to π_2' if output is held constant at q_1 (Figure 8.1). If q is allowed to vary, however, profit rises to π_2 as q rises from q_1 to some higher level, say q_2.

A specific example may further elucidate the indirect profit function. Suppose,

$$\pi = Pq - q^2 \tag{8.7}$$

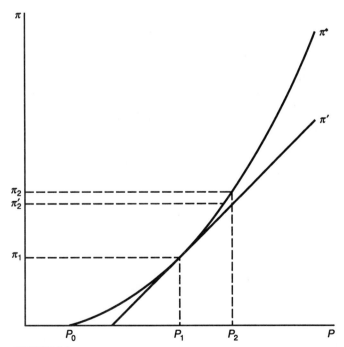

FIGURE 8.1
An indirect profit curve.

Then, $q = P/2$ is the firm's supply function. Through substitution of $(P/2)$ for q in (8.7) we have

$$\pi = \frac{P^2}{2} - \frac{P^2}{4}$$

$$= \frac{P^2}{4} \tag{8.8}$$

which is the indirect profit function. Then, $d\pi/dP = P/2$, and the equation for supply is thus recovered. Clearly, $(d^2\pi/dP^2) > 0$. Profit rises with P at an increasing rate.

8.2 PAID LAND DIVERSION

Consider a farm program in which the government offers to pay farmers for diverting some of their land from production. The payment per acre of land diverted is given by B. Participation involves diverting a fixed proportion $(1 - \beta)$ of the farmer's land where $0 < \beta < 1$. Let the farmer's acreage equal $\bar{a}$. The participating farmer's land diversion is given by $\bar{a}_s = (1 - \beta)\bar{a}$. Acreage planted is given by $a_p = \beta\bar{a}$. The land diversion payment equals Ba_s. The objective in what follows is to assess both the short-run and the long-run effects of such a program.

Before turning to analysis we pause to consider why the government might insist that participation involve idling a fixed proportion of a farmer's land but not the whole farm. Whole-farm removal has not been a popular idea in the United States because of its implications for rural communities. If a large proportion of farms in a county were idled, with farm families going to Florida for the season, then local farm communities could be seriously affected. Businesses might close. Schools would operate at a fraction of capacity. Sunday collection plates would be returned half-empty. Presumably, partial farm removal across wide geographic areas keeps farmers on their land and is less damaging to rural communities than would be whole-farm removal.

Short-Run Analysis

For purposes of short-run analysis, we assume a fixed number of farms, each with fixed amounts of family labor and land. Every farmer must decide whether to participate in the program. If a farmer chooses not to participate, then the quasi-rent function is

$$h_n = Pq_n - C_n(q_n) \tag{8.9}$$

where the subscript n is attached to certain variables in order to indicate nonparticipation and where h equals quasi-rent. The subscript n is not attached to price P because all farmers receive the same market price whether or not they participate in the program. The function $C_n(q_n)$ is the nonparticipating farmer's total variable cost function.

If the farmer chooses not to participate, then the indirect quasi-rent function is given by

$$h_n = h_n^*(P) \tag{8.10}$$

A graphic representation of (8.2) is given by the curve h_n^* in Figure 8.2. It shows the maximum quasi-rent for alternative levels of price P. If $P < P_0$, the farmer produces nothing and quasi-rent equals zero. Presumably P_0 equals the minimum of the nonparticipant's average variable cost curve. For any price P, the slope of h_n^* or the first derivative of h_n with respect to P yields the optimal level of output.

If the farmer decides to join the program, then the quasi-rent function is

$$h_j = Pq_j - C_j(q_j, \beta) + B(1 - \beta)\bar{a}_j \tag{8.11}$$

The subscript j is attached to certain variables in order to indicate farmer participation in the program. Importantly, the participator's total variable cost $C_j(q_j, \beta)$ is higher than the nonparticipator's variable cost $C_n(q_n)$ for all levels of output because program participation involves idling land. The parameter β

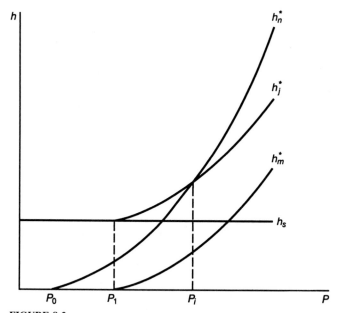

FIGURE 8.2
To participate or not to participate: that is the question.

is a shifter of the cost function; the higher β is, the lower the total variable cost curve. As β approaches 1, the cost function assuming participation tends toward that assuming nonparticipation. Importantly, h_j can be broken up into two component parts, h_m and h_s, where

$$h_m = Pq_j - C_j(q_j, \beta) \qquad (8.12)$$

and

$$h_s = B(1 - \beta)\bar{a}_j$$

Since h_s is a constant, given fixed land $\bar{a}$, maximizing (8.11) merely involves maximizing h_m. This implies that the participating farmer chooses the level of q_j such that marginal cost and price are equal, subject as always to the constraint that price is not below minimum average variable cost. The indirect quasi-rent function for the participating farmer may be expressed, therefore, as follows:

$$h_j = h_m^*(P, \beta) + B(1 - \beta)\bar{a}$$
$$= h_j^*(P, B, \beta) \qquad (8.13)$$

where the function $h_m^*(P, \beta)$ shows the maximum quasi-rent that can be earned from producing a crop for various levels of price P and various levels of β. A graphic representation of $h_m^*(P, \beta)$ is given by h_m^* in Figure 8.2, assuming that β is held constant. It is important to understand that h_m^* lies below h_n^* because a participating farmer must idle land. Also note that for any price above P_1, where P_1 equals the participating farmer's minimum average variable cost of output, the slope of h_n^* exceeds the slope of h_m^*. This means that for any price above P_1, a greater level of output will be produced by the farmer under nonparticipation than under participation. This is, of course, exactly what one would expect. In what follows it will be useful, on occasion, to think of h_m^* as the graph of the indirect quasi-rent function assuming that the government has made land diversion mandatory, with B set equal to zero.

It is now easy to give a graphic representation of the participating farmer's indirect quasi-rent function. The graph of $B(1 - \beta)\bar{a}$, given by h_s in Figure 8.2, is a perfectly flat line since h_s does not vary with price. In order to obtain a graphic representation of the function h_j^*, we add vertically h_m^* and h_s (see Figure 8.2). An increase in B would shift h_s and, therefore, h_j^* upward. An increase in β would lower h_s but raise h_m^*, and the net effect on h_j^* is difficult to ascertain.

The question whether the farmer will participate in the program turns on which option yields the greater quasi-rent. Whether the maximized value of h_n^* exceeds, is less than, or equals the maximized value of h_j^* obviously depends on the level of price. If $P < P_i$ in Figure 8.2, then $h_j^* > h_n^*$ and the farmer joins the program. If $P > P_i$, then $h_j^* < h_n^*$ and the farmer will choose not to join. *If $P = P_i$, the farmer will be indifferent between the two options.* In what follows the critical price P_i will be referred to as an *indifference price*. More formally, P_i is an indifference price if

$$h_n^*(P_i) = h_j^*(P_i, B, \beta) \tag{8.14}$$

Obviously, farmers will be very mindful of price when trying to decide whether to participate in a land diversion program. When price is low, the opportunity cost of allowing some land to stand idle is also low, and if B and β are set appropriately by the government, then participation can be induced. When price is very high, on the other hand, the opportunity cost of diverting land will also be very high. Apparently, raising B but holding β constant would shift h_j^* upward, elevating the indifference price. The effect of raising $(1 - \beta)$ on h_j^*, holding B constant, is uncertain. Raising $(1 - \beta)$ or, equivalently, lowering β, causes the diversion payment from the government to increase. Lowering β elevates the total variable cost curve and lowers the quasi-rent that can be earned growing a crop. It is difficult to determine if one effect will always dominate the other.

We are now in a position to derive a supply curve for the farmer showing how much will be produced at alternative market prices given the opportunity of participating in an acreage diversion program. The indirect quasi-rent curves of Figure 8.2 are plotted again in part *a* of Figure 8.3, only this time

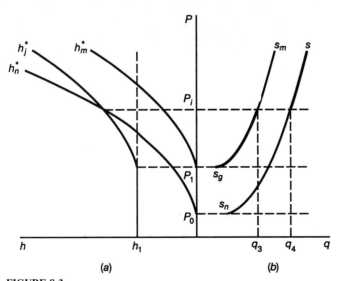

FIGURE 8.3
Deriving a farmer's supply curve under a voluntary land diversion program.

with price P on the vertical axis. In part b, ss_n is the supply curve assuming nonparticipation. For any price $P > P_0$, the quantity produced q_n is given by the slope of h_n^*. If we assume momentarily that the land diversion program is mandatory, such that the farmer must idle land even though B equals zero, then the farmer's supply curve would be given by $s_m s_g$. The output for any price larger than P_1 would then be given by the slope of h_m^*. Getting back to the voluntary program, however, we note that at low prices, below P_i, the farmer participates in the program and moves along $s_m s_g$ as price changes. At high prices, above P_i, the farmer does not participate in the program and moves along ss_n. For price equal to P_i, the farmer is indifferent between participation and nonparticipation, and two output levels q_3 and q_4 are both consistent with the maximization of quasi-rent. The darkened, discontinuous curve ss_g is the farmer's supply curve. This curve coincides with $s_m s_g$ for prices less than P_i and with ss_n for prices above P_i.

The aggregate or market supply curve can be derived recognizing that not all farmers need have the same indifference price. We might expect that efficient farmers, with high net cash returns to acres planted, would have lower indifference prices than would inefficient farmers. We envisage a succession of indifference prices starting from the lowest indifference price P_{is} and ranging up to the highest indifference price P_{ib} (Figure 8.4). Summing laterally the supply curves of all the individual farmers yields the scalloped supply curve SS_g in Figure 8.4. It coincides with the competitive supply curve SS_c for prices above P_{ib}. Changes in participation rates are crucial to understanding why SS_g is more elastic than is SS_c over the price range from P_{is} to P_{ib}. As price increases in this range, nonparticipating farmers expand output exactly as they would under perfectly competitive conditions, through intensifying on fixed acreage. Participants also intensify production, but those who exit the program bring diverted land into production as well.

Market equilibrium is given by the intersection of demand D and supply SS_g. (See Figure 8.4.) In comparison with competition, the government program raises price from P_c to P_g; output is lowered from Q_c to Q_g. It may be noted that if demand intersects SS_g below P_{is}, all farmers would participate in the program. If demand intersects SS_g at a price above P_{ib}, no farmers would participate. As things stand in Figure 8.4, some but not all farmers join the program.

The demand curve in Figure 8.4 may be construed as the lateral summation of a demand for domestic consumption and a demand for exports. On this interpretation of demand, it is clear that the land diversion program, through shifting the supply to the left, lowers farm exports and raises the world price. Whether it makes sense for a country to restrict exports in this manner in a world with many competing food exporters is a good question.

Holding β constant, an increase in B leaves $S_m S_g$ as is but increases all indifference prices. Increasing B, therefore, increases output restriction for demand situations that give rise to partial participation. Holding B constant and increasing β moves $S_m S_g$ closer to SS_c with uncertain effects on indifference

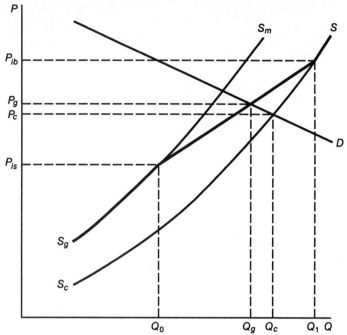

FIGURE 8.4
Short-run market equilibrium under a voluntary land diversion program.

prices. Clearly, however, as β approaches the value of one, all program effects tend to vanish.

It is clear that in the short run all farmers will benefit from a land diversion program. Any farmer has the option of leaving the program and producing output at a price in excess of the competitive level P_c. Other societal groups are not as lucky, however. Consumers pay higher prices for food; taxpayers pick up the tab for paying farmers to idle land.

Assuming that all farmers have identical operations with identical indifference prices is a useful special case to consider in light of subsequent analysis. The resulting supply curve is given by the step function SS_g in Figure 8.5. The equilibrium market price P_g equals P_i for all producers. Equilibrium output is given by Q_g. The uniqueness of the equilibrium level of output Q_g can be ascertained through showing that no other level of output is consistent with equilibrium. Any tendency for output to fall below Q_g would send price above P_i and farmers would expand output; contrariwise, any tendency for output to rise above Q_g would cause price to fall below P_i. The identity of those farmers who participate and those who do not cannot be ascertained, but this element of indeterminacy is unimportant since all farmers are identical.

Short-run increases in quasi-rent or benefits can be easily ascertained graphically on the assumption of identical farm operations and with partial pro-

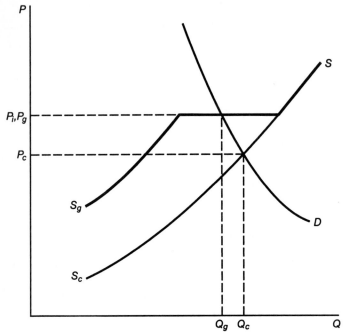

FIGURE 8.5
Short-run market equilibrium assuming identical farmers.

gram participation. The increase in quasi-rent to the nonparticipator equals the area above his or her supply curve and between the price lines corresponding to P_g and P_c. But this increase must be exactly the same for all producers. Therefore, the increase in aggregate quasi-rent equals the area above SS_c in Figure 8.5 and between the price lines for P_g and P_c. Included in aggregate quasi-rent are the land diversion payments.

Long-Run Analysis

For purposes of long-run analysis we retain the assumption that the farming operations of all producers are identical even though the levels of transfer earnings vary among households. In order to assess the long-run effects of land diversion we start with a short-run equilibrium in Figure 8.6 that is also a long-run equilibrium. Initial demand and short-run supply are given by D' and SRS_g' with equilibrium price P_1 and output Q_1. For the marginal producer the return to family labor just equals transfer earnings, assuring a long-run equilibrium.

Now let D increase from D' to D''. The immediate effect is an increase in profits for all producers, who might abandon the program in the short-run, as they do in Figure 8.6. (Zero participation in the subsequent short-run equilib-

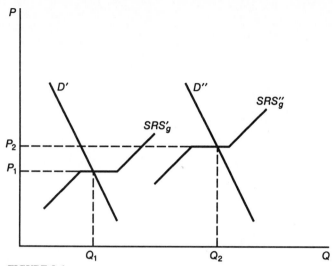

FIGURE 8.6
Deriving the long-run supply curve assuming identical farmers.

rium need not be assumed.) Profits attract entry, however, and as entry occurs, the SRS'_g curve begins to drift toward the right. Market price begins to
slip and, with an increasing cost industry, prices of at least some inputs rise as
well. More particularly, both land rents and the returns to family labor increase in the long run. The indifference price rises with increases in input
prices. Renting land to the government is the more attractive, for any given
price of output, the higher the cost of growing a crop. Entry continues until
excess profit of the new marginal producer vanishes. We assume that this occurs when the short-run supply curve has shifted to SRS''_g (Figure 8.6). The
new equilibrium price and quantity are P_2 and Q_2. Some program participation
occurs, but on a smaller scale than when demand was at D'.

Two points on the long-run supply curve have been derived through the
above experiment, the first given by the intersection of D' and SRS'_g and the
second by the intersection of D'' and SRS''_g. Through experimenting with shifting demands and the consequential shifts of the short-run supply curves, we
can identify many points that lie on the long-run supply curve. The locus of
such points yields the scalloped long-run supply curve SS_g in Figure 8.7. If demand intersects SS_g to the left of Q_0, all farmers participate in the program in
the long run. If demand intersects SS_g between Q_0 and Q_1, as shown in Figure
8.7, participation occurs but is incomplete. If demand intersects SS_g to the
right of Q_1, there will be no participation at all. The long-run supply curve
rises between Q_0 and Q_1 even with identical farm operations, in contrast to the
short-run case (see Figure 8.5), because higher levels of demand and larger
levels of aggregate output cause prices of at least some variable inputs to rise.
The results of this analysis are intuitively appealing. A land diversion program

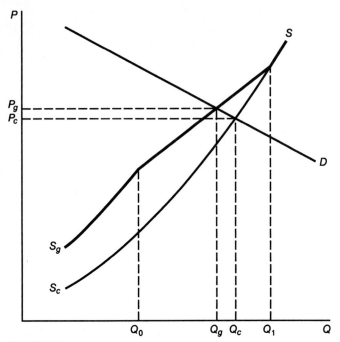

FIGURE 8.7
Long-run market equilibrium under a voluntary land diversion
program.

with given program parameters is less attractive to the farm industry the higher
the level of demand.

This brings us to the question of the long-run implications of land diversion for the distribution of benefits and costs. The profit functions for the
nonparticipating and participating farmer are given by (8.15) and (8.16), respectively,

$$\pi_n = Pq_n - Ra_n - Gk_n - TE \tag{8.15}$$

$$\pi_j = Pq_j - Ra_j - Gk_j + B(1 - \beta)a_j - TE \tag{8.16}$$

(Recall that a equals acreage and k equals producer goods.) Since acreage
planted by the participator a_p can be written βa_j, Equation (8.16) can be rewritten as follows:

$$\pi_j = Pq_j - Gk_j - \left[\frac{R - B(1 - \beta)}{\beta} \right] a_p - TE \tag{8.17}$$

The coefficient for a_p may be correctly interpreted as the real rent the participating farmer must pay for land that is actually planted.

Profit maximization implies equating the price of each input to its value of marginal product. All farmers are assumed to have identical Cobb-Douglas production functions, an assumption that greatly simplifies aggregation as shown in Chapter 3. Aggregating over all nonparticipants in long-run equilibrium, we have

$$R_g A_n = \alpha_1(P_g Q_n) \tag{8.18}$$

where R_g equals rent to land under government intervention, A_n equals aggregate nonparticipating acreage, and Q_n is the associated output. As in Chapter 3, α_1 is the production elasticity for land.

For all participators taken together we have

$$\frac{R_g - B(1 - \beta)}{\beta} A_p = \alpha_1(P_g Q_j) \tag{8.19}$$

where A_p equals participating acreage and Q_j is the associated level of output. Since $A_p = \beta A_j$, where A_j equals land rented by participants, (8.19) can be rewritten in terms of A_j. When this is done and the resulting expression is added to (8.18) we have

$$R_g A = \alpha_1(P_g Q_g) + B(1 - \beta) A_j \tag{8.20}$$

where $A_n + A_j = A$ and $Q_n + Q_j = Q_g$.

Subtracting total land rent under competition from total land rent under the land diversion program yields

$$(R_g - R_c)A = \alpha_1(P_g Q_g - P_c Q_c) + B(1 - \beta) A_j \tag{8.21}$$

where R_c equals land rent under competition. The land diversion program, if effective, causes output to fall and price to rise (see Figure 8.7). As always, the redistributive effect of the program depends in a crucial way on the elasticity of demand. Suppose that demand has unitary elasticity so that $P_g Q_g = P_c Q_c$. Then the increase in land rent equals $B(1 - \beta) A_j$. But $B(1 - \beta) A_j$ equals the government expenditure required to induce $(1 - \beta) A_j$ to stand idle. Thus, the land diversion program effects a redistribution of benefits from taxpayers to landowners equaling $B(1 - \beta) A_j$. Given the assumption of unitary elasticity of demand, the market shares of all nonland inputs are unaffected by the program. To some considerable extent, land diversion is a price support program for land.

Consumers lose from the higher price and, with unitary demand elasticity, the deadweight loss equals the loss of consumer benefits. A land diversion program is a woefully inefficient way of redistributing income relative, say, to direct payments. The reason for this is that diverted land is wasted land. Ironically, the U.S. voting public is outraged by the physical destruction of food but appears to find quite acceptable programs that waste land on a large scale. Here, as so often in the public policy arena, appearances are nearly everything.

If demand is elastic, all nonland input suppliers with upward-sloping supply functions will be made worse off. Landowners will be benefited nonetheless. Output price is elevated on the assumption that at least some farmers participate in the program. The nonparticipator could always bid land away from a participator if the latter could not afford to pay rent in excess of the competitive level in long-run equilibrium. (The welfare implications of land diversion when demand is inelastic are left to the reader.)

8.3 LAND DIVERSION WITH DEFICIENCY PAYMENTS AND PRICE SUPORTS

The land diversion program considered above involved payments for diverted acres. An alternative approach that is important in light of recent major crop programs entails payments that reflect acres planted, market price, and price support protection. Consider a program in which the land diversion provisions are the same as in the previous case. Planted acreage on a participating farm equals $\beta\bar{a}$ and diverted acreage equals $(1 - \beta)\bar{a}$. In contrast to the previous case, however, we now consider a program in which the inducement to participate is based on acres planted and on total production. Specifically, the participating farmer secures the benefits of a price support program that puts a floor on price received for his or her total output together with a payment per acre planted. The latter equals $[P^* - \max(P^+,P)]\bar{y}$ where P^*, P^+, and P equal, respectively, the target price, the support price (often called the nonrecourse loan rate), and the market price; and where $\bar{y}$ is the farmer's established yield based on historical records. Notice that the payment is found by subtracting from the target price the higher of the support price and the market price. Because government payments are based on established as opposed to actual yields, they are referred to here as deficiency payments, in contrast to the direct payments analyzed in Chapter 4.

If the farmer chooses not to join the program, the indirect quasi-rent function is the same as in the previous case, which is to say that it is the same as under competition. A graphic representation is given by h_n^* in Figure 8.8.

If the farmer chooses to join the program, then quasi-rent is given by

$$h_j = [\max(P^+, P)]q_j - C_j(q_j, \beta) + [P^* - \max(P^+, P)]\,\bar{y}\beta\bar{a} \quad (3.22)$$

It is convenient to analyze this rather complicated program by considering first the special case where the support price is relatively low so that it can safely be ignored. We therefore assume P^+ equals zero as a special case. The resulting analysis may then be adjusted at a later point to take account of an effective price support operation.

If the farmer chooses to join the program, then quasi-rent is given by

$$h_j = Pq_j - C_j(q_j, \beta) + (P^* - P)\bar{y}\beta\bar{a} \qquad (8.23)$$

The government payment varies with price but is fixed with regard to choice of output. The indirect quasi-rent function may be expressed as follows:

$$h_j = h_m^*(P, \beta) + h_w \qquad (8.24)$$

where h_w equals $(P^* - P)\bar{y}\beta\bar{a}$ and where $h_m^*(P, \beta)$ is the same as before. A graphic representation of $h_m^*(P, \beta)$ is given by h_m^* in Figure 8.8, with β held constant. This curve is exactly the same as in Figure 8.2; it requires no further explanation. The government payment h_w is a linear downward-sloping function of market price P as given by the curve h_w in Figure 8.8, where P^* equals P_0^*. The intercept h_0 equals $P_0^*\bar{y}\beta\bar{a}$. The slope in absolute value equals $\bar{y}\beta\bar{a}$. When $P = P_0^*$, h_w equals zero. A graphic representation of the participator's quasi-rent function is given by the darkened, kinked curve h_j^* in Figure 8.8. It is obtained by summing vertically the curves h_m^* and h_w.

The indifference price is again given by P_i. If price is less than P_i, the farmer participates in the program. Optimal output is given by the slope of h_m^* just as in the previous case of paid land diversion. If the price exceeds P_i, the farmer does not participate in the program and optimal output is given

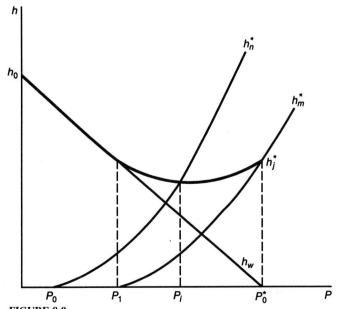

FIGURE 8.8
Modeling the participation decision under deficiency payments.

by the slope of h_n^*. The farmer's supply curve with the option of program participation may again be represented by ss_g in part b of Figure 8.3. This being the case and recalling that we are for the moment abstracting from price supports, the analysis of program effects is very similar to that for the previous case of paid land diversion except in one important respect.

Holding β constant, raising P^* elevates the graph of h_w in Figure 8.8. The indifference price rises and the extent of output restriction, relative to competitive equilibrium, rises as well. Raising P^* in this case is similar to raising B in the case of paid land diversion. But now suppose β is increased, holding P^* constant. Both the steepness and the vertical intercept of h_w in Figure 8.8 rise, but, importantly, the h_m^* curve shifts upward as well. (Payments are made on acres planted, not on acres idled.) The indifference price must therefore rise. Increasing β tends to increase the rate of participation, which tends by itself to raise the equilibrium market price, and to decrease the land diverted by each participant, which tends by itself to lower the market price. Which effect is the greater? If participation is 100 percent in any event, then raising β lowers market price. Otherwise, it is entirely possible that raising β will cause the market price to rise. In the limiting case where $\beta = 1$, however, all farmers would participate and there would be no land diversion or output restriction. Farm benefits would be financed strictly through taxes.

At this juncture, a numerical example might be helpful. Under competitive conditions we assume the total variable cost function for the representative farm is given by $C = q^2$ as in the example considered in Section 8.1. On this assumption, the farm's indirect quasi-rent and supply functions become $h = P^2/4$ and $q = P/2$, respectively. With 1,000 identical farms, the aggregate supply function is given by $Q = 500P$. Let demand be given by $Q = 10,000 - 500P$. In competitive equilibrium, $P = 10$, $Q = 5,000$, and $q = 5$. We assume each farm has 5 acres of land with yield equaling one unit per acre.

Next assume that the government introduces a land diversion program with $\beta = 0.8$ and $P^* = 18$. The established yield for each farm is the competitive yield, i.e., one unit per acre. The indirect quasi-rent and supply functions for the farm that does not participate in the program are exactly the same as under competitive conditions. That is to say,

$$h_n = \frac{P^2}{4} \tag{8.25}$$

and

$$q_n = \frac{P}{2}$$

The total variable cost function for the participating farmer is assumed to be $C_j = 2q_j^2$. Quasi-rent is given by

$$h_j = Pq_j - 2q_j^2 + (18 - P)(0.8)(5) \tag{8.26}$$

Using methods developed in Section 8.1, we can show that $h_m = P^2/8$. The supply function for the farmer that diverts 0.2 of his or her acreage, farming only 4 units of land, is given by $q_j = P/4$. The indirect quasi-rent function for the participator is given by

$$h_j = \frac{P^2}{8} - 4P + 72 \tag{8.27}$$

To find the indifference price we set h_n in (8.25) equal to h_j in (8.26). Solving the resulting quadratic equation yields $P_i = 12.8444$. For this price, $h_n = h_j = 41.24$ with $q_n = 6.42$ and $q_j = 3.21$.

Trial and error can be used to find equilibrium under the land diversion program. Suppose the market equilibrium price equals the indifference price. Then the quantity demanded will equal 3577.8. This quantity exceeds $(1,000)q_j$ and is less than $(1,000)q_n$. Hence, participation will be incomplete, and we know the equilibrium price will indeed equal the indifference price. Letting N_j and N_n equal, respectively, the number of participators and nonparticipators, we have

$$N_j(3.21) + N_n(6.42) = 3577.8 \tag{8.28}$$

and

$$N_j + N_n = 1,000$$

Solving this two-equation system, we find that $N_j = 885.4$ and $N_n = 114.6$. Unfortunately, one farmer will need be drawn and quartered.

We now return to the program that has as one of its components an effective price support operation, i.e., where the price support level is not less than the market price. A graphic representation of the indirect quasi-rent function corresponding to equation (8.22) may now be developed. The curves in Figure 8.8 are reproduced in Figure 8.9. Sections of the curves drawn on the assumption of participation no longer apply because all prices less than P_0^+ are irrelevant. These irrelevant sections are given by the dotted lines. The component of the participating farmer's quasi-rent attributable to the deficiency payment $[P^* - \max(P^+, P)]\bar{y}\beta\bar{a}$ is represented by the kinked line h_w'. This line coincides with the curve h_w in Figure 8.8 for prices larger than or equal to P_0^+ and is perfectly flat for prices less than or equal to P_0^+. The component of the participating farmer's quasi-rent attributable to producing a crop on permitted acreage $[\max(P_0^+, P)]q_j - C_j(q_j, \beta)$ is given by the kinked curve h_m^*. This curve coincides with the curve h_m^* in Figure 8.8 for prices larger or

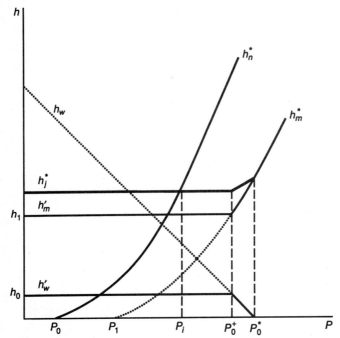

FIGURE 8.9
Modeling the participation decision under deficiency payments and
price supports.

equal to P_0^+ and is perfectly flat for prices less than or equal to P_0^+. Summing
vertically h_w' and h_m' yields h_j^* for the farmer on the assumption of program participation. The indifference price is given by P_i, which is less than P_0^+. It is in
general possible, of course, that P_i could exceed P_0^+.

Turning to the effects of changing program parameters, we note that a
ceteris paribus increase in P^* raises h_w', causing the indifference price to increase. An increase in β elevates both h_w' and h_m'. Again the indifference price
rises. How would the indifference price be affected by an increase in the loan
rate? Raising the loan rate lowers the horizontal segment of h_w' and elevates the
horizontal segment of h_m'. Whether P_i rises or falls turns on whether the profit-
maximizing yield on planted acres exceeds the farmer's established yield. If it
does, the indifference price rises; otherwise the indifference price falls. To see
this, consider a small increment in P^+ beyond P_0^+ in Figure 8.9. The slope of
h_w' is negative and equals $-\bar{y}\beta\bar{a}$ with $\bar{y}$ equaling the established yield. The
slope of h_m' is positive and equals $+y_g\beta\bar{a}$ with y_g equaling the profit-
maximizing yield on permited acres under the program. Does y_g exceed $\bar{y}$? Regardless of the answer, in the limiting case where P^+ equals P^*, deficiency
payments cease to exist, and the resulting program is essentially a voluntary
acreage allotment program as discussed briefly in Chapter 7.

We next derive an aggregate supply curve, given by the kinked curve SS_g in Figure 8.10, that shows how much will be produced at various alternative market prices. (For the moment, ignore the curve labeled SS_g'.) The lowest and highest indifference prices are given by P_{is} and P_{ib}, respectively. We assume that the highest indifference prices exceed the loan rate, but this assumption is not crucial. For all market prices less than P_{is}, all farmers participate. Since the market prices are less than P_0^+, all production plans are based on an effective farm price equal to P_0^+; the level of output equals Q_0 and the supply curve is perfectly inelastic. (Notice that since these possible market prices are less than the support price, nothing would be made available to private buyers!) If the market price is allowed to rise above P_{is}, the participation rate falls and additional land is brought into production. Exiting farmers plant more acres but receive a lower price for their output. It is entirely possible that their yields fall. It is assumed here that increased acreage more than offsets the declining yield such that the outputs of exiting farmers increase. This approach may be justified by empirical evidence suggesting that crop yields are rather insensitive to price. (Alternatively, see Section 8.4 below.) Returning to Figure 8.10, we note that as price rises above P_{ib}, all participation ceases and farmers move along the competitive supply curve.

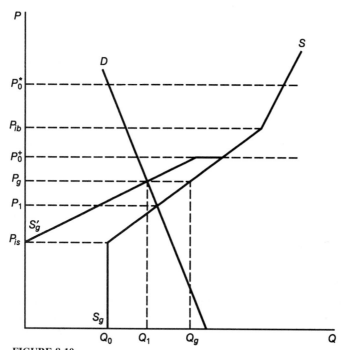

FIGURE 8.10
Market equilibrium under deficiency payments and price supports.

Finding the market equilibrium necessitates derivation of still another supply curve that shows how much will be made available to private buyers at various alternative market prices. Such a curve is given by SS_g' in Figure 8.10. This curve is vital to the analysis because with a price support program available to participants not all that is produced will necessarily be made available to private buyers. Notice that as price rises just a bit above P_{is}, at least one farmer leaves the program. Although the farmer's output may increase by a relatively small amount, all of his or her production becomes available to private buyers because only program participants are eligible for nonrecourse loans. This explains why SS_g' is much flatter in the range of prices from P_{is} to P_{ib} than is SS_g. Note further that once market price tends to rise above P_0^+, total production becomes available to private buyers. This explains the perfectly elastic segment of the SS_g' curve at the market price equal to P_0^+.

We are now in a position to explain how market performance gets determined. The equilibrium price and consumption are given by the intersection of SS_g' and D equaling P_g and Q_1, respectively. The market price is less than the support price. Total production equals Q_g, with the surplus ($Q_g - Q_1$) entering government bins. *Importantly, only the production of nonparticipating farmers is available for private consumption. Participating farmers produce output for government acquisition and disposal.*

Figure 8.10 is useful in comparative-static analysis. If, for example, demand contracts to the left, market price, consumption, and total production decrease. The rate of participation and the government surplus, on the other hand, increase.

How would changes in program parameters affect market performance? Analysis of the effects of changes in β, the proportion of land that may be farmed, is complex and the following discussion is limited to changes in P^* and P^+. A decrease in P^* lowers all indifference prices because land diversion becomes less attractive. Consequently, the relevant parts of SS_g and SS_g' shift outward to the right. Equilibrium market price falls, but total production and consumption increase. The government surplus will decline because participation falls.

Turning to P^+, we make the simplying assumption that the changes in the indifference prices due to changes in P^+ are small and may be ignored or, what amounts to the same thing, that the established yield and the actual yield under the program are about the same. This assumption will allow us to obtain some approximate results. Allowing P^+ to increase beyond P_0^+ in Figure 8.10 has practically no consequences whatever. Equilibrium market price and total production and consumption remain the same. The deficiency payment falls by about as much as quasi-rent from crop production increases. As before, the total production of participants goes to the government. If the support level were raised to and beyond P^*, the program would cease to be a deficiency payment program and a new analysis would be required.

Decreasing P^+ from the level shown in Figure 8.10, from P_0^+, lowers and lengthens the perfectly flat line segment that connects SS_g and SS_g'. In fact, for support prices larger than or equal to P_{is} but less than or equal to P_{ib}, the corresponding flat line segments of SS_g' measure the horizontal distances between the upward-sloping segments of SS_g' and SS_g. This distance increases as P falls. It is clear from Figure 8.10 that a small decrease in P^+ starting at P_0^+ will have no effect on market performance. Consider, on the other hand, successive decreases in P^+ starting from the support level $P^+ = P_g$. Through drawing the appropriate diagram it can be shown that the support program pegs the market price; the government surplus equals, for any support level, the horizontal distance between demand D and the supply curve SS_g. If the support price is set at P_1 in Figure 8.10, there will be no surplus and a decrease in P^+ starting at $P^+ = P_1$ will have no effect on market performance. By way of summary, we may note that for the supply-demand conditions shown in Figure 8.10, the market price will be less than P^+ if P^+ is larger than P_g; the surplus equals $(Q_g - Q_1)$. If $P^+ < P_1$, then the market price will exceed the support price; there will be no surplus. For any P^+ such that $P^+ \leq P_g$ and $P^+ > P_1$, the market price equals the support price and there will be government acquisition of output.

By adding a price support operation to a land diversion program, the government can diminish the expenditure required to finance deficiency payments. Under the conditions assumed here, the resulting tax saving will equal approximately the increased expenditures needed to acquire surplus stocks. Such stocks have market value; they can be sold in the international market, for example. This means the government can save money through linking a land diversion program with a price support operation for participating farmers. As we shall shortly discover, in the 1980s the federal government set P^* and P^+ at high levels, high relative to competitive prices. Participation rates and government stocks soared, and the government once again came under great pressure to idle vast acreages, subsidize exports, and, in general, find new techniques for channeling surpluses into commercial channels of trade. (See Appendixes A and B.)

8.4 LAND DIVERSION AND DIRECT PAYMENTS*

Direct payments are often recommended as an efficient means for generating benefits for farmers and farm input suppliers. This approach is also relatively expensive in terms of treasury outlays, particularly if demand is inelastic. One way of cutting back on treasury outlays is to link the payments with land diversion. For a given target price, land diversion raises market price and diminishes treasury outlays.

In what follows, we consider a program in which the farmer receives a payment per unit of output, per bushel, say, that equals $(P^* - P)$, where as before P^* is the target price and P is the market price. If $P \geq P^*$, no payment is made. The payment per acre planted equals $(P^* - P)y$ where y equals the actual yield, not a fixed or established yield. In order to receive the payment, however, the farmer must divert a given proportion $(1 - \beta)$ of land controlled (owned or rented), just as in the previously considered programs. Short-run and long-run analyses are considered in turn.

Short-Run Analysis

Short-run analysis assumes a fixed number of farms, each with a fixed plant. We suppose the fixed plant consists of given acreage and family labor. The indirect quasi-rent functions for the nonparticipating and participating farmers are given by h_n^* and h_j^*, respectively, in part a of Figure 8.11. Quasi-rent for the nonparticipating farmer increases at an increasing rate with increases in P. The supply curve is given by ss_n in part b and is everywhere upward-sloping. For the participating farmer, on the other hand, quasi-rent remains constant at h_0 for all $P < P^*$. The reason for this is that direct payments are used to assure an effective price no less than P^* no matter how low market price might fall. The positively sloped part of h_j^* is of little interest in that the prices involved are in excess of P^*. There would be no incentive for the farmer to idle land. The supply curve for the participating producer is perfectly inelastic and is given by $s's_g$ in part b of Figure 8.11. At $P = P^*$ the slope of h_n^* exceeds that of h_j^* and quasi-rent of the nonparticipator h_1 exceeds that for the participator h_0 (part a). These results follow because the participators are not free to farm all of their land. When price is close to P^*, farmers will obviously choose not to participate.

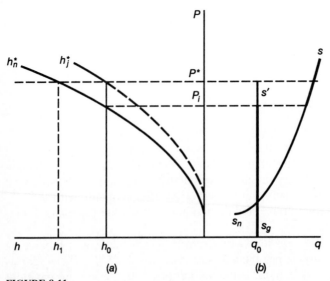

FIGURE 8.11
Deriving the farmer's supply curve under land diversion and direct payments.

The indifference price P_i is given by the intersection of h_j^* and h_n^*. For all $P < P_i$, the producer participates in the program and output equals q_0. For all $P > P_i$, the producer does not participate in the program and, for changes in P, moves along the curve ss_n. The farmer's supply curve, allowing for voluntary participation, is given by ss_g, with a discontinuity at $P = P_i$. It is perfectly inelastic for prices less than P_i and coincides with ss_n for prices larger than P_i.

The aggregate supply curve for all farmers is given by the darkened, kinked curve SS_g in Figure 8.12. (We assume identical operations.) Equilibrium is given by the intersection of demand D and supply SS_g. Demand is positioned in the diagram such that some participation occurs in equilibrium. The program raises market price from P_c to P_g. Aggregate output falls from Q_c to Q_g. Since the program is voluntary and every producer has the option of dropping out of the program and producing at a price in excess of the competitive price, it is clear that every producer benefits from the program in the short run. Importantly, this analysis assumes that program parameters are set in such a manner as to command partial but not 100 percent participation. High price targets tend to expand production. Land diversion tends to contract production. If the target is set high enough, for a given acreage diversion requirement, then the program might expand production beyond the competitive

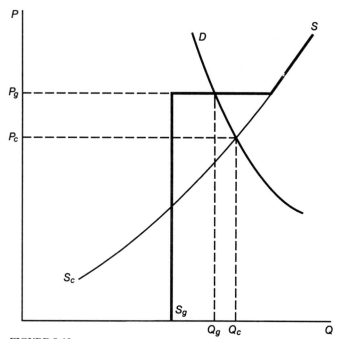

FIGURE 8.12
Short-run market equilibrium under land diversion and direct payments.

level. This would only happen, however, if the rate of participation were 100 percent. The perfectly vertical segment then lies to the right of Q_c. (If the horizontal segment of SS_g fell below the competitive price, then the program would be ineffective.)

An algebraic example is instructive. (The algebra becomes a bit much at this point, and some readers might prefer to concentrate on the results.) Let the production functions for the nonparticipating and participating producer be given by (8.29) and (8.30), respectively,

$$q_n = a_n^{\alpha 1} k_n^{\alpha 2} \tag{8.29}$$

$$q_j = (\beta a_j)^{\alpha 1} k_j^{\alpha 2} \tag{8.30}$$

where a equals fixed acreage and k equals a variable input. Family labor is assumed fixed. (The multiplicative constant α_0 encountered in Chapter 3 may be set equal to 1.) The direct quasi-rent functions are

$$h_n = P a_n^{\alpha 1} k_n^{\alpha 2} - G k_n \tag{8.31}$$

$$h_j = P^*(\beta a_j)^{\alpha 1} k_j^{\alpha 2} - G k_j \tag{8.32}$$

Maximizing h_n (or h_j) with respect to k_n (or k_j) yields

$$k_n = (G P^{-1} \alpha_2^{-1} a_n^{-\alpha 1})^{1/(\alpha 2 - 1)} \tag{8.33}$$

$$k_j = [G(P^*)^{-1} \alpha_2^{-1}(\beta a_j)^{-\alpha 1}] \tag{8.34}$$

Substituting the right-hand sides for k_n and k_j from (8.33) and (8.34) into (8.31) and (8.32) yields the indirect quasi-rent functions. When price P equals the indifference price P_i, we have, by definition,

$$h_n^*(P_i, G, a_n) = h_j^*(P^*, G, a_j, \beta) \tag{8.35}$$

Writing out (8.35) for the specific case in hand and solving for P_i we have

$$P_i = \beta^{\alpha 1} P^* \tag{8.36}$$

This algebraic expression for the indifference price is worth some study. At a glance we can see that the indifference price P_i rises with both β and P^*, which is what we would expect. (Recall that β is the proportion of the farmer's fixed acreage that may be farmed under the program.) Notice also that P_i falls with increases in the productivity of land, providing we take as our measure of the latter, land's production elasticity α_1. This also is what we would expect in that the more productive land is relative to other inputs, the higher the opportunity cost of allowing land to stand idle.

The supply equation for the nonparticipator is derived by substituting the right-hand side of (8.33) into the production function, which yields

$$q_n = a_n^{\alpha_1}(GP^{-1}\alpha_2^{-1}a_n^{-\alpha_1})^{\alpha_2/(\alpha_2-1)} \tag{8.37}$$

Setting P equal to P_i and then using (8.36) to get rid of P_i in favor of P^*, we have

$$q_{ni} = a_n^{\alpha_1}[G\beta^{-\alpha_1}(P^*)^{-1}\alpha_2^{-1}a_n^{-\alpha_1}]^{\alpha_2/(\alpha_2-1)} \tag{8.38}$$

where q_{ni} equals the output of the nonparticipating farmer with price equal to P_i. The expression for q_{ni} can be compared with the optimal output of the participator given by

$$q_j = \beta^{\alpha_1}a_j^{\alpha_1}[G\beta^{-\alpha_1}(P^*)^{-1}\alpha_2^{-1}a_j^{\alpha-1}]^{\alpha_2/(\alpha_2-1)} \tag{8.39}$$

Since total acreage available is fixed, $a_n = a_j$. Also, since $\beta^{\alpha_1} < 1$, we have

$$q_{ni} > q_j \tag{8.40}$$

This is an important result. Let the market price equal the farmer's indifference price. If the farmer participates, he or she receives a price in excess of the market price but must use less land. The effect of the higher price by itself would be to expand output beyond q_{ni}. The effect of the lower acreage by itself would be to decrease output below q_{ni}. *The reduced acreage effect, with its negative sign, outweighs the higher-price effect, with its positive sign, such that participation results in an output less than q_{ni} with price equal to the indifference price.*

Let k_{ni} equal the optimal level of k_n when $P = P_i$. Using (8.33) together with (8.34), it can be shown that $k_{ni} > k_j$. *If market price equals P_i, then producers will farm more land, use more variable input, and produce more output if they do not participate in the program than if they do.*

Long-Run Analysis

The long-run supply curve allowing for a program that involves both direct payments and land diversion is given by the kinked curve SS_g in Figure 8.13. Three demand situations are relevant. If demand for the output is sufficiently low, such that the intersection of D and SS_g yields output Q_0, then the participation rate among producers is 100 percent. Increases in demand in this situation cause market price to rise without a corresponding increase in output. Producers do not respond to changes in market price because as market price rises, say, the direct payment per unit falls by an equivalent amount. If de-

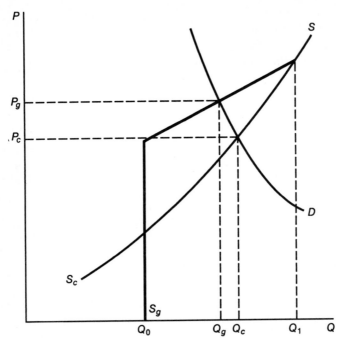

FIGURE 8.13
Long-run market equilibrium under land diversion and direct payments.

mand rises sufficiently, however, the market price will rise to the indifference price, and some farmers will exit the program. Nonparticipating producers expand acreage, the use of variable inputs, and output. In an increasing cost industry, the prices of some variable inputs will rise with increased use. Therefore, the indifference price will rise as well. This explains the upward slope of SS_g between the outputs Q_0 and Q_1. If demand intersects SS_g at some Q larger than Q_1, then participation will not occur and the program becomes irrelevant.

For the purpose of applied welfare analysis we assume that, given values for P^* and β, the demand situation elicits some but not total participation, as in Figure 8.13. The program causes output to fall from the competitive value Q_c to Q_g; price increases from P_c to P_g. Clearly taxpayers and consumers will be made worse off by the program. Consumers ordinarily gain from a direct payment program but not if it is linked, as it is here, with land diversion.

In order to examine the applied welfare effects for farm input suppliers, it is useful to consider the long-run profit functions of farmers depending on whether they do or do not participate in the program. We have

$$\pi_n = Pq_n - Ra_n - Gk_n - TE \tag{8.41}$$

$$\pi_j = P^*q_j - \left(\frac{R}{\beta}\right)a_p - Gk_j - TE \tag{8.42}$$

where the notation is the same as before and recalling that $a_p = \beta a_j$. The real price that a participator pays for land actually farmed, the land that actually enters the production function as an input, equals R/β. To simplify aggregation we assume that all farmers have identical Cobb-Douglas production functions. In long-run equilibrium we have

$$R_g A_n = \alpha_1 (P_g Q_n) \tag{8.43}$$

$$R_g A_j = \alpha_1 (P^* Q_j)$$
$$= \alpha_1 [(P^* - P_g) Q_j + P_g Q_j] \tag{8.44}$$

where R_g is the long-run rent to land with the government program; Q_n and Q_j equal, respectively, the aggregate output produced by nonparticipators and participators, respectively; and $(P^* - P_g) Q_j$ equals total direct payments. It follows that

$$R_g A = R_g (A_n + A_j)$$
$$= \alpha_1 [P_g Q_g + (P^* - P_g) Q_j] \tag{8.45}$$

(We assume a perfectly inelastic supply curve for land.) Subtracting the competitive rent bill from the rent bill under the government program yields

$$(R_g - R_c) A = \alpha_1 [P_g Q_g - P_c Q_c + (P^* - P_g) Q_j] \tag{8.46}$$

If demand is not elastic, so that $P_g Q_g \geq P_c Q_c$, then land benefits from the direct payment–land diversion program. If demand has unitary elasticity, then the annual returns to land in the form of the rent bill rise by land's factor share α_1 of total direct payments. If demand is elastic, it is uncertain on the basis of Equation (8.46) whether landowners will receive any benefits. On other grounds, however, we can be sure that if there is at least some program participation in long-run equilibrium, then landowners will be made better off by the program. Price is elevated above the competitive level. The nonparticipator could always bid land away from a participator who could not afford to pay more than the competitive rent for land.

Notice that some of these results stand in sharp contrast to those associated with the land diversion program analyzed earlier in which the government paid farmers to idle land. Under that program all farmers received the market price for production and, with demand elasticity equal to 1, the entire government expenditure accrued to landowners. Here, under a direct payment approach, the participating producers receive the target price for all that is produced, which encourages intensification of production beyond that associated with the market price.

The difference between the wage bill under a direct payment–land diversion program and under competition is given by

$$W_g L_g - W_c L_c = \alpha_3 [P_g Q_g - P_c Q_c + (P^* - P_g)Q_j] \qquad (8.47)$$

Farm labor benefits from the program if $P_g Q_g \geq P_c Q_c$. Even if demand elasticity equals 1, farm labor benefits because the wage bill rises. This result also stands in contrast to that for the previously analyzed land diversion programs.

8.5   MAJOR CROP PROGRAMS (GRAIN AND UPLAND COTTON)

Attention now shifts to farm programs for the major field crops, which for much of the post–World War II period have relied on land diversion as a key policy instrument. Major crops include corn and other feedgrains (sorghum, barley, and oats), wheat, and cotton. Rice will also be considered briefly. Taken together, these crops account for a large part of the agricultural sector. For example, over the 3-year period 1975–1977, when little land was diverted under farm programs, grain acreage alone accounted for over 96 percent of total harvested crop acreage.

We begin by describing the feedgrain program for 1987 under the Food Security Act of 1985. Since the programs for crops identified above are all quite similar, an explanation of how one works carries over to the others. The second part of this section gives a brief historical account of the evolution of major crop programs since the early 1960s. This account more or less picks up where the discussion of the history of major crop programs in the last chapter left off. The third part of this section centers on some of the likely effects of crop programs and calls attention to the large gaps in our knowledge of what these effects really are.

The 1987 Feedgrain Program

The easiest way to explain the 1987 feedgrain program for corn, sorghum, barley, and oats is to construct an example. Consider a farm that had 200 acres and a corn acreage base of 100 acres. This base equaled the average corn acreage for the farm over the previous 5 years. The program was voluntary, but if the farmer decided to join, then 20 percent of the base, i.e., 20 acres, had to be idled. In addition, the acreage planted to corn had to be less than or equal to 80 percent of the base—80 acres in our example. The major benefits to be derived through participation were deficiency payments and access to price support nonrecourse loans. The deficiency payment equaled the product of three terms: the payment rate, the farm's established corn yield, and the acreage planted to corn. The payment rate equaled the target price for corn minus the larger of the average market price and the loan rate for corn. In 1987, the target equaled $3.03 per bushel; the loan rate was $1.82. The market price, $1.63, was the national weighted average market price received during the first 5 months of the marketing year (September 1987 through January 1988). The established corn yield equaled the average yield for the 1981–1985 crops excluding the years with the highest and lowest yields.

As noted, the loan rate for corn under the 1987 program was $1.82 per bushel. County loan rates were established to reflect the relative value of the commodity at its location. Nine-month loans on the participating farmer's total corn production, or any part thereof, were available from harvest date through May 31, 1988. The farmer had the option of repaying the loan plus accrued interest any time prior to the maturity date, 9 months from the time the loan was made. If the loan was not repaid, the CCC took possession of the corn as full payment of the loan plus interest.

The participating farmer also had the option of idling an additional 15 percent of the corn base acreage for diversion payments. The diversion payment per idled acre equaled $2.00 per bushel times the established yield. Full participation in the program would have involved idling 35 acres in our example, 20 percent plus 15 percent. The sum of the diversion payment plus the deficiency payment described earlier could not exceed $50,000 per person. (Some large farms were able to circumvent this limit through distributing ownership of their operations.)

There was also a so-called 50/92 rule in the 1987 feedgrain program. Under this rule, if the farmer planted between 50 and 92 percent of the permitted acreage to corn (80 acres in our example) and idled the remainder, then payments could have been received on 92 percent of the permitted acreage.

In addition to land diversion and acreage limitations, the participating farmer also had to comply with the sodbuster-swampbuster provisions of the 1985 act. Briefly, these provisions were aimed at discouraging the conversion of highly erodible land and wetland for agricultural production. Farmers who broke out highly erodible fields and planted them to crops or who converted wetlands for the same purpose were ineligible for receiving program benefits.

In the 1987 feedgrain programs, participating farmers received some of their payments in the form of generic commodity certificates. The same was true for farmers participating in the programs for wheat, cotton, and rice. Producers of cotton and rice also had access to the so-called marketing loans. Generic commodity certificates and marketing loans were used to encourage the movement of government stocks into commercial channels of trade, as explained in more detail in Appendixes A and B.

One option not open to feedgrain producers in the 1987 program that had been available in several previous years was that of participating in the farmer-owned grain reserve. This option will be discussed later on in this chapter.

To sum up, the 1987 feedgrain program was voluntary and involved the idling of land, limitations on acreage planted to feedgrains, deficiency and diversion payments, and nonrecourse loans. Deficiency payments were based on established rather than actual yields as in the land diversion model analyzed in Section 8.3. This program was similar in essential respects to those for wheat, cotton, and rice and to those for major field crops for other years in the period since the late 1950s.

Historical Evolution

We turn now to a brief historical account of the origins and predecessors of current programs. Recall from the last chapter that the decade of the 1950s ended on a sour note as regards both the popularity and the effects of programs for major field crops. The corn program involved price supports and voluntary acreage allotments, and the growth in government stocks of corn was careening out of control. The stocks of wheat were also immense in spite of mandatory acreage allotments and heavily subsidized exports. It was difficult politically to tighten up the allotment because to do so would simply have shifted excess capacity, including land, to other crops such as feedgrains. The situation in cotton wasn't much different from that of wheat except that cotton had not only to compete with sources of supply from abroad but with manufactured fibers as well. The mandatory acreage allotment for rice, with its relatively small acreage, was sufficiently tight in light of support prices to keep surpluses from becoming a major problem, but this was the exception, not the rule.

Recognizing that acreage allotment programs tend to shift excess production capacity around from one commodity to another like a hot potato, the federal government first tried land diversion on a fairly large scale in the 1950s. The Agricultural Act of 1956 provided for a two-part soil bank program designed to idle capacity. Under the acreage reserve part, in effect during 1956–1958 for wheat, corn, cotton, rice, tobacco, and peanuts, the CCC was authorized to make payments to farmers for idling allotment acreage on an annual basis. For example, the national acreage payment rate for corn was $44.46 per acre idled in 1958 with variations in rates offered to farmers because of differences in land quality.

Under the conservation reserve, the CCC was authorized to make payments to farmers for shifting general cropland into grass, trees, or other conserving crops on a long-term basis, from 3 to 15 years. Conservation reserve contracts were not offered to farmers after 1960. Cooperating farmers received relatively low annual per acre payments for each year of the contract together with payments for converting cropland to conserving uses, such as trees and cover crops for wildlife. Whereas the acreage reserve centered on high-quality land, the conservation reserve looked to the idling of marginal land.

The soil bank program was rather a half-hearted measure. It was not launched on a sufficient scale and in a manner that brought surplus production under control. It did, however, face up to a major shortcoming of mandatory acreage control, which, as noted, was to shift acreage from program crops to nonprogram crops.

The failure of farm programs in the 1950s was most acute in the case of feedgrains, and it was here that the federal government sought in 1960 to develop a more effective approach. The result was the Emergency Feedgrain Program of 1961, a program that drew upon the previous experience under the soil bank program and became the prototype for major crop programs up to the present time. Briefly, the 1961 program was voluntary, applied to corn and sorghum, and involved diverting or idling a minimum of 20 percent of base acreage. The latter were determined by taking the average of acreage planted in 1959 and 1960 for each farm. Acreage planted plus acreage diverted could not exceed the base. The inducements to enter the program were mainly diversion payments based on acres diverted and the protection afforded by price support loans. The 1961 program was continued in 1962, and its coverage was extended to include barley.

The 1963 program was notable in that it added direct price support payments as an incentive to participate in the program. These payments were made on acreage planted to feedgrains, as opposed to acreage diverted. The payment rate per bushel equaled the difference between the "total support price," somewhat akin to a target price, minus the loan rate. Loan rates were lowered to world prices or less. The total support price for corn in 1963, for example, was $1.25 per bushel. The direct price support payment rate and loan rate were, respectively, 18 cents and $1.07. Notice that the payment rate was not dependent on the market price. The basic elements of the 1963 feedgrain program were continued for 11 years. Importantly, the Food and Agricultural Act of 1965 extended this approach to include wheat and cotton. Government objectives included elevating farm income, keeping loan rates low in order to move commodities into commercial channels of trade, and restraining production.

The Agricultural Act of 1970 added an interesting dimension to major crop programs. This was a limitation on the total payment a participating producer could receive. The limit was $55,000 per program crop per person. A farmer producing feedgrains, wheat, and cotton could receive a payment of no more than $165,000. The limitation on payments reflected a growing concern over the concentration of benefits among the largest and wealthiest farmers. Some of the government checks to large farming operations exceeded $1 million in the late 1960s. The payment limit applied to an individual rather than a total farm operation. A total payment to a family, for example, could have been higher than the limit if the farm had been divided among family members. Students of farm policy had always been aware of the concentration of farm program benefits among the largest farmers, but the use of direct payments brought it out into the open for all to see.

The Agricultural Act of 1970 added still another dimension to present-day crop programs. Deficiency payments were substituted for direct price support payments. In the case of deficiency payments the payment rate per bushel (or other unit of measurement) equaled a target price minus the market price. Importantly, the payments received by participating farmers were sensitive to market prices. Scaling direct payments to the level of market prices as opposed to fixed payments has at least one serious drawback, a drawback that became very obvious in the 1988 drought. A large-scale drought, as in that year, reduces production and raises market prices nationwide. Participating farmers may not only end up with little output to sell from planted acres but may receive no payments on diverted acres as well. Fixed payments, in contrast, tend to reduce risk but at higher potential outlays.

The Agriculture and Consumer Protection Act of 1973 initiated a disaster payments program, which, some have argued, was itself a disaster. Farmers received payments to cover losses due to natural causes such as bad weather that prevented crops from being planted or resulted in very low yields. The program involved a substantial cost to the government because farmers paid no insurance premiums for the protection they received from risk. The major beneficiaries of this program were likely the owners and operators of farms in drought- or flood-prone areas. A program of this sort clearly encourages the expansion of farming into high-risk areas. This approach to protecting farmers from certain risks (mainly those due to inclement weather) has been replaced largely by the all-risk crop insurance program provided by the Federal Crop Insurance Act of 1980. Although the government pays a portion of the insurance premiums, the participation in the program has been low nonetheless.

The Food and Agriculture Act of 1977 contained two innovations, only one of which appears to have gained political acceptability. The innovation that was short-lived based deficiency payments on the production from current plantings, reduced by a program allocation factor but not limited to acreage allotments. The program allocation factor, not to exceed 1, equaled the ratio of needed acreage to harvested acreage or 0.8, whichever was larger. Needed acreage was estimated to satisfy domestic consumption, exports, and ending inventory requirements. The allocation factor was intended to reduce payments and budget outlays in the event harvested acreage became excessive. The acreage controls were later judged to be unsatisfactory in that they invited farmers to plant additional acres in order to take advantage of payments.

The second innovation was the Farmer-Owned Reserve program for the grains, a program that has been in operation in recent years and will likely be around in years to come. Under this program the government induces farmers to share management of their stocks in return for storage subsidies. As originally established, farmers entered grain into the reserve through the non-recourse loan system for a period of three years. The government made payments to farmers to cover storage costs. Two price levels were critical to the program's operation, the release price and the call price. If during the 3-year duration of the loan the market price rose to or above the release level, the farmer was free to market the grain and repay the loan plus interest (figured at a rate less than the market rate); storage subsidies were also phased out. If the price rose above the call level, however, the farmer had to pay off the loan. Sharp penalties were assessed if the farmer sold reserve grain at a price less than the release level. Upper limits were placed on the quantities of grains that could be placed in the reserve. Under the 1985 legislation the release level was set at the higher of 140 percent of the stated loan rate or the target price. Call levels are no longer applicable. With surplus grain flowing out of Uncle Sam's ears in 1986, the 1987 grain programs did not offer farmers the option of committing still more grain to the Farmer-Owned Reserve.

Clearly, the government has been eager to exercise substantial control over management of stocks. Equally clear is the considerable evidence to suggest that the federal government does a poor job in this area. A good case can be made for a program that subsidizes storage cost but allows the market system itself to determine when and how much grain should be stored and the extent to which stocks are scaled back in the face of high prices and other supply-and-demand conditions (see Chapter 5).

The Agriculture and Food Act of 1981 revived the concept if not the language of the acreage allotment and made the rice program analogous to those for other grains. Crop-specific acreage reduction programs, as they were and are now called, put upper limits on the acreage a farmer could plant and still receive deficiency payments and other program benefits. The secretary of agriculture was given considerable flexibility in managing the farmer-owned reserve for grains.

Few pieces of legislation were preceded by as much informed discussion and debate as was the Food Security Act of 1985. Academics, in particular, pulled out all the stops in organizing conferences, identifying alternative approaches, and reviewing the situation. In the end, economic circumstances dictated farm policy as in the past. The bottom was falling out of farm prosperity, and as 1985 approached the main question became what levels of price and income support would be forthcoming. It became clear that the basic framework that had worked before to deliver assistance to farmers—deficiency payments, land diversion, and acreage limitations—would be relied upon once again. The times were too precarious and iffy for experimenting with new, bold approaches. As a consequence the programs enacted under the 1985 act, at least for grains and cotton, followed along pretty much the same paths trodden on before.

Table 8.1 provides information on cropland idled under farm programs together with government payments and farm program costs. As noted previously, the effort to idle cropland under the soil bank program beginning in 1956 lacked vigor. Cropland idled in 1959 and 1960 was all attributable to the Conservation Reserve. Even though cropland idled under the Conservation Reserve began to disappear in the 1960s, other programs, beginning with the Emergency Feedgrain Program in 1961, more than took up the slack. More acreage was diverted, and the acreage diverted was of much higher quality than that diverted under the Conservation Reserve. Over the decade of the 1960s, diverted land averaged 52.7 million acres annually, which equaled about 18 percent of average cropland harvested. Over the period 1973–1982, acreage was diverted on a modest scale or not at all. This was a reflection of the relatively high level of farm prosperity associated with a big jump in farm exports. In the 1980s, starting in 1983, crop programs became very attractive to farmers and the rates of program participation soared. Participating acreage rose to more than 80 percent of base acreage for wheat and corn and to 90 percent for upland cotton in the 1986–1987 crop year. Idled acreage once again rose to high levels, reaching 78 million acres in 1983. This amounted to 25 per-

TABLE 8.1
Cropland idled, government payments, and farm program costs, United States, 1956–1987

| | | | Farm program costs[c] | |
| | Cropland idled[a] (million acres) | Government payments[b] (million dollars) | Feedgrain, wheat, cotton, and rice (million dollars) | All commodities (million dollars) |
Year				
1956	13.6	500	—	—
1957	27.8	962	—	—
1958	27.1	1,074	—	—
1959	22.5	600	—	—
1960	28.7	652	—	—
1961	53.7	1,437	1,189	1,301
1962	64.7	1,692	1,237	1,985
1963	56.1	1,659	2,082	2,925
1964	55.5	2,154	1,753	2,888
1965	57.4	2,445	1,505	2,470
1966	63.3	3,243	1,392	1,384[d]
1967	40.7	3,049	1,096	1,951
1968	49.4	3,397	2,082	3,279
1969	58.0	3,732	3,750	4,183
1970	57.1	3,668	3,166	3,839
1971	37.6	3,076	2,182	2,900
1972	62.1	3,852	3,354	4,073
1973	19.6	2,542	2,135	3,629
1974	2.7	530	1,535	1,106
1975	2.4	794	457	585
1976	2.1	695	368	1,114
1977	0.0	1,490	2,807	3,820
1978	18.3	3,003	3,290	5,656
1979	12.9	1,343	1,642	3,612
1980	0.0	1,257	2,553	2,752
1981	0.0	1,898	1,370	4,036
1982	11.1	3,446	8,989	11,652
1983	78.0	9,212	12,261	18,851
1984	26.9	8,313	2,355	7,315
1985	30.7	7,607	12,445	17,683
1986	47.4	11,674	18,740	25,841
1987	70.5	16,603	19,495	22,408
1988	68.8	14,363	10,525	12,461
1989	48.1	NA	6,668	13,484

[a]Includes long-term diversion such as the Conservation Reserve under the 1950s soil bank program.

[b]Excludes direct payments under the wool program. Includes disaster payments in the mid-1970s and payment-in-kind (PIK) payments in 1983 and 1984.

[c]These figures are on a fiscal year basis. Comparable data are not available for 1956–1960.

[d]A commodity program may give rise to government earnings when surplus products, butter, for example, are sold. This explains why in some years the cost of all programs is less than the cost of major crop programs.

Source: U.S. Department of Agriculture, *Agricultural Statistics*, various years; U.S. Department of Agriculture, Economic Research Service *Agricultural Resources*, various issues; and U.S. Department of Agriculture, Economic Research Service, *Agricultural Outlook*, various issues.

cent of harvested acreage. The government cost of programs for feedgrain, wheat, cotton, and rice rose to over $19 billion in 1987, equaling 87 percent of the cost of all farm programs. Government payments have been highly correlated with idled acres over time.

It should not be supposed that idling 10 percent of base acreage, for example, would cause production to fall by 10 percent. Nonparticipants often increase planted acreage above base acreage in response to higher expected prices caused by whatever land diversion occurs. Land withdrawn from production is often the farmer's less productive land. Studies have shown that diverted land tends to be only 80 to 90 percent as productive as nondiverted land. As might be expected, some small percentage of farmers have not always abided by the rules, planting more acreage than they were supposed to. Writers often refer to percentage reductions in acreage that exceed the associated percentage reductions in production as the result of "slippage," a term applying to a set of factors, some of which were noted above. Because of slippage the effectiveness of diverted acreage has been in the range of 50 to 84 percent in recent years.

Table 8.2 provides information on relevant program variables for grain and cotton for recent years and allows a more detailed account of recent history. Average prices received by farmers are also given to facilitate comparisons with target prices and loan levels. A number of observations are of interest. First, target prices for major crops rose substantially in the early part of the decade of the 1980s and then leveled off as prices received by farmers plummeted. This represented a major and expensive effort on the part of the federal government to shore up farm income in the face of an agricultural depression. (For more detail on the nature and causes of this depression, see Chapter 3.)

Second, the experience gained under the 1981 act teaches a valuable lesson in regard to the importance of program flexibility in an uncertain world. Minimum targets and loan rates were mandated for wheat, corn, and cotton beginning in 1982. Also, loan rates for grains entering the farmer-owned reserve may be, and on occasion have been, higher than the ordinary loan rate used in the price support system. This was the case in 1982, for example, when the reserve loan rate for corn was 45 cents per bushel higher than the ordinary loan rate. In light of the then current inflation and strong export demand, the targets and loan rates set in the 1981 act seemed modest. As inflation was brought under control by tight monetary policy (and a major recession) and as growth in farm exports flagged, prices received by farmers dropped sharply. The result was a build-up of stocks and high levels of government expenditures (see Table 8.1). Wheat stocks, already at a high level, rose by 31 percent from 1981–82 to 1982–83; corn stocks rose by 39 percent. The build-up of stocks was a major reason for the 1983 payment-in-kind program. Under this program farmers received commodities from CCC-owned stocks and from the farmer-owned reserve in return for idling land. The terms were unusually generous,

TABLE 8.2
Program variables for wheat, feedgrains, upland cotton, and rice; and average prices received by farmers, United States, marketing years 1981–82 through 1988–89[a]

Marketing year	1981–82	1982–83	1983–84	1984–85	1985–86	1986–87	1987–88	1988–89	1989–90
Wheat									
Target price	3.81	4.05[b]	4.30[b]	4.38	4.38	4.38	4.38	4.23	4.10
Loan level	3.20	3.55[b]	3.65[b]	3.30	3.30	2.40	2.28	2.21	2.06
Price received	3.69	3.45	3.51	3.39	3.08	2.42	2.57	3.72	NA
Acreage reduction %	—	15	15	20	20	22.5[c]	27.5	27.5	10
Paid land diversion %	—	—	5	10	10	—	—	—	—
Corn									
Target price	2.40	2.70[b]	2.86[b]	3.03[b]	3.03	3.03	3.03	2.93	2.84
Loan level	2.40	2.55[b]	2.65[b]	2.55	2.55	1.92	1.82	1.77	1.65
Price received	2.47	2.55	3.25	2.62	2.23	1.50	1.94	2.25	NA
Acreage reduction %	—	10	10	10	10	17.5	20	20	10
Paid land diversion %	—	—	10	—	—	2.5	15	10	—
Grain sorghum									
Target price	2.55	2.60	2.72	2.88	2.88	2.88	2.88	2.78	2.70
Loan level	2.28	2.42	2.52	2.42	2.42	1.82	1.74	1.68	1.57
Price received	2.25	2.47	2.74	2.32	1.93	1.37	1.70	2.27	NA
Acreage reduction %	—	10	10	10	10	17.5	20	20	10
Paid land diversion %	—	—	10	—	—	2.5	15	10	—
Barley									
Target price	2.60	2.60	2.60	2.60	2.60	2.60	2.60	2.60	2.43
Loan level	1.95	2.08	2.16	2.08	2.08	1.56	1.49	1.44	1.34
Price received	2.48	2.18	2.47	2.29	1.98	1.61	1.81	2.79	NA

Acreage reduction %	—	10	10	10	10	17.5	20	20	10
Paid land diversion %	—	—	10	—	—	2.5	15	10	—
Oats									
Target price	NA	1.50	1.60	1.60	1.60	1.60	1.60	1.55	1.50
Loan level	1.24	1.31	1.36	1.31	1.31	.99	.94	.90	0.85
Price received	1.88	1.49	1.62	1.67	1.23	1.21	1.56	2.61	NA
Acreage reduction %	—	10	10	10	10	17.5	20	20	5
Paid land diversion %	—	10	10	—	—	2.5	15	5	—
Upland cotton									
Target price	70.87	71.00[b]	76.00[b]	81.00	81.00	81.00	79.40	75.90	73.40
Loan level	52.46	57.08	55.00[b]	55.00	57.30	55.00	52.25	51.80	50.00
Price received	55.40	59.50	65.30	58.70	56.80	51.50	63.70	54.80	NA
Acreage reduction %	—	15	20	25	20	25	25	12.5	25
Paid land diversion %	—	—	5	—	10	—	—	—	—
Rice									
Target price	10.68	10.85	11.40	11.90	11.90	11.90	11.66	11.15	10.80
Loan level	8.01	8.14	8.14	8.00	8.00	7.20	6.84	6.63	6.50
Price received	9.05	7.91	8.57	8.04	6.53	3.75	7.27	6.70	NA
Acreage reduction %	—	15	15	25	20	35	35	25	25
Paid land diversion %	—	—	5	—	15	—	—	—	—

[a]Prices are in dollars per bushel for wheat and feedgrains and dollars per hundredweight for cotton and rice. Acreage reductions and paid land diversions are in percentages of national base acres. The first month of the marketing year is June for wheat, barley, and oats; September for corn and sorghum; and August for cotton and rice. NA means not available.

[b]Minimum allowed by law.

[c]A paid land diversion percentage of 2.5 percent was mandatory for program participation. Winter wheat producers had two additional options, 5 percent or 10 percent.

Source: U.S. Department of Agriculture, Economic Research Service, *Policy Research Notes*, various issues; and U.S. Department of Agriculture, National Agricultural Statistics Service, *Agricultural Prices*, various issues.

and diverted land soared to an all-time record as we have already noted. Because of restricted acreage and a serious drought, production of major crops fell substantially, as did end-of-year stocks.

A third observation of interest is closely related to the second. High target prices relative to market prices encourage farmer participation in land diversion programs; participation rates reached high levels during the 1980s. In several years, loan rates were also high relative to market-clearing prices. The federal government, confronted with the prospect of staggering commodity surpluses, looked to both old and new ways of moving surpluses into commercial channels of trade. As described briefly in the previous chapter, Public Law 480 programs dating back to the 1950s were again put into action. These programs provided long-term, low-interest government loans for the purchase of farm commodities by foreign governments with repayment of up to 40 years. They also provided food donations for export, mainly through voluntary relief organizations such as CARE. Of greater importance for the decade of the 1980s, however, were government loan guarantees that assisted exporting firms in making sales to foreign buyers who had difficulty obtaining commercial credit. The CCC guaranteed repayment of loans made by private lending institutions and a significant part of the interest. A blended credit program involved blending or mixing interest-free government loans plus private loans backed by government loan guarantees. In addition to Public Law 480 programs and subsidized private credit for export sales, the government introduced generic commodity certificates and so-called marketing loans, as distinct from nonrecourse loans, in order further to forestall the build-up of surplus stocks.

Table 8.3 shows that government payments were highly concentrated among the largest farms in 1986. Farms with sales less than $100,000 accounted for 86.2 percent of the total number of farms and 43.8 of total payments. Farms with sales in excess of $100,000 accounted for 13.8 percent of the farms and 56.2 percent of the payments. The average payment per farm in 1986 was $1,315 for farms with sales less than $40,000. The average payment

TABLE 8.3
Percentage of total number of farms and direct government payments, by value of sales class, United States, 1986[a]

Farm with sales of	Percentage of total number of farms	Direct government payments	
		Total	Percentage
Less than $40,000	72.9	2,120	17.9
$40,000–$99,999	13.3	3,056	25.9
$100,000–$499,999	12.5	5,574	47.2
$500,000 and over	1.3	1,059	9.0

[a]There were 2.212 million farms in 1986.

Source: U.S. Department of Agriculture, Economic Research Service, *Economic Indicators of Farm Sector: National Financial Summary, 1986*, ECIFS 6-2, December 1987.

per farm with sales in excess of $500,000 was $35,998. It should be borne in mind that the ownership and risk of a farming operation, particularly a large one, may be shared by more than one family.

Economic Effects

The economic effects of the field crop programs described above are difficult to quantify because it is difficult to estimate what farm input and output prices and flows would be in the absence of government intervention. This is particularly true for long-run analysis, which would require estimating the complex interdependencies among output and input prices. Accurate estimates of long-run export demand elasticities would also be required but, as we saw in Chapter 3, the available estimates range all over the board.

Notwithstanding the difficulties noted above, several researchers have tried to measure the effects of land diversion and related programs. Some of the findings are briefly reviewed here. Using a simple, highly aggregative model, Rosine and Helmberger estimated the long-run annual benefits and costs of farm programs for the period 1954–1972. They assumed the demand for exports was perfectly inelastic, an assumption that would appear to be very restrictive in today's economic setting. The 1972 program made substantial use of land diversion programs (see Table 8.1). Rosine and Helmberger estimated that the 1972 program benefits amounted to $274 million for farm labor and $4.2 billion for farmland, the latter in the form of increased annual rent. Labor received 6.1 percent of total benefits. The consumer loss amounted to $2 billion. Cost to the taxpayer was estimated at $5.3 billion. The deadweight or efficiency loss, total costs minus total benefits, amounted to $2.8 billion, which equaled 4 percent of the value of farm output in 1972.

Gardner (1981) estimated the income distributional consequences of farm programs for the crop year 1978–1979, when land was diverted on a much smaller scale than in 1972. Combining his estimated effects of the programs for wheat, feedgrains, cotton, and rice, we find that the farm sector gained $2.9 billion, consumers lost $1.1 billion, and taxpayers paid $2.2 billion in extra taxes, all as a result of the 1978–1979 program.

A recent study of the effects of farm policy by Johnson, Womack, Meyers, Young, and Brandt draws upon a large model of U.S. agriculture developed jointly at the University of Missouri and Iowa State University. The model consists of quantified, interdependent demand-supply relationships for all major commodity markets. The authors estimate what would have happened in the crop years 1986–87 through 1989–90 under a "free market" option, with no price targets and no diverted acres. Their free market option involves limited government intervention in comparison with a regime characterized by programs consistent with the 1981 act, programs that involved direct payments and land diversion. The free market option, relative to the government intervention option, lowered the wheat price by 6 percent, corn price by 9 percent, cotton price by 6 percent, and rice price by 28 percent. Planted wheat acreage rose by 3 percent. The corresponding percentage increases for corn, cotton, and rice acreage were 6 percent, 2 percent, and 5 percent, respectively.

The study by Johnson et al. indicates that the output-reducing effects of acreage diversion programs tend to offset the output-increasing effects of target prices. The move to more market-oriented farm programs would likely increase farm output and lower farm prices, with a salutary impact on U.S. farm exports. These and other research findings are consistent with the theoretical models developed in the earlier sections of this chapter.

Using the estimates provided by Johnson et al., Gardner (1985) calculated the net redistributional consequences of dropping the 1981-style field crop programs for the years 1986–87 through 1989–90. The free market option would have resulted in the following average annual welfare gains and losses: U.S. consumers and taxpayers gain $7.5 billion; foreign buyers gain $1.9 billion; U.S. farmers lose $7.2 billion; and the net efficiency or deadweight gain is $2.2 billion.

That land diversion programs can be used to elevate substantially farm prices and incomes in the short run is beyond question. In the absence of farm programs in such years as 1986 or 1987 (see Table 8.1), real farm prices might have fallen well below those observed over the last 20 to 30 years. According to preliminary estimates, government payments under the wheat program amounted to 75 percent of the farm value of wheat production in 1986. (Wheat producers were getting more money from the government than from the market.) The corresponding percentages for corn and cotton were 52 percent and 48 percent, respectively. There is little or no historical experience to draw upon in estimating what would have happened to the farm sector in the short run if these programs had been suddenly terminated.

When farm prosperity takes a plunge, should the government intervene in order either to soften the landing at a lower plateau or to fill in the valley until prosperity swings up again? The strategy here would not be to use programs to control the major crop sector year in and year out, as in the case of tobacco or milk for fluid consumption. The idea is rather to have the flexibility to put farm programs into action for short periods of time, for 2 or 3 years, say.

A hypothetical graph of total farm quasi-rents over time, with no government intervention, is given in Figure 8.14. The ups and downs in farm prosperity might be explained by changes in the weather and in export demand. Now suppose the government seeks to remove the deep valleys in quasi-rent by diverting land and making direct payments to farmers. The dashed lines in Figure 8.14 are intended to show the extent to which the government seeks to fill in the valleys of farm prosperity with taxpayer and consumer dollars, leaving the peaks as they would otherwise be. With this view of the role of government it might be argued that it is the short-run effects of farm programs, not the long-run effects, that really matter; farm programs would only be in operation for short periods of time. The trouble is that life isn't this simple. Short-run and long-run effects are not independent.

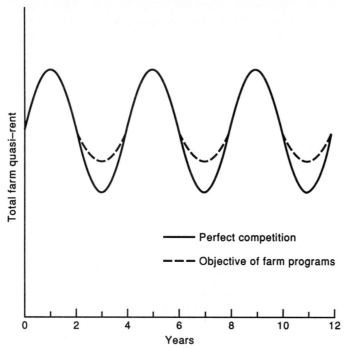

FIGURE 8.14
Altering the cycles of farm prosperity through government intervention.

　　Suppose it becomes common knowledge that the government is willing to divert land and spend billions of dollars annually in periods that would otherwise be characterized by depressed farm income. Previous analysis suggests several reasons why we might expect this policy to lose its effectiveness with the passage of time. First, diverting land on a large scale, even on a periodic basis, tends to undermine the ability of U.S. farmers to compete with foreign producers. The long-run demands for farm commodities with large export markets might be elastic. Although market receipts might rise in the short run as a result of output restriction, they might diminish with the passage of time as foreign producers secure a larger share of world trade.

　　Second, deficiency and diversion payments augment market receipts as a source of farm revenue, but land diversion programs tend to convert such payments into increased rents to land. Land diversion tied to established yields and base acres means that access to program benefits in the long run requires the purchase or rental of land to which base has been assigned, or can be reasonably expected to be assigned in the next farm recession. Recall that in the simple land diversion model analyzed above, assuming unitary demand elasticity meant that the entire government expenditure on payments to farmers accrued to landowners in the long run. Not a penny went to labor. To be sure the real world is a good deal more complicated than that assumed in the land diversion model, but it cannot be denied that farmers will be willing to pay more for land and lenders will be willing to lend more if all land market participants know that costly government programs will be initiated in times of financial strain.

Third, quasi-rent constitutes, basically, the returns to a household's labor and equity capital. The share of program benefits accruing to farm family labor reflects both the relative importance of labor as one among many factors of production plus the elasticity of the labor supply function. As developed in some detail in Chapter 4, these considerations alone raise a serious question as to the extent to which farm programs can elevate returns to family labor in the long run. Field crop production has become increasingly a capital intensive activity. Labor's share of total receipts is small and declining. Statistical analysis further indicates that the farm labor supply function for agriculture as a whole is highly elastic. The labor supply function for the grain and cotton sector must be even more elastic.

Although equity capital has assumed an increasingly important role in the U.S. farm sector, it is also true that there are no barriers preventing the flow of equity capital into the farm sector. Any tendency for the returns to capital invested in farming to become more attractive (higher average returns, lower variability of returns, or both) than returns to capital in the nonfarm sector will tend to raise land rents. The tendency in the long run is for the returns to labor to be no higher than the transfer earnings of marginal farmers and for the returns to equity capital to equal returns in the nonfarm sector. Land rent rises and falls to assure these results whether farm programs are in effect or not.

Returning to Figure 8.14, we note that with the passage of time it might become increasingly more expensive for the government to fill in the valleys of depressed quasi-rent. Of equal importance is the likelihood that the peaks of farm prosperity might sink as valleys were raised. These tendencies reflect the increased cost of production, particularly higher land values, plus the decreased sales in the export market that result from land diversion programs. There is no assurance that the leveling of the terrain would have much effect one way or the other on the *average* returns to farm labor and equity capital over the course of several cycles. It is entirely possible that the average would actually fall.

Finally, Figure 8.14 suggests that the cycles of farm prosperity follow a regular and predictable pattern. This is a great simplification. In practice, cycles of prosperity are irregular and unpredictable. This makes it difficult to decide when a land diversion program should be started and when it should be stopped if the objective is merely to take the pits out of the prosperity cycle. In any event, historical experience suggests that the federal government is willing to continue land diversion on an indefinite basis. Substantial land was diverted, for example, from 1961 through 1972. All the more reason for giving careful consideration to long-run effects in making farm policy choices.

8.6 SUMMARY

Voluntary land diversion programs are today and have been for many years the most important approach to farm price and income problems in the United States. Applicable to feedgrains, wheat, cotton, and rice, these programs offer inducements to farmers to idle land and limit acreages planted to program crops. Inducements include deficiency payments and nonrecourse loans that put a floor on prices received by participating farmers.

Because the land diversion programs of interest are voluntary, theoretical analysis of their economic effects must model the participation decisions of farmers. A useful theoretical construct in this regard is the indirect profit (or quasi-rent) function that shows the maximum profit the farmer can obtain as a function of the level of market price. It is shown that the first derivative of this function (with respect to price) yields the optimum level of output, which is a handy result in the derivation of the farmer's output supply function.

We suppose the farmer derives two indirect quasi-rent functions, one based on participation and the other based on nonparticipation. It is shown that for relatively low prices the graph of an indirect quasi-rent function assuming participation lies above that drawn on the assumption of nonparticipation. Thus, for relatively low prices the farmer participates in the program and the optimum output is given by the slope of the relevant indirect quasi-rent curve. For relatively high prices the graph of the indirect quasi-rent function drawn on the assumption of nonparticipation lies above that drawn on the assumption of participation. Quasi-rent maximization then implies that the farmer stays out of the program. The optimum output equals the slope of the nonparticipating indirect quasi-rent curve. An important concept is that of an indifference price defined as the price that yields the same maximized quasi-rent whether or not the farmer participates in the program. For price changes below the indifference price, the farmer moves along a supply curve that reflects diversion of some proportion of the farmer's land. If market price rises above the indifference price, the farmer leaves the program and moves along a competitive supply curve in response to price changes. In this manner we derive a discontinuous supply curve that shows how much a farmer will produce for various alternative market prices allowing for participation in a land diversion program. The supply curves of all farmers are then aggregated to obtain the marketwide supply curve. The intersection of demand and supply yields market equilibrium.

A land diversion program increases market price and lowers the level of production relative to the competitive outcome. Quasi-rents are increased in the short run. There are good reasons for supposing, however, that with the passage of time the benefits of land diversion programs largely become capitalized into the value of land. The benefits to labor supplied by farm families are likely to be quite limited, even if demand is inelastic. The benefits are negative if demand is elastic. The latter result is of more than passing interest because export markets are of great importance for the very crops for which land diversion programs apply. Long-run demands could well be elastic, which is another way of saying that land diversion programs might seriously impair the competitiveness of U.S. crop producers.

Present-day land diversion programs for feedgrains, wheat, cotton, and rice can be traced back to the soil bank programs of the 1950s and the Emergency Feedgrain Program of 1961. The latter program was an outgrowth of acreage allotment programs that tended to shift acreage from one crop to another without decreasing significantly total farm output and that gave rise to enormous government stocks. The 1970 Farm Bill advanced the somewhat dubious idea that the concentration of benefits among the largest farmers could be lessened through putting an upward limit on the level of deficiency payments that farmers could receive. Loopholes exist that allow the largest farmers to avoid the limitation on the size of payments. Higher market prices generate benefits, at least in the short run, for all farmers regardless of size. More importantly, however, the 1970 bill introduced the idea of deficiency payments based on the difference between a target price and the market price, thus exposing participating farmers to a serious risk. In years of widespread drought, high market prices diminish deficiency payments.

The 1977 Farm Bill was notable for introducing the idea of the Farmer-Owned Reserve for grains as a means for stabilizing commodity markets. Farmers enter grain into the reserve for a 3-year period through the usual nonrecourse loan procedure. The government exerts considerable control over decisions to add to or draw down the level of reserve stocks.

Land diversion programs have been in effect over most of the years since 1956. Many millions of acres were idled annually over the period 1956–1973 and again during 1982–1989. Government expenditures on land diversion programs have often amounted to billions of dollars annually. A disturbing aspect of farm policy has been the tendency to use price support operations to jack up market prices. Government surpluses of farm commodities rise rapidly. Large stocks then became the motivation for idling vast acreages in order to allow moving surplus stocks into consumption and export.

The quantification of the market and welfare effects of land diversion programs for major crops over the last several years poses major problems. Available estimates are neither sufficiently detailed nor precise. In broad terms it appears likely that these programs elevate prices paid by consumers for a variety of foods. Taxpayers have been made worse off. Short-run benefits tend to be concentrated among the largest producers; long-run benefits accrue mainly to landowners. Idled land is wasted land. Land diversion programs are inherently wasteful. Of grave concern is the possibility that land diversion programs have tended to undermine the competitive position of U.S. farmers in international markets. Although these programs have no doubt protected farmers from calamitous drops in income on occasion, as in the decade of the 1980s, the question remains whether alternative programs, such as a simple program of direct payments, would not have worked better.

PROBLEMS

1. For each of the two long-run total cost functions given below, calculate the supply equations and the indirect profit functions. Demonstrate that the first derivatives of the indirect profit functions yield the supply equations.
   (a) $C = 0.4q^2$
   (b) $C = 3q^3$

2. The basic information for this problem and Problems 3, 4, and 5 below is as follows: A farmer has a fixed plant consisting of 100 acres of land. Under competitive conditions the farmer's total variable cost function is $C = q^2$ and the farmer's yield per acre is 0.1. If the farmer participates in a land diversion program, 20 acres must be idled, in which case 80 acres are planted and the total variable cost function becomes $C = 2q^2$.

   Under a voluntary paid land diversion program the farmer has the option of idling 20 acres for a payment equaling 0.4 per acre idled.
   (a) Derive the indirect quasi-rent functions for the farmer with and without program participation.
   (b) Find the indifference price P_i and derive the farmer's supply function allowing for program participation.

3. The basic information is the same as for Problem 2 above. The farmer has the option of participating in a voluntary land diversion program. The payment received is based on acres planted. The payment per acre planted equals a target price minus the market price, all multiplied by the farmer's competitive (established) yield. The latter equals 0.1 per acre, as noted, and the target price equals 16.
   (a) Derive the indirect quasi-rent function assuming program participation.
   (b) Find the indifference price P_i and derive the farmer's supply function allowing for program participation.

4. Given the basic information set forth in Problem 2, find the value of B in a paid land diversion program that would cause the indifference price to equal 10. What would it cost the government, approximately, to secure participation if the market price is just a bit less than 10?

5. Given the basic information set forth in Problem 2, find the value of P^* in a deficiency payment program that would cause the indifference price to equal 10. What would it cost the government, approximately, to secure participation if the market price is just a bit less than 10?

6. *Competitive demand and short-run supply are given by $Q = 10,000 - 750P$ and $Q = 500P$, respectively. There are 1,000 identical farmers, each with 100 acres of cropland. Under a deficiency payment–land diversion program, the farmer has the option of idling 20 acres. The payment per acre planted equals $(P^* - P)\bar{y}$ 80 where $P^* = 13.906$ and $\bar{y}$ equals crop yield in competitive equilibrium. The farmer's total variable cost function with only 80 acres in production is $C = 2q^2$. Find the market equilibrium price and production under the program. How many farmers participate in the program?

7. *Under a voluntary program, the farmer has the option of annually renting his or her *entire* farm to the government for a payment equaling B per acre. Derive the short-run supply function for an individual farmer in light of this option given that land is fixed. Derive the aggregate short-run supply. Analyze the short-run program benefits and costs assuming that in equilibrium some but not all farmers participate in the program.

REFERENCES AND SUGGESTED READINGS

Cochrane, Willard W., and Mary E. Ryan, *American Farm Policy, 1948–1973*, University of Minnesota Press, Minneapolis, 1976.

Gardner, Bruce L., *The Governing of Agriculture*, University Press of Kansas, Lawrence, 1981.

Gardner, Bruce L., ed., *U.S. Agricultural Policy: The 1985 Farm Legislation*, American Enterprise Institute for Public Policy Research, Washington, D.C., 1985.

Hanthorn, Michael, and Joseph W. Glauber, *An Assessment of Marketing Loan Program Options*, U.S. Department of Agriculture, ERS, Agr. Econ. Report No. 581, 1987.

Johnson, D. Gale, ed., *Food and Agricultural Policy for the 1980s*, American Institute for Public Policy Research, Washington, D.C., 1981.

Johnson, Stanley R., Abner W. Womack, William H. Meyers, Robert E. Young, II, and Jon Brandt, "Options for the 1985 Farm Bill: An Analysis and Evaluation," in *U.S. Agricultural Policy: The 1985 Farm Legislation*, American Enterprise Institute for Public Policy Research, Washington, D.C., 1985.

Lee, David R., and Peter G. Helmberger, "Estimating Supply Response in the Presence of Farm Programs," *American Journal of Agricultural Economics*, 67(May 1985):193–203.

Rosine, John, and Peter Helmberger, *An Aggregative Analysis of the U.S. Farm Sector: Past Trends and Future Prospects*, Univ. of Wis. Agr. Exp. Sta. Bul. R2733, June 1975.

U.S. Department of Agriculture, *Agricultural Food Policy Review: Commodity Program Perspectives*, ERS, Agr. Econ. Report No. 530, 1985.

CHAPTER
9

Farm Programs for
Imported Commodities

The previous chapters of this book have centered mainly on U.S. programs for commodities that have historically been exported. In this chapter we focus on policy instruments that can be used to elevate farm prices and incomes for producers of commodities that are both produced domestically and imported on a large scale. Following the pattern set in previous chapters, we first analyze theoretical models designed to generate hypotheses as to the effects of various policy instruments. Attention then centers on the U.S. programs for sugar and wool and the Common Agricultural Policy of the European Community.

9.1 IMPORT QUOTAS, TARIFFS, AND DIRECT PAYMENTS: A COMPARATIVE ANALYSIS

In this section we analyze and compare the economic effects of three alternative programs: import quotas, tariffs, and direct payments. These program alternatives are first examined on the small-country assumption. That is to say, we first assume that variations in U.S. imports do not affect the world price because the United States imports a small proportion of total world exports. The resulting analysis is of value in its own right, but it also serves as a stepping stone to the more difficult case where the United States is a large-world importer, where variation in U.S. imports does affect the world price.

Small-Country Assumption

The U.S. domestic demand and supply for a commodity are given by D and SS_c in part b of Figure 9.1 (ignore for the moment the darkened curves). Subtracting laterally SS_c from D gives the U.S. demand for imports $DMDM$ in part a where M equals imports. The world price is given by P_c, and U.S. buyers are able to buy as much as desired at that price. U.S. transactions do not affect world price. In competitive equilibrium, price equals P_c and the United States consumes Q_3; Q_0 is produced domestically and $(Q_3 - Q_0)$ is imported. By construction $(Q_3 - Q_0)$ equals M_c.

Now suppose that U.S. farmers convince the government of their need for assistance. The objective is to elevate the price received by U.S. farmers to P_0^* in Figure 9.1. An import quota may be used to this end. If U.S. farmers are assured of price P_0^*, they will then increase production from Q_0 to Q_1. What is the maximum level of imports that will assure a price no less than P_0^*? At a price equal to P_0^*, U.S. buyers will want to purchase Q_2. If U.S. farmers produce Q_1, then $(Q_2 - Q_1)$ is the level of quota that will assure a price equal to P_0^* in equilibrium. We assume the quota is allocated gratis among traditional world suppliers in proportion to their exports to the United States in competitive equilibrium. This is important because the domestic price rises above the world level. Other countries will be eager to sell as much as they can in the U.S. market.

Some of the welfare implications of the import quota are readily apparent. Consumers lose area $(a + b + c + d)$. The U.S. farm sector enjoys an increase in quasi-rent in the short run, or increased benefits to farm input suppliers in the long run, equal to area a. The efficiency loss is given by area $(b + c + d)$.

Will foreign suppliers be hurt by this program? If $DMDM$ is inelastic in the relevant range, then the restriction on imports will actually raise total re-

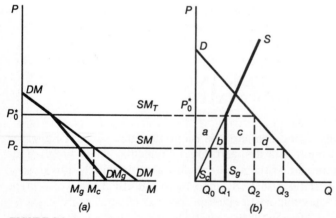

FIGURE 9.1
Effects of import quotas, tariffs, and direct payments for a small importing country.

ceipts to the countries that ship to the United States. It should be borne in mind that whether *DMDM* is inelastic depends on the elasticities of *D* and SS_c.

Some interesting complications may arise. Suppose the imported commodity is an input used in the domestic manufacture of a final consumer good. (Sugar is an important ingredient of candy.) If there is no quota or trade restriction on the final consumer good, the imports of it might rise even as the imports of the raw material decline. What this means, of course, is that demand might be elastic in the long run, when time is allowed for a decline in the relevant domestic food manufacturing industry and a rise in imports of the final good. On the supply side, it would appear likely that the long-run supply is more elastic than the short-run supply. All things considered, whether *DMDM* is construed as a short-run or long-run demand is likely critical to the question whether total receipts to foreign suppliers rise or fall as a result of an import quota. Moreover, if the U.S. domestic demand is sufficiently flat or elastic in the long run, because of imports of the final product, then it might not be possible to raise significantly the raw product price through an import quota.

We now turn to a tariff as an alternative means for elevating the price to U.S. farmers from P_c to P_0^*. A tariff shifts the supply curve for imports upwards. The curve labeled *SM* in part *a* of Figure 9.1 may be shifted upward as far as desired through raising a tariff. Think of it this way. The importing firms in the United States must pay P_c in order to secure possession of the commodity in the world market. They must then pay the tariff for the privilege of bringing the commodity into the United States. (The effects of a tariff could, alternatively, be analyzed as causing the demand *DMDM* to contract.) How high must the tariff be in order to raise the U.S. price to P_0^*? Clearly the answer is $(P_0^* - P_c)$ such that the new supply of imports to U.S. buyers is given by SM_T. With the U.S. price thus raised to P_0^*, consumers lower their purchases from Q_3 to Q_2. Since U.S. producers expand supply from Q_0 to Q_1, imports fall from $(Q_3 - Q_0)$ to $(Q_2 - Q_1)$.

The welfare implications of a tariff equal to $(P_0^* - P_c)$ differ in one important respect from those of an import quota equaling $(Q_2 - Q_1)$. Under the tariff, consumers lose area $(a + b + c + d)$ and U.S. producers gain area a, just as in the case of the import quota. Notice, however, that the U.S. government collects tariff receipts equal to area c or $(P_0^* - P_c)(Q_2 - Q_1)$. This represents a benefit to U.S. taxpayers. *Because of tariff receipts, the deadweight loss equals area (b + d), which is obviously less than the loss caused by the import quota.* Presumably, the exporting countries would much prefer the quota to a tariff because then the area c accrues to them instead of to U.S. taxpayers.

From the selfish viewpoint of U.S. interests, a tariff appears to have a distinct advantage over a quota. As we shall now discover, however, a direct payment program may have an advantage over a tariff.

Suppose the government uses a direct payment program, setting the target price at P_0^*. Taking advantage of the developments in Chapter 4, we see that this changes the U.S. supply from SS_c to the kinked, darkened curve

SS_g in part b of Figure 9.1. Subtracting laterally SS_g from D yields the new kinked demand for imports $DMDM_g$ in part a. The new equilibrium in the world market is given by the intersection of $DMDM_g$ and SM. The equilibrium world price is unaffected, but U.S. imports fall from M_c to M_g. With price left unaffected, U.S. consumers buy Q_3. U.S. farmers expand output from Q_0 to Q_1 and by construction, $(Q_1 - Q_0)$ equals $(M_c - M_g)$.

Under direct payments, producers gain area a, just as in the case of the import quota and the tariff. Taxpayers lose area $(a + b)$, but consumers lose nothing at all. The efficiency loss therefore equals area b, which is, of course, less than for either a tariff or a quota. It should not be supposed, however, that a direct payment program is necessarily to be preferred to a tariff or even a quota. It is likely the case for farm programs in general that the distributional consequences are of much greater significance to politicians than are the deadweight or efficiency losses, which seem to be of interest mainly to economists.

Large-Country Assumption

Having derived the main results for the case of a small importer, we now take up the more general and somewhat more complex case of a large importer, where variation in imports causes variation in world prices. Many of the insights gained from the previous case carry over to this one, but there is at least one new result that may be surprising. Tariffs and direct payments might actually give rise to efficiency gains!

The U.S. domestic demand D, supply SS_c, and export demand $DMDM$ are given in Figure 9.2. The competitive supply curve for imports given by SM_c in part a is now assumed, however, to be upward-sloping. The more the United States buys from other countries, the higher the price that must be

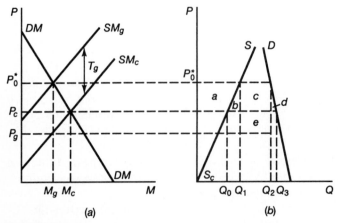

FIGURE 9.2
Effects of import quotas and tariffs for a large importing country.

paid. Competitive equilibrium is given by the intersection of the demand for imports $DMDM$ and the supply for imports SM_c. The competitive world price is given by P_c. U.S. farmers produce Q_0; U.S. consumers buy Q_3; and $(Q_3 - Q_0)$ is imported. By construction, $(Q_3 - Q_0) = M_c$.

Drawing upon analysis of the previous case, we note that the U.S. government can use an import quota equal to $(Q_2 - Q_1)$ in order to elevate the U.S. price from P_c to P_0^*. Consumers suffer a loss equal to area $(a + b + c + d)$; the U.S. farm industry enjoys an increase in benefits equal to area a. The deadweight loss is given by area $(b + c + d)$.

To facilitate analysis of a tariff, we let the competitive supply and demand for imports be given by

$$P_d = a - bM$$

$$P_s = c + dM \tag{9.1}$$

The equilibrium price P and level of imports M can be found using the competitive equilibrium conditions $P_d = P_s = P$. Suppose, however, that the United States places a tariff equal to T per unit on imports. Then $P_s + T = P_d$ because importers must pay P_s in order to gain possession of the commodity in the world market and T per unit for the privilege of selling in the U.S. market. Rearranging, we have $P_s = P_d - T$. Substitute the right-hand side of this equation for P_s in the supply for imports given by system (9.1), letting $P = P_d$. This yields the new model of import demand and supply:

$$P = a - bM$$

$$P = (c + T) + dM \tag{9.2}$$

Solving for M and P, we have

$$M = \frac{1}{b + d}(a - c - T)$$

$$P = \frac{1}{b + d}(ad + bc + bT) \tag{9.3}$$

Clearly, M falls and P rises with increases in the tariff T.

In terms of graphic analysis, increases in T cause the supply for imports in part a of Figure 9.2, to rise from the competitive position SM_c. Upward shifts in SM cause price to rise and imports to fall. How high must T be raised to elevate the U.S. price from P_c to P_0^*? Using graphic analysis, we shift SM up to the point, keeping its slope the same, where it intersects $DMDM$ at the price P_0^*. The vertical distance between SM_g and SM_c equals a particular value for T, namely T_g, that just yields the desired price P_0^*. (Using algebra, we can set P in (9.3) equal to P_0^* and solve for T_g.)

As in the case of an import quota equal to $(Q_2 - Q_1)$, a tariff equal to T_g raises the U.S. price to P_0^*. U.S. farmers expand output from Q_0 to Q_1. U.S. consumers reduce consumption from Q_3 to Q_2. Imports fall from $(Q_3 - Q_0)$ to $(Q_2 - Q_1)$. By construction $(Q_3 - Q_0) = M_c$ and $(Q_2 - Q_1) = M_g$. The world price is reduced from P_c to P_g in part a of Figure 9.2, whether a quota or tariff is used to elevate the U.S. price.

Turning to benefit-cost analysis, we see that the tariff, like the quota, generates a consumer loss in the United States equal to area $(a + b + c + d)$; U.S. farmers again gain area a. To figure the increase in treasury receipts from the tariff we recall that the vertical distance between SM_c and SM_g equals T_g in part a. Clearly, T_g equals $(P_0^* - P_g)$. Therefore, since imports equal $(Q_2 - Q_1)$, the tariff take equals area $(c + e)$ in part b. Adding up the costs and benefits gives the efficiency loss, which equals area $(b + d - e)$. Could the loss be negative? Part b in Figure 9.2 is drawn such that area e does indeed exceed area $(b + d)$; the "loss" is negative. In one fell swoop, the U.S. government can generate a benefit to the domestic farm sector and an increase in treasury receipts that exceeds the consumer loss. *A tariff can generate an efficiency gain.*

On the small-country assumption, a tariff inevitably leads to a deadweight or efficiency loss. On the large-country assumption, it is at least possible that a tariff leads to an efficiency gain. Why the difference? As all young budding economists should know, both monopoly theory and dominant firm theory teach that a large buyer (perhaps competing with a fringe of small buyers) purchasing from a competitive selling industry has market power and might be able to use that power to earn excess profit. The large (monopsonistic) buyer takes advantage of the difference between the price and the marginal cost of an input. In the present model, the United States is rather like a dominant firm, placing a tariff on the commodity in question, causing the price paid to decline, and reaping an efficiency gain.

Care must be exercised, however, in reaching the conclusion that tariffs constitute good public policy. An old cliché regarding sauced geese comes readily to mind. What might be good for one larger buyer such as the United States might be good for other large buyers as well. If the United States places a tariff on automobiles from Japan, why shouldn't the latter place a tariff on U.S. wheat? If all large buyers in the world market try to secure benefits through tariffs, the result will surely be a serious diminution of free trade and the efficiency gains that can be had through comparative advantage. At bottom, our assumption that the buying and selling decisions of the rest of the world can be modeled using demand-and-supply relationships, as in Figures 9.1 and 9.2, is restrictive in that the world market is not characterized by a large number of relatively small, helpless buyers and sellers. The competitive model must be viewed as a rough approximation.

The assumptions of the model given in Figure 9.2 are restrictive in other ways as well. A tariff need not give rise to an efficiency gain even if the United States is the only large buyer in a sea of otherwise atomistic competition. Bothering signs, the U.S. demand and supply in Figure 9.2 are steeply inclined so that a relatively large increase in the domestic price, caused by imposition of a tariff, reduces imports by a small amount. Because the supply for imports SM_c is upward-sloping, reduced imports cause the world price to fall. Importantly, the reduction in U.S. imports is determined solely by U.S. demand and supply and the target price P_0^*. For a given reduction of imports, the fall in the world price depends on the slope of the import supply SM_c. The steeper the slope, the greater the decline and the larger the tariff take.

The student should continue, however, to recognize the distributional consequences of a tariff. Taxpayers, farmers, and farm input suppliers might indeed benefit from a tariff, but consumers end up paying higher prices.

We now compare the effects of a tariff with those of direct payments, keeping the welfare gain to U.S. farmers the same in both cases. The competitive demand and supply curves together with a tariff equal to T_g from Figure 9.2 are reproduced in Figure 9.3. A direct payment program with target price equal to P_0^* causes the U.S. supply curve to shift from SS_c to the kinked curve SS_g, as in part b. As explained previously, this shifts the U.S. demand for imports from $DMDM$ to the kinked curve $DMDM_g$ in part a. A direct payment program causes the world and U.S. domestic price to fall from the competitive level (not shown in Figure 9.3 in order to avoid clutter) to the price P_p given by the intersection of $DMDM_g$ and SM_c. The resulting world price P_p is higher than the world price under the tariff, P_g. U.S. farmers produce the same amount Q_1 in either case. Because direct payments lower the U.S. market

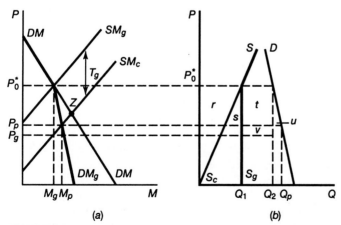

FIGURE 9.3
Effects of tariffs and direct payments for a large importing country.

price, as well as the world price, U.S. consumers enjoy a higher level of consumption with direct payments Q_p than with a tariff Q_2.

Relative to the tariff outcome, direct payments increase benefits to U.S. consumers by the area $(r + s + t + u)$. U.S. producer benefits are the same in both cases. Direct payments cost the U.S. taxpayers area $(r + s)$ plus the tariff receipts, area $(t + v)$, that must now be given up. Relative to the tariff outcome, direct payments lead to an efficiency loss given by the area $(u - v)$. Could this "loss" be negative? Could area u exceed area v? To see the answer to this question, consider a rotation of SM_c around the point Z in part a. That is to say, consider changing the slope of SM_c but always making sure that it intersects $DMDM$ at point Z. As we make SM_c flatter, the world and U.S. market price under direct payments rises above P_p; the area u tends to get smaller, but it does not disappear. Area v, on the other hand, tends to vanish as SM_c gets flatter, and we know that in the extreme case, where SM_c is perfectly flat, the tariff efficiency loss exceeds the direct payment efficiency loss. *We conclude that if the supply for imports from the rest of the world is sufficiently flat, the efficiency loss caused by a tariff will exceed the efficiency loss caused by direct payments.*

Is it possible that the efficiency loss (gain) from direct payments would ever exceed (be less than) the efficiency loss (gain) resulting from a tariff? The answer is yes if only SM_c is sufficiently steep. Problem 2 from the exercises at the end of the chapter provides an example in which both direct payments and a tariff lead to efficiency gains but where the gain from the tariff exceeds that from direct payments.

9.2   THE U.S. SUGAR PROGRAM

Only rarely in the nation's history has Uncle Sam been able to keep his sticky fingers off the sugar market. In 1789, the government imposed a tariff on imported sugar, and, except for a few years in the early 1890s, we have had tariffs ever since. The tariffs were seen at first as a means for raising government revenue, but by 1894, the objective had veered away from raising revenue in favor of subsidizing the domestic beet and cane sugar producers. The Sugar Act of 1934 as amended set the stage for sugar policy for many years. The main provision of the resulting programs involved assigning sugar quotas to domestic areas and foreign countries. Other provisions involved benefit payments to growers, acreage restrictions, an excise tax on sugar, minimum wages for field workers, and the protection of children from labor exploitation.

In 1974 world sugar supplies were tight, and the sugar program was allowed to expire at the end of the year. The period from 1976 to 1980 was characterized by considerable price volatility; sugar policy was something of a muddle, with no clear-cut or consistent strategy. All of that changed with the 1981 Act, however, which established a sugar program that harked back to those established under the 1934 act. The main instrument is strict quotas on sugar imports.

According to a study by Ives and Hurley, with the U.S. Department of Commerce, the current sugar program has (1) maintained the domestic price of sugar at several times the world level; (2) cost consumers more than $3 billion annually; (3) encouraged a 40 percent rise in imports of some sugar-containing products (candy, for example) that compete with domestically produced products; (4) caused a sharp reduction in raw sugar imports; and (5) caused a 40 percent reduction of the U.S. sugar refining industry.

Amplifying some of the above points, we note that over the 6-year period 1982–1987, following the 1981 act, the average annual world price of raw sugar equaled 6.37 cents per pound. This was 30 percent of the corresponding average for the United States, which equaled 21.16 cents. High sugar prices encouraged consumers and food manufacturers to switch to sugar substitutes. Over the period 1982–1987, U.S. per capita sugar consumption declined 15.6 percent, from 73.7 to 62.2 pounds; U.S. per capita consumption of high-fructose corn syrup, on the other hand, increased by 79.8 percent, from 26.3 to 47.3 pounds. Per capital consumption of low-caloric sweeteners expanded as well. It is possible, of course, that sugar substitutes would have laid claim to an increasing share of the sweeteners market even in the absence of the sugar program. If so, high sugar prices have surely had the effect of speeding the process along.

High sugar prices in the United States, relative to the world market, also encouraged the substitution of imported sugar-containing products for those produced domestically. There are many such products including candy, animal feed, syrups, and cookies and cakes. The imports of sugar-containing products increased dramatically after passage of the 1981 act. In the 6-year period prior to 1981, the imports of sugar-containing products increased by 39.3 percent. The corresponding increase for the 6-year period following 1981 was 220.9 percent. Many factors, including changes in the trade value of the dollar, were likely responsible for the large increase in the imports of sugar-containing products. The high domestic sugar price was one factor among several.

If the U.S. demand for imports were inelastic in the relevant range, then import quotas would have increased total revenue to the sugar exporters, our three largest suppliers being the Dominican Republic, the Philippines, and Guatemala. Given the substitution possibilities in both U.S. sugar production and sugar consumption, it seems likely that the long-run demand for sugar imports is elastic. In any event, the evidence suggests that quota-holding countries, most of whom are desperately poor, have been badly hurt by the U.S. sugar program. Regarding these countries, Ives and Hurley write (p. 41):

> While they have received a price substantially above the world price for exports to the U.S., they have seen sharply lower sales. In 1988, the United States will import from the CBI countries [Caribbean basin nations, excluding Cuba] and the Philippines about one-fifth of the amount it purchased in the year before the quota program began. For the first twelve-month quota, imports from the thirteen countries were limited to 1.36 million tons, representing foreign exchange earnings of $518 mil-

lion. By the 1985/1986 quota, imports were restricted to 871,000 tons, equivalent to $331 million. The 1988 quota limits imports to 483,500 tons, with an approximate value of $140 million. (The information in brackets was added.)

Turning to benefit-cost analysis, we note that according to Babcock and Schmitz, the sugar program resulted in consumer losses of $2.7 billion and producer benefits of $1.35 billion in 1983. The efficiency or deadweight loss was estimated at $1.35 billion. The production of sugar is heavily concentrated among large producers, reflecting the backward integration of sugar processing mills into sugar production. This means that program benefits are also heavily concentrated among the largest producers. The four largest Florida processor-growers accounted for roughly 11 percent of total U.S. sugar production in 1983. On the assumption they received an equal percentage of the producer benefits estimated by Babcock and Schmitz, these four processor-growers enjoyed benefits as sugar producers averaging $37.1 million dollars in 1983. Thirteen processor-growers in Hawaii accounted for roughly 18 percent of total U.S. sugar production in 1983. If we assume they also received an equal percentage of total producer benefits for that year, then the average benefit for the 13 was $18.7 million. A more refined benefit-cost analysis would need to take an explicit account of the short-run losses to processor-growers caused by the reduced demand for sugar refining capacity.

9.3   THE U.S. WOOL PROGRAM

The legislative authority for the present wool program is the National Wool Act of 1954, as amended and extended by the Food Security Act of 1985. Prior to 1954, the price of wool was supported through a market price support program, which resulted in large government-owned stocks of wool. (Large and growing government stocks of farm commodities have often been the immediate cause of changes in farm programs.) The 1954 act described wool as "an essential and strategic commodity which is not produced in quantities and qualities in the United States to meet the domestic needs." In 1977 the Wool Act was amended to say that wool is not only an essential and strategic commodity but that it is energy-efficient as well! Here, as is so often the case in farm policy, the official reasons given for having a farm program are not to be taken seriously.

The wool program uses direct payments in order to bring the average price received by all wool producers up to an announced target level. (A producer need not receive the average price, of course.) Let P^* and P equal the target and market price, respectively. The payment rate per dollar of wool sold PR is then defined as

$$PR = \frac{P^* - P}{P} \qquad (9.4)$$

The direct payment to the ith producer is given by $PR(P_i q_i)$ where P_i equals the market price received by the ith producer and q_i equals annual output. Take an example. In 1985 the target price (it's called the support price in the literature) was $1.65 per pound. The average *market* price received by all producers equaled $0.633. The payment rate PR, calculated using (9.4), equaled 1.607. If the ith producer received 90 cents per pound for high-quality wool in the marketplace, then the direct payment per pound equaled (1.607) (90¢) or $1.45; the *effective* price received by the farmer equaled $2.35, the sum of the payment rate and the market price. If the ith producer received 50 cents per pound for low-quality wool, then the direct payment per pound equaled 80 cents, which when added to the market price received meant an effective farm price of $1.30. The market price differential between high- and low-quality wool was 40 cents per pound. The market indicated to the producer that high-quality wool was, at the margin, worth 40 cents per pound more than was low-quality wool. Under the wool program this information was distorted in that the effective price differential at the farm level was increased to $1.05. Clearly, the present program for wool encourages the production of high-quality wool more than it does the production of low-quality wool.

Table 9.1 provides information pertinent to the wool program for the years 1970–1988. The direct payment per pound varied considerably over this period from 0 to 111.2 cents, exceeding the market price itself in 8 of the 19 years. The direct payments are concentrated among the largest producers, as we would expect. In 1985, 27,832 wool producers, the smallest producers, received payments averaging $53; the largest 43 producers received payments averaging $151,569.

In spite of heavy subsidization, U.S. wool production has declined steadily. Sheep producers receive about 75 percent of their sheep income from selling lambs for meat. The lamb market has been depressed for several reasons, including keen competition from abroad.

Figure 9.4 can be used to guide some approximate benefit-cost calculations under 1985 economic conditions. To simplify matters we assume wool is homogeneous and that the short-run supply curve S is linear. In response to the $1.65 target price, the wool industry produced 88 million pounds in 1985. How much would the industry have produced had there been no program? To answer this question we note that the demand confronting U.S. wool producers is perfectly elastic at the world price. This is so because the U.S. now imports more wool than it produces domestically and, more importantly, because the U.S. accounts for less than 2 percent of world production. The market price for wool is determined in a world market. In the absence of the wool program the 1985 price of wool would still have equaled about 63.3 cents per pound.

A study by the U.S. Department of Agriculture suggests that the elasticity of the short-run supply equals 0.3. Consider the formula for the arc elasticity of supply:

TABLE 9.1.
Wool: shorn wool production, support price, average market price received by producers, direct payment, total government payments, U.S., 1970–1988

Year	Shorn wool production (million lb)	Support price (cents/lb)	Market price received (cents/lb)	Direct payment (cents/lb)	Total government payments[a] (million $)
1970	161.6	72	35.5	36.5	64.0
1971	160.2	72	19.4	52.6	102.3
1972	158.5	72	35.0	37.0	68.0
1973	143.7	72	82.7	0.0	0.0
1974	131.4	72	59.1	12.9	14.5
1975	119.5	72	44.7	27.3	40.9
1976	111.1	72	65.7	6.3	7.0
1977	107.3	99	72.0	27.0	28.9
1978	102.9	108	74.5	33.5	36.1
1979	104.9	115	86.3	28.7	30.8
1980	105.4	123	88.1	34.9	37.5
1981	109.8	135	94.5	40.5	47.0
1982	106.1	137	68.4	68.6	71.9
1983	102.9	153	61.3	91.7	116.9
1984	95.5	165	79.5	85.5	92.3
1985	87.9	165[b]	63.3	101.7	103.8
1986	84.8	178	66.8	111.2	106.9
1987	84.7	181	91.7	89.3	84.5
1988	89.2	178	138.0	40.0	41.4

[a]Includes unshorn lamb payments and promotion deductions.

[b]Altered to comply with Gramm-Rudman.

Source: Agricultural Stabilization and Conservation Service, *ASCS Commodity Fact Sheet: Wool; Summary of 1989 Support Program and Related Information*, U.S. Department of Agriculture, April 1989.

$$AE = \frac{Q_0 - Q_1}{Q_0 + Q_1} \div \frac{P_0 - P_1}{P_0 + P_1} \qquad (9.5)$$

We take Q_0 and P_0 as the quantity and price with the program in effect and Q_1 and P_1 as quantity and price absent the program. We know that Q_0 equals 88 million pounds; P_0 equals \$1.65; P_1 equals 63.3 cents; and AE equals 0.3. Solving for Q_1, we have Q_1 equals 67.3 million pounds.

Using the formula for computing the area of a rectangle, we find that area *a* (Figure 9.4) equals \$68.4 million; area *b* equals \$10.5 million. The estimated short-run loss to wool producers due to termination of the wool program equals \$79 million, which exceeds the market value of production. Consumers are unaffected in that the demand for U.S. wool is perfectly elastic. Termination of the program would save the government \$89 million and yield a \$10 million gain in "economic efficiency." (The discrepancy between the estimated tax saving and the total government payments given in Table 9.1 is explained in part by footnote *a* of the table.) Notice that the efficiency gain as a

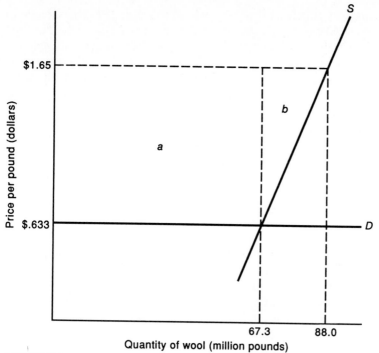

FIGURE 9.4
Welfare effects of U.S. wool program.

percentage of the producer loss equals 12.7 percent. The corresponding percentage for the sugar program is 50.0 percent. These research results support theoretical analysis, which, recalling that the sugar program relies on import quotas, suggests that import quotas are an inefficient means for generating farm sector benefits relative to direct payments.

Aside from being rough and ready, the above applied welfare analysis is limited to the short run. Long-run analysis would require knowledge of the long-run supply function.

9.4 THE COMMON AGRICULTURAL POLICY OF THE EUROPEAN COMMUNITY

We now turn to the Common Agricultural Policy (CAP) of the European Community (EC). Less now than it once was, this policy is an excellent example of a program that places heavy reliance on tariffs to elevate farm prices and returns to farm resources.

The CAP has its genesis in the Treaty of Rome signed in 1957. Under this treaty a customs union was formed by six nations: Belgium, France, West Germany, Italy, Luxembourg, and the Netherlands. These nations were later joined by Denmark, Ireland, and the United Kingdom in 1973; by Greece in 1981; and by Portugal and Spain in 1986. (The ten members of the customs union prior to 1986 will be referred to later as the EC-10.) A customs union is a form of economic integration that requires the elimination of all internal tariffs, import quotas, and other trade impediments; the abolition of impediments to flows of capital and labor among member countries; the creation of a common external tariff on trade with nonparticipating countries; and the apportionment of tariff revenues among the member countries according to an agreed formula. The objective behind the creation of the EC was to allow free competition to flourish in a large geographic area that had historically been riddled with trade impediments during times of peace and trenches during times of war. Aside from the benefits of greater political cooperation, a customs union of the size of the EC can claim many economic benefits including mainly the efficiency gains from the free operation of comparative advantage in a large market.

The CAP has been a major manifestation of European economic integration, having become fully operational in the late 1960s. Although each commodity program has its own unique features and institutions, three policy instruments lie at the heart of major programs for cereals, dairy products, beef and veal, and sugar. First, the CAP relies heavily on market price supports achieved through government purchases and removals. Support levels are referred to as *intervention prices* in the EC. A network of intervention centers throughout the EC has been established in order to purchase commodities at intervention prices and to store the resulting surpluses for later resale and disposal.

Second, tariffs are used to prevent imports from undercutting high domestic prices and taking advantage of price support operations. A tariff is set equal to the pegged internal price minus world price on a daily basis. Since the latter varies the tariff varies as well and it is therefore referred to as a variable levy. Such a system provides stability and protection to the domestic market regardless of the volatility of world prices.

A third important instrument of the CAP is the widespread use of export subsidies, referred to as *export restitutions* in the EC. Export subsidies equaling the differences between domestic and world prices are needed to move surpluses from storage to the international market.

Understanding what the economic consequences of the CAP have been over the last two decades requires that careful attention be given to both short-run and long-run analysis. We propose to undertake such analyses with the aid of Figure 9.5, which will prove to be not nearly as complicated as it might first appear.

Let the demand and short-run supply for the EC be given by DD_e and SRS_e in part *b*. The short-run supply function for farm output is often judged to be highly price inelastic, and for simplicity we imagine SRS_e is perfectly inelastic. Long-run supply is given by LRS_e. Corresponding to DD_e and SRS_e is the short-run offer curve given by $XSXD$ in part *a*, with that part of the curve

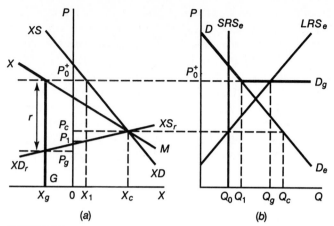

FIGURE 9.5
Short-run and long-run effects of the EC's common agricultural policy.

in the first quadrant, labeled XD, being the EC's short-run demand for imports and that part in the second quadrant, labeled XS, being the EC's short-run supply for exports. The offer curve for the rest of the world is given by $XD_r XS_r$ in part a. That part of the curve in the first quadrant, labeled XS_r, is the rest of the world's (ROW's) supply of exports to the EC. That part of the curve given in the second quadrant, labeled XD_r, is the ROW's demand for exports from the EC. The EC's long-run offer curve is given by XM. In worldwide short-run equilibrium, price equals P_c, given by the intersection of XD and XS_r. The EC imports $(Q_c - Q_0)$, which equals X_c by construction. (Figure 9.5 was drawn such that the short-run market equilibrium is also the long-run equilibrium.)

We next suppose a farm program (the CAP) is begun with the objective of raising the price to EC farmers from P_c to P_0^+ (Figure 9.5). This can easily be done by placing a tariff on imports of such magnitude as to force the EC price up to P_0^+. If imports are lowered through a tariff from $(Q_c - Q_0)$ to $(Q_1 - Q_0)$, then the EC price will be elevated to P_0^+ in the short run. Following the analysis developed earlier in this chapter, we know that the tariff must be set at such level as to elevate XS_r (see part a) to the point where it intersects XD at price P_0^+. The tariff must therefore be set equal to $(P_0^+ - P_1)$. Farmers will be happy, at least for the moment, and tariff revenue to the EC equals $(P_0^+ - P_1) X_1$.

The program raises quasi-rents and increases the returns to family labor above the transfer earnings of marginal farmers. This means that additional European households will want to organize family farms. With an inelastic supply of land, land prices and rents rise as land is farmed more intensely than before. Farm production in the EC expands. As the short-run supply shifts to the right, the EC eventually becomes self-sufficient with EC farmers producing Q_1 in part b. At this point, tariff receipts dry up and the tariff (the variable levy) can no longer be counted on as an effective instrument of policy. New devices must be brought to bear on the process of price determination.

Enter the market price support program. The intervention price is set at P_0^+, with the EC promising to buy unlimited quantities at this price. The EC's domestic demand changes from DD_e to the darkened, kinked curve DD_g. Its long-run offer curve changes from XM to the darkened, kinked curve XG. In long-run equilibrium, the EC price is maintained at P_0^+; EC production rises from Q_0 to Q_g; and EC consumption falls from Q_c to Q_1. The world price falls from P_c to P_g. A tariff equal to or slightly exceeding $(P_0^+ - P_g)$ will be sufficient to protect the EC market from cheap imports. The EC no longer imports X_c but instead exports its surplus $(Q_g - Q_1)$. By construction, $(Q_g - Q_1) = X_g$. Since the domestic price exceeds the world price, an export subsidy or restitution per unit of output equal to r in part a must be paid to move EC surpluses into the world market. Instead of being a source of funds, as in the short run, the CAP has become a cause of expenditure.

Aside from disturbing influences, this appears to be the essential history of the CAP. With a major assist from technological change, the CAP has turned the EC from a major importer of temperate zone products into a major exporter. According to a study by the Australian Bureau of Agricultural Economics, the EC market price support level for wheat exceeded the world price by 65 percent over the period 1967–68 through 1982–83. The corresponding percentage for barley and maize was 56 percent. As a recent example, we note that for January 1989 the U.S. farm-level price for wheat equaled $150.27 per metric ton. The EC import levy and domestic price support level equaled, respectively, $133.41 and $199.68, both on a metric ton basis. The EC export subsidy, the real-world counterpart to r in part a of Figure 9.5, equaled $67.27 per metric ton.

Controls over production in the EC have been practically nonexistent, and agricultural production since the late 1960s has risen consistently by about 2 percent a year; EC consumption, on the other hand, has risen annually by only 0.5 percent a year. The study by the Australian Bureau of Agricultural Economics estimated that the CAP has lowered world prices of temperate zone products by 16 percent on average.

The above findings are consistent with the data given in Table 9.2. Over the period 1970–1986, the EC-10 switched from being a net importer of beef, butter, total grain, and wheat to a net exporter. The EC-10 imports of total grain, for example, amounted to 18.7 percent of total world grain exports in 1970; EC-10 exports equaled 9.5 percent of world exports in 1986. In the case of soybeans, the EC has remained a large world importer, but, importantly, there is no variable levy on soybeans. Because of the General Agreement on Tariffs and Trade, many feedgrain substitutes enter the EC either duty-free or at a low rate. Since prices of feedgrains in the EC are high relative to world prices, EC farmers have been eager to purchase the feedgrain substitutes that escape tariffs upon entering their market. Such substitutes include soybean

TABLE 9.2
Total world exports and EC-10 and U.S. net trade, selected farm commodities, 1970 and 1986[a]

| | Net trade (1,000 metric tons) | | | | | |
| | Total world | | EC-10 | | U.S. | |
Commodity	1970	1986	1970	1986	1970	1986
Beef	2,900	4,841	−593	485	−806	−745
Butter	947	1,227	−46	215	3	24
Soybeans	12,571	26,065	−5,671	−9,808	11,773	20,142
Total grain	119,236	204,683	−22,308	19,534	39,802	63,388
Wheat	56,479	100,925	−6,456	15,190	20,140	27,569

[a]EC-10 does not include Portugal and Spain. See text.

Source: Mark Newman, Tom Fulton, and Lewrene Glaser, *A Comparison of Agriculture in the United States and the European Community*, Economic Research Service, U.S. Department of Agriculture, June 1987.

and other oilseed meals, corn gluten feed, and manioc. (Manioc or cassava comes from a tropical plant with starchy roots grown mainly in Thailand.) In 1982, the EC negotiated voluntary export restraints with major suppliers that severely reduced EC imports of manioc. Of great concern to countries supplying feedgrain substitutes is the growing subsidization of oilseed production in the EC through direct payments. The production of oilseeds in the EC has increased sharply since 1981.

Now that the EC has changed from being a net importer of several major farm commodities to a net exporter, the budget cost of elevating farm prices has soared. (The cost to consumers was always high.) More in response to budget strain, it seems, than to complaints about unfair competition from competing food exporters and exploited consumers, the governing bodies of the EC have been looking for ways of cutting back or at least holding in check farm subsidies. Some restraint has been shown in determining market price support levels, with reductions made mandatory by increases in production beyond targeted levels. Milk production quotas were assigned to dairy farms in 1984 as an alternative to a sharp reduction in the support level. Land set-aside programs have been recently envisaged for the grains.

Increasingly, the EC is looking toward the so-called coresponsibility levies as a means of defraying program costs. *Coresponsibility levies* are producer taxes used to partially finance export subsidies. For an analysis of such levies, the reader is referred to Section 4.5 of Chapter 4. That section discusses the economic effects of assessments on U.S. dairy farmers intended in part to lower treasury outlays on the support program for milk components allocated to manufacturing. A major conclusion is that a 5 percent assessment or levy on producer receipts is less effective in lowering surpluses than is a 5 percent reduction in the support level. Also, the levy tends to increase the proportion of producer benefits financed by consumers in comparison with a lowered support level. A coresponsibility levy already assessed in the EC's sugar program was extended to milk in 1977 and to grains in 1986.

Finally, although recently emerging as a major exporter of farm products, the EC remains the largest market for U.S. farm exports, particularly for oilseeds and oilseed products, animal feeds, and grains. At present, the EC continues to be a net importer of tea, coffee, and bananas.

9.5   SUMMARY

Farm commodity programs that are used to elevate farm prices and quasi-rents vary depending on whether the commodity is exported or imported. This chapter, in contrast to previous chapters, centers on programs that are of interest mainly for farm commodities that are both produced domestically and imported on a large scale. Sugar and wool in the United States are prime examples.

The policy instruments of main interest are import quotas, tariffs, and direct payments. Consider a set of programs that generate the same level of benefits to the farm sector. If we assume that the United States is a small-world importer, such that variation in U.S. imports has no affect on the world price, then it can be shown that a direct payment program is the most efficient way of generating benefits to the farm sector, followed by tariffs and import quotas in that order. Direct payments increase domestic production but keep the consumer price at the world level. Tariffs and quotas elevate the domestic price above the world price, but tariffs bring in revenue to the treasury, allowing taxes to fall. Import quotas allow foreign countries to sell their imports to the United States at the high domestic price. The total revenue to foreign suppliers rises if the U.S. demand for exports is inelastic in the relevant range and falls if demand is elastic.

The results of theoretical analysis change in some important respects if we assume that the U.S. is a large-world importer, where variation in its imports do affect appreciably the world price. That import quotas are the least efficient way of generating farm sector benefits continues to be the case. It can be shown, however, that tariffs and direct payments can actually lead to efficiency gains if only the supply of imports to the United States is sufficiently steep. Too much can be made, however, of the possible efficiency gains from tariffs and direct payments. If all the large trading partners in the world community try to secure such gains, the result would surely be the loss of efficiency associated with comparative advantage and free trade.

Three real-world programs are considered that illustrate the use of policy instruments for farm commodities that are both imported and produced domestically. The U.S. programs for sugar and wool illustrate import quotas and direct payments. The European Community's Common Agricultural Policy illustrates the use of tariffs. Import quotas on sugar have raised U.S. sugar prices far above world levels, which has (1) cost U.S. consumers billions of dollars annually; (2) caused the imports of sugar-containing products, such as candy, and the consumption of high-fructose corn syrup to increase sharply;

and (3) caused the total receipts to foreign suppliers to fall off drastically. Unfortunately, the foreign suppliers of sugar to the United States are some of the poorest nations of the world, such as the Dominican Republic, the Philippines, and Guatemala. These nations desperately need foreign exchange to further their economic development. The main beneficiaries of the U.S. sugar program are the large sugar companies that have integrated cane sugar production and milling. These companies each receive benefits amounting to several million dollars annually as a result of the program.

The U.S. wool program uses direct payments to elevate the effective prices received by producers. Because of the manner in which the calculations are made, the program subsidizes more heavily producers of high-quality wool than it does the low-quality producers. Over the period 1980–1988, the market price of wool averaged 53.8 percent of the support or target price. As would be expected, payments are heavily concentrated among the largest wool producers.

The European Community (EC) is a customs union (free-trade area) formed in 1957 by the Treaty of Rome and now consisting of 12 countries. The EC's Common Agricultural Policy (CAP), which became operational in the late 1960s, relied on tariffs to elevate the prices received by EC farmers for a wide range of farm products. Tariffs were effective because the EC was a food deficit region. Due both to a high price policy and technological growth, the EC has become a food surplus region and a large food exporter. Protection of the EC farm sector now requires, in addition to tariffs, price support programs and export subsidies. High budgetary costs appear to be pushing the CAP in the direction of production controls and land diversion programs.

PROBLEMS

1. U.S. demand and supply are given by $Q_0 = 10 - P$ and $Q_s = \frac{1}{4}P$, respectively. The United States is a small-world importer. The world price equals 4. Transportation costs and multiple currencies are ignored. Find the equilibrium U.S. price, production, consumption, imports, and receipts to foreign suppliers under the following regimes:
   (a) Perfect competition.
   (b) A quota is placed on imports causing the U.S. price to rise to 7. Calculate the consumer loss, producer gain, and the efficiency loss.
   (c) A tariff is placed on imports causing the U.S. price to rise to 7. Calculate the consumer loss, producer gain, tariff receipts, and the efficiency loss.
   (d) The target price is set equal to 7 under a direct payment program. Calculate the consumer gain, producer gain, taxpayer loss, and efficiency loss.
2. U.S. demand and supply are given by $Q_d = 10 - P$ and $Q_s = \frac{1}{4}P$, respectively. The supply of imports to the United States is $M = 1 + \frac{1}{8}P$. Transportation costs and multiple currencies are ignored. Find the equilibrium U.S. price, production, consumption, and imports for each of the following regimes:
   (a) Perfect competition.
   (b) A quota is placed on imports causing the U.S. price to rise to 7. Calculate the consumer loss, producer gain, and the efficiency loss.

CHAPTER

10

Agriculture and the Environment

Production activities nearly always entail the production of waste products along with the products desired for ultimate human consumption. The household chore of putting out the garbage every week reminds us that consumption activities also give rise to waste products. In the literature on environmental pollution, waste products are often referred to as *residuals,* a terminology that is adopted here. Residuals or waste products would be of little concern if they were biodegradable and nontoxic, and could be bundled in neat packages to be hauled away to underutilized landfills. Unfortunately, the disposal of the residuals from production and consumption activities is often much more complicated than this.

The problems caused by the inevitable absorption of residuals by the environment receive attention in the media almost on a daily basis. Examples are plentiful and frightening, with environmental pollution reaching from below the earth's surface to the stratosphere. For many years, plans have been going forward in the United States for geologic repositories for the long-range internment of highly toxic nuclear wastes from nuclear power plants. No one really knows what to do with the stuff. The groundwater in many states contains several kinds of pesticides thanks largely to farmers who are spreading millions of pounds of toxins across the length and breadth of the land annually. In the summer of 1988, East Coast residents were shocked by the hospital wastes that washed up on their beaches. Certain types of chlorofluorocarbons, widely used in insulation, refrigerants, aerosol propellants, and cleaning agents, threaten the ozone layer in the atmosphere, which absorbs harmful ultraviolet radiation from the sun. The burning of fossil fuels in power plants, industrial boilers, and cars annually spews millions of tons of sulfur and nitrogen oxides into the atmosphere, with the United States and the United Kingdom being two of the world's worst offenders. One result is acid rain that threatens human health, wildlife, and forests.

According to a recent article in the *New York Times* (April 13, 1989), the Environmental Protection Agency estimates that in 1987 manufacturers alone released 22.5 billion pounds of hazardous substances. This figure includes 2.7 billion pounds of chemicals released into the air, a form of pollution with virtually no controls; 9.7 billion pounds discharged into streams and other surface waters; 3.2 billion pounds injected into underground wells; 2.7 billion pounds dumped in landfills; and 2.6 billion pounds sent to waste treatment and disposal facilities. These estimates are probably on the low side in that the discharges of small manufacturers were not counted.

Environmental pollution is not new to our age. One expects that on occasion even cavedwellers had to clear away from their dwellings the bones and waste from the great beasts they had killed and devoured. There are reasons for believing, however, that the problems of pollution are becoming ever more ominous. The industrial production and energy conversion characteristic of the modern age has placed new strains on the capacity of the environment to absorb residuals. New exotic residuals like polychlorinated biphenyls (PCBs) and spent nuclear fuel pose problems of disposal never before encountered. The tremendous increase in population by itself probably is straining the absorptive capacity of the environment quite aside from the introduction of new residuals. The global nature of environmental pollution has now intensified to the point where mechanisms are needed to resolve not only the conflicting interests of people living in different countries but in different hemispheres as well.

This chapter centers on environmental degradation as an economic problem, a problem arising out of the failure of the market system to allocate efficiently the nation's resources as between goods and services purchased in markets, on the one hand, and the protection of the services provided by the environment, on the other. Although interest centers on agriculture and the environment, the lessons learned have widespread applicability. We begin by developing a model of optimal resource use in a setting where farms engaged in food production generate residuals that degrade environmental services. External effects and external costs and benefits are defined. The meaning of market failure is explained as part of an analysis of optimal resource allocation in a model that explicitly recognizes the values of environmental services. Many of the previous chapters have been concerned mainly with income redistribution. In what follows, however, our interest will be directed toward economic efficiency; income redistribution will be largely ignored. Later sections of the chapter take up the damages to the environment caused by soil erosion and the use of chemical fertilizers and pesticides. Government programs designed to protect environmental services from agricultural pollution will also be critically examined.

10.1 OPTIMAL RESOURCE ALLOCATION
AND THE ENVIRONMENT

Consider the case where farmers have the option of using inorganic nitrogen fertilizer as one among several inputs. The government regulates the use of nitrogen fertilizer by putting an upper limit on the annual amount that may be applied per acre. Let F equal this upper limit. If the upper limit F is large enough, it will not be binding, and farmers will be free to apply as much fertilizer as they desire. We let F_c equal the lowest level of F such that the regulation is not binding. For the moment, we ignore the government's motivation in the regulation of fertilizer use. We simply take regulation as a given.

The profit function for a representative farm in the long run is given by

$$\pi = Pq - C(q, F) - TE$$

where, as before, P equals price, q equals output, and TE equals transfer earnings. The total variable cost function, recalling that TE is fixed, is given by $C(q, F)$. Total variable cost rises with increases in q but falls with increases in F. (We ignore all $F > F_c$.) Graphic representations of the farm's average variable cost and marginal cost curves are given in Figure 10.1 for two alternative levels of F, F_0 and F_1, where $F_1 > F_0$. Clearly, decreasing F lowers the amount of fertilizer use for any price level and elevates the cost curves. The farm's supply curve is shifted to the left by decreases in F. Thus, if we let price equal P_0 in Figure 10.1, output equals q_0 with low fertilizer use and q_1 with high fertilizer use.

Figure 10.2 allows aggregative analysis. Demand for food is given by D. If the regulation of fertilizer use is ineffective, that is to say, if $F \geq F_c$, then the long-run supply curve is given by S_c, the perfectly competitive supply curve. Let the supply curve associated with $F = 0$ be given by S'. Presumably, there exists an entire family of supply curves, all sandwiched between S' and S_c, each one associated with an alternative level of permitted fertilizer use.

With ineffective control of fertilizer use, market price and output are given by P_c and Q_c. This is the competitive market solution. Market performance reflects the desires of people for food, as reflected by demand, plus the costs of providing the output as reflected by the farmers' cost and supply curves.

An environmental problem may now be posed. Suppose that not all nitrogen fertilizer is taken up by the crops that are being produced. Some is washed away by rain and flows into rivers and lakes. Through percolation, some enters groundwater. The absorption of nitrogen by the environment would not be a cause for concern were it not for evidence that nitrate contamination causes health problems, particularly among infants. The contamination of surface and groundwater by nitrogen residuals is an example of an external

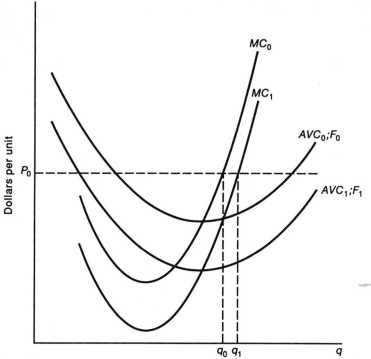

FIGURE 10.1
Average variable and marginal cost curves with two levels of fertilizer application.

effect that gives rise to external costs. External costs include the costs of purifying drinking water or the costs of human health disorders, or both. Animal health may also be adversely affected. *Because full external costs are not borne by farmers, such costs can have no effect on the level of food production.*

Before continuing with our analysis of the regulation of fertilizer use, we digress in order to define more fully the meaning of external effects and external costs and benefits. A firm's production activity is said to have an *external effect* if it alters or shifts production functions of other firms or utility functions of households. The definition of the external effect of a household's consumption activity follows accordingly. An external effect is said to give rise to an external cost if it decreases the outputs of other firms for any given set of inputs used by those firms or if it decreases the utilities of consumers for any given set of consumption goods. River pollution may increase production costs of downstream firms and decrease the utilities of people who enjoy fishing. The external effects of production and consumption activities might, on the other hand, give rise to external benefits as opposed to costs. A beautiful front yard may give enjoyment to passersby, enjoyment that may not redound to the benefit of the owner as he or she toils with water sprinklers and lawn mowers.

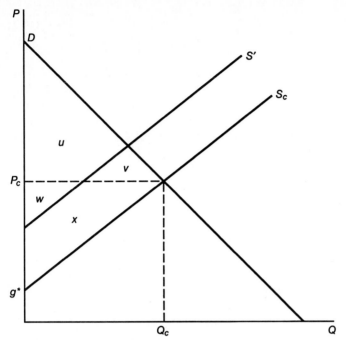

FIGURE 10.2
Market effects of disallowing fertilizer.

The celebrated bee keeper produces honey, but the many bees buzzing hither and yon also facilitate the pollination of cherry blossoms. In what follows, however, we shall not take time to dally in the orchard or smell the roses. Our concern is with power plants that belch smoke, with farmers who spread toxic materials on the land, with municipalities that dump human excrement in rivers and bays, and with manufacturers that dump dangerous chemicals in landfills.

Returning to our analysis of the regulation of fertilizer use, we see that a classic economic problem has arisen from our assumptions. *What is the optimum tradeoff between food production, on the one hand, and safe drinking water, on the other?* In order to answer this question we need to derive three functions. The first to be developed below shows the willingness of society to pay for food in varying quantities that depend on the extent of water contamination. A second function shows the willingness of society to pay for drinking water of varying purity. A third function shows the amount of taxes that must be collected to assure enforcement of the government's regulations. In what follows we abstract from the multiple uses of the nation's water supply and concentrate on water required for direct human consumption.

In order to analyze the benefit-cost implications of environmental policy, we let the equations for demand and supply in the presence of government regulation be given by

$$P = a - bQ$$

$$P = g + dQ$$

(10.1)

where g, the vertical intercept of the supply function, is a downward-sloping function of fertilizer use F. That is, $g = g(F)$. The higher the permitted use of F, the lower is g. When $F = F_c$, we will let $g = g_c$. A more general formulation would allow for nonlinear demand and supply functions and the possibility that changes in F alter both the position and the shape of the supply curve. The basic principles to be developed, however, would not be greatly different. (It can be shown, however, that if restricting fertilizer use alters the slope of the supply curve, then producer surplus could be increased.) Given our assumption of linearity, the equilibrium values for P and Q are given by

$$P_0 = \frac{ad + bg}{b + d}$$

$$Q_0 = \frac{a - g}{b + d}$$

(10.2)

Consumer surplus TCS is given by area h in Figure 10.3 or by

$$TCS = \tfrac{1}{2}(a - P_0)Q_0$$

$$= \tfrac{1}{2}b\left(\frac{a - g}{b + d}\right)^2$$

(10.3)

where the second expression for TCS is obtained through substitutions for P_0 and Q_0 using (10.2). Consumer surplus is our approximate measure of the willingness of consumers to pay for the privilege of buying food at price P_0. Similarly, the producer surplus TPS is given by area k or by

$$TPS = \tfrac{1}{2}(P_0 - g)Q_0$$

$$= \tfrac{1}{2}d\left(\frac{a - g}{b + d}\right)^2$$

(10.4)

Producer surplus measures the willingness of all farm input suppliers to pay for the privilege of selling their inputs to farmers, given that farmers receive a price for their output equal to P_0. Adding (10.3) and (10.4) yields the expression for what we will call food surplus FS. We have

$$FS = \frac{(a - g)^2}{2(b + d)}$$

(10.5)

The food surplus FS shows the willingness of consumers to pay for the privilege of buying food together with the willingness of farm input suppliers to pay

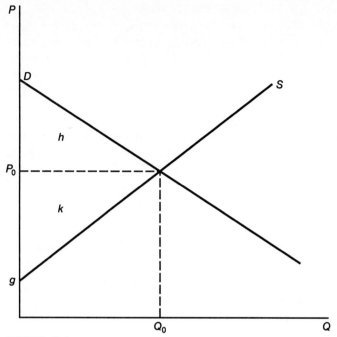

FIGURE 10.3
Measuring consumer and producer surpluses for given level of
fertilizer application.

for the privilege of selling their inputs to the food production industry. It is
clear from (10.5) that assigning successively higher values to g would cause FS
to decline. Notice that if $a = g$, there would be neither food output nor a food
surplus. This extreme case is of little practical significance, however, since nitrogen fertilizer is not indispensable to food production.

Since $g = g(F)$, we have

$$FS = \frac{[a - g(F)]^2}{2(b + d)} \tag{10.6}$$

Equation (10.6) gives the expression for food surplus as a function of fertilizer
use. Using the chain rule of calculus, it can be shown that FS is positively related to F. It is clear from (10.5), after all, that the lower g is, the higher FS is.
But the higher the permitted use of F is, the lower g is. Therefore, F and FS
are positively related. When $F = F_c$, the supply function is the competitive
supply given by S_c in Figure 10.2, as previously noted. Food surplus equals
area $(u + v + w + x)$. When $F = 0$, the supply curve is given by S' in Figure
10.2. Food surplus equals area $(u + w)$. The cost of avoiding entirely the pollution of water caused by food production in competitive equilibrium is given
by the area $(v + x)$, providing we ignore the government cost of regulation

A graphic representation of equation (10.6) is given by the *FS* curve in the second quadrant of Figure 10.4, with permitted fertilizer use *F* plotted on the horizontal axis. *This curve shows the maximum amount of money FS that consumers and farm input suppliers would be willing to pay for the privilege of consuming and producing food depending on the permitted use of nitrogen fertilizer.* The point *FS'* is associated with no fertilizer use; FS_c is associated with fertilizer use under perfect competition with no effective government regulation.

As fertilizer use increases, the nitrogen residuals *NR* that enter the nation's freshwater supply rise, and we need a function that relates the two. For this purpose let $F = F(NR)$. (Of course, *NR* could just as well be expressed as a function of *F*.) A graphic representation of the relationship between *F* and *NR* is given by the curve labeled *NR* in the third quadrant of Figure 10.4. We have assumed a particular shape for this curve for illustration, but the crucial aspect is that it be upward-sloping. (We ignore nitrate residuals from other sources, septic tanks, e.g., that might also enter the nation's water supply.)

The 45° line in the fourth quadrant is simply a graphic representation of the identity that asserts $NR = NR$. It is introduced here simply because it is useful in the graphic derivation of the important relationship given by the curve labeled *WF* in the first quadrant of Figure 10.4.

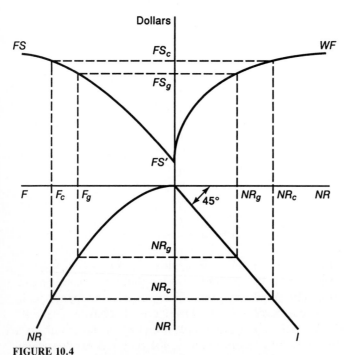

FIGURE 10.4
Willingness to pay for food production and consumption
opportunities for alternative levels of fertilizer application.

The WF curve shows the willingness of society to pay for the privilege of both consuming and producing food as a function of the degree of water pollution. The relationship is positive because the greater the permitted use of fertilizer, the greater the amount of food, and the greater the amount of nitrates to be found in the nation's drinking water. We can derive the *WF* curve graphically by making like a spider. Let $F = F_c$. Using the *FS* curve, F_c maps into FS_c, and we draw a dashed, horizontal line at this level in the first quadrant. Using the *NR* curve in the third quadrant together with the *I* curve in the fourth quadrant, we see that F_c maps into NR_c, which yields a dashed vertical line in the first quadrant. The intersection of dashed lines FS_c and NR_c in the first quadrant locates one point on the *WF* curve. Other webs can be drawn to locate as many such points as we please, which allows our drawing the *WF* curve.

A mathematical representation of this relationship can be easily derived. Since $F = F(NR)$, we have, using (10.6):

$$FS = \frac{[a - g(F(NR))]^2}{2(b + d)} \qquad (10.7)$$

A numerical example might be helpful. Let demand and supply be given by $P = 10 - Q$ and $P = g + Q$, respectively. Then, $FS = \frac{1}{4}(10 - g)^2$. If $g = 4 - \frac{1}{2}F$ and $F = (NR)^{1/2}$, then $FS = \frac{1}{16}[144 + 24(NR)^{1/2} + (NR)]$. This equation for *FS* corresponds to the *WF* curve in the first quadrant of Figure 10.4.

If food production involved introducing minute traces of nitrates in the water supply that caused damage to neither plant nor animal life, then we would have no environmental problem. Perfect competition with free fertilizer use would result in economic efficiency. The economic and environmental problem arises out of the possibility, as already noted, that nitrates could be inimical to human health.

We therefore postulate a functional relationship that shows the maximum amount of money that members of society would be willing to pay collectively, WW, for the nation's supply of drinking water depending on the amount of nitrate residuals it contains. This relationship is assumed to reflect both the costs of removing residuals from drinking water and, because complete purification may be impossible or too costly, the health hazards associated with consuming at least some contaminants. Presumably, the dirtier the water, the less society would be willing to pay for it. A graphic representation of this function is given by the *WW* curve in the first quadrant of Figure 10.5.

The *WF* curve derived in Figure 10.4 is redrawn in Figure 10.5. We may now sum vertically the *WF* and *WW* curves in order to obtain the *GW* curve in Figure 10.5. This curve shows the gross amount of money people would be willing to pay for food and water, depending on the level of nitrate residuals the government allows in the nation's water supply. In order to obtain the net

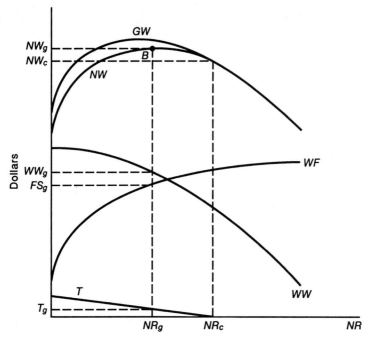

FIGURE 10.5
Maximizing net benefits through regulation of the level of fertilizer
application.

amount of money society would be willing to pay, we must at last face up to
the cost of regulation.

Regulating the amount of nitrogen fertilizer used by farmers might prove
to be a costly business. Taxes will need be collected to assure compliance.
Presumably, the smaller the amount of fertilizer use permitted, the greater the
cost of regulation. The curve labeled T in Figure 10.5 is assumed to show the
government expenditure required to keep nitrogen residuals NR out of the nation's water supply. Taxes fall to zero, of course, if the permitted level of F
equals F_c. In that case no regulation is required.

In order to obtain a curve that shows the *net* willingness of people to pay
for food and drinking water, depending on the level of water contamination,
we subtract vertically the T curve from the GW curve. The resulting curve is
given by NW in Figure 10.5.

Our criterion for finding the optimal permitted level of fertilizer use is
simple enough. *We assume the government's objective is to maximize the willingness of society to pay for food and water net of the cost of government regulation.* This maximum point is given by point B along the NW curve, linking
together the maximum net willingness to pay for food and water NW_g with the
optimum level of water pollution NR_g. The optimum quantity of nitrate resid-

uals NR_g may be linked, working backward, to the optimum levels of fertilizer use F_g (see Fig. 10.4) and the optimal levels of food and water surpluses FS_g and WW_g. The student should take note that whereas some people might benefit from the government program, others will be hurt. In our analysis one individual's willingness to pay is treated the same as the willingness to pay on the part of any other individual. All dollars are given equal weight without regard to who gets and who gives.

The above graphic analysis may be supplemented by a brief mathematical treatment. Letting $WS = f(NR)$, $WW = w(NR)$, and $T = t(NR)$, we have

$$NW = f(NR) + w(NR) - t(NR) \tag{10.8}$$

Maximizing NW, we take the first derivative of NW with respect to NR and set it equal to zero. This yields

$$\frac{d(FS)}{d(NR)} - \frac{dT}{d(NR)} = -\frac{d(WW)}{d(NR)} \tag{10.9}$$

Notice that both $dT/d(NR)$ and $d(WW)/d(NR)$ are negative. The derivative of FS with respect to NR minus that for T is the marginal benefit of a small increase in NR. The marginal benefit results from an additional food surplus together with reduced taxes. The derivative of WW with respect to NR, on the other hand, is the marginal cost to society of a small increase in NR. The marginal cost results from the decreased willingness to pay for drinking water.

Thus, equation (10.9) involves the following familiar idea. To find the optimum, consider successive increments in NR. If the value of the extra food plus the tax saving associated with an increment in NR (the marginal benefit) exceeds the lost value of water purity (the marginal cost), we allow NR to increase. We increase NR by small increments up to the point where the extra benefit just equals the extra cost. At this point the willingness to pay for food and water net of government cost is maximized. Decreased water contamination beyond this point lowers society's net willingness to pay. The marginal conditions for a maximum given by (10.9) are satisfied at point B in Figure 10.5.

The above analysis provides an example of a competitive market that does not lead to efficient market performance. In the absence of government regulation, farmers will apply more than the optimum amount of nitrogen fertilizer. The fundamental reason for this is that in making their production decisions, farmers do not incur the social costs of the degradation of the nation's supply of drinking water. As a consequence, the costs of water contamination have no bearing on food production and consumption decisions. Food production and fertilizer use are excessive. This discussion points toward an important definition.

A market system is said to result in *market failure* if there exists a government program that improves economic efficiency. Such is the case here. (Some writers also define market failure to include an objectional income distribution.) Government regulation of fertilizer can be used to lower the extent of water pollution. The cost includes higher taxes and higher food prices, but net benefits result from the increased purity of the nation's drinking water. It should not be thought, however, that external costs inevitably lead to market failure. Two conditions must be met in the present context before it can be said that a market fails: (1) External costs must exist. (2) Some form of government intervention must exist that leads to an increase in society's willingness to pay for both environmental services and the market output, allowing for the taxes required to operate the program. The invisible hand of the market system, to use Adam Smith's famous characterization, may indeed give rise to environmental pollution, but it is always possible that the clumsy hand of government might make matters worse.

Returning to Figure 10.5, we note that the shape and position of the WW curve are merely illustrative. If the WW curve were downward-sloping, as we would expect it to be, but if it were rather flat as well, then the maximum of the NW curve might occur at $NR = NR_c$. There would then be no need for government intervention. The high cost of government regulation would also push the optimum level of NR in the direction of NR_c.

Still another interesting polar case occurs if the maximum lies on the vertical axis. This might happen in the case of a very dangerous residual from a chemical for which good substitutes exist. The pesticide DDT is a possible example.

Direct regulation is not the only way of limiting the application of nitrogen fertilizer. One alternative is to place a tax on fertilizer, recognizing that the higher the tax, the greater the substitution of other inputs. Presumably, a tax that is sufficiently high would cause fertilizer applications to cease entirely. Another alternative to regulation is payments to farmers who are willing to forgo or restrict their use of fertilizer. Instead of a stick, use the carrot.

An altogether different approach is to focus attention directly on the discharging of nitrate residuals into the environment, without attempting to control fertilizer use per se. More specifically, the government might regulate the amount of residuals each farmer is allowed to discharge into the nation's water supply. Taxes (fines) on discharges or payments to farmers to avoid discharges are alternatives to regulation. Putting limits on discharges allows farmers to search for alternative technologies that limit the sacrifice of food production associated with decreased levels of contamination. There may be alternative ways of applying fertilizer with varying levels of discharges. Manure is not spread on frozen fields that border lakes and rivers. Farmers who farm highly erodible land, to take another example, might be encouraged to adopt low tillage methods in order to keep fertilizer from washing into surface waters.

Limiting residuals directly would not appear to be particularly feasible in the present case of nonpoint-pollution. Thousands of farms are involved over a wide heterogeneous geographic area. Of even greater importance, however, is the difficulty of monitoring the extent of discharges by each farmer. Identifying the specific sources of nitrates in groundwater is virtually impossible. Regulating the flow of discharges into the environment is more plausible in the case of paper mills that pump contaminated water into a river. Power plants that burn coal in the generation of electricity are another example.

A final illustrative approach involves controlling neither fertilizer use nor nitrate residuals but simply using sufficient government revenues to finance water purification programs that assure water purity does not fall below some minimum standard. For example, the federal government might subsidize municipal water treatment plants and the purchase of distilled water by residents of rural areas.

We may now take up the question of optimal policy given that many avenues may be open to the government for protecting the environment. Choose some particular approach and find the maximum net willingness to pay for food and water. In the case of fertilizer regulation, find point B in Figure 10.5. Do the same for every possible approach. The approach that leads to the highest possible net willingness to pay is the optimal policy.

The above theoretical model calls attention to the basic elements of environmental quality control problems in general. A considerable amount of information is required for intelligent public policy. First, we require information on the benefits to society associated with an increased flow of marketable products allowed by increasing the flow of pollutants into the environment. The nature and magnitude of these benefits will vary from one industry to another. In the case of the farm industry, attention centered on the increased level of food output and on the decreased costs of food production and lower food prices. Second, we require information on the costs of increasing the flow of residuals into the environment. The costs take the form of decreased wildlife and recreation values, poorer human health, and perhaps increased costs for some products. Third, information is needed on the taxes needed to operate the program. Finally, the above information is required for each of several alternative approaches that might be used to protect the environment.

It is easy, of course, for the economist to sit back and say we need information on this and we need information on that, and it is up to others—to engineers, hydrologists, and medical researchers—to provide the necessary data. Getting the data required to optimize efficiency poses enormous difficulties, however. Perhaps the most formidable difficulties arise out of the need to assess the costs of environmental degradation. The values of environmental services are of central importance, but these services are not bought and sold in a market. In most instances, there are no market prices that economists can use to estimate, for example, how much people would be willing to pay for the right to breathe air of varying purity.

A further serious limitation of the above theoretical model is that it does not take explicit account of risk and uncertainty, and the dynamics of environmental change are largely ignored. The extent to which nitrogen fertilizer contaminates surface water depends on rainfall, which is impossible to predict. The lag times between pollution and the subsequent problems of human health may persist for many years. Depletion of the ozone layer, for example, may be the present generation's unlovely bequest to future generations.

Many of the problems associated with actually using the above model or some variant thereof to guide environmental policy will become more apparent when we turn more explicitly to agriculture in the next two sections of this chapter.

10.2 SOIL EROSION: PROBLEMS AND POLICIES

What is soil erosion and why is it a problem? Soil erosion is the movement of soil by water and wind. Rain drops dislodge soil, and running water may carry it away to a valley site or to rivers and lakes. Wind may dislodge soil, particularly dry soil, and move it for many miles, perhaps for hundreds of miles as in the Dust Bowl years of the 1930s. The soil moved by erosion is, of course, the topsoil, which usually contains organic matter and plant nutrients that are important to crop yields. In time, erosion may cause gullies to form that make land unsuitable for cultivation and increase field crop production costs. It is possible, too, for poor soil to be deposited on top of better soils, thus lessening productivity.

Soil that reaches rivers and lakes may have several harmful effects. Soil carried as suspended sediment may be damaging to wildlife and reduce recreational opportunities such as fishing, boating, and swimming. Suspended sediment imposes clean-up costs for water used for residential and some industrial purposes. When eroded soil becomes sediment, it gradually reduces the life of lakes and reservoirs. Increased plant nutrients stimulate algae growth, decreasing fish populations and reducing recreation values provided by the environment. Sediment in rivers may, over time, cause flooding. Additional dredging operations also may be needed to clean channels for barge traffic. When soil erosion carries pesticides into rivers and lakes, a whole new set of issues arise.

From the above discussion it is clear that soil erosion causes problems, but are the problems of such nature as to warrant government intervention? In other words, does soil erosion give rise to market failure as defined above?

The External Costs of Soil Erosion

Two kinds of problems may be caused by soil erosion: (1) the additional on-farm costs due to lower soil productivity, and (2) the off-farm costs due to sedimentation. The recent research on soil erosion indicates that from the point of view of the need for government intervention, off-farm costs are probably a good deal more serious than are on-farm costs. Some explanation for why this is likely the case is in order.

The basic reason why on-farm costs due to erosion probably do not necessitate government intervention is because a market exists for topsoil, namely the market for farmland. The logic of the argument may be advanced by a simple example. Consider a farmer who owns a farm and plans to grow one more crop before retiring and selling the farm. Allowing soil erosion to occur increases profit but lowers the value of the farm. Profit π is positively related to the amount of erosion allowed thus: $\pi = \pi(E)$, where E equals soil lost through erosion. The sales value of the farm V is negatively related to E thus: $V = V(E)$. Maximizing current wealth, the present value of the sum of profit plus the sales value of the farm after the crop is harvested and sold, implies that the discounted marginal gain from depleting the soil equals the discounted marginal cost of lost soil as reflected in the decreased value of the farm. The marginal gain associated with allowing E to increase is the increase in profit. The marginal cost is the decrease in the sales values of the farm. The one must be balanced off against the other. Importantly, the on-farm cost of soil erosion is born by the farmer in terms of decreased value of the farm.

Determining the optimum soil conservation practices for a farmer under real-world conditions poses serious problems, and it would be remarkable if farmers, landowners, and land buyers and sellers did not make mistakes. Crop production often gives rise to some erosion, depending on farm management practices and the nature of the land in terms of topography, soil structure, source of water, and the like. Farmland is highly heterogeneous. Conditions can vary widely on the same farm. Topsoil can be replenished, but it is an expensive business, and there are substitutes for topsoil such as fertilizers. As soil erodes, yields fall unless technological change and substitute inputs more than compensate for the lost soil. Dynamics and uncertainty are important factors in the optimization problem in that no one knows what the demands for food will be in the future or, more importantly, what new inputs will become available. The argument heard on occasion that the needs of future generations are not given sufficient weight in "mining" farmland overlooks the role played by land speculators, by people who invest their money in land ownership in anticipation of future price movements. Soil conservation choices are hard choices to make, but there is no assurance whatever that government officials can do a better job of efficiently protecting soil productivity and the value of investments in land than can the farmers and landowners themselves.

In addition to theoretical arguments, empirical research indicates that the effects of soil erosion on crop yields in the United States have been of minor importance. Pierre Crosson has reviewed the various studies that have been made and, looking to the future, concludes (p. 46), "the estimated long-term erosion induced losses of soil productivity are small to negligible compared to the technology-induced increase in yield expected over the next 50 years by an impressive array of experts."

If a case is to be made for government intervention in the area of soil conservation, it appears that attention had better be shifted away from on-farm to off-farm costs. Off-farm costs include loss of recreational values, damage to lake and reservoir storage, damage to water transportation systems, and increased municipal and industrial water treatment costs. By their very nature, off-farm costs are external costs that do not appear in the profit functions of farmers. These costs are not reflected in the prices we pay for food.

Estimation of off-farm costs is difficult, but Clark, Haverkamp, and Chapman have made a valiant effort to do just that. Excluding some costs for which data are not available, they estimate that the annual off-farm costs of soil erosion range from $3.2 billion to $13 billion, with $6.1 billion being a best-guess estimate. The wide range immediately suggests the difficulty of estimation and the roughness of the resulting estimates. Even so, these estimates are the best we have, and they suggest that the off-farm costs of erosion are large and warrant study of instruments the government might use to avoid them.

Soil Erosion and Public Policy

The distinction between on-farm and off-farm costs, with the latter being the more likely cause of market failure, has important implications for an analysis of public policy. We begin by reviewing what soil conservation policy has been.

U.S. soil conservation policy over the last several decades can be traced back to the Soil Conservation and Domestic Allotment Act of 1936 as amended, most recently by the Food Security Act of 1985. Traditionally, conservation policy has relied mainly on education, technical assistance, and cost sharing. Personnel from the Extension Service and the Soil Conservation Service have called attention to the problem of erosion and to techniques for soil conservation. Technical assistance has involved mapping farms and recommending practices for each field. Depending on the field, recommendations might include the establishment of permanent vegetative cover, contour or strip-cropping systems, low- or zero-tillage, and pond construction for water retention. Cost sharing has been made available under yearly or long-term contracts. It has been estimated that farmers bear approximately half the cost of approved conservation practices, with the government picking up the remainder. Government expenditures have been quite limited, however, with conservation program outlays averaging only $200 per commercial farm in the early 1980s (see Robinson).

The Food Security Act of 1985 revived the idea of a land conservation reserve as it first appeared in the 1950s as part of the soil bank program. The basic idea is simply to retire erodible land from production, an idea that is particularly attractive politically in periods of surpluses and low prices. The new Conservation Reserve Program (CRP) encourages farmers, through 10–year contracts with the U.S. Department of Agriculture (USDA), to stop growing crops on highly erodible cropland and to plant such land to cover crops instead. One objective of the program is to have 40 to 45 million acres committed to the reserve by 1990. The CRP offers farmers annual per acre payments plus one-half of the cost of establishing a permanent cover. Under a novel feature, farmers with eligible fields submit bids indicating the annual sums they would require in order to participate in the program.

As of 1989, 30.6 million acres had entered the Conservation Reserve, surpassing the 28.7 million acres of peak enrollment under the soil bank program in 1960. About 6 percent of the enrolled land has been planted to trees. The average rental rates for the 30.6 million acres was $48.71 per acre.

In addition to the CRP, the Food Security Act of 1985 contained conservation compliance provisions that discourage farmers from the reckless production of crops on highly erodible land. The act also contained the so-called sodbuster and swampbuster provisions. Under the conservation compliance provision, if crops are produced on fields that are highly erodible without locally approved conservation plans, producers may lose eligibility for major crop programs. Conservation compliance applies to land where annually tilled crops were produced at least once during the period 1981–1985 and will apply to all highly erodible land in annual crop production by 1990. (Land is considered highly erodible if potential soil loss is more than eight times the rate at which soil can maintain continued productivity.) Farmers had until January 1, 1990, to develop and begin implementing a conservation plan. The sodbuster provision discourages the conversion of highly erodible land for crop production. If erodible grassland or woodland is used for crop production, without an approved conservation plan, the farmer may lose eligibility for participation in major crop programs. "Sodbuster" applies to highly erodible land that was not tilled annually from 1981 to 1985. The swampbuster provision discourages the conversion of natural wetlands to cropland. Producers who convert wetland to cropland after December 23, 1985, may lose their eligibility for major crop programs. Farmers who fail to comply with conservation compliance and the sodbuster and swampbuster provisions risk losing their eligibility for price and income supports, crop insurance, government loans, and the annual payments under the soil conservation programs.

Turning to policy evaluation, we may be sure that present land conservation policy is far from optimal. It appears that off-farm cost, not on-farm cost, is the main reason for market failure. The market for topsoil is very likely the nation's number one defense against erosion that destroys land productivity. The evidence indicates, moreover, that on the assumption of continued investment in research and development, new inputs and new technologies can be relied upon to increase yields in spite of soil erosion.

Whether the nation spends too much or too little on preserving farmland productivity through erosion control is unclear. It seems quite likely, however, that what is spent is not spent wisely. Expenditures are spread somewhat evenly over the landscape instead of being concentrated in areas where farmland erosion is the most severe. Under the Agricultural Conservation Program, conservation plans for individual farms are drawn up that are never put into practice. Substantial conservation funds have been used to increase crop yields with little concern for controlling erosion. Subsidies for applying fertilizer and lime and installing irrigation systems are examples of yield-increasing practices that have little to do with erosion.

Recent innovations that link conservation practices with participation in farm price and income support programs may cause decreased participation on the part of farmers with highly erodible land and increased participation by others. To the extent farmers are the best judge of soil conservation practices that efficiently conserve land productivity, the substitution of government decisions for private decisions through cross compliance may be a step in the wrong direction. Although preservation of wetlands and grasslands may be laudable objectives, the question remains whether the programs authorized by the 1985 legislation will be effective. Conservation objectives will not be achieved in areas where nonprogram crops are grown or in periods of prosperity when farm programs are unattractive.

Finally, the importance of off-farm cost raises the question whether landscape erosion control is the best way of avoiding sedimentation. At present the specific sources of the sediment that clouds surface waters and clogs rivers and harbors is largely unknown except in a few isolated cases. Where, then, should conservation practices be put to work? Some researchers are calling attention to small sediment detention reservoirs and grassed areas along the borders of streams as the best ways of checking the damage caused by sediment. The idea behind detention reservoirs is to capture the sediment upstream from areas where damage occurs.

10.3 PESTICIDES: PROBLEMS AND POLICIES

Pesticides include herbicides that kill weeds, insecticides that kill insects, and fungicides for controlling plant diseases. Although first applied to crops in the United States in 1924, pesticides were not used extensively until after World War II. The growth in pesticide use and the proliferation of products available since then, particularly in the case of herbicides, has been phenomenal. Over 50,000 pesticide products are now registered for use by the Environmental Protection Agency. The introduction of pesticides contributed greatly to the rapid technological growth in agriculture since World War II, at least as growth is conventionally measured without regard to external costs.

The External Costs of Pesticide Use

Although first perceived as miracle inputs by farmers and others, doubts began to take root with the passage of time, particularly following the publication of Rachel Carson's *Silent Spring*. Resistent strains of insects developed. Insects that were formerly benign, held in check by insect predators, became voracious consumers of crops. Beneficial insects were also killed. Most pesticides are poisonous to humans, ranging from those that are mildly poisonous to those that are deadly. They are therefore risky inputs to manufacture and risky to apply. Society is accustomed, however, to occupational hazards and to the need for regulations that assure safe working conditions.

What has begun to arouse the citizenry are the pesticide residues that degrade the environment and have started to show up in the food we eat, the water we drink, and the air we breathe. A recent USDA publication (by Nielsen and Lee) estimates that at present the drinking water of 50 million people in the United States comes from groundwater that is potentially contaminated with agricultural chemicals, including fertilizer residue. Over 97 percent of rural America's drinking water comes from underground sources. In 1980, 40 percent of the U.S. population relied on public water supplies drawn from underground sources. Because of the interaction between surface water and groundwater, contamination of the latter may in time contaminate the former in some areas.

What are the effects of pesticide residuals on human health? To what extent do these residuals degrade the environment, with undesirable effects on fish and animal populations? These are good questions, but the answers that can be given on the basis of presently available data and scientific studies are very poor indeed. At present the widespread concern regarding pesticide residuals is based as much on what we don't know as on what we do know. It is the uncertainty that provides cause for alarm and a hospitable climate for chemophobia.

Available evidence suggests that some pesticides may cause cancers, reproductive abnormalities, and central nervous system disorders. The evidence comes from a variety of sources including experiments with animals and from accidents in which people have been exposed to large doses of pesticides. What is needed, however, is information on the long-term effects of low doses of pesticides, particularly as regards human health. Effects may not be observed for several years or even decades, allowing plenty of room for other health-affecting factors to cloud cause-and-effect relationships for pesticides. It is also important to bear in mind that synthetic pollutants are not the only source of carcinogens. Indeed, some scientists have argued that such pollutants are of small importance relative to the carcinogenic material found in nature. Toxic molds, for example, are found in wheat, corn, and nuts. The browned and burnt material consumed at meal time contains potent carcinogens. Lest such findings drive one to drink, it should be noted that alcohol consumption is another major source of carcinogens.

Pesticide Policy

The Federal Insecticide, Fungicide, and Rodenticide Act (FIFRA) of 1947, as amended, together with several sections of the Federal Food, Drug, and Cosmetic Act (FFDCA) of 1938, as amended, authorize the Environmental Protection Agency (EPA) to regulate pesticides and their uses. (See the 1986 General Accounting Office study cited at the end of this chapter.) Under FIFRA, particularly as amended in 1972, the EPA is authorized to register pesticides, to specify the terms and conditions for their proper use, and to remove unreasonably hazardous products from the market. Under FFDCA, the EPA is authorized to establish the maximum acceptable levels of pesticide residuals in foods and animal feeds in order to protect human health, at the same time assuring the nation of an adequate supply of food. Significant amendments to FIFRA were enacted in 1972, which shifted the emphasis of regulation from consumer protection and product performance to public health and environmental protection.

What does pesticide registration entail? The EPA may register a product only if it will not cause unreasonable risks to people and to the environment, taking into account the benefits of an increased supply of food. Registrations are essentially licenses for specified uses of the product. A registration might indicate, for example, that a specific insecticide may be applied to soybeans. Once registered, the EPA relies on warnings and instructions for use stated on the product's label as the means for regulating risks to people and the environment. Regulatory decisions including registrations are based in part on health and environmental effects data requested by the EPA and supplied by pesticide producers.

Under the 1972 amendments to FIFRA the EPA was directed to assess the safety of about 35,000 pesticide products that had been previously registered and to reregister only those products that satisfied new health and environmental criteria. Amendments added in 1978 sanctioned registrations and reregistrations on the basis of assessments of the effects of the 600 basic chemicals used in pesticide manufacture as opposed to the many thousands of resulting mixtures sold as pesticide products.

The maximum pesticide residues allowed in food under FFDCA are called *tolerances,* and the EPA must establish tolerances or exemptions from tolerances for all pesticide products as a prerequisite for registration. Tolerances are established on the basis of data on toxicity submitted by pesticide manufacturers. Although the EPA is charged with the responsibility for setting tolerances, the Food and Drug Administration is responsible for monitoring most of the nation's food supply to assure that consumers are not exposed to unsafe levels of pesticide residues.

A final element of federal pesticide policy has come to be known as *special review*. Suppose that at some point in time new evidence becomes available suggesting that the riskiness of a registered pesticide is greater than previously thought. The EPA then conducts a special benefit-cost analysis, which becomes the basis for deciding whether the pesticide in question should have its uses further restricted or whether the pesticide should be withdrawn from the market, either immediately or after some appropriate period of time allowing for the smooth adjustment of production techniques.

Passing dandy laws is one thing; funding and creating effective programs is quite another. Members of Congress, industry trade representatives, environmentalists, and other voices have joined in a lusty chorus condemning the EPA's performance of its various functions. Whether the criticisms are justified or not, it is clear that the legislative objectives for the EPA were determined with inadequate attention given to the complexity of the means whereby objectives could be achieved and to the funds and personnel that would be required to make sure the work was done both properly and in a timely fashion. It is easy to argue in retrospect that the federal government should never in the first place have allowed the use of pesticides without checking their health and environmental implications. At the least this suggests that the new inputs spawned by biological research and genetic engineering should be examined closely before they are turned loose in the agricultural sector.

In any event, it is clear that up to this point in time, U.S. pesticide policy has been a disappointment; it has not protected the public health and the environment from the risks of pesticide residues. Pesticide products are still being used in large numbers and in massive quantities with little information on their long-run health and environmental effects. The present risks are very real even though we may discover in time that pesticides have not had significant detrimental effects on human health. A 1986 General Accounting Office (GAO) evaluation of the EPA's performance of its various functions is a litany of failed expectations. Regarding conditional registration, pending final assessment, the GAO concludes (pp. 98–99):

> Our review of the legislative history indicates that both the Congress and EPA anticipated that conditional registration of new active ingredients would be for exceptional purposes. Since 1978 EPA has conditionally registered a large proportion—about 50 percent—of all new pesticide active ingredients even though some of the required health and environmental test data were not submitted to and evaluated by EPA.

Regarding reregistration, the GAO concludes (pp. 54–55):

> While much of the population is exposed daily to pesticides in food and the environment, EPA has limited assurance that human health and the environment are adequately protected from possible unreasonable risks of older pesticides.... Based on current program and resource projections, it appears that reregistration will extend into the 21st century.

Regarding pesticide residues in food, the GAO concludes (p. 70):

> Because tolerance reassessments are dependent on the data received and reviewed by EPA under the pesticide reregistration program, probably not until the 21st century will the safety of all older tolerances and exemptions have been reassessed according to current scientific standards. Until EPA obtains complete data and reassesses existing tolerances, the potential of many pesticide residues to cause genetic change, birth defects, cancer, and other chronic health effects cannot be fully determined.

Regarding inert ingredients in pesticides, ingredients used as solvents, thickeners, and propellants, the GAO concludes (p. 89):

> EPA has only recently begun to review inert pesticide ingredients, although some inerts were known to be hazardous to humans and insufficient information existed to determine the potential risks of many others.

Regarding special reviews of pesticides of concern, the GAO concludes (p. 118):

> EPA, industry, and environmental groups all agree that EPA's special review process for addressing pesticides of concern is taking too long to complete, contrary to EPA's goal of doing these reviews quickly. Special reviews have taken from 2 to 6 years or longer to complete, and the hearing process which may follow a special review may take up to 2 years or longer. During this period of review and hearings, the public and the environment may be exposed to potentially hazardous pesticides.

What to do? Many suggestions have been made to make pesticide regulation work better. A user-fee system, for example, could be applied to pesticide registration activities with new statutory authority for allocating the resulting funds to the EPA. Recently, the EPA has called for new legislation that would remove a judicial appeals process that chemical companies could use to delay the removal of potentially dangerous chemicals. Some writers, however, have questioned whether regulation can be made to work. Antle and Capalbo point out that the regulatory approach is based on the presumption that social benefits and costs of each pesticide can be determined with regulatory decisions based on that information. They conclude (p. 169):

> In practice this is difficult if not impossible to do, largely because the costs of the information needed to implement this kind of policy are high, if not infinite (the information cannot be had at any price).
>
> An alternative approach to pesticide policy could be based on the ecological premise, that chemical-based pest-management technology is undesirable because it is in conflict with basic ecological principles and therefore will continue to cause hazards to human health and the natural environment. Under this approach, the goal of public policy would be to discourage chemical-intensive technology and to encourage substitutes for it.

The concerns of Antle and Capalbo are shared by many people, scientists and laypeople alike, and it is out of these concerns that the plea for *sustainable agriculture* has emerged. While sustainable agriculture means different things to different people, it would be highly misleading to equate sustainable agriculture with low input agriculture, as some writers are wont to do. Sustainable agriculture entails not fewer inputs but a different mix of inputs in which the use of pesticides is severely curtailed and the use of other inputs, particularly farm labor and management, is increased. Sustainable agriculture involves some farming practices that could be characterized as being old-fashioned. Linking crop and livestock enterprises on the same farm, deep tilling of the soil, and rotations of several crops are examples. In some respects, however, sustainable agriculture is futuristic in that it looks toward using biological pest controls and integrated pest management. Integrated pest management pits pesticides, labor, and knowledge (of pest life cycles, pest-predator relations, and pest-plant relations) against the remarkable and frustrating capacity of plant diseases to spread and of insects to eat and multiply. This mode of farming involves the observation of pest numbers and selective, carefully targeted applications of pesticides. The use of pesticices in integrated pest management stands in contrast to the repeated and heavy applications of pesticides on a fixed schedule with little or no regard for need or the environment. The adjective "sustainable" is obviously intended to promote, not just describe, and its use reflects the belief that the heavy and widespread use of pesticides is or may be a dead-end street, that increasing genetic resistance and secondary pest outbreaks will make present practices unprofitable in the long term, and that environmental degradation will eventually force an alternative mode of farming.

Perhaps the most persuasive argument in favor of sustainable agriculture is that regulation has not worked very well. Perhaps regulation can be made more effective through tighter legislation and more expenditures. Other policy approaches include taxing farm chemicals (pesticides and commercial fertilizers), linking farm program deficiency payments with agricultural practices that use little or no pesticides, and research programs designed to find substitute inputs that entail less risk to the public health and the environment.

Finally, it would be a grave mistake to suppose that a movement away from the heavy reliance on farm chemicals would be detrimental necessarily to farmers and all farm input suppliers. A substantial scaling back of farm chemicals would lower production and elevate farm prices, much as idling land under farm programs has done (see, for example, Osteen and Kuchler). Agricultural chemicals are likely better substitutes for labor than is land, however. It appears possible that after a transitional period, farm incomes would rise and that the long-run demand for farm family labor would increase. Consumers, on the other hand, would most certainly pay higher food prices and farm exports would fall. The Food and Drug Administration could devote more of its resources to scrutinizing imported farm products, which is what domestic farmers think the Food and Drug Administration should do anyway. Domestic consumers would need become accustomed once again to fruits and vegetables that have been nibbled by bugs but which no longer glow in the dark.

10.4 SUMMARY

Production and consumption activities nearly always give rise to waste products or residuals. Short of launching such residuals into space, they must be absorbed by the environment, and this can cause serious problems. Pollution tends to destroy the quality of services provided by the environment such as clean air, pure water, and even sunshine. Of major environmental concern in the farm sector are soil erosion and the uncertainty as to the long-run effects of pesticides.

Environmental protection involves a trade-off, a trade-off between the quantity of goods and services provided by industries and the quality of services provided by the environment. In general, the more we get of one the less we get of the other. Under a pure market system, with no government intervention, firms are free to pollute water and air to whatever extent they desire in their quest for profit. They can ignore external costs, defined as costs to society associated with production but which do not appear in the private profit accounts of firms. Such costs can, therefore, have little or no effect on how products are produced and in what quantities. The main concern, of course, is that unfettered competition will lead to a suboptimum trade-off between quantity of products and quality of environmental services, with the former being too large and the latter being too low. A possible role for government intervention is to correct the imbalance.

This chapter presents a model that shows how the government can select an environmental policy that maximizes efficiency and is in that sense optimal. For illustrative purpose we consider inorganic nitrogen fertilizer that can be used to lower the costs of producing food but that also gives rise to nitrate residuals in the nation's water supply, residuals that apparently can have serious health consequences. Consider increments in fertilizer use starting from a position in which fertilizer is totally banned. From the viewpoint of efficiency, it makes sense to allow an increment of fertilizer use to occur if the willingness of society to pay for the extra food enjoyed plus the tax savings associated with less stringent controls exceed the willingness of society to pay to avoid the increase in water pollution. In other words, fertilizer use should be expanded as long as marginal benefits exceed marginal costs. Maximum efficiency is achieved when marginal benefits just equal marginal costs and the willingness of society to pay for both food and water, net of the taxes required to finance the government program, is maximized. It might happen that if the residual in question is rather harmless and/or if the cost of government controls is very high, the free market solution might be optimal. Alternatively, it might be discovered that a government program that lowers fertilizer use below the free market level, perhaps even to zero in the case of a dangerous chemical, increases society's net willingness to pay for food and water. Such cases are referred to in this chapter as cases of market failure. The market is said to fail because government intervention increases economic efficiency.

There may be several approaches the government could use to lower nitrate residuals in the nation's water supply, including control of fertilizer use, direct limitations on discharges of nitrate residuals, taxes on fertilizer, and payments to farmers to induce them not to use fertilizer. Choosing optimal public policy involves maximizing the net willingness of society to pay for food in varying quantities and water of varying purity for each approach and then choosing that approach associated with the maximum of the maxima. One must not view the model developed in this chapter as a recipe the government can easily follow to achieve optimal policy. In most cases involving environmental pollution, an optimization model will call for data that are extremely difficult to obtain. Measuring the willingness of society to pay for water depending on how dirty it is, for example, is not easy. At the very least, however, the model of this chapter calls attention to a range of considerations that must be taken into account in choosing government policies if the resulting choices are to be sensible ones. In broad terms, three questions may be asked. How much does society want the extra production that can be achieved if further environmental contamination occurs? How much does society want to avoid the further erosion of the quality of environmental services? How much does it cost taxpayers to foot the bill for government programs that would be needed to control contamination?

Turning to applied problems, we explore both soil erosion and pesticides as possible sources of market failure in the farm sector. Soil erosion occurs when wind or water moves soil from one spot to another. Erosion tends to lower the productivity of cropland and, more importantly, causes the destruction of recreation opportunities, damages water storage facilities, increases water transportation costs, and increases the potential for floods. Instruments the government can use to curtail erosion include education of farmers; technical assistance; cost sharing; tying farm program benefits to the adoption of effective conservation practices; denying participation in farm programs to farmers who convert sodland and swampland into cropland; and providing farmers with payments for putting highly erodible land into conservation reserves for long periods of time. Developing sensible land conservation policy requires recognition of the likelihood that the external costs of greatest importance are off-farm costs, not the costs of reduced land productivity. Unfortunately, the sources of the sediments causing the most serious off-farm damage are difficult to ascertain.

The large-scale introduction of pesticides in farm production has been an important source of cost savings. The major long-run beneficiaries have been consumers who have enjoyed paying lower prices for food. The blessing to consumers may have been a mixed one, however, in light of possible food contamination. The blessings to society as a whole must be discounted because pesticides pollute both ground and surface waters and damage wildlife. The Environmental Protection Agency and the Food and Drug Administration are charged with the responsibility for balancing the benefits and costs of pesticide use through regulation. Balancing the benefits of a cheaper food supply against the benefits of a cleaner, healthier environment is virtually impossible to perform with any degree of precision; the performance of the relevant government agencies up to this point in time has received scant applause from the public gallery. The trouble is that we know very little now and we may not even learn much in the future as to the long-term effects of low dosages of pesticide contamination on human health. The uncertainty in regard to the effects of pesticide use has prompted many people to urge the government to move the farm sector away from heavy reliance on pesticides in favor of a more labor-intensive farming system that uses traditional methods, such as crop rotations, together with the new products of biological research. Pesticide use would be much more selective than it is at present.

PROBLEMS

1. Under competitive conditions the demand and supply for food are given by $P = 10 - Q$ and $P = (1.0)Q$. A dangerous farm chemical is used, however, that contaminates the nation's drinking water. Policy A forbids the use of the chemical, which elevates the supply function to $P = \frac{3}{2}Q$. Policy B allows farmers to use the chemical, but then removes the chemical residual from the water before consumption. The cost of policy B to taxpayers equals 6. Which is the more efficient policy? Explain.

2. The demand and supply for food are given by $P = 10 - Q$ and $P = g + Q$, respectively, where g is a parameter that depends on the maximum amount of nitrogen fertilizer farmers are permitted to use per acre. It is assumed that $g = 4 - 0.01F$ and that $NR = 0.01F$, where F equals the maximum allowable amount of fertilizer per acre and NR equals the level of nitrate residuals found in the nation's supply of drinking water. Society's willingness to pay for drinking water WW depends on the extent of contamination according to the function $WW = 20 - (NR)^2$. Under competition with no regulation on fertilizer use, $F = 400$.

   (a) Suppose $F = 0$. Compute the increase in FS and the decrease in WW associated with an increase in F equal to 50 where FS equals society's willingness to pay for the opportunity to produce and consume food. Would it make sense for society to allow F to rise to 50? Explain.

   (b) Find the optimum level of water contamination and the associated values for the quantity and price of food. Compare these values with those under perfect competition.

3. *The government announces a voluntary program in which farmers are assured of a price no less than P^* if they refrain from using pesticides. With pesticides, a farmer's total variable cost function is $C = q^2$. Without pesticides, the function is $C = 2q^2$. Demand is given by $P = 100 - Q$. There are 100 identical farmers.

   (a) Find the indifference price.

   (b) Find the minimum target price that assures 100 percent participation. (Hint: See the analytical methods developed in Chapter 8.)

REFERENCES AND SUGGESTED READINGS

American Agricultural Economics Association Soil Conservation Task Force, *Soil Erosion and Soil Conservation Policy in the United States,* Occasional Paper No. 2, American Agricultural Economics Association, January 1986.

Ames, Bruce N., Renae Magow, and Lois Swirsky Gold, "Ranking Possible Carcinogenic Hazards," *Science,* 236(1987):235–271.

Antle, John M., and Susan M. Capalbo, "Pesticides and Public Policy: A Program for Research and Policy Analysis," in *Agriculture and the Environment,* T. T. Phipps, P. R. Crosson, and K. A. Price, eds., Resources for the Future, Washington, D.C., 1986.

Batie, Sandra S., "Agriculture as the Problem," *Choices,* Third Quarter, 1988, pp. 4–7.

Carson, Rachel, *Silent Spring,* Houghton Mifflin, Boston, 1962.

Carter, Harold O., and Carole Frank Nuckton, eds., *Chemicals in the Human Food Chain: Sources, Options, and Public Policy,* Agricultural Issues Center, University of California, Davis, 1988.

Clark II, Edwin H., Jennifer A. Haverkamp, and William Chapman, *Eroding Soils: The Off-Farm Impacts,* the Conservation Foundation, Washington, D.C., 1985.

Crosson, Pierre, R., "Soil Erosion and Policy Issues," in *Agriculture and the Environment,* T. T. Phipps, P. R. Crosson, and K. A. Price, eds., Resources for the Future, Washington, D.C., 1986.

Dicks, Michael R., Felix Llacuna, and Michael Linsenbigler, *The Conservation Reserve Program: Implementation and Accomplishments, 1986–87,* Economic Research Center, U.S. Department of Agriculture, Statistical Bulletin Number 763, Washington, D.C., January 1988.

Freeman III, A. Myrick, Robert H. Haveman, and Allen V. Kneese, *The Economics of Environmental Policy,* Wiley, New York, 1973.

Lichtenberg, Erik, and David Zilberman, "Problems of Pesticide Regulation: Health and Environment Versus Food and Fiber," in *Agriculture and the Environment,* T. T. Phipps, P. R. Crosson, and K. A. Price, eds., Resources for the Future, Washington, D.C., 1986.

Nielson, Elizabeth G., and Linda K. Lee, *The Magnitude and Costs of Groundwater Contamination from Agricultural Chemicals: A National Perspective,* Economic Research Service, U.S. Department of Agriculture, Agricultural Economic Report Number 576, Washington, D.C., October 1987.

Osteen, Craig, and Fred Kuchler, *Potential Bans of Corn and Soybean Pesticides: Economic Implications for Farmers and Consumers,* Economic Research Service, U.S. Department of Agriculture, Agricultural Economic Report Number 546, April 1986.

Robinson, Kenneth L., *Farm and Food Policies and Their Consequences,* Prentice-Hall, Englewood Cliffs, NJ, 1989.

Tietenberg, Tom, *Environmental and Natural Resource Economics,* 2nd ed., Scott, Foresman, Glenview, IL, 1988.

U.S. General Accounting Office, *Pesticides: EPA's Formidable Task to Assess and Regulate Their Risks,* GAO, RCED-86-125, Washington, D.C., 1986.

U.S. General Accounting Office, *To Protect Tomorrow's Food Supply, Soil Conservation Needs Priority Attention,* Report to the Congress, B-114833, Washington, D.C., February 1977.

APPENDIX
A

Generic Commodity Certificates

The Food Security Act of 1985 authorized the secretary of agriculture to implement several program activities to reduce and/or avoid commodity surpluses. The simplest way to avoid surpluses, of course, is to drop the price support program. It is easy for economists to make such a recommendation but much harder for politicians to carry it out. Recent program activities designed to diminish the surplus problem have included lowering loan rates, expanding export promotion programs, offering marketing loans, and issuing generic commodity certificates. Generic certificates are explained and analyzed in this Appendix. Marketing loans are considered in Appendix B.

Farmers who participated in the 1986 and 1987 grain programs received part of their government payments (deficiency, diversion, or both) in the form of generic commodity certificates. Under this program a corn producer due $5,000, for example, might receive a government check for $3,000 and a piece of paper or certificate with a face value of $2,000. Certificates had expiration dates set at 8 months from the time of issuance. How might this certificate be used? There are three options. First, the farmer could return the certificate to the government for cash at the expiration date. If this were all there was to it, the program would be of little interest.

To understand a second option, let us suppose further that the farmer commits 1,000 bushels of corn to the nonrecourse loan program and receives $1.82 per bushel or $1,820 in return. The loan is for a typical 9-month period, and the farmer is expected to pay monthly storage costs of 3 cents per bushel. The farmer accepts an obligation through taking out a nonrecourse loan. Either the loan must be repaid with interest, or the collateral must be turned over to the government at the expiration of the loan. Assuming that the market price stays well below $1.82, the farmer at the end of the 9-month period would ordinarily turn over the 1,000 bushels of corn as repayment of the loan. The net revenue would equal the initial loan minus total storage cost or $1,550.

Under the second option, the farmer has the right to use part of the generic certificate as an alternative method of discharging the loan obligation. Here's how it works. The CCC announces posted county prices for corn (and other commodities) all across the land estimated in such manner as to approximate, at least, the local cash price. Suppose the posted price for the county in which our hypothetical farmer resides exactly equals the local market price, assumed to be $1.30 per bushel. Under the program the farmer is entitled to surrender part of the value of the certificate to the government, namely $1,300 as a means of discharging his or her obligation under the loan. The figure $1,300 is calculated by multiplying the 1,000 bushels under loan times the posted county price $1.30. The remainder of the certificate, $700, could be converted to cash as under the first option described above or the third option described below.

Now let's see why the second option might be better than the first from the farmer's point of view. Under the program the farmer would have had the certificate in hand at the time of harvest, when the commodity was eligible to go under loan. Upon taking out the loan the farmer receives $1,820 in cash, which, when added to the certificate, equals $3,820. But to obtain this sum of money under the first option, the farmer must pay the storage cost for holding the commodity for 9 months ($270) and wait until the expiration date on the certificate or at least near this date, to collect the $2,000. If the farmer chooses instead to use the certificate to discharge the loan obligation, at the very same time the loan is taken out, then he or she will have a commodity worth $1,300 that could be sold immediately, plus the $1,820 received via the loan, plus the remaining certificate value of $700. These three components also sum to $3,820, but the farmer would need to pay no storage cost. Furthermore, only a $700 certificate would need to be held until the expiration date. It pays to use the certificate to discharge the loan obligation. The main saving arises out of not having to pay storage costs.

The third optional use of certificates reflects two of their characteristics not yet explained. Generic commodity certificates could be bought and sold, and they could also be used to buy commodities owned by the government or under loan. Now suppose that the local grain elevator is storing wheat owned by the government. Assume the posted county price for wheat is $2.30, but that the local market price is $2.40. Our hypothetical farmer receives a $2,000 certificate under the corn program but the certificate is generic; it can be used to buy any of a very long list of commodities owned by the government at any of many locations. Under these circumstances, the $2,000 certificate is worth more to the elevator than its face value. Why? Because the elevator could use the $2,000 certificate to purchase 869 bushels of wheat from the government ($2,000 ÷ $2.30), selling the newly acquired wheat for $2,085. Thus, the elevator would be willing to pay up to $2,085 for the farmer's $2,000 certificate. From the point of view of the elevator, the certificate is a special kind of money that can be used to buy government stocks at bargain basement prices. Even if the posted county price were not less than the market price, the local elevator might desire to buy the farmer's certificate at a premium. The elevator might be able to sell it to some other commodity merchant who is in a position to buy a government-owned commodity at some other market location for less than the local market price. Wherever the posted county prices are less than local market cash prices, profits can be made by buying cheap from the government, with the aid of certificates, and selling dear. Such arbitrage has the effect of lowering market prices to posted county levels.

A third option open to our hypothetical farmer, then, is to sell all or part of the generic commodity certificates in the market for certificates. Whether the second or third option or some combination of the two is the most profitable alternative depends on the level of storage cost, the rate of interest, and the extent to which the certificate's market price is above its face value.

In order to understand the economic effects of using generic commodity certificates, it is important to remember that the government is under an obligation not to sell the stocks it owns at prices less than the announced release prices, release prices that exceed loan rates. In a period of depressed farm prices, as in 1986 and 1987, government storage can become expensive and puts Uncle Sam in the unenviable position of being a residual supplier of commodities in world trade. Generic commodity certificates were used by wheat and corn producers, particularly the latter, to move wheat and corn under loan into grain markets. These commodities would otherwise have ended up in government hands. A significant quantity of government-owned wheat also found its way into the market for domestic consumption and export. Marketing firms made profits through arbitrage in light of the federal government's effort to determine local market prices. Hanthorn and Glauber (see p. 236) estimate that certificates lowered both corn and wheat prices in 1986 and in 1987. The downward price pressure was particularly strong in the case of corn.

APPENDIX B

Marketing Loans

Under a marketing loan scheme, farmers have the option of repaying their nonrecourse loans at less than the loan rate. The Food Security Act of 1985 provided for mandatory marketing loans for upland cotton and rice. Such loans were possible for feedgrains, wheat, and soybeans at the discretion of the secretary of agriculture. Loan repayment rates differ among commodities but generally are set at the world price, a minimum percentage of the loan rate, or at the greater of the two. Had such a program been applied to corn, for example, the participating farmer would have had the option of repaying the loan at the world market price or 70 percent of the loan rate, whichever is higher.

In order to understand the economic effects of the marketing loan program, consider Figure B.1. The market price of corn P and the price received by farmers P_y are measured along the horizontal and vertical axes, respectively. With active international trade, perfect competition, and no transportation costs, P_y and P would be equal and the relationship between them would be given by the 45° line. We assume a price support program is in effect, however, letting P^* equal the support price. Consider an option under which the farmer takes out a loan, repays the loan at 70 percent of the loan rate, and sells the crop, all at the same point in time. (Whether the farmer would ever exercise this option is another matter, which we will get to soon enough.) In this case we have

$$P_y = P^* + P - (0.7)P^*$$
$$= P + (0.3)P^* \tag{B.1}$$

The graph of Equation (B.1) is given by LL' in Figure B.1.

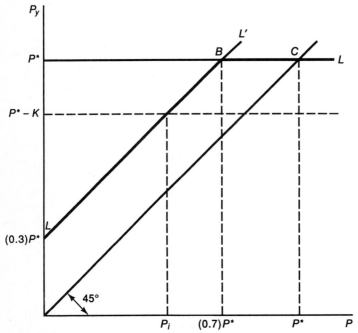

FIGURE B.1
Relationship between the market price and alternative support prices.

As a second option, suppose the farmer takes out a loan, repays it at the world or market price, and sells the crop, again all at the same point in time. We then have

$$P_y = P^* + P - P$$
$$= P^* \tag{B.2}$$

The graph of this relationship is a flat line.

According to the legislation, the loan may be repaid at the higher of the market price and $(0.7)P^*$. Thus,

$$P_y = P^* + P - \max(P, 0.7P^*) \tag{B.3}$$

The graph of this relationship, given by the darkened curve LL in Figure B.1, is kinked, starting at the vertical intercept $(0.3)P^*$ and passing through points B and C. In the absence of storage cost, marketing loans would be of little interest to farmers who enjoyed the ordinary nonrecourse loan as an alternative. The reason for this is simple. The marketing loan is merely an option, it is not mandatory. For any market price less than P^*, the farmer could always secure a farm price of P^* via the nonrecourse loan program.

The story changes with the explicit introduction of storage cost per bushel equal to K. The net price $(P^* - K)$ is plotted in Figure B.1. We can now compare $(P^* - K)$ with P_y as calculated using (B.3). For all market prices less than P_i, the farmer maximizes price received by taking out a loan, paying the storage cost, and turning over the commodity to the government when the loan expires. The net or real price to the farmer is $(P^* - K)$. For low market prices it pays the farmer to stick to the usual nonrecourse loan program. For all prices larger than P_i but less than P^*, on the other hand, it would pay the farmer to take out a marketing loan and sell the commodity. The price received is then given by Equation (B.3) and no storage cost need be incurred. Because the farmer is indifferent between a marketing loan and the usual nonrecourse loan at $P = P_i$, the price P_i may be viewed as the indifference price. Clearly, then, marketing loans can be used to move commodities into commercial trade channels rather than into government bins depending on market prices, storage costs, and program parameters.

In the above example, the farmer faced the possibility of repaying the loan at 70 percent of the support price. If this percentage is decreased toward 0 percent, allowing the farmer to repay at the market price, then the horizontal segment of LL would tend to extend to the vertical axis. At the 0 percent limit, the marketing loan option would assure the farmer of a price no less than P^*. The resulting program would be identical to a direct payment program with the target equal to P^*.

Turning to market analysis, we let the competitive supply equation be given by

$$P_y = bQ \qquad (B.4)$$

where it is assumed the market price and the price received by the farmer are equal. The graph of this relationship is given by SS_c in Figure B.2. We now seek to determine a relationship that shows how much farmers will produce at various alternative market prices under a program that involves both nonrecourse and marketing loan options. We will start by first deriving a supply curve on the assumption, which we will maintain only for a moment, that the relationship between the market price and the farm price is given by Equation (B.3) as graphed in Figure B.1. That is to say, we will start by deriving a supply curve, SS' in Figure B.2, on the assumption that the farmer adopts the marketing loan option. The support price is given by P^*. For all market prices larger than $(0.7)P^*$, $P_y = P^*$ and farmers produce Q_1; the curve SS' is perfectly inelastic for this range of prices. (Prices larger than P^* may be ignored since they would render the program ineffective.) For market prices less than $(0.7)P^*$, use Equations (B.3) and (B.4) in order to derive the relationship between Q and the market price P as follows:

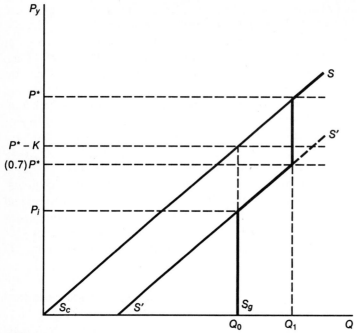

FIGURE B.2
Derivation of supply with ordinary price support and marketing loan options.

$$P = -0.3P^* + bQ \tag{B.5}$$

For all market prices less than $0.7P^*$, the supply curve SS' has the same slope as SS_c but lies further to the right. For any market price less than P^*, farmers receive a higher price and produce more than under perfect competition. Notice, however, that SS' is not the supply curve we are seeking. It is based on Equation (B.3), an equation giving the relationship between P and P_y on the assumption that the farmer takes out a marketing loan willy-nilly.

Again letting the storage cost equal K per unit, we plot $(P^* - K)$ in Figure B.2. When the market price equals P_i, the farmer receives $[P_i + P_i + (0.3)P^*]$ under the marketing loan option. Under the nonrecourse loan option, the price received equals $(P^* - K)$. Since the output is the same for either option, we know that $(P^* - K)$ and $[P_i + (0.3)P^*]$ are equal. Since the farmer would be indifferent as between the two options, P_i may properly be viewed as an indifference price. For all prices less than P_i, the farmers participate in the nonrecourse loan program, receive $P^* - K$, and produce in total Q_0. For all prices above P_i and below P^*, the farmers exercise the marketing loan option and move along SS'. The supply curve showing how much farmers would produce at alternative market prices given both the nonrecourse and marketing loan option is given by the darkened, kinked curve SS_g in Figure B.2. It is perfectly inelastic for prices less than P_i and coincides with SS' for prices above P_i. We hasten to add, however, that market prices will never fall below P_i; part of the SS_g curve is never involved in actual price determination. It is important to understand why this is true.

Earlier in this book, in Chapter 4, we saw that a price support or nonrecourse loan program makes the demand curve confronting farmers perfectly elastic at the support price, rendering that part of the supply curve lying below the support price ineffective. The previous analysis ignored storage cost, however. With storage cost taken into consideration, a simple nonrecourse loan program would make the demand confronting farmers perfectly elastic at $(P^* - K)$.

A program that involves the twin options of a nonrecourse loan and a marketing loan makes the demand curve confronting farmers perfectly elastic at the indifference price P_i. Any tendency for prices to fall below P_i would cause farmers to switch from marketing to nonrecourse loans. Commodity acquired by the government through the nonrecourse loan system would not be allowed to enter the marketing channel at a price less than P^*. What this means is that any tendency for price to fall below P_i would be immediately thwarted by government acquisitions. Therefore, the demand curve confronting farmers becomes perfectly elastic at the indifference price P_i when farmers enjoy both the nonrecourse and marketing loan options.

We are now in a position to explain the determination of market performance. The supply curve SS_g from Figure B.2 is reproduced in Figure B.3. Demand is given by DD under perfectly competitive conditions and by DD_g under the farm program. The intersection of DD_g and SS_g gives market equilibrium price P_2 and output Q_g. (Equilibrium price equals P_i given the position of DD.) To maintain price at P_2, the government acquires $Q_g - Q_2$ under the nonrecourse loan system. Notice that if DD began shifting to the right, holding SS_g constant, government acquisitions would eventually decline to zero. If DD is high enough, the perfectly elastic tail of DD_g, arising out of the government program, would not come into play in determining market performance; equilibrium price would then rise above P_i. For any equilibrium market price in excess of P_i, the market performance attained could be exactly duplicated by a direct payment program if only the target price were chosen appropriately.

This brings us to our main conclusion. Consider a farm program that offers farmers both the usual nonrecourse loan and marketing loan options with given program parameters. The economic effects of such a program can be exactly duplicated by a program that involves both direct payments and market price supports if only the target price and the price support level are chosen appropriately.

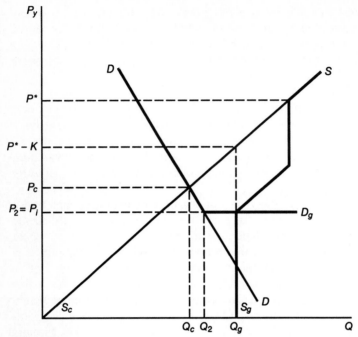

FIGURE B.3
Market performance with ordinary price support and marketing loan options.

APPENDIX
C

AGSEC: A Computer Simulation to Teach Agricultural Policy[*]

AGSEC is a computer simulation program designed to help students understand the effects that farm policy tools have on the following economic variables: commodity prices, farm income, production, exports, stocks, and the
cost of government programs. For the sake of simplicity, AGSEC deals with a
single commodity (corn). The effects of policy choices estimated by supply-
demand equations are representative of the U.S. corn market from 1985 to
1990. AGSEC puts the player in the position of secretary of agriculture, with
an opportunity to try various kinds and levels of agricultural policies. These
policy decisions are made in four successive years to coincide with presiden-
tial elections. After each year, the player can choose new values for any or all
policy variables. The economic effects of each year's decisions are transformed into an overall popularity rating and individual popularity ratings for
four interest groups: farmers, taxpayers, consumers, and the European Community (EC).

AGSEC has a beginner and an advanced version. In the beginner's version, the starting situation is always the same so the player can see the direct
effects of policy decisions. In the advanced version, the starting situation and
other variables are selected randomly. This latter version provides considerable flexibility and forces the player to deal with uncertainty. The player can
get experience with many different situations by playing AGSEC several
times.

[*]Creators Earl Brown and Bruce Gardner are professors in the Department of Agricultural and
Resource Economics, University of Maryland, College Park.

AGSEC can be used by individuals for self-paced instruction with or without additional reference material. AGSEC can be used with groups, such as students, farmers, and county agents, as part of a formal learning situation to increase understanding and to stimulate interest and discussion. Also, AGSEC can be used at fairs and exhibits to attract attention.

Instructors and advanced students interested in learning about the assumptions and economic and political structure of AGSEC should refer to the technical guide in the help menu.

AGSEC is easy to use. Basic instructions are shown on each opening screen, and there is an extensive help menu with more complete instructions, definitions, and suggested strategies.

AGSEC requires the following minimum hardware and software:

1. An IBM-PC or fully compatible computer with 256K RAM, 130K disk space, and a color monitor
2. Any version of DOS

INDEX